A TRANSLATOR'S HANDBOOK
on
PAUL'S FIRST LETTER TO
THE CORINTHIANS

Helps for Translators Series

Technical Helps:

Old Testament Quotations in the New Testament
Short Bible Reference System
New Testament Index
The Theory and Practice of Translation
Bible Index
Fauna and Flora of the Bible
Manuscript Preparation
Marginal Notes for the Old Testament
Marginal Notes for the New Testament
The Practice of Translating

Handbooks:

A Translator's Handbook on the Book of Joshua
A Translator's Handbook on the Book of Ruth
A Translator's Handbook on the Book of Amos
A Translator's Handbook on the Books of Obadiah and Micah
A Translator's Handbook on the Book of Jonah
A Translator's Handbook on the Gospel of Mark
A Translator's Handbook on the Gospel of Luke
A Translator's Handbook on the Gospel of John
A Translator's Handbook on the Acts of the Apostles
A Translator's Handbook on Paul's Letter to the Romans
A Translator's Handbook on Paul's First Letter to the Corinthians
A Translator's Handbook on Paul's Letter to the Galatians
A Translator's Handbook on Paul's Letter to the Ephesians
A Translator's Handbook on Paul's Letter to the Philippians
A Translator's Handbook on Paul's Letters to the Colossians and to Philemon
A Translator's Handbook on Paul's Letters to the Thessalonians
A Translator's Handbook on the Letter to the Hebrews
A Translator's Handbook on the First Letter from Peter
A Translator's Handbook on the Letters of John

Guides:

A Translator's Guide to Selections from the First Five Books of the Old Testament
A Translator's Guide to Selected Psalms
A Translator's Guide to the Gospel of Matthew
A Translator's Guide to the Gospel of Mark
A Translator's Guide to the Gospel of Luke
A Translator's Guide to Paul's First Letter to the Corinthians
A Translator's Guide to Paul's Second Letter to the Corinthians
A Translator's Guide to Paul's Letters to Timothy and to Titus
A Translator's Guide to the Letters to James, Peter, and Jude
A Translator's Guide to the Revelation to John

HELPS FOR TRANSLATORS

A TRANSLATOR'S HANDBOOK
on
PAUL'S FIRST LETTER TO
THE CORINTHIANS

by

PAUL ELLINGWORTH

and

HOWARD HATTON

UNITED BIBLE SOCIETIES

London, New York,
Stuttgart

Books in the series of *Helps for Translators* may be ordered from a national Bible Society or from either of the following centers:

United Bible Societies	United Bible Societies
European Production Fund	1865 Broadway
D-7000 Stuttgart 80	New York, NY 10023
Postfach 81 03 40	U.S.A.
West Germany	

L.C. Cataloging in Publication Data

Ellingworth, Paul.
    A translator's handbook on Paul's first letter to the Corinthians.

    (Helps for translators)
    Bibliography: p.
    Includes index.
    1. Bible. N.T. Corinthians, 1st--Translating. 2. Bible. N.T. Corinthians, 1st--Commentaries. I. Hatton, Howard, 1929- . II. Title. III. Series.
BS2675.5.E38 1985   227'.206   85-1142
ISBN 0-8267-0140-X

ABS-1988-300-1,550-L-2-08578

Contents

List of Tables

Preface

A Translator's Handbook on Paul's First Letter to the Corinthians is another volume in the series of Handbooks in the United Bible Societies' Helps for Translators series. Special attention has been given to the structure of the discourse so that the translator will be able to understand the movement and the logical progression of the sections of this letter and how they contribute to the message of the whole.

The Revised Standard Version (RSV) and the Today's English Version (TEV) translations are shown at the beginning of each section. They are reproduced again at the beginning of the discussion of each verse. However, the discussion follows RSV, and references to words and phrases from the verse under discussion are printed in boldface so that the translator can easily locate desired information. TEV is kept before the translator as a possible model for a meaningful translation. References to TEV and to other translations are in quotation marks and are identified, as are references to quotations from passages elsewhere in RSV.

As is true for both Handbooks and Guides in the series, this volume concentrates on exegetical matters that are of prime importance for translators, and it attempts to indicate possible solutions for translational and linguistic problems that may occur. Translators' Guides provide important information in a relatively condensed form, using a format that makes it possible to retrieve the information easily. Handbooks such as this volume are biblical commentaries that deal with the full range of information important to translators. However, the authors do not attempt to provide the kind of help not directly related to translating, which other scholars and theologians may be seeking, since much of that information is available elsewhere.

A limited Bibliography is included for the benefit of those who are interested in further study. Details of interest to translators with advanced training in textual studies and exegesis are included in the footnotes.

A Glossary is provided that explains technical terms according to their usage in this volume. The translator may find it useful to read through the Glossary in order to become aware of the specialized way in which certain terms are used. An Index gives the location by page number of some of the important words and subjects discussed in the Handbook, especially where the Handbook provides the translator with help in rendering these concepts into the receptor language.

A special word of thanks is due to Mrs. Ruth Binnington of Edinburgh, who typed the first fair copy of the exegetical material.

Abbreviations Used in This Volume

<u>Bible Texts, Versions and Other Works Cited</u>
(for details see Bibliography, page 339)

AT	American Translation
BJ	Bible de Jérusalem
Brc	Barclay
CLT	Common Language Translation
DuCL	Dutch common language version
FrCL	French common language version
GeCL	German common language version
ItCL	Italian common language version
JB	Jerusalem Bible
KJV	King James Version
Lu	Luther, Revidierter Text
Mft	Moffatt, The Bible: A New Translation
NAB	New American Bible
NEB	New English Bible
NIV	New International Version
Phps	Phillips
PoCL	Portuguese common language version
RSV	Revised Standard Version
TEV	Today's English Version
ThCL	Thai common language version
TNT	Translator's New Testament
TOB	Traduction Oecuménique de la Bible
UBS	United Bible Societies

<u>Books of the Bible</u>

Gen	Genesis	1,2 Cor	1,2 Corinthians
Exo	Exodus	Gal	Galatians
Lev	Leviticus	Eph	Ephesians
Num	Numbers	Phil	Philippians
Deut	Deuteronomy	Col	Colossians
Psa	Psalms	1,2 Thes	1,2 Thesalonians
Isa	Isaiah	1,2 Tim	1,2 Timothy
Matt	Matthew	Heb	Hebrews
Rom	Romans		

Translating 1 Corinthians

The purpose of this and other Handbooks is to provide Bible translators in various parts of the world with help in understanding and translating the scriptures. This means that the Handbooks are both less and more than other commentaries.

They are less than other commentaries because they do not normally include much material on the historical background or literary criticism of the various books of the Bible; nor do they systematically describe the ways in which biblical passages have been interpreted in different church traditions and at different times. Still less do they claim to discuss the importance of the biblical text for systematic theology or religious philosophy. To these limitations of content may be added certain limitations of form. The Handbooks are intended to be read by translators, some of whom have only a limited knowledge of Hebrew and Greek, and most of whom do not speak English as their mother tongue. For this reason, Hebrew and Greek words are seldom quoted, even in transliteration, and some explanations are given (for example, of idioms quoted from English translations of the Bible) which a native speaker of English would not need.

These limitations on the form and content of this Handbook are deliberate. They reflect an overriding concern for helping translators to understand the meaning of the biblical text, as a necessary condition for translating it. Even in this area it is necessary to be selective. We do not claim to have mentioned every possible meaning of every text. Our guiding principle has been to provide translators with material for answering the two questions which are vital for their work: "What does the text mean?" and "How can we translate it?"

In agreement with this aim, this Handbook is based on the third corrected edition (1983) of the UBS *Greek New Testament*. Its text is the same as that of the 26th edition of the Nestle-Aland *Novum Testamentum Graece*, 26th edition 1979, as corrected in 1981. In these editions, square brackets— [ ] —are used to enclose words, or parts of words, whose presence or position in the text is disputed.

Although this Handbook is based on the Greek text, every effort has been made to explain the text in such a way that the Handbook can be used by translators who know little or no Greek. Occasionally, footnotes may include technical information requiring some knowledge of Greek.

Two English translations of 1 Corinthians are printed in this Handbook: the Revised Standard Version (RSV) and Today's English Version (TEV). RSV is a rather literal translation, and therefore a good guide to the grammatical structure of the Greek text. TEV is an accurate representation of the meaning of the text, and a useful example of how it may be restructured in translation.

This Handbook often refers to translations of 1 Corinthians in other, mainly European, languages. These are quoted in a rather literal English retranslation. Our purpose in doing this is not to suggest that European languages are in any way more developed, or translations in them better, than those in other parts of the world. We have used these translations in two main ways: first, to illustrate how different interpretations of the Greek text affect the translation; and second, to provide examples of how the meaning of the text has been expressed in particular translations.

References to other translations, whether in English or in other languages, should be understood as suggestions and possible helps, not as perfect models to be followed without question. The responsibility for finding the closest natural equivalent of the original text belongs to the translators. No translation in another language, no commentary, and no handbook can take this responsibility away.

In 1 and 2 Corinthians, Paul is writing to a church which he knew well. In many places he answers questions put to him by the Christians at Corinth, and tries to solve problems which have arisen in their church. Often he refers to people and events without giving many details of them. This sometimes creates problems for the translator.[1] For example, much of 1 Corinthians is concerned with what happened when the Christians at Corinth met together. It is important to realize that these activities included teaching, discussion, and even passing judgment, in addition to what modern Christians might describe as "worship." No one term covers it all. Again, it is important (though difficult) to decide where Paul is speaking in his own name, and where he is referring to, or even quoting from, a letter he had received from Corinth. These and many other difficulties are discussed in detail in this Handbook; but sometimes we have to admit that no one today can be sure of the situation in Corinth at the time Paul wrote.

Outline

The outline of 1 Corinthians is generally clear. The only serious problem is caused by the fact that Paul sometimes starts from a particular question, and answers by appealing to fundamental Christian beliefs. He may therefore seem to be wandering from the point; but this is not really so. The following divisions may be suggested:

Introduction: 1.1-9
Divisions in the Church: 1.10—4.31
Immorality in the Church: chapter 5
Lawsuits between Christians: 6.1-11
The use of the body: 6.12-20
Christian marriage: chapter 7
Dealings between Christians and pagans: 8.1—11.1
The gifts of the Holy Spirit, including love: chapters 12—14
The resurrection: chapter 15
Practical matters: 16.1-12
Conclusion: 16.13-24.

---

[1] Some of these problems are discussed in P. Ellingworth, 1980, "Translating 1 Corinthians"; The Bible Translator 31.234-238.

Chapter 1

1 Paul, called by the will of God to be an apostle of Christ Jesus, and our brother Sosthenes,

2 To the church of God which is at Corinth, to those sanctified in Christ Jesus, called to be saints together with all those who in every place call on the name of our Lord Jesus Christ, both their Lord and ours:

3 Grace to you and peace from God our Father and the Lord Jesus Christ.

1 From Paul, who was called by the will of God to be an apostle of Christ Jesus, and from our brother Sosthenes—

2 To the church of God which is in Corinth, to all who are called to be God's holy people, who belong to him in union with Christ Jesus, together with all people everywhere who worship our Lord Jesus Christ, their Lord and ours:

3 May God our Father and the Lord Jesus Christ give you grace and peace.

In New Testament times, letters in Greek usually began in the form "A to B, greeting." In this letter, A is represented by the contents of verse 1, B by the contents of verse 2, and verse 3 gives the greeting. Paul follows this introduction form, but develops it and gives it a Christian content. Groups of translators should decide in principle how they are to translate the beginnings of New Testament letters, since these are all very similar. They should also consider how letters usually begin in their own languages, and follow that pattern as far as possible.

Verses 1-3 are a single sentence in the Greek. Here, as in many other parts of Paul's letters, translators may find it more natural in their own languages to divide this long sentence into several sentences. They may also need to restructure it, that is, translate its various parts in a different order. For example, the German common language translation (GeCL) restructures verses 1-3 in the following way: "Paul and Sosthenes write this letter to the church in Corinth. We greet everyone . . . We pray to God . . . to give you grace and peace."

GeCL assumes that both Paul and Sosthenes "write this letter." But this assumption is not certain, since from verse 4 onward Paul uses such phrases as "I [not "we"] always give thanks" (Today's English Version [TEV]).[1] In other letters, such as 2 Corinthians and 1 Thessalonians, Paul seems to think of Silas and Timothy as real coauthors and rarely speaks of himself alone. It is likely, then, that although Paul and Sosthenes share in the greeting, Paul alone is the writer.

---

[1] W.F. Lofthouse, 1946-47, "Singular and Plural in Paul's Letters," The Expository Times 58.179-182, shows how careful Paul is in the use of "I" and "we" forms. He quotes with approval C.H. Dodd, Romans, page 107: "Paul rarely if ever says 'I' unless he is really speaking of himself personally, even if he means to generalize from the particular instance."

[3]

If, then, Paul is the only author, it may be good to translate verse 3 before verse 2. For example, "I, Paul . . . , together with brother Sosthenes, pray that God . . . may give you grace and peace. I am writing to the church . . . at Corinth . . . ."

1.1	RSV	TEV
	Paul, called by the will of God to be an apostle of Christ Jesus, and our brother Sosthenes,	1 From Paul, who was called by the will of God to be an apostle of Christ Jesus, and from our brother Sosthenes—

The Greek text says literally, "Paul called apostle of Christ Jesus, through the will of God, and Sosthenes the brother." The phrase "called apostle" does not mean that Paul was merely given the name "apostle" as Jesus gave the name "Peter" to Cephas. "Called apostle," as many translations show, means "called to do the work of an apostle" or "called to be a messenger of Jesus Christ." "Apostle" is related to a Greek verb meaning "send" and often means "someone sent as a messenger." Jesus used it this way. Paul is called to follow Jesus, and he is also sent out as one of his messengers (compare Mark 3.14).

The words **by the will of God** probably refer both to Paul's calling and to his appointment as an apostle. Christ, though, was the one who appointed him directly. The work of God and that of Christ are closely connected, both here and in verse 2. GeCL combines the word "called" with the phrase "by the will of God" and translates this clause simply as "Paul, whom God called to be an apostle of Jesus Christ."

Called refers to one particular event in the past, so TEV translates it as "was called," not "has been called." However, this past event is mentioned because it had consequences at the time when Paul wrote this letter. It is because Paul was once called, that he now has the authority of an apostle. Paul will have much more to say about this later (especially 1.10; 3.5; 4.1).

Translators in languages which do not have a passive form of the verb may prefer to render the clause **called by the will of God** as "whom God decided to call . . . ." Some languages can translate this phrase in an idiomatic way by saying "whom God set his heart to call."

Most translations, like TEV, keep the word "apostle" and explain it in a glossary or word list. Phillips (Phps) first edition translated it as "messenger" in order to show that not everyone who preached the Christian message was an apostle. Sosthenes, for example, does not have this title.

Brother in this verse, as often in the New Testament, refers to a male, but elsewhere in 1 Corinthians the word for "brother" includes women too (see for example 1.10). Jews sometimes called one another "brothers" even when they were not of the same family (for example, 2 Maccabees 1.1). And early Christians often called one another "brother" even when they were of different nationality or race. However, the main meaning of **brother** in this verse is "fellow Christian." It should be translated this way in languages where the word "brother" refers only to an actual family member. In certain languages, though, it can be translated in an idiomatic way as "elder," or "younger," or "elders and youngers" when it is plural. One may therefore translate this phrase as "my fellow Christian, Sosthenes."

To the church of God which is at Corinth, to those sanctified in Christ Jesus, called to be saints together with all those who in every place call on the name of our Lord Jesus Christ, both their Lord and ours:	To the church of God which is in Corinth, to all who are called to be God's holy people, who belong to him in union with Christ Jesus, together with all people everywhere who worship our Lord Jesus Christ, their Lord and ours:

The meaning of this verse is clear, but the grammar in Greek is awkward: it says literally "to the church of God which is in Corinth, made holy in Christ Jesus, called saints." Paul begins by speaking of the church as a group, and then goes on to speak about its members. The Revised Standard Version (RSV) **those** and TEV "all" are not in the Greek text, but help to make the transition from the singular **church** to the plural **saints.** GeCL breaks the sentence after **the church of God which is at Corinth,** and the Italian common language version (ItCL) even begins a new paragraph:

> . . . we write to the church of God which is found in Corinth.
> We greet you, united with Jesus Christ . . . ."

The Greek word for "church," as it is used in the New Testament, may mean either a local Christian community, as in this verse, or all Christians everywhere. In certain languages where the word for church refers to a "building" or a group of people who meet in a particular building, it may be necessary to translate this word as "God's people" or "those who believe in God." Translators may be tempted to use a capital letter for "church" when it means "all Christians," but they should remember that such a distinction will be lost when the translation is read aloud.

In some languages it may be necessary to show that Corinth was a city, not a country or district such as Galatia. In such a case one may say "in the city of Corinth," to show that it is an important center of population.[2]

The words **saints** and **sanctified** are related to each other. Both of these words express the idea that Christians "belong" (TEV) to God and are therefore set apart to serve God's purposes alone. This fact is made clear in TEV's translation, "God's holy people" and "who belong to him." The **saints** and **sanctified** are like Israel in Old Testament times whom God chose as his people for a special purpose. So the more important meaning behind these two words is the idea that Christians belong to God. It follows from this that Christians must live good lives, but it is the idea of belonging to God, not that of sinlessness, which is basic here. There is no suggestion here, however, that special individuals may have the title "saint." "Saints" in the New Testament are always a community of Christians.

There is a slight difference of meaning, though, between **saints** and **sanctified. Called to be saints,** like "called . . . to be an apostle" (TEV) in verse 1, refers to a single past event. The tense of the word translated **sanctified,** on the other hand, expresses the idea of a past event whose consequences stretch into the present time.

---

[2] See Euan Fry, October 1979, "Cities, towns and villages in the Old Testament," The Bible Translator 30.434-438.

Another point that translators need to keep in mind about these two words is that in biblical Greek, as well as in Hebrew, writers often used related words such as **saints** and **sanctified** to add emphasis to their message. In some languages, however, this may sound heavy and awkward. Translators may need to find some other way to convey emphasis. GeCL, for example, uses two expressions which are unrelated: "set apart for God and called to be God's people." In other languages it may be best to use a single strong expression such as "whom God has set apart for himself" or "whom God has made his own people." The meaning of "set apart" here refers to being set apart for God, *for* separation *from* other people.

In Christ Jesus is a very common expression in Paul's writings, but its meaning is not clear. Paul probably means that a Christian's new life depends closely and entirely on Christ. TEV's rendering "in union with Christ Jesus" gives this meaning. Other possible translations are "and whose whole lives are lived with Jesus Christ," "who depend entirely on Jesus Christ," or "whose lives are lived close to Jesus Christ."

There is no difference in meaning between Christ Jesus and Jesus Christ. GeCL and ItCL, for example, have "Jesus Christ" in both places. Translators should use whichever order is more natural in their own languages. In some places in the New Testament "Christ," on its own, is a title meaning "Messiah," meaning "the one whom God has chosen to be king." In this verse and normally in all of Paul's writings, he uses "Christ" simply as a name.

It is possible from the standpoint of Greek grammar to connect the clause **together with all those who in every place call on the name of our Lord Jesus Christ** with either (a) **Paul . . . and our brother Sosthenes** in verse 1, or (b) **to the church of God which is at Corinth,** or with (c) **called to be saints.** Choice (a) is least likely. It does not seem that all Christians are joining Paul and Sosthenes in greeting the Christians at Corinth. Choices (b) and (c) have almost the same meaning; both refer to the Christians in Corinth. TEV shows that it chooses (b) by repeating the word "all" and by its ordering of the clauses in the sentence. ItCL says "Moreover, our letter is for all those who confess Jesus Christ, our common Lord, wherever they are." The words "is for" are perhaps too strong, since in much of 1 Corinthians Paul deals with the particular problems of this one church. An additional reason for choosing (b) is that this is certainly the meaning of 2 Corinthians 1.1-2. However, it is possible to choose (c) as the meaning. RSV has done this.

The word **place** in the phrase **every place** was sometimes used by the Jews to mean a synagogue. In a similar way Paul may have used it to mean a Christian meeting place, which at that time would normally have been a person's home. It is therefore possible to translate **every place** as "wherever they meet."

The phrase **call on the name of** has the essential meaning of "worship." TEV translates it this way. In the Old Testament it often has the meaning "ask the Lord for help," for example Joel 2.32. This verse is quoted both in Acts 2.21 and in Romans 10.13. To call upon someone's "name" is a natural Hebrew way of speaking about "calling for help" from the owner of the name. Such language was used in the Old Testament about speaking to God, and it is used in the New Testament about Christ. The phrase **call on the name of** also involves the ideas of praise and thanksgiving.

Both their Lord and ours is the most probable meaning of the Greek phrase, which can be translated literally as "theirs and ours." It can also mean "in every (meeting) place, both theirs and ours." This second meaning is a little easier grammatically; but the first, namely **their Lord and ours,** makes much better sense. It also fits the major theme of this letter, which is "unity" among Christians. In some languages an appositional construction such as **Christ, their Lord and ours** is difficult to translate. In such cases a translator can render this as "Christ, who is both their Lord and our Lord" or "Christ, who commands both them and us."

<u>1.3</u>   RSV   TEV

    Grace to you and peace from God our Father and the Lord Jesus Christ.

    May God our Father and the Lord Jesus Christ give you grace and peace.

This verse is exactly the same as Romans 1.7b. Please consult the *Translator's Handbook on Paul's Letter to the Romans*, pages 13-14.

In some languages this verse may be translated as a prayer, as in GeCL: "We pray God . . . to give you grace and peace."

The appositional construction **God our Father** is unnatural in many languages. Translators in such languages may say "God, who is our Father."

The phrase **Lord Jesus Christ** may be rendered as "Jesus Christ who is our Lord." However, in some languages one cannot possess the person who controls. In such a case a translator may say "Jesus Christ who controls us."

Grace in Greek is related to the word for "greeting" which was commonly used at the beginning of Greek letters. **Peace** was similarly used in Jewish letters. In the language of the early Christians, to pray that someone might receive **grace** was more than an ordinary greeting. And **peace** for Christians, as in the Old Testament, was more than the absence of war or a peaceful feeling which an individual might have inside himself. Christians understood these terms as related to the nature of God. The two, therefore, overlap in meaning, both with one another and also with "righteousness," which TEV often translates as being "right with God." **Peace** in the New Testament refers to a total state of well-being or good spiritual health which God gives to a person. **Grace,** depending on the context, can have any one of three meanings: (a) God's generosity in giving his love to people who do not deserve it, (b) the total sum of God's gifts considered as a whole, or (c) individual gifts. In this verse, meaning (b) is the most likely. It is difficult, though, to express this wide meaning in common language translations (CLTs). Such words as the English "grace" have lost much of their meaning, not only among non-Christians but also in the churches. In languages where there has not been a long history of Bible translation, one may often combine the meanings (a) and (b) by saying "May God be kind and generous toward you," "May God show his goodness," or "May God give you what you need."

RSV   **1.4-9**   TEV

Blessings in Christ

    4 I give thanks to God^a always for you because of the grace of God which was given you in Christ Jesus, 5 that in every way you were enriched in him with all speech and all

    4 I always give thanks to my God for you because of the grace he has given you through Christ Jesus. 5 For in union with Christ you have become rich in all things, including all speech

[7]

knowledge— 6 even as the testimony to Christ was confirmed among you— 7 so that you are not lacking in any spiritual gift, as you wait for the revealing of our Lord Jesus Christ; 8 who will sustain you to the end, guiltless in the day of our Lord Jesus Christ. 9 God is faithful, by whom you were called into the fellowship of his Son, Jesus Christ our Lord.

[a] Other ancient authorities read *my God*

and all knowledge. 6 The message about Christ has become so firmly established in you 7 that you have not failed to receive a single blessing, as you wait for our Lord Jesus Christ to be revealed. 8 He will also keep you firm to the end, so that you will be faultless on the Day of our Lord Jesus Christ. 9 God is to be trusted, the God who called you to have fellowship with his Son Jesus Christ, our Lord.

If it is more natural to use a complete sentence as a section heading, such sentences as "God Blesses Us Through Jesus Christ" or "Paul Gives Thanks for Blessings" may be used.

The first part of this section contains Paul's expression of thanksgiving to God. In this thanksgiving, as in the greetings in verses 1-3, Paul follows a pattern which was commonly used in letters of his time. But he fills this thanksgiving pattern with Christian content. Most translations divide verses 4-8 into several sentences. In the Greek, however, it is a single sentence. Translators should begin by analyzing these verses into "kernel" or simple sentences, following the method suggested in E.A. Nida and C.R. Taber, *The Theory and Practice of Translation*, pages 51-55. In languages which do not have a passive form of the verb, verses 4-9 will cause special problems. When translators in such languages analyze these verses into kernel sentences, they will need to identify the person performing or initiating the action (agent) and the person to whom the action is done or toward whom the action proceeds (goal). Sometimes, though, there is another person or thing which the agent uses to perform the action on the goal; for example, "Though him [Christ] God [agent] made all things [goal]" (John 1.3). Christ performs the "instrumental" role. When the translator puts this sentence into the active it will usually be rendered "God made all things through Christ" or "God used Christ to make all things." In the Greek text of this chapter, passive verbs appear in each verse in the section 4-6, while in verse 7 there is a noun which RSV translates literally as **the revealing,** showing that the noun is really an event with an implicit agent and goal. TEV translates this Greek noun as the English passive "to be revealed." In verse 4 TEV identifies God as the agent or performer of the action, "he has given you," but in verse 5 both RSV and TEV make no attempt to identify the agent of the action **you were enriched.** If the translator decides that God is the one who "makes rich," then God would also be the one who "confirms" or "firmly establishes the testimony" in verse 6. God is also the agent of the action "revealing" in verse 7.

This section develops the idea of God's grace, which has already been mentioned in verse 3. The meaning of grace becomes gradually more specific. In verse 4 Paul is thinking of God's gifts as a whole. In verse 5 he gives examples of particular gifts, though the Greek word for "grace" is not used. In verse 7 he uses a related word, which TEV translates "blessing," and which always has the meaning of a specific gift.

I give thanks to God*a* always for you because of the grace of God which was given you in Christ Jesus,

a Other ancient authorities read *my God*

I always give thanks to my God for you because of the grace he has given you through Christ Jesus.

Always, like the words **every** and **all** in verse 5, may be an example of the vivid exaggeration that is often found in Hebrew and Aramaic speech (compare, for example, Mark 10.25). If **always** is translated literally into languages where such exaggeration is not used, readers may feel that Paul does nothing else but **give thanks.** In such languages it will be better to use some expression meaning "repeatedly" or "very often."

Most of the Greek manuscripts have "my God" (TEV) instead of just **God,** but two important manuscripts omit "my," and RSV, the New English Bible (NEB), and the New International Version (NIV) follow these. The United Bible Societies' (UBS) Greek New Testament, which is the same as Nestle-Aland twenty-sixth edition, includes "my," but Nestle-Aland twenty-fifth edition omitted it. It is possible that scribes added the word under the influence of Romans 1.8; Philippians 1.3; and Philemon 4. It is known that scribes tended to add words more often than they omitted them. In languages where "my God" would signify that one owned God, translators may say "the God whom I worship."

Give thanks is simply "thank" in Greek and may be translated this way if it is more natural. In any case this verb should be translated as an action or event.

For you translates the Greek expression which really means "about you" or "concerning you." It can also be translated as "because of what you are" or "because you have become Christians." It certainly does not mean "on behalf of you."

Please refer to the comments in the introduction to this section (1.4-9) on how to translate passive verbs. God is the agent or the doer of the action in the clause **because of the grace of God which was given you.** One way to translate this phrase is "God has been very generous to you."

Grace: see the introduction to this section, verses 4-9. Here, to speak of God as "giving grace" may be awkward. In some languages the word for "give" requires a more definite object. Perhaps the verse could be restructured as follows: "I thank my God for what he has done for you. He has been good to you. He has done his work in you through Jesus Christ."

In this verse Paul becomes very specific about the reason for his thanksgiving. First, he says in a general way that he is thankful **for you** Christians in Corinth. Next, he states that it is **because of** what God has given them through Christ that he is thankful.

The words **in Christ Jesus** may be connected with **given** or **you.** If these words are connected with **you,** it is possible to rephrase this expression as "given to you as Christians." However, the first choice, "given in (through) Christ Jesus," is more likely, but there is not much difference in meaning between the two choices. Please see the comments on verse 2 concerning the translation of the phrase **in Christ Jesus.**

that in every way you were enriched in him with all speech and all knowledge—	For in union with Christ you have become rich in all things, including all speech and all knowledge.

This verse probably expresses in greater detail the same reason for thanksgiving which Paul mentions in verse 4, **the grace of God which was given you.** So one may translate the beginning of verse 5 as "that is, because." GeCL shows the connection between these two verses in the following way: "That shows itself in (the fact) that you have become enriched in everything . . . ."

The verb **you were enriched,** as has already been explained in the introduction to this section, refers to the activity of God. So **in him** must mean "in Christ." TEV's "in union with Christ" is a clearer translation. In some languages the phrase **you were enriched** would refer to literal wealth or riches; but that is not the meaning here. It may be wise therefore to render this phrase as "you have received an abundance of all good things" or "God has given you an abundance of all good things."

RSV translates a single emphatic Greek word in two different ways, twice as **all** and once as **every** for the sake of variety. TEV renders this word as "all" each time it appears in this verse. There is no difference in meaning, and each group of translators must decide whether repetition or variety is more effective in their own language.

Speech (literally "word" in the Greek) and **knowledge,** like "wisdom" in verse 17, are important words in 1 Corinthians. It is likely that people in Corinth were using these and other terms to preach a false Gospel. So in this verse, and in many other passages, Paul tries to give these words a real Christian meaning. Translators need to decide in each context in 1 Corinthians whether Paul is using the words (a) in a general, neutral sense, (b) to refer to the false teaching, for example, "what you call wisdom," or (c) in a specifically Christian sense. It will then be easier to decide how, if necessary, to use different words in one's own language to give these differences of meaning. In this verse Paul probably uses these terms in a general sense.

The Greek word for **speech** also means "word" and "reason." It occurs in 1.17 (with "wisdom"); 1.18; 2.1,4,13; 4.19,20; 12.8; 14.9,19 (twice),36; 15.2,54. In this verse **all speech** probably means "all kinds of Christian speaking." ItCL renders it as "preaching." In 1 Corinthians this term very rarely refers to a single word. More commonly it means a message, whether revealed directly by God (14.36) or spoken through human beings.

The Greek word for **knowledge** here is used also in 8.1,7,10,11; 12.8; 13.2,8; 14.6. Translators should avoid words which suggest information or technical ability when they translate the word **knowledge.** In this verse **all knowledge** suggests "knowledge about all spiritual realities."

Detailed Comment on
"Knowledge" and "Wisdom" in 1 Corinthians

The theme of knowledge and wisdom is probably more important in 1 Corinthians, especially in chapters 1—2, than in any other book of the New Testament.

The Greek words to be considered are (1) the verb *ginōskō*, "I know," and (2) its related noun *gnōsis*, "knowledge"; (3) *oida*, another verb meaning "I know"; (4) the noun *sophia*, "wisdom," and (5) the related word *sophos*, which is used both as an adjective, "wise," and as a noun meaning "a wise person." There is also (6) one occurrence of the verb *sunoida*, a compound of *oida*, which is used negatively in 4.4 to mean "I am conscious of nothing [against myself]," that is, "my conscience is clear (TEV).

Apart from (6) there is no sharp distinction in meaning between these terms. They are, however, used in various ways, some of which reflect the circumstances in which this letter was written.

The best guidance for the translator is to be found by paying careful attention to the ways in which these words are used each time they occur. In other words, each occurrence must be translated in the way which most naturally fits the context. Sometimes the immediate context gives very little help, as for example in 13.9,12, where "to know" is used absolutely, that is, without a grammatical object, and therefore with no indication of the kind of knowledge referred to. Similarly, in 8.2 Paul speaks very generally of someone who "imagines that he knows something," but who in fact "does not yet know as he ought to know" (RSV). In such difficult cases the whole passage must be read carefully to discover the kind of knowledge Paul has in mind.

Fortunately for the translator, Paul usually gives clear indications of what he means by "knowledge" or "wisdom." A major distinction is that between knowledge of persons and knowledge of facts. Many languages express these two types of knowledge by the use of different words or phrases. In Paul's writings, knowledge of persons is usually indicated by the use of a direct object; for example, "I know John." Knowledge of facts is often indicated by the use of a subordinate clause, which may be either a statement of the kind "I know that 2 and 2 make 4," or an indirect question such as "I do not know whether he will come," meaning "Will he come? I do not know" (see 1.16; 7.16; 14.16).

The distinction between knowledge of people and knowledge of facts is not, however, absolute. In fact, most occurrences of *ginōskō* in 1 Corinthians refer to knowledge of personal qualities or activities, such as "the things of God" (RSV "the thoughts of God," 2.11) or "the mind of the Lord" (2.16, quoting Isa 40.13). These are closer to personal knowledge than to knowledge of facts, and should be translated accordingly.

A more difficult problem is the translation of those passages where Paul makes a contrast between (a) natural human wisdom or knowledge, sometimes called "the wisdom of this world," and (b) the knowledge or wisdom which has its origin in God or in Christ. Paul usually makes it quite clear which kind of knowledge or wisdom he has in mind. In 2.4, for example, he speaks of "plausible words of [human] wisdom" in contrast to "demonstration of the Spirit and of power." Every effort should be made to translate these two kinds of wisdom or knowledge by the same word or phrase in the receptor language; otherwise the basis of the contrast is lost. In most languages this will be possible. If it is quite impossible, a note should be added stating that the same terms are used in the Greek.

Nevertheless it is only natural that the two kinds of knowledge or wisdom operate in different ways. In this letter human wisdom is especially associated with eloquent speaking. Paul generally rejects any claim to this (see 1.17; 2.1,4,5,13). Occasionally, however, he does speak of knowledge and wisdom as being positively associated with his own teaching and preaching; see, for example, 2.6,7; 12.8.

One symptom of the contrast between human and divine wisdom is that divine wisdom is associated with power, while human wisdom is not (see 1.24; compare 1.30; also 12.8; 13.2). This, however, is not part of the meaning of the words for knowledge and wisdom themselves; it is something made clear by the context.

One of Paul's favorite expressions is the rhetorical question "Do you not know?"(3.16; 5.6; 6.2,3,9,15,16,19; 9.13,24). This is usually a way of tactfully reminding the readers of the facts which they had previously learned as part of Christian instruction. In two places, 11.3 and 12.2-3, Paul moves from what the readers know already to new things which he wants them to "know" or "understand." In both cases the reference is to factual rather than personal knowledge.

In a few places such as 8.1,4, "we know" seems to introduce a reference to a letter which had been sent to Paul from the Christians at Corinth. In such places Paul begins by indicating a point of agreement or common ground with his correspondents, but then he goes on to correct something they have written. Some translations put what "we know" in quotation marks (as RSV does in 8.1); other translations add words such as "as they say" (TEV) or "as you say" (NEB) to make the meaning clear.

Some aspects of knowledge and wisdom found in other books of the Bible are not prominent in 1 Corinthians. For example, Paul does not often use "know" in the sense of having practical skill, "knowing how to" do something. The closest Paul comes to it is in 3.10, where he describes himself as a "wise," that is, "skillful" master builder; and in 6.5, where "wise" means having the necessary understanding to judge a legal dispute. Nor does Paul use "know" in this letter in the sense of having sexual relations.

1.6	RSV	TEV

even as the testimony to Christ was confirmed among you—	The message about Christ has become so firmly established in you

RSV understands this verse as being merely an aside by Paul. The dashes in RSV are equivalent to parentheses. However, it also seems that Paul is expanding on the beginning of verse 5. God enriched the Christians in Corinth more and more as the Christian message took deep root in their lives. RSV shows this fact by the use of **even as,** although TEV omits a connective word in order to divide the sentence. In any case, the meaning seems to be that people received spiritual gifts as the result of Christian preaching.

TEV's translation "has become . . . firmly established" is probably more correct than RSV's **confirmed.** The context does not seem to contain the idea of one thing's being confirmed or guaranteed by another. Translators in some languages will need to render the passive expression "firmly established" as, for example, "God has firmly established . . . in your lives." One may even use a more idiomatic expression and say "The message about Christ has put its roots down firmly in your lives" or "God has caused the message about Christ to put its roots . . . ."

The Greek word translated **testimony** also means "witness," implying then that the testimony is "about" Christ rather than "by" him. TEV brings this meaning out clearly by saying "the message about Christ."

The Greek may mean either **among you** or "in you" (TEV). Since much of this letter is concerned with relations of Christians with one another, **among you** suits the wider context better. The GeCL first edition made this wider context more explicit by rendering this as "in your (local) church."

1.7	RSV	TEV

so that you are not lacking in any spiritual gift, as you wait for the revealing of our Lord Jesus Christ;

that you have not failed to receive a single blessing, as you wait for our Lord Jesus Christ to be revealed.

In many languages it will be more natural to make verse 7 a separate sentence, although 6 and 7 are one sentence in the Greek. Perhaps one could begin the verse with "As a result, you have not failed . . . ."

The exact meaning of **you are not lacking in any spiritual gift** is uncertain. The possibilities are:

(a) there is not one of God's gifts which you do not have (TEV and NEB have this interpretation);

(b) there are none of God's gifts which you do not have enough of;

(c) there is not one of God's gifts which you have less of than any other gifts (the King James Version [KJV] seems to take this meaning).

Possibility (a) is the most likely; (b) is somewhat weaker, but otherwise is not much different from (a); and (c) is not supported by the context, where Corinth is not being compared with other churches.

The Greek word translated as **spiritual gift** and TEV as "blessing" is related to the word for "grace"; but it always has the meaning of a specific gift from God. GeCL makes this meaning fully explicit by translating "the gifts which God's Spirit gives."

As you wait . . . : in the second half of verse 7 Paul turns his attention from what Christ has already done for the Corinthian Christians to what he will do. The word translated **wait** is a strong one. It does not suggest a passive attitude but one of eager expectation. NEB's translation "wait expectantly" brings out the full meaning. A number of languages can render this element of "expectantly" by an idiom; for example, "as you set your face and eyes waiting for."

For the revealing: the Greek noun rendered as **revealing** is the term from which the English word "apocalypse" is derived. It is often used in speaking about the End Time. Although the Greek uses a noun, **revealing** is an event or action and will need to be translated as a verb in many languages, as TEV has done. In other languages it may be necessary to show that Paul is teaching about Jesus' return to earth in order to judge everyone. In this case one may say, for example, "as you wait for Jesus Christ to appear." But if a translator is of the opinion that God is the doer of the action **revealing**, one may say "as you wait for God to reveal Jesus Christ" (see the introduction to this section for a discussion on translating these passive verbs).

who will sustain you to the end, guilt-   He will also keep you firm to the end,
less in the day of our Lord Jesus Christ.   so that you will be faultless on the Day
                                            of our Lord Jesus Christ.

Many translations begin a new sentence at this point. It is not necessary,
though, to follow TEV's example in translating the word for "also." Paul has not
previously mentioned anything else which Christ has done. **Who** in RSV and "he" in
TEV refer to Jesus Christ in verse 7. This fact needs to be made clear in languages where the translator has rendered the latter part of verse 7 as "for God to
reveal Jesus Christ."

The Greek verb which is translated **will sustain you** is the same as that
which is translated "confirmed" or "firmly established" in verse 6. GeCL renders
this as "he will help you to remain firm on this ground to the end." In some languages it will be necessary to explain the "ground" on which the Corinthian
Christians will "remain firm." The meaning is that Christians must not lose their
faith in Christ no matter what tests or temptations they meet. One can say "He
will also keep you from losing your faith."

RSV and TEV are certainly correct in using the expression **to the end** in this
verse. The context speaks clearly about the final "Day" (TEV), or the Day when
Jesus Christ will return.

The central idea of the word **guiltless** is not that the Corinthians will be
prevented from doing anything wrong until Christ comes again, but that Christ
will "keep them firm" in their trust in him. He will keep them from renouncing
their faith or denying him even under persecution, so that in the final judgment he
may pronounce them innocent. GeCL expresses this same idea in a negative way:
"so that no one can accuse you (successfully)."

Day: for Paul, "the Day of the Lord" has become, not just God's judgment
day, but the day when Christ comes to glory. Translators should use a phrase
similar to this, to avoid readers raising the objection: "Why should one day more
than another belong to God?" Translators should also avoid any phrase which
might be understood as meaning "Sunday."

Most manuscripts and most translations have **our Lord Jesus Christ** as in
verse 7 (NEB is an exception). Two important manuscripts omit **Christ** in verse 8,
perhaps because the scribes wished to make the sentence less heavy or repetitious. There is no reason why **Christ** should not be omitted here, since there is
no loss in meaning (see Metzger, pages 543-544; the UBS Greek text puts **Christ** in
square brackets). GeCL, having used the full phrase "our Lord Jesus Christ" in
verse 7, speaks simply of "his judgment day" in verse 8. One could also say here,
"on the day when he returns."

God is faithful, by whom you were   God is to be trusted, the God who
called into the fellowship of his Son,   called you to have fellowship with his
Jesus Christ our Lord.   Son Jesus Christ, our Lord.

God is faithful: the word **faithful,** which is chosen by RSV, often means the attitude of an inferior to a superior, as in the phrase "faithful servant," "faithful hound." That is not the meaning in this verse. TEV's "trusted" is a better translation. Another way to render this phrase is "You can trust God." In languages which must show the reason for "trusting," one may say "You can trust God that he will do these things." Some CLTs have placed these words at the end of the sentence in order to emphasize them; for example, ItCL says ". . . and God keeps his promises."

By whom you were called: many languages must show that God is the agent of the action **called.** Translations such as TEV and NEB make this explicit. GeCL says "God himself has called you."

Perhaps the most important word in this verse is the one which RSV and TEV translate **fellowship.** NEB replaces this noun by a verb having the same meaning: "to share in the life of his Son." "Share in," of course, simply means "participate in." The text implies that the **fellowship** into which God calls Christians is the fellowship or communion which he himself has with his Son. So the word which translators use here should not refer specifically to the kind of **fellowship** which Christians have with one another in the church.

TEV puts the clause "God is to be trusted" in apposition with the phrase "the God who." In languages which do not employ appositional constructions such as this, the translator should use two separate sentences; for example, "You can trust God. He is the one who called you . . . ."

	1.10-17	
RSV		TEV

Divisions in the Church

RSV	TEV
10 I appeal to you, brethren, by the name of our Lord Jesus Christ, that all of you agree and that there be no dissensions among you, but that you be united in the same mind and the same judgment. 11 For it has been reported to me by Chloe's people that there is quarreling among you, my brethren. 12 What I mean is that each one of you says, "I belong to Paul," or "I belong to Apollos," or "I belong to Cephas," or "I belong to Christ." 13 Is Christ divided? Was Paul crucified for you? Or were you baptized in the name of Paul? 14 I am thankful[b] that I baptized none of you except Crispus and Gaius; 15 lest any one should say that you were baptized in my name. 16 (I did baptize also the household of Stephanas. Beyond that, I do not know whether I baptized any one else.) 17 For Christ did not send me to baptize but to preach the gospel, and not with eloquent wisdom, lest the cross of Christ be emptied of its power.	10 By the authority of our Lord Jesus Christ I appeal to all of you, my brothers, to agree in what you say, so that there will be no divisions among you. Be completely united, with only one thought and one purpose. 11 For some people from Chloe's family have told me quite plainly, my brothers, that there are quarrels among you. 12 Let me put it this way: each one of you says something different. One says, "I follow Paul"; another, "I follow Apollos"; another, "I follow Peter"; and another, "I follow Christ." 13 Christ has been divided[a] into groups! Was it Paul who died on the cross for you? Were you baptized as Paul's disciples? 14 I thank God that I did not baptize any of you except Crispus and Gaius. 15 No one can say, then, that you were baptized as my disciples. (16 Oh yes, I also baptized Stephanas and his family; but I can't remember whether I baptized anyone else.) 17 Christ did not send me to baptize.

bOther ancient authorities read *I thank God*

He sent me to tell the Good News, and to tell it without using the language of human wisdom, in order to make sure that Christ's death on the cross is not robbed of its power.

a Christ has been divided; *some manuscripts have* Christ cannot be divided.

The introduction to this letter is now over, and Paul begins to discuss the problem of divisions in the church. This subject will continue to be important until 4.21.

Paul marks the beginning of a new section in three ways. First, the words I **appeal** are often used by Paul at the beginning of paragraphs. Second, when Paul uses the word **brethren** to address his readers, it usually marks a new stage in his argument, or a change of theme. Third, the Greek text in verse 10 uses a common word with the meaning "but" or "and." This word often indicates a new idea. However, RSV and TEV do not translate it, and this is in accordance with good English style.

Although verse 10 begins a new section, this section has points of contact with verses 1-9; for example, the unity of the Christian community, and Paul's authority as an apostle.

The TEV section heading "Divisions in the Church" may also be rendered as "The Corinthian Christians are Divided" or "The Corinthian Christians Quarrel."

1.10	RSV	TEV

I appeal to you, brethren, by the name of our Lord Jesus Christ, that all of you agree and that there be no dissensions among you, but that you be united in the same mind and the same judgment.

By the authority of our Lord Jesus Christ I appeal to all of you, my brothers, to agree in what you say, so that there will be no divisions among you. Be completely united, with only one thought and one purpose.

I appeal to you: Greek, like many other languages, has various verbs with the meaning "ask." Some are more formal than others, like the English "request." The most important verbs of "asking" in Paul's letters are *parakaleo* which is used here, and *erotao* which is used in Philippians 4.3. Both of these are relatively informal. The word *deomai* which is used in 2 Corinthians 5.20 and 10.2, is more formal or official. In each case, however, the context determines the shade of meaning to be given in translation. In the present verse Paul uses *parakaleo* with no particular emphasis, except that it is placed at the beginning of the sentence and the section.

Brethren: as RSV shows, there is no "my" (TEV) in Greek. TEV supplies this for stylistic purposes, as it is good natural English to use a possessive pronoun with words indicating family relationships. Translators in other languages will need to determine what is natural in their own languages. "Brothers" (TEV) here, as in other places in 1 Corinthians, refers to "fellow Christians," not actual family members.

By the name of is literally "in the name of." In Jewish thought someone's name involved his power and personality. This meant that when an important person sent someone else to speak or act in his name, that messenger must be heard and obeyed as if the one who sent him were there in person. TEV's rendering "By the authority of" conveys the meaning well in English; but in some languages it may be necessary to say, for example, "on behalf of." Paul speaks here as an apostle, that is, someone sent by Christ (see the comments on verse 1).

That all of you agree is literally "that all of you say the same (thing)." But the rest of the verse shows that Paul is not asking the Corinthian Christians to recite some fixed saying or formula.

The relation between the last three clauses of this verse needs to be made clear. Literally, the structure is: (a) in order that you all say the same (thing), (b) *and* that there be no divisions among you, (c) *but* that you be united. On the surface it looks as if Paul is contrasting (a) and (b) with (c). If we examine this verse more closely, however, it becomes clear that (a) is a general statement which (c) repeats in greater detail. (b) says the same thing as (c), but in a negative way. It may be helpful, then, to begin a new sentence at the end of (a), so that the contrast between (b) and (c) may be clearer. ItCL does this: ". . . I request you to put yourselves in agreement. Let there be no quarrels among you, but be united . . . ."

The Greek word which is translated **dissensions** is the origin of the English word "schism," but it does not yet have this technical meaning. In Mark 2.21 it is used to describe a tear in a garment. Similarly, the word which is translated **united** in verse 10 is used in Mark 1.19 of mending nets which have been torn.

We want to stress that Paul is writing to all the Christians in Corinth. They evidently all met in a single place. There were not separate churches or denominations as in a modern city. Paul is speaking here about divisions in the "thoughts" and "purposes" of the Christians. Some of them were showing loyalty to a particular leader, and this was destroying the unity of the church. This is the point of TEV's "so that there will be no divisions among you." At this point in the letter Paul is trying to prevent divisions from arising in the future, although later in the letter he speaks about divisions which have already arisen (see, for example, 11.18-19).

Some translators will need to render the English noun "divisions" (TEV) by a verb or verbal expression. One could say "so that you will not divide yourselves into groups."

There is no great difference in meaning between the expressions **same mind** and **same judgment**. These two terms are used in the Greek to add emphasis, and translators must consider whether the same is true in their own language. If there is a distinction, the word for **mind** (TEV "thought") suggests "perception" as compared with **judgment**.

1.11	RSV	TEV

For it has been reported to me by Chloe's people that there is quarreling among you, my brethren.

For some people from Chloe's family have told me quite plainly, my brothers, that there are quarrels among you.

Reported: the verb which TEV translates as "have told . . . quite plainly" does not necessarily have this strong sense. It more probably means only "report," "inform," or "tell" (compare NEB). Paul is trying to approach this delicate subject very gently, so he uses great tact. The phrase is literally "for it has been reported to me concerning you, my brothers."

The word **it** in **it has been reported** is a "dummy subject." This is a device used in English to create a grammatical subject so that there will be a complete sentence. In many languages translators can change the passive sentence to active and say, for example, "Some people from Chloe's family have informed me . . . ."

Chloe's people: no one knows whether Chloe's people were relatives, or other dependents such as slaves or former slaves. TEV renders this phrase as "Chloe's family," but other CLTs are divided on this matter. "Chloe's group" is a possible translation.

Quarrels here refers to strong arguments between church members as to who their spiritual leader and teacher was (see verse 12). Such quarreling involved only words, not physical violence. If a language requires that one state what the quarreling was about, one may say "that you are quarreling among yourselves as to who your leader is."

For **my brethren,** see the discussion on this expression at verse 10. Please note the great affection which is expressed by the word "my" before "brothers" (TEV).

1.12   RSV   TEV

What I mean is that each one of you says, "I belong to Paul," or "I belong to Apollos," or "I belong to Cephas," or "I belong to Christ."

Let me put it this way: each one of you says something different. One says, "I follow Paul"; another, "I follow Apollos"; another, "I follow Peter"; and another, "I follow Christ."

What I mean is that is literally "but I say this." This phrase introduces in greater detail an explanation of what Paul has just said in verses 10-11. GeCL translates this as "you know what I mean." ItCL says "I (will) explain myself."

Each one of you is probably an exaggeration (see the comment on verse 5). The Corinthian readers would have understood it in this way. If, however, readers of a modern translation are likely to understand such a phrase literally, translators should use an expression such as "you are saying many different things."[3]

Or I belong to Christ: this is the meaning given by all translations which we have consulted. Some commentaries think that here Paul is speaking in his own name. If so, the translation would be "but I belong to Christ." However, the translation given by RSV and TEV is more likely, and TEV's rendering "I follow" is more natural English. In the Gospels the words "follow Christ" literally mean "walking about with Jesus wherever he led his followers." However, pupils often did this with their teacher too. So the word "follow" also has the wider meaning "acknowledge someone as teacher." That is what Paul means here. These words could be translated, "I have Christ as my teacher" or "Christ is my teacher." However, in the ancient world the relationship between a teacher and his

_____

3 There is a similar problem in John 2.10, where the Greek is just "everyone," but TEV correctly translates "Everyone else serves the best wine first . . . ."

followers was often closer and more personal than in a western school today. It was similar to the relationship between an Indian guru and his followers.

1.13 RSV	TEV
Is Christ divided? Was Paul crucified for you? Or were you baptized in the name of Paul?	**Christ has been divided***a* **into groups! Was it Paul who died on the cross for you? Were you baptized as Paul's disciples?**

a Christ has been divided; *some manuscripts have* Christ cannot be divided.

This verse contains several problems. One has to do with the text itself, while the others are concerned with punctuation. Most Greek manuscripts make the first question an open one: "Is Christ, then, divided?" The second question, on the other hand, expects the answer "No": "Surely it was not Paul who was crucified for you?" A few manuscripts make the first question correspond to the second: "Surely Christ is not divided?" This, though, is less likely to be what Paul wrote. The difference between the two questions is one of emphasis rather than meaning. Thus TEV translates the first one as a statement: "Christ has been divided into groups!" The second is translated as a question: "Was it Paul who died on the cross for you?"

TEV makes it clear that Paul is not thinking of an individual being cut up into pieces. He is thinking of the church, the Christian community in Corinth, as the body of Christ. He means that since there is only one Christ, it is unthinkable that those who believe in him should be divided into rival parties. In some languages it may be necessary to make the implicit information explicit by translating "Christ has only one body, the church, and it cannot be divided."

The oldest Greek manuscripts had no punctuation. It is therefore possible to read the first part of this verse as either a question, an exclamation, or a statement. There is little difference between what is called a rhetorical question and a statement. A rhetorical question is one which is asked, not to obtain information, but to give more emphasis or impact. For example, NEB's "Surely Christ has not been divided among you!" would have almost the same meaning if a question mark were put in place of the exclamation mark. Paul used many of these questions in 1 Corinthians. In fact, sometimes there is a whole series of them in a section such as 4.7-8, and especially 9.1-12. When translators deal with rhetorical questions, they have to decide, first of all, whether for Paul himself the question is a real one or a rhetorical one. Secondly, translators must decide whether their own languages use rhetorical questions. If these are not natural in a translator's language, they should be rendered as emphatic statements. If the rhetorical question is positive, then the corresponding emphatic statement must be negative: "Who cares?" means "Nobody cares!" Whereas, if the rhetorical question is a negative one, the corresponding emphatic statement will be positive: "Aren't you ashamed?" means "You should be ashamed!"[4]

Another punctuation problem occurs between the second and last parts of this verse. Should they be punctuated as one (double) question, or as two separate

---

4 For a detailed study of rhetorical questions, see Beekman and Callow (1974), chapter 15.

questions? Translators need to decide how the three sentences are related to each other. For many languages it will be helpful to follow TEV. One should then make the first part of the verse a statement, and render the second part as two separate questions. The translator should then omit RSV's **or**.

Crucified for you: TEV uses the simpler expression "died on the cross . . . ." It does this in order to make the meaning of **crucified** clear, especially near the beginning of this letter. Paul was writing to people who knew about the Roman method of execution called "crucifixion." But in some parts of the world today, readers of Bible translations may know nothing about this method of executing people. They may even think of the cross as mainly an article which stands in churches. In such cases it will be important to use some expression which means "died" (TEV) or "was killed." And since this is the first time that Paul refers to crucifixion in this letter, one can say something like "died on a cross." It is also important not to talk about some other kind of execution here, since Paul is, of course, referring to an actual historical form of execution.

Were you baptized . . . ? The meaning of this question is quite general: "Did someone baptize you in the name of Paul?"

Baptized in the name of Paul: in verse 10 TEV translated **in the name of** as "by the authority of." Here, where the meaning is different, TEV renders this phrase "as Paul's disciples." Some of the meaning, though, is lost in TEV. Baptism, from the earliest times, involved literally naming the name of Christ (see Matt 28.19 for a command from Christ which uses the formula "in the name" in both RSV and TEV). GeCL has a note on the word "name" in its glossary. It says "with this naming of the name, the person baptized is given over to belong to Jesus, his Lord, and is placed under Christ's protection." One can rephrase **were you baptized in the name of Paul** as "When they baptized you, did they use Paul's name?" or "Did they baptize you as if you belonged to Paul?" or ". . . so that you would belong to Paul?"

<hr>

1.14   RSV   TEV

I am thankful[b] that I baptized none of you except Crispus and Gaius;

       I thank God that I did not baptize any of you except Crispus and Gaius.

[b] Other ancient authorities read *I thank God*

There is good evidence to support either RSV's **I am thankful** or TEV's "I thank God." The UBS Greek text includes "God" in the third edition, so TEV follows it. The difference, though, is so slight that TEV does not think it worth indicating in a footnote. Everywhere else Paul uses the full expression "I thank God." So it would be natural for scribes to add "God" in this verse to make it agree with the other passages, and to fill out the meaning. The phrase "I thank" would be very clumsy in English by itself, and Paul certainly means something more specific than "I am thankful," as TEV makes clear.

| lest any one should say that you were baptized in my name. | No one can say, then, that you were baptized as my disciples. |

Lest any one should say: this rendering by RSV is too literal. The Greek may also mean "with the result that"; in other words, something did not happen. This seems a better meaning here. Paul is glad that he baptized so few people at Corinth, because the result now is that no one can say that Paul baptized on his own authority or in order to found a party of his own in the church. TEV's "then" means "consequently" and helps to make the meaning clear. GeCL makes the whole statement positive: "Otherwise you would say afterwards that *I* had become your Lord through baptism!"

Instead of **you were baptized** many Greek manuscripts have "I baptized." Paul probably didn't write it this way, but many translations will need to make clear the doer of the action "baptize" in this verse. It was most likely Paul. However, it would be just as correct to render this as "they baptized you to become my disciples" or "that you received the rite of baptism in order to become my disciples."

| (I did baptize also the household of Stephanas. Beyond that, I do not know whether I baptized any one else.) | (Oh yes, I also baptized Stephanas and his family; but I can't remember whether I baptized anyone else.) |

In this verse Paul corrects verse 14 and also adds something which he had forgotten while dictating. RSV and TEV show this by using parentheses. This extra thought of Paul must be kept in its place. Translators should not remove this personal touch of Paul by putting verse 15 after verse 16. TEV's "Oh yes" is good English style. One could also say "Oh, I remember now!"

Household has more than the literal meaning "house." It can mean "family" as in TEV, or even include unrelated dependents who are living in the same house. But there is nothing in this verse to indicate whether or not the **household** or "family" included children.

RSV and TEV translate the second half of the verse rather literally. Although some scholars disagree, the context suggests the slightly stronger translation "I cannot remember baptizing anyone else." GeCL has "but otherwise, I really do not know of anyone else whom I baptized."[5] The word **anyone** is singular. One could say "any other person."

| For Christ did not send me to baptize but to preach the gospel, and not with | Christ did not send me to baptize. He sent me to tell the Good News, and to |

---

5 The word which RSV translates "whether" may also mean "that," as in 7.16. See C. Burchard, 1961, "*Ei* nach einem Ausdruck des Wissens oder Nichtwissens Joh 9:25: Act 19:2: I Cor 1:16: 7:16," Zeitschrift für die Neutestamentliche Wissenschaft 52.73-82.

eloquent wisdom, lest the cross of Christ be emptied of its power.

tell it without using the language of human wisdom, in order to make sure that Christ's death on the cross is not robbed of its power.

Paul now summarizes the argument of this section. **Christ . . . send me** points back to verse 10 where Paul claimed the "authority of our Lord Jesus Christ." It also recalls verse 1, where Paul emphasizes strongly that he is "called . . . to be an apostle." "Apostle" and "send" are related words in Greek.

RSV's **For** links this verse with the whole previous argument, rather than directly with verse 16. It links up in particular with verses 14-15. A literal translation like **For** does not show this connection. So TEV, like NEB, omits this word and puts verse 17 in one paragraph with 14-15 in order to make this linking clear.

This verse also prepares the way for the following verse by introducing the themes of *telling the Good News, wisdom,* and *the cross.* It is for this reason that some CLTs begin a new paragraph here and not at verse 18. Paul uses the contrasting terms "not baptism but preaching" like a hinge to move from one stage in his argument to the next. The problem with beginning a new paragraph at verse 17 is that verse 16 makes a weak ending to a section. We must remember that translations will be read aloud in church.

In verses 11-16 Paul has used a rather simple and informal style with unusually short sentences. But in verse 17 Paul's thoughts begin to be more condensed and his style becomes less clear. This is because he starts to write about things which are more theological in nature. It is for this reason that TEV repeats "and to tell it," preparing the reader for new thoughts. The meaning is almost "and, what is more, to tell it without using the language of human wisdom." In certain languages it will be helpful to begin a new sentence at the words "and to tell." One can then restructure the first part of this verse as follows: "Christ did not . . . but rather to preach the Good News. I should preach, then, without . . . ."

The Greek word which TEV translates as "language" is the same word which was translated "speech" in verse 5. And there is little difference of meaning between the word translated **wisdom** here, and "knowledge" in verse 5. **Wisdom** is the key word in this section and is used with various shades of meaning. Each time it occurs, translators should ask themselves two questions: (1) does this wisdom refer to true wisdom which comes from God, or (2) is Paul speaking in an ironic way about so-called human wisdom, apart from God? If it is this second meaning, it may be necessary for the translator to add additional words such as TEV's "human" in this verse in order to make the meaning clear.

In verse 17 the context shows that **wisdom** is used in a negative sense. In fact, Paul uses it this way until verse 24. For this reason TEV rightly adds "human." Still better is Phps' translation, "the persuasiveness of clever words." The word "clever" in English often has the negative or ironic meaning which Paul wants to give to **wisdom** in this verse. Paul is trying to show the contrast between the superficial impressiveness of clever talk, and the message about the deep and real power of the cross. So Paul says at the end of this verse that the two cannot be combined.

Emptied of its power or "robbed of its power" (TEV) both render the Greek correctly. The Greek word means literally **emptied** and is the same word which is used in Philippians 2.7 of Christ's "emptying himself." Possible translations are "so that Christ's death on the cross is not useless" or "so that all the power of Christ's death is not taken away."

Christ the Power and the Wisdom
of God

18 For the word of the cross is folly to those who are perishing, but to us who are being saved it is the power of God. 19 For it is written,
"I will destroy the wisdom of the wise,
and the cleverness of the clever I will thwart."
20 Where is the wise man? Where is the scribe? Where is the debater of this age? Has not God made foolish the wisdom of the world? 21 For since, in the wisdom of God, the world did not know God through wisdom, it pleased God through the folly of what we preach to save those who believe. 22 For Jews demand signs and Greeks seek wisdom, 23 but we preach Christ crucified, a stumbling block to Jews and folly to Gentiles, 24 but to those who are called, both Jews and Greeks, Christ the power of God and the wisdom of God. 25 For the foolishness of God is wiser than men, and the weakness of God is stronger than men.

18 For the message about Christ's death on the cross is nonsense to those who are being lost; but for us who are being saved it is God's power. 19 The scripture says,
"I will destroy the wisdom of the wise
and set aside the understanding of the scholars."
20 So then, where does that leave the wise? or the scholars? or the skillful debaters of this world? God has shown that this world's wisdom is foolishness! 21 For God in his wisdom made it impossible for people to know him by means of their own wisdom. Instead, by means of the so-called "foolish" message we preach, God decided to save those who believe. 22 Jews want miracles for proof, and Greeks look for wisdom. 23 As for us, we proclaim the crucified Christ, a message that is offensive to the Jews and nonsense to the Gentiles; 24 but for those whom God has called, both Jews and Gentiles, this message is Christ, who is the power of God and the wisdom of God. 25 For what seems to be God's foolishness is wiser than human wisdom, and what seems to be God's weakness is stronger than human strength.

The TEV section heading "Christ the Power and the Wisdom of God" may also be translated as "The Power and the Wisdom of God is Christ." This section heading reflects the phrases at the end of verse 24, and so the translation should resemble the words used in verse 24, to help highlight the theme. Most translations which use section headings make a single section of verses 18-31 as TEV has done. But GeCL inserts an extra heading, "How God Acts," before verse 26.

This section is carefully written and full of effective contrasts and repetitions. Barrett, for example, describes verses 22-24 as "Paul's most brilliant epigrammatic description of the world in which the Gospel is preached, and of the Gospel itself." The translator should try to keep the balance and repetition which is present in the Greek wherever this can be done naturally. But where repetition would produce a heavy effect, it should be avoided.

For the word of the cross is folly to those who are perishing, but to us

For the message about Christ's death on the cross is nonsense to those

who are being saved it is the power of God.	who are being lost; but for us who are being saved it is God's power.

As TEV shows, **word** refers not to a single word but to the "message" about Christ's death on the cross.

Of the cross, which TEV translates as "about Christ's death on the cross," can also be rendered as "that Christ died on the cross."

Is folly . . . is the power of God: the word translated **is** has rather more emphasis in Greek than in English. This repetition of **is** helps to balance the two halves of the verse. However, it is used to express a contrast in meaning, as the word **but** shows. Translators should therefore consider whether **is** means the same in the two halves of the verse, or whether, in their own language, it would be clearer to translate the clause **is folly** as "seems folly (nonsense)." The underlying thought is that **those who are perishing** fail to understand the message about the cross, whereas Paul and his readers **who are being saved** understand it as what it really is, namely "God's power" (TEV). In a number of languages it may be necessary to place the phrase "those who are being lost" (TEV) at the beginning of the verse, and restructure the whole verse in the following way: "Those who are being lost think that the message about Christ's death on the cross is nonsense, but we who are being saved see it as the power of God." TEV's "lost" does not refer to someone losing his way, but to someone who is on his way to destruction.

The parallel between the two halves of this verse is partly broken by the addition in the second half of **to us,** which a few Greek manuscripts wrongly omit. The context shows clearly that these words refer to all Christians, including both Paul and his readers.

The meaning of the word translated **power** is quite general. Often, especially in the plural, it can mean a "mighty act" in the sense of a miracle; but verse 22 shows that Paul does not mean it that way in this verse. Paul is thinking mainly of the power which God himself has and uses, not the power which he shares with believers. Translators should therefore avoid using a word here which suggests, for example, physical power or physical violence. Possible translations of the final part of this verse are "it is through Christ's death on the cross that God shows how powerful he is" or "we see how powerful God is because of how Christ died."

1.19	RSV	TEV

For it is written, "I will destroy the wisdom of the wise, and the cleverness of the clever I will thwart."	The scripture says, "I will destroy the wisdom of the wise and set aside the understanding of the scholars."

Some scholars have thought that verses 18-31 are from a sermon based on the quotation from Jeremiah 9.24 in verse 31. Jewish preachers sometimes put their text at the end of a sermon. However, Paul seems to link his thinking more closely to the quotation from Isaiah 29.14 in this verse, especially to its key word "wisdom."

RSV's **For** should be omitted in translation, as it is vague and possibly misleading. Paul seems to mean "What I have just said is confirmed by scripture when it says . . . ."

It is written is literally "it has been written." The tense of the verb in Greek implies that what has been written in the past remains valid in the present. Paul often uses this phrase to introduce quotations from the Old Testament. RSV's rather literal translation **it is written** may not be enough to tell some readers that the quotation is from the Old Testament. TEV renders this phrase as "the scripture says." In a number of languages, though, one cannot talk about scripture's "talking" or "saying." In these languages only humans or other living beings can talk. In such cases the translator may say "In a passage of the Scriptures we find the following" or "One may read in the Scriptures the following." GeCL has the excellent translation "God has said." ItCL has "the Bible says," but has to add a glossary note explaining that this is not the whole Bible, but what Christians would now call the Old Testament. It is better to avoid the word "Bible" and to translate "the holy writings" or to follow the example of GeCL.

Like most of Paul's quotations, this one is taken from the Septuagint (the Greek Old Testament), though Paul as a rabbi could have quoted the Hebrew text (see Acts 22.3; Phil 3.5). Books were bulky and expensive, and Paul very likely could not take them with him on his frequent travels. So he made many of his quotations from memory. Sometimes, therefore, he gave the general sense rather than the exact wording. This is what he does here. At the end of the quotation, in place of the Septuagint's rendering "I will hide," Paul writes "I will set aside." He may be thinking of Psalm 32.10 (Psa 31.10 in Greek), where the phrase "set aside" (TEV) is used twice about God's "setting aside" the plans of the Gentiles.

As often in Old Testament poetry, the two lines of the quotation mean the same:

I will destroy	**the wisdom**	**of the wise**
I will thwart	**the cleverness**	**of the clever**

In some languages, including English, it is not natural to write poetry in pairs of synonymous parallel lines. It may be better, then, to combine the two lines into one. The key word **wisdom** must be kept because it is important in the following verses. But Paul does not use **cleverness** again in 1 or 2 Corinthians. If a translator decides to translate both halves of the quotation, the **and** may be omitted since it may suggest that something new is about to be said. In this case, **I will** may be repeated.

On **wisdom**, see comment on 1.17. **Clever** and **cleverness** are often used in a bad sense in English. There is nothing negative about the Greek words themselves; Paul is saying essentially the same thing in both halves of the sentence. But it is clear from the context that both **wisdom** and **cleverness** are used in an ironic, negative sense, of human intelligence used without God's help. Both halves of the sentence imply that God will prevent the plans made by this kind of human wisdom from being realized. It may be necessary to make this explicit by translating, for example, "I will prevent the plans of those who think they are wise or clever from coming into effect."

Translators should also consider whether the subject of this quotation is one about which poetry would naturally be written in their own language. TEV translates this verse as prose in the Old Testament (Isa 29.14). Speakers of each language normally have their own views of what subjects are suitable for poetry.[6]

RSV	TEV
Where is the wise man? Where is the scribe? Where is the debater of this age? Has not God made foolish the wisdom of the world?	So then, where does that leave the wise? or the scholars? or the skillful debaters of this world? God has shown that this world's wisdom is foolishness!

TEV's translation "So then" is not in the Greek, but is added in the English to indicate that Paul is about to draw a conclusion from the Old Testament verse which he has just quoted. This is good English style and may also be useful in other languages. Other ways to indicate this transition are "In that case," "If this is the case," or "If God is going to do this."

RSV's literal translation **Where is** . . . does not mean much in some languages, and may even be understood as "Tell me where he is." It is actually a rhetorical question (see the comments on 1.13). TEV is right to expand the phrase to "where does that leave . . . ?" One can also translate this as "what can we say about . . . ?" or "of what importance are . . . ?"

The Greek singular forms, **wise man, scribe,** and **debater,** refer to groups of people, so TEV is correct to translate by using plurals. **Wise man** may refer to Greek philosophers. These were people who had great knowledge and were highly respected. **Scribe** probably refers to Jewish teachers of the Law. These were people who had a deep understanding of the Law and could explain it to others. **Debater** refers to people who were skilled in arguing.

The rhythm and structure of the Greek sentence makes it appear that **of this age** refers to the **debater** only. However, the meaning of the whole sentence suggests that all three groups are **of this age.** NEB makes this meaning explicit: ". . . limited, all of them, to this passing age?" Where the grammar and the meaning of a text appear to disagree, the translator must translate the meaning. TEV's rendering "of this world" is a more accurate English translation of the Greek.

The Greek uses two different words for **world:** *aiōn* and *kosmos.* These occur in this verse as follows: ". . . the skillful debaters of this *aiōn*? God has shown that the wisdom of the *kosmos* is foolishness!" *Kosmos* is repeated in verse 21, where it is translated "people" (TEV), though earlier editions of TEV had "men." TEV is probably right in thinking that there is little difference in meaning here, and that the two words are used in Greek for variety. RSV's **age** indicates that in some contexts *aiōn* refers to time, not place. *Kosmos,* though, refers particularly to the people of the world, as in 1.21 (see TEV). In this passage, as often in Paul's writings, both ideas are included. On the one hand, there is **this age** or "this world" (TEV) in which the powers of evil reign. On the other hand, there is "the world (or, age) to come" which was foretold in the Old Testament, and now has begun with the coming of Christ. But God must still complete it by a great act in which he will transform the whole universe. The context, therefore, supports TEV in using the same word "world" twice.

The Greek for **Has not God made** refers to a single past event, which, as the context shows, was the death of Christ.

Has not God made foolish the wisdom of this world? One can render this as a statement: "The fact is, God has demonstrated that the wisdom of wise people is foolishness."

---

6 See K.R. Crim, 1972, "Translating the Poetry of the Bible," <u>The Bible Translator</u> 23.102-109.

　　　　RSV　　　　　　　　　　　　　　TEV

For since, in the wisdom of God, the world did not know God through wisdom, it pleased God through the folly of what we preach to save those who believe.

For God in his wisdom made it impossible for people to know him by means of their own wisdom. Instead, by means of the so-called "foolish" message we preach, God decided to save those who believe.

If one compares RSV with TEV, it is clear how much TEV has changed the structure of the Greek in order to bring out the meaning more clearly. **For since** introduces the reason why **it pleased God . . . to save those who believe.** There is a contrast involved between the first and second parts of this verse. TEV's "Instead" makes this contrast clear.

World: see the comments on verse 20 for a discussion of this word.

Most translations and commentaries assume that verse 21 refers to two sorts of wisdom: God's wisdom and human wisdom. RSV's rather literal translation does not make this clear. It is even grammatically possible that **through wisdom** repeats the meaning of **in the wisdom of God,** but this is most unlikely. The words translated **through wisdom** may also mean "by means of wisdom." Paul's point, though, is not that human wisdom was evil in itself, but that people refused to use it in the right way.

The Greek word translated as **it pleased** often refers to a formal decision made by someone in authority. TEV's "decided" brings out this meaning.

TEV's "so-called" is not in the Greek, but is added to make clear in English that Paul is using the word "foolish" ironically, not in a serious way. Other languages will have different ways to convey irony; for example, "what people call the foolish message we preach."

As TEV shows, the word which Paul uses here for "preaching" means, not the act of preaching, but its content. So "the . . . message we preach" (TEV) is a better translation than RSV's **what we preach.** Paul is not contrasting the "use of words" and some other kind of action, but is contrasting the "foolish" message about Christ's death, and the so-called "wisdom" of skillful debaters.

The verb **believe** in a number of languages will require an explicit object. One can say, for example, "believe in him."

Translators may need to change the order of the clauses in the second sentence. For example, one can restructure this as "Instead, God decided that he would use the so-called 'foolish' message that we preach in order to save those who believe in him."

　　　　RSV　　　　　　　　　　　　　　TEV

For Jews demand signs and Greeks seek wisdom,

Jews want miracles for proof, and Greeks look for wisdom.

For translates the same Greek word as **since** in verse 21. It is difficult to see what the purpose of this word is, and TEV, NEB, and other translations omit it.

Demand and **seek** translate Greek verbs that are similar in meaning. They are probably used for variety. RSV's **demand** is probably too strong. The meaning of **seek** is "to gain" or "expect to get." "Expect" would be closer to the meaning here, or some phrase like "want someone to give them."

Signs: especially in John's writings, the Greek word for "sign" sometimes means a miracle which does not only astonish people, but shows the meaning of what God is doing. TEV's "miracles" is a better translation in this verse. The phrase "want miracles" can also be rendered as "want to see miracles."

TEV's "for proof" is not in the Greek. Most CLTs which we consulted omit it (except FrCL). In favor of adding these words, it may be said that there is evidence in the New Testament of people asking for, or being given, miracles as signs that God was at work in Jesus (see, for example, Matt 12.38-42; Luke 7.20-21; 11.29-32; John 14.11; 1 Cor 2.4). If the words "for proof" are added, it may be necessary in some languages to explain what is being proved. This may be done by adding a few words, such as "proof that God is at work"; this is implied in verse 21. In any case, the idea of logical or mathematical proof should be avoided. What Paul means here is powerful convincing evidence; the Jews whom Paul mentions would have accepted miracles as such evidence. Paul is probably thinking, in fact, of miracles like the ten plagues in the Old Testament, which convinced the king of Egypt that he should set the Israelites free.[7] The evidence seems to show, then, that "for proof" should be omitted.

In verses 22-24 two different Greek words are used for "non-Jews," namely **Greeks** and **Gentiles.** It is most unlikely that Paul intended to refer to two separate groups of people. **Greeks** was most often used to mean, not just the Greek nation, but non-Jewish pagans in general. The translation of **Jews** and **Greeks** in verse 22, as well as **Gentiles** in verse 23, should avoid suggesting that Paul means every individual Jew and Gentile. He has experienced that many Jews ask for signs, and many Greeks seek wisdom, and based on that experience he has made a general statement about the two groups. In certain parts of the world it will be necessary to take care that the terms used for "Jews" and "Gentiles" are not considered insulting. "Gentiles" means generally "non-Jews." So any reference to particular groups, such as Greeks, Arabs, or Christians, should be avoided. "Gentiles," though, is not a common-language word; the TEV word list explains it as "a person who is not a Jew." One may also say "non-Jews" (see ItCL, for example).

1.23	RSV	TEV

but we preach Christ crucified, a stumbling block to Jews and folly to Gentiles,	As for us, we proclaim the crucified Christ, a message that is offensive to the Jews and nonsense to the Gentiles;

TEV's "As for us" is added to show that **we** is emphatic in the Greek. This is a natural style in many other languages too. In languages which have an exclusive "we," it is important to understand that **we** in this verse refers to "Paul and the other evangelists." It does not necessarily include Sosthenes (verse 1), and probably not the readers of Paul's letter. It is even possible, in the light of 2.1-2, that **we** here means no more than "I, Paul." This is a common way for Paul and other writers to speak. However, it is safer to translate this pronoun as the exclusive **we** in this verse.

---

[7] See L.A. Rood, 1960, "Le Christ comme dynamis theou," Litérature et theologie pauliniennes, pages 93-108 (A. Descamps, editor).

Preach (TEV's "proclaim") translates a word often used of a herald or town crier making public announcements. It is often employed in the New Testament in speaking of apostles and other people who told the good news about Jesus. It does not usually refer to preaching to the Christian community. Translators should certainly avoid using a word which only means preaching in a church building.

Usually Paul uses **Christ** as a proper name, equivalent to "Jesus" (see comments on verse 1). This verse is one of the places, however, where the name may keep some of its original meaning of "Messiah," the one whom God chose to be king. It is not just the story of Jesus being put to death on the cross which is "offensive to the Jews" (TEV), but the claim that the one whom God has chosen to rule over and liberate his people had died as a criminal. However, most translations keep **Christ,** even here as a proper name, because "Messiah" is as difficult for most present-day readers to understand as it would have been for non-Jews in Paul's time. See the TEV word list on "Christ."

The tense of the verb which is translated **crucified** suggests an event whose effect continues into the present. Whether translators can easily convey this or not depends on the tense structure of verbs in the receptor language.

The word **stumbling-block** originally meant "an object which trips someone up." It may mean "something which makes a person fall in such a way as to be (physically or spiritually) destroyed." TEV's translation, "a message that is offensive," is probably adequate. In more colloquial English we could say the Jews "could not swallow" or "could not stomach" this message. Other languages will have equivalent figurative expressions. GeCL's "for the Jews, that is blasphemy" is a possible translation, but perhaps a little too strong. The underlying meaning in this context is probably that Jews rejected the message about Christ's death on the cross because it was so completely different from what they expected of the Messiah.

Grammatically the **stumbling-block** may be either Christ, the cross, or the message about Christ's death on the cross. The difference in meaning is slight, since the three are closely connected. "Christ," or "Christ as having been crucified," fits in best with verse 24.

The final phrase **and folly to the Gentiles** may be rendered as "and the Gentiles feel that it is nonsense."

RSV   TEV

but to those who are called, both Jews and Greeks, Christ the power of God and the wisdom of God.

but for those whom God has called, both Jews and Gentiles, this message is Christ, who is the power of God and the wisdom of God.

The end of verse 23 and the beginning of verse 24 contain a contrast of three things: **a stumbling-block to Jews, folly to Gentiles,** and **but to those who are called . . . .** Normally the Greek words showing this contrast would be translated as "on the one hand . . . on the other hand." However, "on the one hand" cannot be used here in English, since the contrast involves three factors, not two: **Jews, Gentiles,** and **those who are called.** Translators must decide how these three factors are related. The context seems to show that the important contrast is between Jews and Gentiles on the one hand, and Christian preachers on the other. To make this clear, TEV rightly leaves out of verse 23b any elements of contrast between Jews and Gentiles.

At the end of the verse, **of God** is repeated in Greek as in RSV, TEV, and other translations. Paul wishes to emphasize that Christ is not wise or powerful in human terms—even though God makes him "our wisdom" (verse 30). In some languages it may be necessary to translate these phrases as "Christ, who is the power which comes from God, and the wisdom which comes from God" or "Christ, who shows that God is powerful and wise."

1.25	RSV	TEV

For the foolishness of God is wiser than men, and the weakness of God is stronger than men.

For what seems to be God's foolishness is wiser than human wisdom, and what seems to be God's weakness is stronger than human strength.

In this verse Paul may be speaking ironically, or putting himself for the moment in the position of the Gentiles who found the Christian message foolish, and of the Jews who considered the cross a sign of weakness. TEV's "seems to be" shows this irony.

Paul avoids the Greek noun for **foolishness** which he has used before. Instead he employs the related adjective that is probably more emphatic. Paul also avoids speaking directly about the **foolishness** of God. TEV's added phrase "what seems to be" shows Paul's reluctance. This phrase can also be translated as "what looks like" or "what appears to be." GeCL has "God acts against all reason—yet he is wiser than all humans."

Men translates a Greek term which refers to human beings, both male and female. TEV's "human wisdom" and "human strength" give the right meaning.

In verses 22-24, Paul has three times mentioned the Jews first and the Gentiles second. In the present verse, although neither group is named, the order is reversed: the Gentiles (Greeks) who are interested in wisdom are referred to by implication, before the Jews who are interested in power (or miracles, see comments on verse 22). If translators find it strange or confusing in their own language, they should not hesitate to put verse 25b before verse 25a.

RSV	**1.26-31**	TEV

26 For consider your call, brethren; not many of you were wise according to worldly standards, not many were powerful, not many were of noble birth; 27 but God chose what is foolish in the world to shame the wise, God chose what is weak in the world to shame the strong, 28 God chose what is low and despised in the world, even things that are not, to bring to nothing things that are, 29 so that no human being might boast in the presence of God. 30 He is the source of your life in Christ Jesus, whom God made our

26 Now remember what you were, my brothers, when God called you. From the human point of view few of you were wise or powerful or of high social standing. 27 God purposely chose what the world considers nonsense in order to shame the wise, and he chose what the world considers weak in order to shame the powerful. 28 He chose what the world looks down on and despises and thinks is nothing, in order to destroy what the world thinks is important. 29 This means that no one can boast in God's presence. 30 But

wisdom, our righteousness and sanctification and redemption; 31 therefore, as it is written, "Let him who boasts, boast of the Lord."

God has brought you into union with Christ Jesus, and God has made Christ to be our wisdom. By him we are put right with God; we become God's holy people and are set free. 31 So then, as the scripture says, "Whoever wants to boast must boast of what the Lord has done."

This section consists of two closely related sentences (verses 26-29 and 30-31). Long sentences in Paul's writings are often a sign of tense emotion. Translators may have to convey this emotion in other ways, depending on what is natural in the receptor language. Paul also shows by various examples of balance and repetition that he is coming to the climax of his argument.

The links with verses 18-25 are close. The theme is still weakness and folly, contrasted with strength and wisdom.

Call in verse 26 echoes **those who are called** in verse 24 (see comments on verses 2 and 24). However, in this section, especially in verses 26-29, Paul moves from the theme of what God did generally in Christ, to what he has done specifically for Christians in Corinth.

1.26   RSV   TEV

For consider your call, brethren; not many of you were wise according to worldly standards, not many were powerful, not many were of noble birth;

Now remember what you were, my brothers, when God called you. From the human point of view few of you were wise or powerful or of high social standing.

For (TEV "Now") is omitted by some CLTs. Barrett expands the sentence somewhat: "You can see what I mean, brothers, by looking at your calling as Christians." The English "Now," especially at the beginning of a sentence, is often an expression of time, but also indicates the beginning of a new stage in a story or argument. If a new paragraph is opened here, many languages will be able to show the connection with the previous section without using the word "Now."

Consider can be literally "look at" (imperative) or "you look at" (indicative), with little difference of meaning. Most translations agree with RSV and TEV in choosing the imperative. TEV uses the word "remember" because, as the context shows, Paul is asking his readers to figuratively look at the past event of their being called to be Christians.

Your call probably means "the circumstances in which you were called" or "what you were like when God called you to follow Christ." One may also say "Please remember what kind of people you were before God called you" or ". . . when God called you."

On **brethren**, see the comments on verses 1 and 10. TEV adds "my" as in verse 10.

According to worldly standards is literally "according to (the) flesh." This phrase has the same meaning as "of the world" that is repeated three times in verses 27-28, and translated there by TEV as "what the world thinks" or "considers."

There is a question whether **according to worldly standards** refers only to **wise,** as the structure of verse 26 in Greek seems to suggest, or whether it refers also to **powerful** and **of noble birth.** RSV and NEB prefer the first construction; TEV and ItCL prefer the second. The main difficulty with TEV is that "from the human point of view" adds nothing to the meaning of "high social standing." It is probably better, then, to follow RSV. One could say, for example, "Few of you were wise from the human point of view. Not many of you were powerful or highly born."

Worldly standards, like TEV's equivalent phrase "human point of view," is a correct translation of the Greek "according to (the) flesh." In some parts of Paul's letters, the word for "flesh" means "sinful human nature," but in this passage sin is not specially emphasized. The same is true of the word for "world," used in verses 27-28 with the meanings "human beings" or "human society." Men and women are included in both expressions.

Of noble birth is literally "well-born" or "from a good family." Paul writes for a society in which social standing was determined more by birth than by wealth.

1.27	RSV	TEV
	but God chose what is foolish in the world to shame the wise, God chose what is weak in the world to shame the strong,	God purposely chose what the world considers nonsense in order to shame the wise, and he chose what the world considers weak in order to shame the powerful.

The transition to the second part of the comparison which began in verse 26 is marked by a strong **but** which TEV omits. Many languages will need to retain the **but.** This second part of the comparison is much longer than the first, and contains more repetition within itself, as RSV shows. Translators should ask themselves whether in their languages such repetition produces effective emphasis or just a heavy, boring sentence. TEV weakens the effect of this repetition by adding the word "purposely," which is also implied in the second half of the sentence.

In verses 27-28 the Greek is literally "the foolish things . . . the weak things . . . the strong things . . . the low and despised things . . . the things that are." But in contrast, verse 27 talks about "the wise people." The reason appears to be that wisdom is essentially a characteristic which belongs to people. Translators may wish to follow TEV at this point.

In the world may mean "that part of the world which consists of foolish, weak, low, and despised things (or people)," but is more likely to mean the same as "worldly standards" in verse 26. The word **what** may be rendered as "the things that."

Purpose and result are closely related in both the Old and the New Testament, and the same Greek conjunction can be used to introduce either purpose or result. The Greek word appears three times in verses 27-28, and again in verse 31. It is a question of whether it should be translated "in order that" or "with the result that." "In order that" is more appropriate in verses 27-28, and probably "with the result that" in verse 31. In verses 27-28 Paul is speaking of a process which has already begun, but which will be completed at the last judgment. In that judgment human values are turned upside down. The key words in Paul's description of this process are **to shame** and its opposite "to boast" (verse 29), looking forward to the phrase "bring to nothing" in verse 28 and the Old Testament quotation in verse 31. It is also likely that these words are looking back to the word "destroy" in the quotation in verse 19, where a different Greek word is used. Paul's linking of these four words confirms that **shame** is not just an inward feeling of humiliation; it is the state of being "publicly humilated" or "reduced in status." Many languages can express this idea in an idiomatic way; for example, "lose face," "lose eye."

1.28	RSV	TEV

God chose what is low and despised in the world, even things that are not, to bring to nothing things that are,

He chose what the world looks down on and despises and thinks is nothing, in order to destroy what the world thinks is important.

What: see the comment on verse 27.

Low is the opposite of "noble birth" (TEV "high standing") in verse 26 and means "lowly-born" or "from an unimportant family."

Despised is the most common meaning of the following Greek word, which in 6.4 TEV translates "of no standing." This Greek word is related to the word "for nothing." Paul may be thinking of this when he adds **even things that are not.** Similarly, the following phrase means "in order to destroy the things that (the world thinks) are (something)." The words in parentheses are implied. "Something" means "something important." This way of understanding **despised** becomes clear if the UBS Greek text is followed. The first part of the verse may be translated "and God has chosen what the world considers as lowly-born and despises (x) things which do not exist." Other manuscripts add "and" at the point marked (x). But the omission of "and" suggests not only that the same group is being spoken about, but also that the two phrases, before and after (x), mean essentially the same thing.

The last part of the verse is translated clearly by GeCL: ". . . for he (God) wanted to reduce to nothing those who are something before men."

1.29	RSV	TEV

so that no human being might boast in the presence of God.

This means that no one can boast in God's presence.

This verse describes the result of the process described in verses 27-28.

No human being: as in verse 26, the Greek word for "flesh" is used to mean **human being** (TEV "no one"). This verse says literally "so that all flesh should not boast before God." But the negative "not" really contradicts "all," so that the sentence means "so that no flesh (that is, no one) should boast before God." The thought is similar to that of verse 23, since the phrase "Jews and Gentiles" was often used to mean the same as "all flesh," that is, the whole human race.

The word for **boast** is difficult to translate in this passage, because Paul gives it a bad meaning, and then in verse 31 he quotes an Old Testament text in which it has a good meaning. The essential ideas are (1) being happy, (2) showing happiness openly, and (3) speaking about the reasons for one's happiness. However, in some contexts **boast** may also include the idea of someone saying that he is better in some way than someone else. In verse 29 Paul means that in God's presence it is foolish and wrong to compare one human being with another. So this verse may be translated "This means that no one can say in God's presence that he is superior to anyone else."

In the presence of God may be translated "knowing that God is there" or ". . . present."

1.30 RSV	TEV
He is the source of your life in Christ Jesus, whom God made our wisdom, our righteousness and sanctification and redemption;	But God has brought you into union with Christ Jesus, and God has made Christ to be our wisdom. By him we are put right with God; we become God's holy people and are set free.

The reference to boasting in the previous verse anticipates the quotation in verse 31, and the present verse may be understood as an example of what Paul means by "boasting in the Lord" in the next verse.

In RSV the first **He** refers to God, but **whom** refers to Christ. This should be made clear in translation, if necessary, by using nouns in place of pronouns, or by some other equivalent change. TEV uses "God" in the first instance, and the name "Christ" in the second.

Your is emphasized like "we" in verse 23.

The first part of the verse may be understood in two ways: (1) "It is only in Christ Jesus that you are related to God"; or (2) "the fact that you are Christians (in Christ) has its origins in God." The difference is one of focus rather than meaning. The second alternative is slightly more probable. For a comment on the phrase **in Christ Jesus,** see verse 2.

Whom God made our wisdom may be understood in such a way as to emphasize **our.** The meaning in this case may be restated: "Christ is (or, has) the only kind of wisdom we care anything about, and God has given us this kind of wisdom." However, it is more likely that emphasis falls on **wisdom,** and that the meaning is "Christ has become for us the very personification of wisdom, God's wisdom." This meaning may be translated "Through (or, in) Christ, God gives us his own wisdom." There is evidence that passages in the Hebrew Old Testament and the Deuterocanon, which personify wisdom, influenced Paul and other New Testament writers. TEV uses "God" in the first sentence of this verse and again in the second sentence. Many languages will find this too repetitive, as it is clear who the agent of the action "has made" is. One can simply say ". . . and has made Christ . . . ."

The relation among the four nouns **wisdom, righteousness, sanctification,** and **redemption** is not clear. The structure of the Greek sentence appears to separate **wisdom** from the others and to join **righteousness** and **sanctification** closely together. Commentators are generally agreed that these four nouns, which represent four actions by God, are not to be understood as a series of separate stages in the Christian life. In "glorifying" or "boasting" about Christ, Paul heaps up nouns to describe what God has done in Christ. It is possible to think of our wisdom as a general description of Christ, and the other nouns as indicating various aspects of his work. If so, TEV is right to divide the sentence after wisdom.

The second half of this verse, which TEV translates as a separate sentence, includes more abstract nouns like wisdom. TEV translates these by verbs, since they indicate events.

Righteousness in this verse, like sanctification and redemption, are nouns which refer to something which is done by God through Christ. TEV makes the meaning clear. In some languages it may be necessary to translate "God puts us right with himself."

Sanctification, as TEV shows, is related to a community: "we become God's holy people." The word does not mean individual saintliness. It refers to God's claiming Christians and setting them apart, like Israel in Old Testament times, to be his special people. One could render this as "people who are dedicated to God" or "God's special people."

Redemption sometimes suggests the payment of a ransom. But often, in both the Old and the New Testament, it simply refers to "freedom" or "liberation" from the power of evil. The great example of this was the liberation of Israel from slavery in Egypt at the time of the exodus. No payment was involved in that liberation. In certain languages redemption or "are set free" (TEV) can be translated as "have received our freedom." FrCL translates "set free from sin."

In the second half of this verse many translators will need to identify God as the agent of all the events. This verse may be restructured as follows: "God has put us right with himself through Christ, and has made us like his people and set us free."

1.31	RSV	TEV
	therefore, as it is written, "Let him who boasts, boast of the Lord."	So then, as the scripture says, "Whoever wants to boast must boast of what the Lord has done."

This verse is awkward and even meaningless when it is translated literally: "in order that as it is written, 'Let he who boasts, boast in the Lord.' " As we suggested in the comments on verse 27, the Greek probably expresses result rather than purpose, like "so that" at the beginning of verse 29. An expanded restructuring would be "So now, as a result of all God has done for us in Christ (verse 29), we know what the scripture means when it says, 'If anyone is going to boast, let him boast in the Lord.' " "In the Lord" probably means "of what the Lord has done" (TEV), though the text in its Old Testament setting means "in God."

The previous verse has emphasized that God is the source of all that Christ has become for Christians, and of the Lord (TEV "of what the Lord has done") may mean "what God has done in Christ." Similarly, the quotation may mean for Paul, "If anyone is going to boast, let it be about how God has changed him through Christ" (compare verse 30a).

In this verse, unlike verse 29, the word for boast has a good meaning. The corresponding Hebrew word appearing in Jeremiah 9.24 is often used in praising God. In languages where it is necessary to use different expressions for (a) showing happiness openly with words, and (b) claiming to be superior to someone else, a translator should choose (a) here. In such cases it may be helpful to add a footnote which states that in Greek, the same verb is used in verse 29 and 31. In verse 31 the meaning which Paul gives to the Old Testament text is probably "Whoever wants to say why he is happy must say it is because Christ has made his life so much better than it was before."

On TEV's "as the scripture says," see the comments on verse 19.

Chapter 2

The Message About the Crucified Christ

1 When I came to you, brethren, I did not come proclaiming to you the testimonyᶜ of God in lofty words or wisdom. 2 For I decided to know nothing among you except Jesus Christ and him crucified. 3 And I was with you in weakness and in much fear and trembling; 4 and my speech and my message were not in plausible words of wisdom, but in demonstration of the Spirit and of power, 5 that your faith might not rest in the wisdom of men but in the power of God.

ᶜ Other ancient authorities read *mystery* (or *secret*)

1 When I came to you, my brothers, to preach God's secret truth,ᵇ I did not use big words and great learning. 2 For while I was with you, I made up my mind to forget everything except Jesus Christ and especially his death on the cross. 3 So when I came to you, I was weak and trembled all over with fear, 4 and my teaching and message were not delivered with skillful words of human wisdom, but with convincing proof of the power of God's Spirit. 5 Your faith, then, does not rest on human wisdom but on God's power.

ᵇ God's secret truth; *some manuscripts have* the testimony about God.

The place of this section in the wider structure of 1 Corinthians may be seen from several points of view. First, this section develops in greater detail what Paul has said about himself and his work in 1.14-17. Second, it is the third and most personal of the three sections which contrast the Christian message with human wisdom (1.25; 1.26-31; and 2.1-5). Third, this section, especially verses 4-5, rounds off all that Paul has said since 1.17. It thus prepares the way for another major division (see introduction to 2.6-16).

The main features which mark these verses as a separate section are (1) the emphatic **I**, which is the first word in the Greek; (2) **brethren,** which is often used by Paul to mark a new stage in his argument (see also 3.1; 4.6; 7.24; 10.1; 12.1; 14.6,20,39; 15.1,31,50; 16.15; similarly 11.33; 15.58); and (3) the final statement about wisdom and strength which ends this stage of the argument in 2.5.

The TEV section heading, "The Message about the Crucified Christ," can also be rendered as "The Message about Christ Who Was Crucified" or "Paul Preaches about Christ Who Was Crucified."

When I came to you, brethren, I did not come proclaiming to you the testimony ᶜ of God in lofty words or wisdom.

When I came to you, my brothers, to preach God's secret truth, ᵇ I did not use big words and great learning.

The emphatic I makes a contrast with "your call" (TEV's "what you were")
in 1.26. Not only are the Corinthian readers weak, but even Paul himself is weak
from the human point of view. Paul may also be contrasting himself in an indirect
way with false preachers in Corinth. This idea is possibly even stronger in verse 3,
which begins with the same emphatic I.

When I came . . . I did not come repeats the Greek verb for "come." TEV
and NEB remove this repetition completely, and other translations simplify it; for
example, Jerusalem Bible (JB): "When I came to you, it was not . . . ." Some
translators may need to expand When I came to "When I came to visit you."

Brethren should be translated "fellow Christians" or "fellow believers" in
languages where the word "brother" only refers to an actual family member. In
certain languages, though, this word may be rendered in an idiomatic way; for
example, "elders and youngers."

It is not certain whether Paul wrote the testimony of God or "God's secret
truth" as in TEV. TEV translates the Greek word for "mystery" (*musterion*), while
RSV translates the word for "testimony" (*marturion*); these Greek words can be
easily confused with each other. The manuscript evidence is evenly divided;
Nestle-Aland 25th edition has "testimony," while the UBS text and Nestle-Aland
26th edition have "mystery." Commentators and translators are similarly divided
like RSV and TEV.[1] Scribes may have changed "mystery" to testimony because
they were looking back to 1.6. Less probably, they may have changed testimony
to "mystery" because they were looking forward to 2.7. A good reason to pick
"mystery" is that Paul usually speaks of the Christian "mystery" as something
which is revealed. He uses such language here: "preaching," verse 1; "demonstration," verse 4 (see the comments). For these reasons we choose the reading of the
UBS text, which the TEV text follows.[2]

If "mystery" is chosen as the text, it may be either "a secret truth belonging to God" or "a secret truth about God." The first is more likely since, as
the context shows, Christ is the content of this secret truth.

RSV's I did not come proclaiming is more literally "I came not according to
superiority of word or wisdom preaching to you . . . ." The meaning is "when I
came, it was not to proclaim . . . ." TEV's "big words" should not be understood
literally as meaning that Paul used only short and simple words. The term which
is translated words means "message," as in 1.18. Here it may have the added
meaning of "argument" or "reasoning." There is a close connection between words
and wisdom, as in 1.17. The Greek for words or wisdom means "message, that is,

---

[1] "Testimony" is preferred by RSV, Dutch common language translation
(DuCL), GeCL, ItCL, NEB, New American Bible (NAB), JB, Bible de Jérusalem
(BJ), and "mystery" by TEV, French common language translation (FrCL),
Translator's New Testament (TNT), Moffatt (Mft), Goodspeed (American
Translation [AT]), Phps, Barclay (Brc), and Traduction Oecuménique de la Bible
(TOB). Many translations give the alternative reading in a note.

[2] So R.E. Brown, 1958, "The Semitic Background of the New Testament
Mysterion" (I), <u>Biblica</u> 39.426-448.

wisdom" (see the Detailed Comment at 1.5). It is for this reason that TEV replaces **or** with "and."

RSV's **lofty,** which TEV renders as "big," translates a Greek noun which may mean simply "prominence" or "authority," as in 1 Timothy 2.2. But in the present verse Paul may be comparing himself with other preachers. Translator's New Testament (TNT) takes this latter view: "I came to you with no superiority in speech or wisdom."

TEV's "use . . . great learning" can also be rendered "show off my education"; French common language translation (FrCL) has ". . . impressive education."

2.2	RSV	TEV

For I decided to know nothing among you except Jesus Christ and him crucified.

For while I was with you, I made up my mind to forget everything except Jesus Christ and especially his death on the cross.

For shows that the function of this verse is to explain in greater detail what has been said in verse 1. The Greek is literally "For I did not decide to know anything . . . ," meaning **I decided to know nothing . . . .** Although the form of verse 2 is negative, it may be translated positively, as in TEV's rendering: "I made up my mind to forget everything."

The Greek verb translated **decided** indicates an act of judgment, but its use with **know** is unusual; how can one decide what to know? TEV's positive statement, "I made up my mind to forget everything," helps to solve this problem in English. GeCL has "I had decided," since the Greek verb can refer to an event which took place earlier than those mentioned in verse 1; that is, it can refer to a decision which Paul made before he reached Corinth. GeCL continues: ". . . not to bring you anything else than Jesus Christ." ItCL has "I had decided not to teach anything else than Christ." This whole sentence may also be rendered as "I had decided that I would not teach anything else than the story about Jesus Christ."

As we have already stated in the comments on 1.23, Paul generally uses **Christ** as a proper noun. But here it may have its original meaning, "the Messiah." The word for **and** in the phrase **and him crucified** could then show a contrast. In order to demonstrate this contrast, we should translate these two phrases as "Jesus as the Messiah—but a crucified Messiah!" or "Jesus as the Messiah—but a Messiah whom they put to death on a cross."

TEV rightly adds "especially," to show that the last words of this verse are emphasized. As in 1.23, the tense of the verb "crucify" indicates a past event whose consequences stretch forward into the present. FrCL has "and more precisely, Jesus Christ nailed on the cross." NEB has a similar rendering.

2.3	RSV	TEV

And I was with you in weakness and in much fear and trembling;

So when I came to you, I was weak and trembled all over with fear,

As in verse 1, the emphatic words **And I,** with which the verse begins, suggest a contrast, either between Paul and the reader's self-confidence, or more probably, between Paul and the self-confidence of the false preachers.

I was translates a Greek verb which has various meanings, but its tense indicates a particular event. It may introduce a reference (1) to Paul's state when he arrived in Corinth from Athens (Acts 18.1); (2) to his state during his stay in Corinth (which Paul, as he looks back, thinks of as a single event); or (3) even to a state into which he fell during his eighteen months in Corinth (Acts 18.11). More literal translations such as RSV leave the choice open. (1) is supported by verse 1 and is chosen by TEV. However, it would mean that Paul is not saying anything essentially new in the present verse. Many translations agree with TEV. TNT chooses (2): "all the time I was with you I was weak . . . ." Apart from verse 1, the wider context seems to suggest (2). This would include the content and manner of Paul's teaching throughout his stay in Corinth. (3) does not seem likely, simply because Paul does not give enough detail. Regardless of which time setting the translator chooses for the first clause, the last two clauses of the verse may be restructured as "my physical condition was very weak, and I was shaking all over with fear," or "my body was very weak, and I was so afraid that I shook all over."

TEV combines the words **fear** and **trembling** into "trembled all over with fear." This is probably correct, as these two words are often linked together by their basic meaning.

<table>
<tr><td>2.4</td><td>RSV</td><td>TEV</td></tr>
</table>

RSV	TEV
and my speech and my message were not in plausible words of wisdom, but in demonstration of the Spirit and of power,	and my teaching and message were not delivered with skillful words of human wisdom, but with convincing proof of the power of God's Spirit.

We do not know why Paul uses two such similar words as **speech** and **message.** Perhaps he does it simply for emphasis. If this is true, the translator must decide whether, in his own language, emphasis is not better conveyed by a single, strong expression. If there is any difference in meaning between the two expressions, the word for **speech** may, as in verse 1, refer to Paul's reasoned argument (compare Acts 18.4). **Message,** on the other hand, refers more specifically to his preaching about the life, death, and resurrection of Jesus. NEB translates the second term as "gospel." In languages which do not have a passive form of the verb, one can render the first part of this verse as "and I did not teach and preach the Good News with . . . ," or "and I did not use . . . as I taught and preached the Good News."

The Greek words translated **in plausible words of wisdom** raise some serious problems. The first point is that "human" (TEV) is almost certainly not in the original text; it was added by some scribes here, as in 1.17, to make the meaning clear. TEV added it for this reason. Out of many other forms of the Greek text, the most likely ones may be translated (1) "by persuasive words of wisdom" and (2) "by persuasion of wisdom." There is little difference of meaning between these two. (1) is probably the most correct form of the text, but there is the problem that the adjective translated "persuasive" is found nowhere else in Greek literature. It is formed, however, in the same way as certain other Greek adjectives.

The words which are translated **in demonstration of the Spirit and of power** may be connected in various ways. TEV, like many commentators and translators, understands **of the Spirit and of power** to be what is called a hendiadys. This is a figure of speech in which two words, connected by "and," are used to express a single idea. The *Concise Oxford Dictionary* (COD, sixth edition) gives as an example of hendiadys in current English the phrase "nice and warm." So in this verse **the Spirit and . . . power** would mean "the power of God's Spirit" (TEV). TEV adds the word "God's" to show more clearly what RSV means by **Spirit** with a capital S. Capital letters cannot be heard when a text is read aloud, so TEV's rendering is better.

The whole phrase, **in demonstration of the Spirit and of power,** may be understood in two main ways: (1) "proof of the fact that God's Spirit was powerfully at work," or (2) "proof that is based on the fact that God's Spirit is powerfully at work." (2) appears to suit the context better. The activity of God's Spirit was self-evident; it needed nothing else to prove it. Paul's message was proved to be true by signs that God's Spirit was powerfully at work. It is in this way that most modern translations understand the text, though some express this interpretation more clearly than others. Among the clearest are Moffatt (Mft), "the proof supplied by the Spirit and its power," and Traduction Oecuménique de la Bible (TOB), "they [my word and preaching] were a demonstration made by the power of the Spirit."

Translators should avoid using a word for "proof" (TEV) which suggests a logical or mathematical demonstration which has nothing to do with faith. That is why TEV uses the phrase "convincing proof" to translate a single Greek word. It may have been perfectly clear to believers that God's Spirit was at work, but there were other people who thought that the whole thing was "nonsense" (1.23), just as there were people on the day of Pentecost who thought the apostles were drunk (Acts 2.13).

The final clause of this verse may be restructured in the following way: ". . . but rather my teaching and preaching were attended with signs which convinced people that God's Spirit was working powerfully."

The Greek preposition *en* occurs in both halves of this verse and is repeated in verse 5. RSV translates it as **in.** A more probable meaning is "with" (TEV) or "by means of" in verse 4, and "on" or "on the basis of" in verse 5. Translators should avoid giving the impression that "the power of God's Spirit" (TEV) is just a tool in Paul's hands. Perhaps one could say "I did not preach and teach using skillful words of human wisdom, but God proved my preaching and teaching to be true by the power of his Spirit."

2.5	RSV	TEV

that your faith might not rest in the wisdom of men but in the power of God. — **Your faith, then, does not rest on human wisdom but on God's power.**

In this verse Phps' translation conveys very well the force of the Greek preposition *en* as meaning "on the basis of." It says, "God's purpose was that your faith should not rest upon man's cleverness but upon the power of God."

The words **your faith** may be rephrased as "your trusting in Christ."

Might not rest in (TEV "does not rest on") can be stated as "is not the result of" or "is not caused by." One may rephrase this verse in the following way: "So, it is not human wisdom which caused you to trust in Christ, but the power of God."

God's Wisdom

6 Yet among the mature we do impart wisdom, although it is not a wisdom of this age or of the rulers of this age, who are doomed to pass away. 7 But we impart a secret and hidden wisdom of God, which God decreed before the ages for our glorification. 8 None of the rulers of this age understood this; for if they had, they would not have crucified the Lord of glory. 9 But as it is written,

"What no eye has seen, nor ear
    heard,
nor the heart of man conceived,
what God has prepared for those
    who love him,"

10 God has revealed to us through the Spirit. For the Spirit searches everything, even the depths of God. 11 For what person knows a man's thoughts except the spirit of the man which is in him? So also no one comprehends the thoughts of God except the Spirit of God. 12 Now we have received not the spirit of the world, but the Spirit which is from God, that we might understand the gifts bestowed on us by God. 13 And we impart this in words not taught by human wisdom but taught by the Spirit, interpreting spiritual truths to those who possess the Spirit. d

14 The unspiritual e man does not receive the gifts of the Spirit of God, for they are folly to him, and he is not able to understand them because they are spiritually discerned. 15 The spiritual man judges all things, but is himself to be judged by no one. 16 "For who has known the mind of the Lord so as to instruct him?" But we have the mind of Christ.

d Or *interpreting spiritual truths in spiritual language;* or *comparing spiritual things with spiritual*
e Or *natural*

6 Yet I do proclaim a message of wisdom to those who are spiritually mature. But it is not the wisdom that belongs to this world or to the powers that rule this world—powers that are losing their power. 7 The wisdom I proclaim is God's secret wisdom, which is hidden from mankind, but which he had already chosen for our glory even before the world was made. 8 None of the rulers of this world knew this wisdom. If they had known it, they would not have crucified the Lord of glory. 9 However, as the scripture says,

"What no one ever saw or heard,
    what no one ever thought could
      happen,
    is the very thing God prepared
      for those who love him."

10 But c it was to us that God made known his secret by means of his Spirit. The Spirit searches everything, even the hidden depths of God's purposes. 11 It is only a person's own spirit within him that knows all about him; in the same way, only God's Spirit knows all about God. 12 We have not received this world's spirit; instead, we have received the Spirit sent by God, so that we may know all that God has given us.

13 So then, we do not speak in words taught by human wisdom, but in words taught by the Spirit, as we explain spiritual truths to those who have the Spirit. d 14 Whoever does not have the Spirit cannot receive the gifts that come from God's Spirit. Such a person really does not understand them; they are nonsense to him, because their value can be judged only on a spiritual basis. 15 Whoever has the Spirit, however, is able to judge the value of everything, but no one is able to judge him. 16 As the scripture says,

"Who knows the mind of the Lord?
    Who is able to give him
      advice?"

We, however, have the mind of Christ.

c But; *some manuscripts have* For.
d to those who have the Spirit; *or with words given by the Spirit.*

TABLE 1

THE STRUCTURE OF 1 CORINTHIANS 2.6-16

Negative (the world's ignorance)	Positive (Christian wisdom)
verses	
6 [but] not a wisdom of this age . . .	[but] we do impart wisdom
7	But . . . a secret and hidden wisdom . . .
8 None of the rulers of this age understood this . . .	
9 ("No eye has seen (it) . . .	But . . . God has prepared (it) . . .")
10	. . . God has revealed (it) . . .
11 No one comprehends . . . except the Spirit of God.	
12 (have received not the spirit of the world	[But] but the Spirit which is from God)
13	we . . . understand . . . 13 And we impart this in words
not taught by human wisdom	but taught by the Spirit . . .
14 [But] the unspiritual man does not receive the gifts . . .	
15	[But] the spiritual man judges all things . . .
16 "For who has known the mind of the Lord . . . ?"	But we have the mind of Christ.

This Table is based as far as possible on RSV. Words in square brackets are present in the Greek but not in RSV.

Some translations subdivide this section by beginning new paragraphs at verses 10 (JB), 10b (NEB), 13 (TEV, GeCL, Mft, Phps) or 14 (RSV). This suggests that there is no clear-cut division here. Other translations, such as ItCL, New American Bible (NAB), and TNT treat this section as a single unit. There are two stylistic features here which seem to support this: (1) In contrast with 2.1-5 and 3.1-2, Paul uses "we" rather than "I" throughout this section. TEV does not make this clear, but RSV does. (2) The entire section is held together by a series of contrasts between the *ignorance* of the world's "rulers" and the *true wisdom* which God gives to mature Christians. We will discuss both of these statements in greater detail later; each of them raises general questions.

(1) What does Paul's "we" mean in this passage? As we noted previously, it may mean no more than "I," but this is unlikely when we contrast the surrounding verses. Nor is there anything in this passage, or in the letter generally, to suggest that Paul means "Sosthenes and myself" (see comments on 1.1). However, "we" will certainly not include all the readers of this letter, since this section is about "a message of wisdom to those who are spiritually mature," and in 3.1-2 Paul stated clearly that not all his readers were in this state. The remaining possibilities are that "we" means (a) "Paul and his fellow apostles" or "fellow evangelists," or (b) "Paul together with those of his readers who are spiritually mature." If (a) is correct, the "we" would be exclusive. On the whole it seems likely that the "mature" are a group which is distinct from those who "proclaim" the "message of wisdom." This would exclude (b).

(2) There is a zig-zag movement throughout this section between positive statements about *true Christian wisdom,* and negative statements about the *real ignorance* of the world and the powers that rule it. This zig-zag movement is summarized in Table 1. Notice that in verses 11 and 16, there are rhetorical questions expecting the answer "No." These rhetorical questions are equivalent to negative statements, and translators may render them as such if this is more natural in the receptor language. See the detailed comments on 1.13 for a discussion of rhetorical questions.

(3) In this section Paul stops talking ironically about his opponents' word "wisdom." Rather he repeatedly defines it as only *human wisdom* which is really *ignorance.* This is contrasted with *true Christian wisdom* which is more closely related in this section to the work of the Holy Spirit.

2.6	RSV	TEV

Yet among the mature we do impart wisdom, although it is not a wisdom of this age or of the rulers of this age, who are doomed to pass away.

Yet I do proclaim a message of wisdom to those who are spiritually mature. But it is not the wisdom that belongs to this world or to the powers that rule this world—powers that are losing their power.

Yet marks the beginning of a new section. Despite all that Paul has said earlier against human wisdom, there is a true Christian wisdom, and this is the theme of the following verses. Another way of rendering the word **Yet** is "having said all this . . . " or "even though I have spoken the way I have . . . ."

Greek has no indefinite article "a," so one of the meanings of the absence of the definite article "the" is "a." Here there is no article before **wisdom,** and

Paul may mean "a certain kind of (true) wisdom" which is in contrast with the "human wisdom" that he attacked in verses 4-5. Various translations, including FrCL, ItCL, Goodspeed (American Translation [AT]) and TOB understand the verse this way. In that case one may say "Having said all this, I do proclaim a certain kind of wisdom to those . . . ."

RSV's **among** before **the mature** is probably a better translation than TEV's "to." AT translates this quite clearly: "Yet there is a wisdom that we impart when we are with people who have a mature faith." Who are these "spiritually mature" (TEV) people?[3] There is no evidence that they are "perfect" (KJV) in the sense of being without defect. Nor is there any suggestion that Paul thought of human beings as permanently divided from birth into classes, the highest of which are called "perfect." This would contradict what Paul says about God's giving the Holy Spirit to all Christians (see chapter 12, especially verse 13). Chapter 3.1-2 gives a clue to the central meaning of this word: it is a dynamic term describing the maturity which is a product of Christian growth. Keeping this in mind, the words "spiritually mature" may also be rendered as "people who trust in Christ very strongly," or it could be phrased idiomatically as "people who have hearts high enough to recognize and understand spiritual truths."

Impart (TEV "proclaim") translates a common Greek word for "speak," which is how TEV translates it in verse 13. Paul uses this verb more commonly in 1 Corinthians than in all the other letters which are attributed to him. He tends to use it in referring either to speaking in tongues (chapter 14), speaking to mature Christians (here and in 3.1), or speaking on his own authority (2 Cor 11.17; compare 1 Cor 9.8). However, he seldom uses it in referring to basic Christian preaching. TEV's "proclaim" does not make the meaning clear, but on the other hand, RSV's **impart** is not common language. Other translations find ways of distinguishing this "special" speaking or teaching: GeCL first edition "open up"; NAB "express"; Barclay (Brc) "teach." For Paul, "speaking wisdom" is more than talking about wisdom; his preaching is a means by which God allows his wisdom to appear.[4]

The second half of this verse contains a statement with two negatives (see Table 1) and raises two related questions:

(1) Is the main idea that of space (world) or time (**age**)?
(2) Are "the powers of this world" human or superhuman?

We raised the first question in the comments on 1.20. In the present verse the ideas of space and time are very closely connected. The underlying idea, which links both space and time, is that the present order of the universe is temporary. A translator, then, may render the Greek *aiōn* by **age** or a similar expression meaning a long period of time. References to time at the end of this verse (literally "who are passing away") and in verse 7 (**before the ages**) favor such a translation. On the other hand, verse 8 speaks of the power of these forces at the present time, or in the world as it is, or both. In verse 12, as several times in chapter 1, the other Greek word for "world," *kosmos*, means human society organized in opposition to God, but without any direct reference to time. Some

---

3 See W. Baird, 1959, "Among the mature: The idea of wisdom in 1 Corinthians 2.6," Interpretation 13.425-432.
4 P. Bormann, 1960, "Zum Verständnis von 1 Kor 2, 6-8," Theologie und Glaube 50.94-98.

modern translations such as NEB, NAB, and JB, in addition to RSV, have **age**. But TEV and many other translations use "world," favoring the idea of "space."

The second question, concerning **the rulers of this age**, does not affect translation into certain languages such as English. But translators into many other languages may have to decide whether the **rulers** are human or nonhuman. Verse 8 does not settle this question; **the rulers of this age** may be either people like Caiaphas, Pilate, and the Roman emperor, or the supernatural powers of evil which are ultimately responsible for Christ's death (compare Col 2.10,15). A majority of scholars think that supernatural powers are intended here.[5]

In some languages it may be difficult to reproduce TEV's appositional construction, "powers that rule this world, powers that are losing." In such languages one can add the words "these are" to the final clause and say ". . . these are the powers that are losing their power."

Not a wisdom of this age may be expressed as "not wisdom which humans teach."

Translators in certain languages will find it helpful to restructure **of the rulers of this age** as "that the rulers of this world possess."

Who are doomed to pass away: Pass away (TEV's "losing their power") is the Greek word which is translated "to bring to nothing" or "destroy" in 1.28. The passive present participle "being destroyed" sometimes means "passing away" or "disappearing," without any reference to destruction. This present participle may refer either to something which is happening already, as in TEV, or to a future event which is certain to happen, as in RSV. In spoken English, for example, "I'm coming" is more likely to mean "I will certainly come soon" than "I am already on the way." Translations, then, vary in the time setting of this verb. Brc, for example, has "they are already passing from the scene," while ItCL has "who will soon be destroyed," considering this a future event. Paul seems to use this verb in 6.13, and most clearly in 15.24,26, to mean "destroy," referring to the future. In 13.8,10,11, where the probable meaning is "disappear," the reference is also to future events.

2.7	RSV	TEV

But we impart a secret and hidden wisdom of God, which God decreed before the ages for our glorification.

The wisdom I proclaim is God's secret wisdom, which is hidden from mankind, but which he had already chosen for our glory even before the world was made.

The strong **But** at the beginning of this verse indicates that Paul is returning to positive statements after a series of negative ones. Please see verse 6 for comments on **we impart**. The contrast here is between the "human" wisdom of verse 5 and "God's . . . wisdom" (TEV).

TEV's "The wisdom I" can be rendered as "This wisdom which I."

---

[5] However, M. Pesce's detailed Paolo e gli arconti a Corinto (Brescia 1977) argues that the "rulers" are the Jewish authorities. So do A.W. Carr, 1976, "The rulers of this age—1 Corinthians 2:6-8," New Testament Studies 23.20-35; and T. Ling, 1956, "A note on 1 Corinthians ii.8," Expository Times 68.26. Against this view, W.J.P. Boyd, 1957, "1 Corinthians ii.8," Expository Times 68.158.

The meaning of the word which RSV translates **secret** may either refer to speaking in a mysterious way, or that God's wisdom is (or was) itself **secret.** RSV and TEV follow this second interpretation. As we noted on verse 1 of this chapter, the "mystery" of the Gospel is usually, for Paul, something which has been revealed. The "secret" is now an open secret, not because people have discovered it for themselves, but because God has revealed it. Translators should take care that the word chosen for **secret** is not too strong. Otherwise it will seem as if Paul is contradicting himself.

The tense of the verb suggests that the **wisdom** has been **hidden** not only now, but also in the past. The rest of the verse confirms this. In languages which do not use the passive voice, the phrase **hidden wisdom** or "hidden from mankind" (TEV) may be restructured as "which he has hidden from humanity." However, TEV's "from mankind" is not in the Greek text and may be too general. What Paul means is that the wisdom was hidden from previous generations, and also from those at the present time who are not "spiritually mature."

If translators follow TEV's restructuring of this verse, it may be helpful to repeat the information "is the wisdom which he had" after the word "but" in the second half of this verse.

The verb which is translated **decreed** is used in the New Testament to refer to something which God decided or fixed as part of his eternal plan or purpose (see Acts 4.28; Rom 8.29-30; Eph 1.5,11). The words **God decreed** may also be translated as "God decided" or "God set his heart (mind) to do." TEV's "chosen" is less exact.

For **before the ages,** see comments on verse 6. TEV brings out the meaning.

Glorification or "glory" (TEV), in English and some other languages, is a word which is seldom used outside church circles. Unfortunately, few modern translations can find a better word. Part of its meaning is "what Christians have to boast about" (see 1.29-31). More generally it means living so close to God or Christ that some of the wonder and power of God's own life is shared with believers. This is the basis for GeCL's translation: "Already, before God created the world, he formed a plan to give us a share in his glory. But he kept this plan hidden." TNT has a detailed glossary note on "glory."[6] In certain languages it will be helpful to translate this term as "honor." The final sentence can then be restructured as "But God had already decided before he made the world that this wisdom would bring honor to us."

<table>
<tr><td>2.8</td><td>RSV</td><td>TEV</td></tr>
</table>

RSV	TEV
None of the rulers of this age understood this; for if they had, they would not have crucified the Lord of glory.	**None of the rulers of this world knew this wisdom. If they had known it, they would not have crucified the Lord of glory.**

By itself, the word which is translated **understood** (TEV's "knew") could mean "has known" or even "know," but the context is clear that the past tense **understood** or "knew" is correct. This Greek word refers to personal knowledge and sharing rather than just knowing facts. **The rulers of this age** (see comments

---

6 See also E. Fry, 1976, "Translating 'glory' in the New Testament," The Bible Translator 27.422-427.

on verse 6) had no share in this kind of wisdom. GeCL translates "None of the rulers of this world experienced anything of this."

The Lord of glory is of course Christ. Such expressions may be best rendered by a phrase such as "our glorious Lord," or better yet, "the Lord who shares God's glory" (GeCL). But translators need to be careful not to give the impression that Christ shares only a part of God's glory.

2.9   RSV   TEV

But as it is written,	However, as the scripture says,
"What no eye has seen, nor ear	"What no one ever saw or heard,
heard,	what no one ever thought could
nor the heart of man conceived,	happen,
what God has prepared for those	is the very thing God prepared
who love him,"	for those who love him."

This verse, together with the first part of verse 10, has some serious problems of grammar, punctuation and text. However, the general meaning remains clear.

The best way of understanding the structure of this passage is to think of the entire quotation, together with the introductory words **as it is written**, as being in parentheses (see Table 1). The main line of thought, then, would be like this: "None of the rulers of this age understood this . . . . But . . . God has revealed to us." Within this main contrast there is a second contrast between the first two lines and the last line of the quotation itself. TEV's "But" of verse 10 thus repeats the stronger **But** at the beginning of the present verse, which TEV translates "However." This interpretation is based on the UBS Greek text, which is discussed in the first comment on verse 10.

The quotation from the Old Testament in this verse is not a complete sentence, as RSV shows. There is nothing in the text which corresponds to TEV's "is the very thing." Another way of understanding the quotation would be "This is what scripture means when it speaks about what no one ever saw or heard . . . ." The third line can be expanded to make a complete sentence, and to smooth over the change of subject from **no eye** or "no one" (TEV) to **God**. One could say, for example, "This is what God prepared for those who love him." RSV chooses another possibility: it links the quotation with the first part of verse 10; but this is a slightly less natural way of rendering the Greek. RSV also removes emphasis from the last line of the quotation. Such a rendering goes against the general structure and movement of the passage which we have outlined above. For more information, see the punctuation note in the UBS Greek New Testament.

The words which RSV translates **eye, ear,** and **heart** refer to different aspects or functions of the human personality. TEV shows this quite clearly, and since these words refer to things that people do, TEV is correct to translate them by verbs. In biblical thought, the heart has more to do with the mind than the emotions; hence TEV's translation, "what no one ever thought could happen." TEV adds "ever" to show that the quotation is quite general in its application; it does not refer to a particular situation.

The two instances of the word **what** in the quotation may be translated as "the thing that no one . . . heard, or that no one . . . ."

In certain languages it will be necessary to add the word "which" between "things" and "God" (TEV) in the last sentence, and say, for example, "is the very thing which God . . ." or "happened to be the very thing which God . . . ."

Those in the last sentence should in many languages be identified as "people"; for example, "for those people who love him."

So far we have spoken about "the quotation," but in fact there is considerable doubt about where it comes from, and indeed whether it is one quotation or more than one. The introductory words strongly suggest that Paul intends to quote from the Old Testament, but if so, the quotation is very inaccurate, especially toward the end. Sources suggested for various parts of the quotation include Isaiah 52,15; 64.4; and Sirach 1.10.[7]

2.10　　　　RSV	TEV
God has revealed to us through the Spirit. For the Spirit searches everything, even the depths of God.	But[c] it was to us that God made known his secret by means of his Spirit. The Spirit searches everything, even the hidden depths of God's purposes.

[c] But; *some manuscripts have* For.

It is not certain how this verse is linked to verse 9. Some manuscripts have "But," others "For" (see TEV footnote). The manuscript evidence is equally divided, and editions of the Greek New Testament, translations, and commentaries disagree. "But" makes good sense if the structure which we have outlined in Table 1 is correct. The only slight difficulty is that Paul repeats the "but" of verse 9, using a less strong Greek word after the parenthesis of the quotation.

Paul states in the first part of this verse, with greater emphasis than before, that God has now revealed his "mystery," and that this revelation takes place by means of the (Holy) Spirit. TEV's "his" before "Spirit" is not in the Greek, but is added to make the meaning clear. "Secret" in "his secret" is taken by TEV to refer to the "wisdom" which is mentioned in verses 7-8. If the translator follows this interpretation, it will be helpful to say "his secret wisdom" in this verse.

In the phrase **through the Spirit** it will be necessary in many languages to make the underlying causative action clear. One could restructure this first sentence as "God caused his Spirit to make known to us his secret wisdom."

Most translations, like RSV and TEV, put a period or full stop after the first part of verse 10. Many omit the **For** which follows, expecting the reader to see for himself that the second half of the verse explains and develops the first half.

---

7 Readers interested in following the search for the source of this quotation should consult P. Prigent, 1958, " 'Ce que l'oeil n'a pas vu,' 1 Cor 2:9: Histoire et préhistoire d'une citation," Theologische Zeitschrift 14.416-429; M. Philonenko, 1959, "Quod oculus non vidit, 1 Cor 2:9," Theologische Zeitschrift 15.51-52; A. Feuillet, 1963, "L'énigme de 1 Cor. II, 9," Revue Biblique 70.52-74; E. von Nordheim, 1974, "Das Zitat des Paulus in 1 Kor 2:9 und seine Beziehung zum koptischen Testament Jakobs," Zeitschrift für die Neutestamentliche Wissenschaft 65.112-120; K. Berger, 1976, "Zur Diskussion über die Herkunft von 1 Kor. ii.9," New Testament Studies 24.269-276. See comments on 1.19.

The words which are translated **searches** (see Rom 8.27) and **depths** (see Rom 8.39; Eph 3.18) may have been borrowed by Paul from language used by his opponents. It may be appropriate, then, to translate these rather unusual words by terms which are unusual in one's own language, to suggest that they may have a special meaning. Mft, along with AT and TOB, extends the metaphor of **depths** to include **searches** also: "the Spirit fathoms everything, even the depths of God." The idea is that of searching to the bottom of deep water.

2.11	RSV	TEV

For what person knows a man's thoughts except the spirit of the man which is in him? So also no one comprehends the thoughts of God except the Spirit of God.

It is only a person's own spirit within him that knows all about him; in the same way, only God's Spirit knows all about God.

RSV's **For** may make it difficult for the reader to realize that this verse introduces a new thought. It is probably better to omit this word as TEV does. The thought in this verse, which is found in the Old Testament (Prov 20.27) and in "common human experience" (Barrett), is that in order to understand something, one must compare it with something similar. Specifically, it is the human in man which enables him to understand human things; and similarly, it is only God's Spirit which can understand the things of God. If human beings are to understand these things, it can only be because God allows them to share in his own Spirit.

RSV uses the present tense for the verb **know**, but a different tense is used in the second half of the verse, where the same Greek verb is translated **comprehends**. Paul may have changed the tense for variety, but the second half more probably means "who has ever known the things of God . . . ?" It is therefore more emphatic than the first half.

The first half of the verse is clumsy and not very clear in detail, though there is no doubt about its general sense. A literal translation would be "For who of men knows the things of a man except the spirit of man which (is) in him?" The singular "man" means "any man," humans in general, not a particular individual. (The word for **man,** of course, includes women too.) TEV's word "him" in the phrase "knows all about him" is ambiguous—it can refer either to "the Spirit" in verse 10 or to "a person" in this verse. It may be necessary to translate this as "knows all about himself" or "knows all about that person."

The rhetorical question in the first half of the verse is equivalent to a strong negative statement. The second half of the verse confirms this. There is, however, a difference between the two sections. The first half expresses something which Paul thinks his readers will readily accept; the second half is a new idea which follows the first.

TEV's "that knows all about him" or ". . . about God," gives the meaning of the Greek text, which is literally "the things of man/God," but TEV's "all" is not in the text. NEB has "what a man is" and "what God is"; AT's "a man's thoughts" and "the thoughts of God" may be too specific.

RSV   TEV

Now we have received not the spirit of the world, but the Spirit which is from God, that we might understand the gifts bestowed on us by God.	We have not received this world's spirit; instead, we have received the Spirit sent by God, so that we may know all that God has given us.

To change the order of clauses in this verse would make the sequence of thought clearer; but none of the translations which we have consulted do this. Between verses 11 and 12a there is a slight jump in Paul's argument, and verse 12b goes back to fill the gap. It would therefore be possible to translate "But we do understand the gifts which come from God, because he has given us, not the spirit of the world, but his own Spirit."

The clause **the Spirit which is from God** can be rendered as "the Spirit whom God has sent," or one may restructure the sentence as "instead, God has sent his Spirit to us."

Please see the comments on 1.20 on the phrase **the world.**

What Paul means by "knowing" or "understanding" the **gifts bestowed on us by God** can be understood by remembering that "to know" in biblical language includes the meaning "to experience" or "to participate in." TEV and other translations consider that **the gifts** refers to more than just "spiritual gifts" as in chapter 12. GeCL says, for example, "what God has done for us."

2.13   RSV   TEV

And we impart this in words not taught by human wisdom but taught by the Spirit, interpreting spiritual truths to those who possess the Spirit.[d]	So then, we do not speak in words taught by human wisdom, but in words taught by the Spirit, as we explain spiritual truths to those who have the Spirit.[d]
[d] Or interpreting spiritual truths in spiritual language; or comparing spiritual things with spiritual	[d] to those who have the Spirit; or with words given by the Spirit.

This verse, like the first part of verse 11, is stylistically heavy in the Greek, and its meaning is not entirely clear. Part of the reason may be that Paul is piling up words, including several repetitions, in order to emphasize his theme. Translators may need to simplify the structure of this verse.

As Paul's argument develops, it becomes more and more difficult to understand **we** as referring to Paul alone. The meaning, at least from this point to the end of the chapter, appears to be "we spiritual people." These are probably the same people as the "mature" of verse 6 and the "we" who have the "mind of Christ" in verse 16.

RSV's **this** is a plural in Greek which refers to the gifts which Paul has just mentioned. TEV leaves the connection with verse 12 for the reader to understand. **And** at the beginning of the sentence really means "also," showing that Paul is about to say something new; he is saying that we not only understand God's gifts by means of his Spirit, but what is more, we speak about them.

The clause **we impart this in words not . . .** may be restructured as "when we speak, we do not use words . . . ."

Words not taught by human wisdom is the most likely translation here. However, there is another possibility, which is different in grammar but similar in meaning: "not in learned words of human wisdom."

The phrase **taught by human wisdom** will be difficult for some translators. Other ways of rendering this phrase are "which arise out of human wisdom" and "which come from human wisdom."

After the clear statement of verse 12, there should be no need for a translator to repeat that **the Spirit** is God's Spirit. This is shown not only by the capital S but by the context.

The end of this verse is literally "interpreting" or "comparing spiritual things with spiritual (things or people)." There are two problems here: The first one is the meaning of the verb. The second is whether the second "spiritual" refers to things or people.

The Greek verb *sunkrino* is not used anywhere else in the New Testament except in 2 Corinthians 10.12, where it occurs twice and means "compare." RSV seems to follow its meaning in the Septuagint of Genesis 40.8 and Daniel 5.7, where it means "interpret." This gives better sense in the immediate context here. Following **we impart**, though, the meaning "compare" may have been suggested by verse 11. TEV has the rendering "explain." In both places where Paul uses this verb, it is accompanied in the immediate context by another verb (here *anakrino* in verses 14-15). Both verbs have the same root, *krino*, which means "judge." Here, as earlier in speaking about wisdom, Paul seems to be taking up a word which is used by his opponents in Corinth. He reuses it to express what he believes to be the true Christian message. There is a play on words here. How far it is possible to reproduce this play on words in translation depends on the words which are available to a translator in his or her language. It also depends on the meaning of the related word *anakrino* in verses 14-15 (see the comments).

This leads to the second problem. If the verb *sunkrino* is taken to mean "compare," the end of the sentence may mean either "comparing spiritual things with (other) spiritual things," as in the second part of RSV's footnote, or may mean "comparing spiritual things in spiritual (words)," "words" being borrowed from the first part of the sentence. Neither of these alternatives, especially the second, gives very clear sense. It is more likely, then, that the verb means **interpret.** If this is the meaning, the translation possibilities are either "interpreting spiritual things to spiritual people" or "interpreting spiritual things in spiritual words," as in the first part of RSV's footnote. Against the second alternative, "spiritual words," it may be said (a) that nowhere else does Paul speak of "spiritual words"; (b) that the immediate context (verses 15 and 3.1) mentions spiritual people. A majority of translations agree with the TEV text. JB follows a different Greek text which is supported by two important manuscripts and translates "we teach spiritual things spiritually." Dutch common language translation (DuCL), AT, and Brc agree with the TEV footnote.

The term "spiritual people," at least in English, can be easily misunderstood as the wrong kind of "boasting." It is important, therefore, for a translator to discover the precise meaning of "spiritual," and of the opposite term which is so often translated "natural" (see the RSV footnote). TEV's translation of Jude 19 as "who are controlled by their natural desires, who do not have the Spirit" helps to make the meaning of "unspiritual" or "natural" clear. Paul and other New Testament writers were deeply influenced by Hebrew thought. So they did not make a sharp distinction between body, mind, and soul or spirit. The Hebrew word for "flesh" usually meant human nature with its weakness; the word for "soul" meant human nature with special reference to its inner life and vitality; and the word for "spirit" referred to the "breath of life," which was not essentially part of man at all, but was breathed into him by God (Gen 2.7). However, here Paul is making a distinction between human beings who are governed by their own inner (sinful) nature, and those who are governed by the spirit of God. In this setting, RSV's "unspiritual" and TEV's "whoever does not have the Spirit" (verse 14; compare verse 12) are quite precise translations.

In some languages one cannot talk about "having the Spirit." In cases like this a translator may say "who have the Spirit living in them."

2.14	RSV	TEV

The unspiritual[e] man does not receive the gifts of the Spirit of God, for they are folly to him, and he is not able to understand them because they are spiritually discerned.

Whoever does not have the Spirit cannot receive the gifts that come from God's Spirit. Such a person really does not understand them; they are nonsense to him, because their value can be judged only on a spiritual basis.

[e] Or *natural*

Some of the problems of this verse have been covered in the comments on verse 13. Once more, Paul turns from positive to negative statements, using a "but" which both RSV and TEV omit in translation, feeling that the contrast can be understood in English without this word.

Translations often rightly put "God's Spirit" (TEV) where the text has only "Spirit." In the same way it is possible that scribes added the word "God's" to make the meaning clear. The UBS Greek New Testament accepts "God's" as part of the original text.

There is nothing in the Greek which corresponds to **the gifts,** but the thought is so close to that of verse 12 that RSV and TEV are right to add a reference to God's gifts in the present verse only.

The clause **the gifts of the Spirit of God** may also be rendered as "that God's Spirit gives."

Folly is the word used in 1.18,21, and 23. **They are folly to him** may be rephrased as "he considers them to be nonsense."

RSV keeps the two clauses, **for they . . . understand them,** in the same order as the Greek, but TEV changes the order to show more clearly the relation between them. The second clause is literally "and he cannot understand."

Them, in both RSV and TEV, refers to the gifts of the Spirit. **Understand** is the word which was translated "know" in verse 11. In this verse it refers to particular events, implying "Even when they see what happens when God gives the gifts of his Spirit to people, they do not realize what is happening." It is also possible, in the light of the words "all things" in verse 15, that **understand** refers to something more general. In that case, "he does not understand anything" is a possible translation.

The Greek *anakrino*, which TEV translates as "judged" and RSV **discerned** (see comments on verse 13), refers to the process of examination and investigation which leads up to a judgment, rather than just to a verdict in the law court or to God's final judgment. In Acts 17.11 the meaning is that the Jews in Beroea were examining the Scriptures carefully, in order to see whether what the Christians were saying was true. In this verse the meaning of *anakrino* is that it is only with the help of God's Spirit that the Spirit's own gifts can be examined and understood. In certain languages which do not naturally use a passive form of the verb, it may be helpful to render this final clause as "because a person can judge their value only if he has the Spirit living in him."

2.15	RSV	TEV

The spiritual man judges all things, but is himself to be judged by no one.

Whoever has the Spirit, however, is able to judge the value of everything, but no one is able to judge him.

Before concluding his argument with a final quotation in verse 16, Paul adds two brief statements in this verse. The first is positive and the second, negative.

On **the spiritual man,** see the comments on verse 13. Commentators note that **the spiritual man** could be Christ himself. This is most unlikely! One important reason is that "Christ" simply cannot be the meaning of verse 13, which is the immediate context of this verse. It is only because the spiritual person has, or is controlled by, the Spirit that he has the supernatural power to examine and understand everything (compare verse 11). There is no suggestion here that the spiritual person has the right in himself because he has some kind of higher rank.

To be judged by no one: the meaning of these words is determined by the first half of the verse and is also related to the text of previous verses. The person without the Spirit (unspiritual) is not qualified to examine anyone who has the Spirit. He cannot because he himself does not have the means by which he can understand the Spirit itself, or comprehend what the Spirit gives to other people. Paul works out the practical implications of this verse in chapter 4. In the light of 4.3-4, the meaning of 2.15b is probably "no one," no human being, as in TEV. TEV also makes a stronger English sentence by using the active "is able to judge" rather than the passive **to be judged.** In languages which do not employ the passive, it would be well to follow TEV's example here.

2.16	RSV	TEV

"For who has known the mind of the Lord so as to instruct him?" But we have the mind of Christ.

As the scripture says,
   "Who knows the mind of the Lord?
      Who is able to give him
            advice?"
We, however, have the mind of Christ.

This quotation is from Isaiah 40.13 and is fairly accurate. **For** is not part of the quotation but an introduction to it in the Greek text (see other examples in 10.26 and in Rom 10.13). TEV adds "as the scripture says" to make this point clear, especially for people hearing the passage read aloud. In some languages the scripture cannot "speak" or "say" anything. In such cases a translator may say "we read in the Scriptures" or "it is written in the Scriptures."

In the context of this verse Paul makes no difference in meaning between **mind** and "Spirit," so his quoting a text about the Lord's **mind** can be used in an argument about the Spirit.

RSV's **so as to instruct him** brings out the connection between the two lines of the quotation. TEV, on the other hand, is closer to the meaning of the Hebrew text than to that of the Septuagint, from which Paul quotes.

As in verse 11, the translation "who has ever known" may be more precise than "knows" (TEV). In languages which cannot talk about "knowing" a mind, the question **who has known the mind of the Lord?** may be rendered as "who knows what the Lord is thinking?"

But we have the mind of Christ: it is important, though difficult, to get the emphasis of this sentence right. RSV's literal translation, and even TEV, throws stress on the final word, **Christ.** The Greek sentence, however, does not stress **Christ.** It is therefore likely that Paul is here taking it for granted that Old Testament texts which speak of "the Lord" refer to Christ. The point of this verse is rather "No one, humanly speaking, can enter into the mind of Christ. Yet because God has given his Spirit to mature Christians, they can now say that they, in contrast to everyone else, do have Christ's mind." TNT attempts to convey this in translation: "But we do possess Christ's mind." The thought is similar to that of Philippians 2.5, though the language is different.

In some languages it may be necessary to render **we have the mind of Christ** as "we think the way Christ does."

Chapter 3

The structure of this chapter and of the following one is not entirely clear, though commentaries generally agree that important new sections begin at 3.1 and 5.1. Most editions of the Greek text, and most translations and commentaries, also make a break before 3.18. JB expresses the relation between 3.18-23 and the rest of the chapter by a heading "Conclusions." The only other division in the UBS Greek text is before verse 10; but most translations and commentaries either make another paragraph before verse 5, or break before verse 5 and not before verse 10. Translations also vary according to whether they begin a new paragraph at the beginning of verse 9 (GeCL), in the middle (TEV), or at the end (RSV). On this question, see the detailed comments below. The simplest way of relating verses 1-3, 5-9a, and 9b-17 to one another is to think of verses 1-4 as announcing the general theme, "Fellow workers of God," while verses 5-9a and 9b-17 develop this theme with the help of the images of farming and building. As usual, however, none of these divisions are absolutely clear-cut.

| RSV | **3.1-4** | TEV |

Servants of God

1 But I, brethren, could not address you as spiritual men, but as men of the flesh, as babes in Christ. 2 I fed you with milk, not solid food; for you were not ready for it; and even yet you are not ready, 3 for you are still of the flesh. For while there is jealousy and strife among you, are you not of the flesh, and behaving like ordinary men? 4 For when one says, "I belong to Paul," and another, "I belong to Apollos," are you not merely men?

1 As a matter of fact, my brothers, I could not talk to you as I talk to people who have the Spirit; I had to talk to you as though you belonged to this world, as children in the Christian faith. 2 I had to feed you milk, not solid food, because you were not ready for it. And even now you are not ready for it, 3 because you still live as the people of this world live. When there is jealousy among you and you quarrel with one another, doesn't this prove that you belong to this world, living by its standards? 4 When one of you says, "I follow Paul," and another, "I follow Apollos"—aren't you acting like worldly people?

The link with the previous section is shown mainly by the phrase **spiritual men,** but is also made clear by repeated references to what people are "not able" to do (2.14; 3.1,2; see comments on verse 1). Within the wider context, the reference to divisions in verse 3 takes up the theme which Paul announced in 1.11. Then his mention of Paul and Apollos in verses 4-5 (compare also verse 22) recalls 1.12. Other less important links will be mentioned in the detailed comments.

However, there are even stronger indications that Paul is changing his theme. The section begins with the same emphatic **I** which Paul used at the beginning of a section in 2.1. He appeals to his readers as **brethren** (see comments on 1.10). Most clearly of all, he no longer speaks about "we," as in 2.6-16, but of **I** and **you,** contrasting himself with his readers. It is tempting to connect the themes of the two sections, 2.1-5 and 3.1-4, both of which begin with the unusual and emphatic **I.** Paul preached a simple message, both because he himself was weak (2.1-5), and also because his hearers were immature (3.1-4). This does not imply that Paul would have preached to mature Christians a message different from that of the cross; indeed, 2.8 suggests the contrary. Paul means rather that the full implications of the death of Christ, as part of God's eternal plan (2.7), could only be understood by mature Christians.

The TEV section heading "Servants of God" may also be rendered as "We serve God" or "We apostles are God's servants."

3.1	RSV	TEV
	But I, brethren, could not address you as spiritual men, but as men of the flesh, as babes in Christ.	As a matter of fact, my brothers, I could not talk to you as I talk to people who have the Spirit; I had to talk to you as though you belonged to this world, as children in the Christian faith.

The function of the first Greek word (literally "And I"), which RSV translates **But I,** has just been discussed. TEV adds "As a matter of fact," to emphasize Paul's change of theme as well as the shift from "we" language to "I/you" language. Another way of rendering this is "As for me . . . I."

Brethren: here Paul is addressing himself to all the Christians in Corinth, both male and female. In some languages one must say, for example, "my fellow Christians." There is no "my" in the Greek; the word is added for reasons of English style.

Address (TEV's "talk") is the common Greek word translated "impart" or "proclaim" in 2.6 (see the comments). In both places Paul is speaking about his personal way of transmitting the Christian message.

It is often very difficult to translate comparisons, and the one in this verse, **not address you as . . . but as . . . ,** presents difficulties. The text literally translated is "I could not talk to you as spiritual but as fleshly, as to children in Christ." The main problem here is that of making the positive side of the comparison real. TEV's "as though you belonged . . ." does not do this adequately. The meaning is more probably "I could not talk to you as I would talk to people who have the Spirit. Rather, I had to talk to you as people who really do belong to this world, as people who are like children in the Christian faith."[1]

Spiritual men (TEV "people who have the Spirit"): see 2.13,15.

In certain languages the sequence "Spirit; I . . ." in TEV presents difficulties. One may say "Spirit; but I . . . ," or "Spirit. Instead I . . . ."

Translators are often tempted to see distinctions where none are intended in the text, and to define words more strictly than New Testament usage would

---

[1] GeCL uses *wie*, suggesting an unreal comparison, rather than *als*.

allow. The single Greek word which RSV translates **men of the flesh** illustrates these dangers. The Greek word in this verse is *sarkinos*; in verse 3 the corresponding word is *sarkikos*. In some contexts these are distinguished, *sarkinos* meaning "made of flesh," as in 2 Corinthians 3.3, and *sarkikos* meaning "having the character of flesh," as in 1 Corinthians 9.11. (See the comment on "flesh" in 1.26.) *Sarkikos*, therefore, more often has a bad meaning, referring to human beings in rebellion against God. However, in 1 Corinthians 3.1-4, most commentators and translators agree that there is no difference in meaning between these two words.

Paul's language is flexible. On the one hand there are people described as "unspiritual" (2.14), as having "the Spirit of the world" (2.12), as being "of the flesh" (3.1,3), and as "behaving like ordinary men" (3.3) or like "children" (3.1). On the other hand there are those who are **spiritual men** (3.1; compare 2.11-14) and are therefore "spiritually mature" (2.6). The only important distinctions within each of these sets of terms is that some include a time element and others do not. In the present passage, especially verses 2 and 3, expressions of time are important.

In some languages it will be helpful to render the clause "you belonged to this world" (TEV) as "you were people who were controlled by this world" or "you were people who were under the control of this world."

Even in chapter 2 Paul does not rigidly separate different categories of people. Now in chapter 3 he is more directly concerned with the process of growth which leads to Christian maturity and a life which is entirely under the control of the Holy Spirit. This theme of Christian progress is implied in the reference to **babes** here, and in two different expressions which are translated "not ready" in verse 2. The last phrase in verse 1, therefore, modifies what Paul has said earlier, so that one might well translate it "as people who belong to this world, or at least as children in the Christian faith."

In Christ means "in the Christian faith" (TEV), or one may say "like children in your understanding of the Christian faith."

3.2   RSV   TEV

RSV	TEV
I fed you with milk, not solid food; for you were not ready for it; and even yet you are not ready,	**I had to feed you milk, not solid food, because you were not ready for it. And even now you are not ready for it,**

This verse and the first part of verse 3 form a balanced whole:

I fed you with milk, not solid food;	**for you were not ready for it**

[what is more]

even yet you are not ready [to take it],	**for you are still of the flesh.**

The first half of verse 2, which is literally "I gave you milk to drink, not solid food, for you were not yet able," will almost certainly need two modifications in translation. First, translators will need to avoid suggesting "I did not give you solid food to drink." One can avoid this mistake, either by omitting "to drink," or by adding "to eat" after **solid food,** or by using some general verb like the

English "to feed." This verb can have either solid or liquid food as its object. Second, it will be necessary in most languages to say what the readers were "not ready" for (TEV). TNT has "for you could not yet take it," where "take" has the meaning "swallow" or "digest."

The wording of the phrase translated **even yet** (TEV's "even now") is a little difficult in the Greek,[2] probably because Paul is emphasizing it strongly, but the meaning is quite clear.

3.3	RSV	TEV
	for you are still of the flesh. For while there is jealousy and strife among you, are you not of the flesh, and behaving like ordinary men?	because you still live as the people of this world live. When there is jealousy among you and you quarrel with one another, doesn't this prove that you belong to this world, living by its standards?

For the first clause, see comments on verse 2.

Of the flesh, in contrast with "of the Spirit," means "controlled, not by the Holy Spirit, but by natural human impulses." As the rest of the verse shows, these impulses are essentially the tendency toward self-centeredness. There is no reference in this passage to sexual sins.

While there is jealousy: while may refer to time and mean "as long as"; so also TEV, NEB. It may refer to space and mean "where." It may also have a logical meaning, "whereas" (KJV) or "since." This last meaning seems to fit the context best and is preferred by most commentators. ItCL has "Your discords and divisions show that you still think and behave like others" (that is, non-Christians). In other languages one may need to render this as "You are jealous of each other and quarrel with each other. This shows . . . ."

KJV, following many Greek manuscripts, adds "and divisions" after "jealousy and strife," but the UBS Greek text omits this word. Scribes may have added it from Galatians 5.20, the only other place in the New Testament where it is used. The phrase **there is jealousy** may be rendered as "you are jealous of each other."

RSV's **among you** and TEV's "with one another" translate the same Greek phrase, which comes before **jealousy and strife** and applies to both nouns.

The last part of the verse forms a rhetorical question which, as we discussed in the comments on 1.13, will often be translated as a statement rather than a real question. One might say, for example, "When there is . . . this proves that you belong to this world . . . ." In languages in which rhetorical questions are natural, it is an advantage to keep this and the following rhetorical question in verse 4 in translation. The reason is that these rhetorical questions are followed by a real question in verse 5a, to which the answer is given in verses 5b and 6.

RSV is misleading to keep the Greek **and** before **behaving,** as it gives the impression that something new is to be said. Actually, this final phrase is explaining **are you not of the flesh.** TEV shows this fact clearly by dropping the **and.**

The last few words of this verse are literally "and walk according to man." "Walk" is a common biblical metaphor for "live" in the sense of "behave." Many

---

[2] B and p[46] improve the Greek by omitting *eti.*

languages will be able to follow this metaphor. Thai common language translation (ThCL) has "walk your life."

Men in this passage means virtually the same as **flesh** and includes women, too.

<u>3.4</u>   RSV   TEV

For when one says, "I belong to Paul," and another, "I belong to Apollos," are you not merely men?

When one of you says, "I follow Paul," and another, "I follow Apollos"—aren't you acting like worldly people?

This verse expands and illustrates the meaning of verse 3, but does not do it logically. So RSV's **For** is a weak connection. It may be omitted in translation.

I belong can be rendered in many languages as "I am a disciple of."

The last part of the verse needs expansion in some languages, including English. The literal answer to the question **are you not merely men?** is clearly "Yes, we are." But verse 3 has shown that the question is not intended literally. It describes a purely human way of life lived apart from the Holy Spirit. For this reason Barrett renders this clause as: ". . . are you not men—that and nothing more?" One may also translate this clause as a statement; for example, "you are acting like worldly people!" or "you are acting according to human standards!"

RSV   **3.5–9**   TEV

5 What then is Apollos? What is Paul? Servants through whom you believed, as the Lord assigned to each. 6 I planted, Apollos watered, but God gave the growth. 7 So neither he who plants nor he who waters is anything, but only God who gives the growth. 8 He who plants and he who waters are equal, and each shall receive his wages according to his labor. 9 For we are God's fellow workers; you are God's field, God's building.

5 After all, who is Apollos? And who is Paul? We are simply God's servants, by whom you were led to believe. Each one of us does the work which the Lord gave him to do: 6 I planted the seed, Apollos watered the plant, but it was God who made the plant grow. 7 The one who plants and the one who waters really do not matter. It is God who matters, because he makes the plant grow. 8 There is no difference between the man who plants and the man who waters; God will reward each one according to the work he has done. 9 For we are partners working together for God, and you are God's field.
You are also God's building.

This section develops the thought that Paul and his fellow evangelists, especially Apollos, are workers in God's field or vineyard. What holds verses 5–9a together is the theme of what Paul and Apollos are and what God is. This common theme is developed by the use of Greek neuter pronouns translated **what** (verse 5), **anything** (verse 7), and **equal** (verse 8). See the detailed comments below concerning these pronouns.

There is a transition at the beginning of verse 5 from a rhetorical question to a real one. TEV and many other translations mark this transition with a new paragraph. In the Greek text it is marked by a word which often means "therefore," but which RSV translates **then** and TEV "after all." Its function here is not to introduce a logical deduction, but to show that Paul is passing to another aspect of the same theme.

3.5	RSV	TEV
	What then is Apollos? What is Paul? Servants through whom you believed, as the Lord assigned to each.	**After all, who is Apollos? And who is Paul? We are simply God's servants, by whom you were led to believe. Each one of us does the work which the Lord gave him to do:**

Many Greek manuscripts have the more commonplace "who?" (masculine) in place of the more striking "what?" of the UBS Greek text. RSV follows the UBS text literally, but in some languages it may be necessary, or at least more natural, to follow the example of TEV and other CLTs and use the word "who."

Another possibility would be to restructure the sentence to read, for example, "But what makes Apollos or Paul important?" "Important" may seem to be an overtranslation, but the verse as a whole is not negative (Paul does not say "only servants . . . "), and "to be something" (verse 7; RSV "is anything") is a natural idiom for "to be important" (compare Gal 6.3).

TEV's "God's" is not in the Greek text, but in view of the emphatic references to God in verses 6, 7, and 9 of this chapter, "God's" is probably what Paul means. "Christ's," though, as in 2 Corinthians 11.23, is also possible.

The Greek word for **servants** refers to people who had a higher status than slaves, but no special importance. Barrett comments that the word in this verse was often used of a waiter. GeCL translates this word as "helpers." NEB slightly restructures this final clause as "God's agents in bringing you to the faith." Mft goes further in the same direction: "They are simply used by God to give you faith."

You believed refers to a particular time in the past. But Paul does not, of course, suggest that the readers have now stopped believing. Rather, he refers to the time when "you came to the faith" or "began to believe." In languages which need an object after **believed,** one may say "believed in Jesus Christ" or "believed in the Gospel."

As elsewhere in the New Testament, **the Lord** is almost certainly Christ rather than God (compare, for example, Luke 7.13,19; John 20.20; Acts 2.36; 1 Cor 7.10,12,25; 9.14).

The Lord assigned to each: the Greek is concentrated and very difficult. It says literally "to each as the Lord gave." Here the meaning is most likely "each of us evangelists." TEV and other CLTs are probably right in thinking that what "the Lord gave" (TEV) was a task of planting or watering (verse 6) rather than, at least directly, a special spiritual gift.

There seems to be no special reason for the change in this verse from Paul's normal order, "Paul-Apollos," to "Apollos-Paul." However, translators should maintain the present order to be faithful to the Greek text.

3.6	RSV	TEV

I planted, Apollos watered, but God gave the growth.

I planted the seed, Apollos watered the plant, but it was God who made the plant grow.

I is emphasized in order to balance **Apollos**. There is no central contrast between Paul and Apollos; both are contrasted with God. TEV's "seed" and "plant" are not in the Greek text, and the second phrase could mean "Apollos watered the ground"; but the meaning "the plant" is more likely in the context. Many other languages will also need objects after the verbs "planted" and "watered," as in TEV.

This verse, like 4.15 and Acts 18.1-17, suggests that Paul had established the church in Corinth, and that Apollos came later.

The strong **but** before **God** throws emphasis on the name **God**.

3.7	RSV	TEV

So neither he who plants nor he who waters is anything, but only God who gives the growth.

The one who plants and the one who waters really do not matter. It is God who matters, because he makes the plant grow.

RSV's **So**, which TEV omits, is often used in Greek to introduce a logical sequence, similar to TEV's "then" in verse 21 of this chapter. The point of this verse can be understood best by looking back for a moment. Verse 5a asked the real questions, "What then is Apollos? What is Paul?" to which the first short answer was "servants." The end of verse 5, and still more verse 6, explained the meaning of "servants" by telling what work went with this position. Now verse 7 states the conclusion that neither Paul the planter, nor Apollos the waterer, is important; but God is the one who "made the plant grow." One may translate the word **anything** as "really are not important," and expand **only God** to "The important person is God . . . "; in many languages a new sentence should begin with such a clause, as in TEV.

3.8	RSV	TEV

He who plants and he who waters are equal, and each shall receive his wages according to his labor.

There is no difference between the man who plants and the man who waters; God will reward each one according to the work he has done.

This verse is so closely connected with the content of the previous verses, that most translations rightly omit the Greek word for "and" or "but" which KJV translates "Now." The first part of the verse in Greek says literally "The planter and the waterer are one thing," continuing the series of neuter pronouns which began in verse 5. Translations vary in how they understand this clause, depending mainly on whether they think of the planter and waterer as (1) equal in status or (2) sharing in the same work. RSV and TNT choose "equally important" (compare

DuCL, ItCL); Mft has "on the same level"; Phps opts for "alike insignificant." In favor of (2) are NEB's "they work as a team" and GeCL's "both work at the same work." TEV's rendering "there is no difference" also follows (2). In favor of (1) is the fact that the context explicitly states that the work of the planter and waterer are different. But favoring (2) is the fact that verse 5 has linked Paul and Apollos as servants, and the wider context of this chapter contrasts the unity of the evangelists' work with the disunity of the parties in Corinth. It appears, therefore, that (2) gives the better sense.

The Greek word which is translated as **wages** (TEV's "reward") has two meanings: the literal meaning "pay" or "wages," as in 9.17-18 (TEV), and the figurative meaning "reward," usually referring to something good. It is the same Greek word that RSV translates "reward" in verse 14. "Reward" is probably the better translation in this verse, as it helps to prepare the reader for reference to the final day of judgment in verse 13.

<u>3.9</u>	RSV	TEV

For we are God's fellow workers; you are God's field, God's building.

For we are partners working together for God, and you are God's field.

You are also God's building.

As the paragraph division in TEV, NEB, and other translations shows, the last part of this verse makes a sudden but natural transition from farming to building. This image of building is developed in verses 9b-17. There is, however, no grammatical break in the Greek, which is literally "for of-God, of-God building you-are." Translators need to decide carefully whether in their languages they tend to put such transitional statements with the preceding or the following section of the text. GeCL, for example, treats the whole of this verse as an introduction to the following paragraph, while RSV and other translations take it as the conclusion to verses 5-9. TEV makes the break sharper than it is in Greek by putting 9a at the end of the previous paragraph, and letting 9b begin a new paragraph. In these comments we shall follow TEV, which reflects natural English usage.

RSV's **For** is a weak conjunction which is often omitted in translation. Here it introduces the conclusion to this part of Paul's argument. It is also possible that **For** links 9a with verse 8a, leaving 8b as an aside which anticipates verses 10b-15. If this is so, it would be possible to restructure verses 8 and 9 as follows, taking TEV as a base: "There is no difference between the man who plants and the one who waters, for we are partners working together for God, and God will reward each one according to the work he has done."

The pronoun **we** in this verse is exclusive, referring only to Paul and Apollos.

There are two main ways of understanding the first part of this verse: (1) "we are God's fellow-workers" (NEB text) or (2) "we are fellow-workers in God's service" (NEB footnote). Brc refuses to choose between these two options, and translates "we work together and we work for God." In favor of (1) it may be said that it largely includes (2) and adds something extra which gives a more precise meaning that fits in well with the context.

In place of the metaphor **God's field**, some translators may prefer to use a simile; for example, "like a field that God is working in."

[63]

It would be possible to translate **God's building** as "the building on which God is working," but in verse 16, even immature Christians are described as being already God's temple. TEV's paragraphing shows that Paul introduces here a new thought, which he will develop in verses 10-17.

RSV   3.10-17   TEV

RSV	TEV
10 According to the grace of God given to me, like a skilled master builder I laid a foundation, and another man is building upon it. Let each man take care how he builds upon it. 11 For no other foundation can any one lay than that which is laid, which is Jesus Christ. 12 Now if any one builds on the foundation with gold, silver, precious stones, wood, hay, straw— 13 each man's work will become manifest; for the Day will disclose it, because it will be revealed with fire, and the fire will test what sort of work each one has done. 14 If the work which any man has built on the foundation survives, he will receive a reward. 15 If any man's work is burned up, he will suffer loss, though he himself will be saved, but only as through fire. 16 Do you not know that you are God's temple and that God's Spirit dwells in you? 17 If any one destroys God's temple, God will destroy him. For God's temple is holy, and that temple you are.	10 Using the gift that God gave me, I did the work of an expert builder and laid the foundation, and another man is building on it. But each one must be careful how he builds. 11 For God has already placed Jesus Christ as the one and only foundation, and no other foundation can be laid. 12 Some will use gold or silver or precious stones in building on the foundation; others will use wood or grass or straw. 13 And the quality of each person's work will be seen when the Day of Christ exposes it. For on that Day fire will reveal everyone's work; the fire will test it and show its real quality. 14 If what was built on the foundation survives the fire, the builder will receive a reward. 15 But if anyone's work is burnt up, then he will lose it; but he himself will be saved, as if he had escaped through the fire. 16 Surely you know that you are God's temple and that God's Spirit lives in you! 17 So if anyone destroys God's temple, God will destroy him. For God's temple is holy, and you yourselves are his temple.

In this passage, and already at the end of verse 9, Paul may be thinking of the Jewish Festival of Tabernacles, during which temporary building materials were used to cover a permanent framework or foundation.[3] In any case, Paul is not speaking about a building itself but about the building process. This is, then, another dynamic image like that of the plant in verses 6-9.

3.10   RSV   TEV

RSV	TEV
According to the grace of God given to me, like a skilled master builder I laid a foundation, and another man is building upon it. Let each man take care how he builds upon it.	**Using the gift that God gave me, I did the work of an expert builder and laid the foundation, and another man is building on it. But each one must be careful how he builds.**

[3] J.M. Ford, 1974, "You are God's 'Sukkah' (1 Corinthians iii. 10-17)," New Testament Studies 21.139-142.

There is a considerable degree of doubt as to whether the words **of God** are part of the original text. However, a majority of the editors of the UBS Greek New Testament voted to include them. Scribes may have omitted them, either as too repetitious, or because they were comparing this passage to Romans 12.6 and Galatians 2.9. In any case, **of God** is implied in the text.

Grace for Paul can only be a gift of God (see comments on 1.3), though there is no specific gift mentioned here. God gave Paul what he needed to found the church at Corinth. TEV's "gift" is a more accurate English translation. RSV's **given to me** must mean "that God gave me" (TEV). **Grace** can also be translated as "ability." In some languages it will be necessary to restructure the clause "using the gift that God gave me" (TEV) as "I used the gift (ability) which God gave to me."

The word which is translated **master builder** is the word from which the English "architect" is taken. The Greek word described someone who not only drew up plans but also directed the building work and assigned different tasks to different workmen. However, Paul probably intended the first meaning here, since in verse 5 he says that the work of assigning tasks is Christ's own function.

Foundation: certain cultures do not use foundations at all, and their languages may have no word for this type of building part which the Greeks and many modern cultures use in building houses and other structures. Such cultures construct their houses on stilts or poles. In such cases one may say, for example, "the center pole" or "the pole which holds up the building."

Another man is building upon it probably refers to Apollos, but Paul is not using the experience of Apollos and himself as the basis for more general statements. This is shown by the repeated **each man** of verses 10,13, and "any man" of later verses. The present tense in the verb, **is building,** does not necessarily refer to the time at which Paul is writing. It may refer to any stage after the founding of the church at Corinth, including the work of Apollos, which in verse 6 was referred to in the past tense. It is possible to render this clause as "upon which another man is building," or one can begin a new sentence after **foundation** and say ". . . foundation. Another man is building upon it."

3.11	RSV	TEV
	For no other foundation can any one lay than that which is laid, which is Jesus Christ.	For God has already placed Jesus Christ as the one and only foundation, and no other foundation can be laid.

In verses 10 and 12 the **foundation** may refer to Paul's first preaching about Christ rather than to Christ himself (2.1-2). But in this verse Paul is saying that Christ himself is the foundation. This verse may well be a nonfigurative aside which is inserted by Paul into a passage otherwise full of figurative language.

In this verse Paul's thought moves from his elementary teaching about Christ to Christ himself. **For** may be understood as marking this change in his argument. RSV and TEV retain this word, though many translations such as NEB and GeCL omit it. Bible de Jérusalem (BJ) uses "indeed," and TOB has "as for the foundation, no one can lay another . . . ."

TEV reverses the order of RSV to show that the second statement is a basis for the first. **Is laid** means "is already there," "already in place," permanently, not simply "the foundation I laid when I first came to Corinth." The foundation in this sense cannot be laid twice in different places.

In languages which do not normally use a passive, one may restructure this verse as "For God has already placed Jesus Christ as the one and only foundation. So no one can lay any other foundation."

3.12	RSV	TEV

RSV	TEV
Now if any one builds on the foundation with gold, silver, precious stones, wood, hay, straw—	Some will use gold or silver or precious stones in building on the foundation; others will use wood or grass or straw.

In this verse Paul uses figurative language again and turns his attention to the materials used in building. The return to figurative language is marked by **Now**, which TEV omits. The word **if** introduces a real or fulfilled condition: Paul has already said that people have been building on the foundation he has laid (see, for example, verse 10). Barrett translates this first phrase as "Whatever anyone builds . . . ." The **any** is quite general, as TEV shows by the plural "Some." TEV's "others" is a good English translation, for it brings out the implied contrast between valuable and cheap building materials. Translators in some languages will have to add the word "people" after the words "Some" and "others": "some people"; "other people."

TEV's "in building" is a difficult construction. One may also say "when they build upon."

The foundation refers to verse 11, where the same word is mentioned. Translators in certain languages will need to make this reference clear by saying "this foundation."

Many commentators are uncertain as to the exact meaning of the two Greek words which are translated **precious stones** and **straw**. Concerning the first word, most translations pick **precious stones**, and this fits in well with the reference to **gold** and **silver**, and with such descriptions as those found in Isaiah 54.11-12; Revelation 21.18-21. In some cultures, however, it seems strange to use jewels in a building—though this was done in India in building the Taj Mahal. For this reason NEB translates this word as "fine stone," that is, stone of finest quality, which is the meaning of the second phrase in the Septuagint of 1 Kings 7.9-11 (3 Kingdoms 7.46-48 in Greek). As for the second word, **straw** is the most likely meaning, although "stubble" is possible. Other scholars feel that "reeds" is intended, since reeds are often a symbol of weakness in the Old Testament. The translator must keep in mind that in this context the point is that wood, grass, and straw will burn, while gold, silver, and jewels or fine stones will not.

3.13	RSV	TEV

RSV	TEV
each man's work will become manifest; for the Day will disclose it, because it will be revealed with fire, and the fire will test what sort of work each one has done.	And the quality of each person's work will be seen when the Day of Christ exposes it. For on that Day fire will reveal everyone's work; the fire will test it and show its real quality.

This verse is remarkable for the number of synonyms which Paul uses to describe the idea of "revealing" or "making clear." These synonyms are **become manifest, will disclose it,** and **it will be revealed.**

TEV's "the quality of" is implicit in the Greek and becomes explicit in the last part of the verse, where Paul says that "fire will test it and show its real quality."

The phrase **will become manifest** or "will be seen" (TEV) may be expressed as "will be revealed" or "will be known." But in languages which do not use passives, one may say "people will see." It may also be helpful to place this phrase at the beginning of this verse and say "And people will see the quality of . . . when the Day of Christ . . . ."

The Day is one of the expressions used in the Old Testament of the time when God will judge his people, or the world. In the New Testament it has the added meaning of the day of Christ's return (see 1 Thes 5.4 and also 1 Cor 1.8). TEV translates "Day of Christ" because throughout this passage Paul shows that Christ is central to God's purposes from beginning to end (see verses 11,23). If, however, "Day of Christ" is not clear to the intended readers of the translation, **the Day** may be translated "the Day of Judgment" or "the day when Christ comes to judge."

For the Day will disclose it, because it will be revealed with fire: the Greek may mean (1) "the Day is revealed in fire," or (2) "each man's work is revealed by fire," that is, by whether or not it can be burnt. The reasons for (1) are that "Day" is the nearest noun in the Greek that can serve as the subject of the verb **be revealed,** and that (2) would make Paul repeat himself. RSV is ambiguous. FrCL clearly picks (1): "that day will manifest itself by fire." Out of all the translations which we consulted, only TEV explicitly chooses (2). GeCL has just one sentence, reducing the seeming repetition in the Greek: "On that day, the worth of each person's work will be tested in fire."

Test does not seem to be used in the technical sense of testing or proving gold while refining it. The context speaks of destruction and survival on the Day of Judgment, rather than speaking of purification. It is therefore better to use an expression which has the wider meaning of a **test** that one either passes or fails.

Some Greek manuscripts add "itself" between the **fire** and **will test.** Some copyists may have omitted this word because it adds nothing to the sense. But others may have added it to strengthen the sentence. The emphatic "itself" following a noun is rare in Paul's writings. So it is probably better to omit "itself," as the UBS Greek text does.

3.14   RSV   TEV

If the work which any man has built on the foundation survives, he will receive a reward.

If what was built on the foundation survives the fire, the builder will receive a reward.

Any man may refer to either men or women.

RSV's **foundation** is not expressed in Greek but is present in the underlying meaning. TEV fills out the meaning at various points even more than RSV.

Survives is in the future tense in Greek, referring to the Day of Judgment. The meaning is that only work with good building materials will remain standing after the fire. This initial clause may be rephrased as "If someone builds on that foundation with material which doesn't burn . . . ," or the whole verse can be restructured as follows: "God will reward the person who builds on this foundation with material that doesn't burn."

Reward: see the comments on verse 8.

3.15   RSV   TEV

If any man's work is burned up, he will **But if anyone's work is burnt up, then**
suffer loss, though he himself will be **he will lose it; but he himself will be**
saved, but only as through fire. **saved, as if he had escaped through the**
fire.

The first part of this verse parallels the structure of verse 14. It expresses a contrast which TEV rightly brings out by adding "But." Translators should consider what resources are available in their own language to express (1) the contrast between verse 14 and 15a; (2) the wider contrast between what happens to the work and what happens to the builder himself; (3) the qualifications which are introduced at the end of the sentence. In most translations which we consulted, either (1) or (2) is left unexpressed.

Is burned up, like "survives" in verse 14, is in the future tense in Greek, referring to the Day of Judgment.

He will suffer loss is too general a translation. Three other translations are possible: (1) he will be punished (GeCL); (2) he will lose his work (TEV), that is, it will be burnt up; (3) he will lose the reward for his work (Barrett, FrCL, ItCL, TNT). (1) is an unusual meaning of the Greek word, though Paul may be thinking of its use in the Greek of Proverbs 19.19. (2) adds nothing to what has been said already. (3) makes a good contrast with verse 14b and may be the best solution.

He himself will be saved emphasizes the contrast between the person himself and the work he has done. He will be like someone who narrowly escapes death by running through flames. Literally, he will not be condemned and destroyed by God at the last judgment, although his work on earth has been destroyed.

But only as through fire is too literal a translation. TEV's "as if he had escaped through the fire" rightly fills out the meaning of the Greek. "As if," though, suggests that Paul is not thinking specifically of the judgment fires. The rendering "like someone who has been pulled out of the fire" probably is a more general and accurate meaning.

3.16   RSV   TEV

     Do you not know that you are   **Surely you know that you are**
God's temple and that God's Spirit **God's temple and that God's Spirit lives**
dwells in you?   **in you!**

Paul turns rather abruptly from drawing lessons from himself and Apollos to addressing his readers. He applies to them a conclusion which is drawn partly from the previous verses, though using different language. This verse, like verse 8b, anticipates the following section, where the "if any one" language of verses 12, 14, and 15 is resumed in verse 17. However, in other respects verse 17 carries on the new thought of verse 16, so a new paragraph is not needed at that point.

Do you not know is a negative rhetorical question which is equal to the positive statement "You certainly know that you are God's temple . . . ," or "I am sure that you know that . . . ," or "I am sure that you are aware of the fact that . . . ."

The main problem in understanding and translating verses 16-17 is to decide whether Paul is referring to the Christians at Corinth individually, or as a body of believers, or both. It seems more natural to apply the image of the **temple** to the church as a whole, though in 6.19 it probably refers to individual Christians. It is also possible that the words "if any one" in verse 17 refer to one or more individuals who are a threat to the church at Corinth. Moreover, Paul seems to purposely use a plural relative pronoun "which" in verse 17, meaning "you yourselves," where a singular "which (temple)" would have been grammatically more correct. Paul's general tendency in this passage is to make positive statements about unspecified individuals in Corinth. Some translators may prefer to use a simile instead of the metaphor **God's temple**; for example, "you are like a temple which belongs to God."

Temple may be rendered as "God's house," "God's dwelling place," or "the big house where people worship God."

The most likely meaning of the end of the verse is **in you** (whether as a group or as individuals), though "among you" is possible, as in verse 18.

3.17	RSV	TEV

If any one destroys God's temple, God will destroy him. For God's temple is holy, and that temple you are.

So if anyone destroys God's temple, God will destroy him. For God's temple is holy, and you yourselves are his temple.

Any one can be rendered in some languages as "any person."

It is by no means certain that the verb which is translated **destroy** has the same meaning in the first and second clauses. The Greek word has the general meaning **destroy**, but sometimes has the narrower meanings "corrupt (morally)," "ruin (financially)," or "seduce (sexually)." None of these last three meanings is possible in the second clause, since God is the subject; but the meaning of the two clauses may well be "If anyone corrupts God's temple, God will destroy him." DuCL uses different words having the same meaning, and GeCL uses the same words to show the play on words in the Greek. "Corrupts" would make a good connection with the thought that God's temple is holy. Compare 2 Corinthians 6.14—7.1.

Him is emphatic; literally "that one" or "that person."

For **will destroy**, some Greek manuscripts have "destroys," but this is less likely to be what Paul wrote.

God's temple is holy really means "God's temple belongs to him alone." See comment on 1.2.

And that temple you are is literally "which (plural) you (emphasized) are." The meaning is "you individually make up God's temple" rather than "you yourselves are holy."

RSV	3.18-23	TEV

18 Let no one deceive himself. If any one among you thinks that he is wise in this age, let him become a fool that he may become wise. 19 For the wisdom of this world is folly with God. For it is written, "He catches the wise in their craftiness," 20 and again, "The Lord knows that the thoughts of the wise are futile." 21 So let no one boast of men. For all things are yours, 22 whether Paul or Apollos or Cephas or the world or life or death or the present or the future, all are yours; 23 and you are Christ's; and Christ is God's.

18 No one should fool himself. If anyone among you thinks that he is wise by this world's standards, he should become a fool, in order to be really wise. 19 For what this world considers to be wisdom is nonsense in God's sight. As the scripture says, "God traps the wise in their cleverness"; 20 and another scripture says, "The Lord knows that the thoughts of the wise are worthless." 21 No one, then, should boast about what men can do. Actually everything belongs to you: 22 Paul, Apollos, and Peter; this world, life and death, the present and the future—all these are yours, 23 and you belong to Christ, and Christ belongs to God.

In this section Paul rounds off the argument about the danger of party divisions and the rival ideas of wisdom, which he introduced in 1.18. The break with the preceding verses is not sharp, though he uses the form **Let no one** for the first time. Some commentators see a clear distinction between **if anyone** in verse 18 and the same words in verse 17. They feel that verse 17 is referring to a possible happening, whereas verse 18 is referring to a real fact. On the other hand, it is possible that it was those who claimed to be **wise** who were in danger of corrupting or destroying the church.

3.18   RSV   TEV

Let no one deceive himself. If any one among you thinks that he is wise in this age, let him become a fool that he may become wise.

No one should fool himself. If anyone among you thinks that he is wise by this world's standards, he should become a fool, in order to be really wise.

The imperative form **Let no one** is not commonly used in English and some other languages. TEV's "No one should" is better modern English. Translators need to find the best way to render imperatives in their languages rather than following an English model literally.

TEV's "fool himself" is a good common language rendering which equals RSV's **deceive.** The phrase has nothing to do with the terms for "folly" or "madness" which Paul uses in other places. Other possible translations are "delude" or "be under any illusion" (Phps).

The punctuation of the next part of the sentence is uncertain. All translations consulted appear to agree with TEV and RSV. Westcott and Hort's Greek New Testament, which some commentators follow, makes a balanced sentence[4] such as is often found in the writings of Paul (see verses 4-5) and other biblical writers:

---

[4] An A B B' A' structure, known as chiasmus. See also comments on 15.57-58.

A. If anyone thinks he is wise   let him become a fool   A'.

B.   among you   in this world   B'.

This links **among you** with **wise,** giving the meaning "If anyone thinks he is wise by the standards of your group," just as in the following clause "in this world" means "by this world's standards" (TEV). If this argument is correct, a possible alternative to RSV and TEV would be "Anyone who thinks he is wiser than the rest of you should become a fool by this world's standards."

As in verses 12-15, the **If** almost certainly implies that some people in Corinth did "think they were wise," so one may translate this clause, **If any one thinks that he is wise,** as "Anyone who thinks he is wise . . . ."

On **wise,** see comments on 1.5,19.

For a discussion of the word translated **age,** see the comment on 2.6. "World" (TEV) is a better translation here.

The word for **fool** was often used by followers of popular teachers in the ancient world to refer to people outside their group, or to nonthinkers generally. The contrast in this verse is with the kind of philosophical speculation which some people at Corinth seem to have called "wisdom." "Madman" is therefore too strong a translation here. Paul does not use the words for **fool** and "folly" (verse 19) outside this part of 1 Corinthians.

TEV's "really" is not in the Greek, but is necessary in good English to bring out the contrast with "by this world's standards," and to prepare for verse 19.

3.19 RSV	TEV
For the wisdom of this world is folly with God. For it is written, "He catches the wise in their craftiness,"	For what this world considers to be wisdom is nonsense in God's sight. As the scripture says, "God traps the wise in their cleverness";

For the wisdom of this world is not as clear as TEV's rendering "what this world considers to be wisdom." Paul's point is that the "world's wisdom" is not "real wisdom." This first clause may also be rendered as "what people of this world (humans) consider to be wisdom." For Paul, wisdom and folly always have to do with people, so this clause could even be translated as "what the world calls wisdom, God calls folly."

On **folly,** see comment on "fool", verse 18.

On **it is written,** see comments on 1.19, where the same phrase is used. The quotation in this verse is from Job 5.13, though its language (**catches** and **craftiness**) is stronger than that of the Septuagint and does not agree exactly with the Hebrew text.

3.20 RSV	TEV
and again, "The Lord knows that the thoughts of the wise are futile."	and another scripture says, "The Lord knows that the thoughts of the wise are worthless."

And again is a standard way in biblical Greek of introducing the second and later items in a series of quotations (compare Rom 15.10-12; Heb 1.5; 10.30). TEV's "and another scripture says" is better English style.

The quotation in this verse is from Psalm 94.11 and follows the Septuagint, except that it replaces "men" by "wise (men),"[5] perhaps under the influence of the quotation in verse 19. This quotation, even more than the first, develops and supports the statement in verse 19a about "what God calls folly."

The word for **thoughts** can mean thoughts expressed in "reasoning" (Mft) or "arguments" (NEB, JB). These renderings would fit in well with Paul's argument. Psalm 94 is concerned with thoughts which only God can know about, and Paul expresses this idea in 4.5 when he says that "the Lord . . . will disclose the purposes of the heart." For the moment, though, Paul seems more concerned with views which wrongly claim to be wisdom. So he puts emphasis on the final word **futile.** Both RSV and TEV make this emphasis clear.

Futile may also be expressed as "useless" or "meaningless."

3.21   RSV   TEV

So let no one boast of men. For all things are yours,

No one, then, should boast about what men can do. Actually everything belongs to you:

So (TEV's "then") introduces the conclusion of Paul's argument. One could also phrase this first sentence as "So then, no one should boast . . . ."

For a discussion of the imperative form **let no one boast,** see verse 19.

For a discussion on **boast,** see comments on 1.29. This word is used twice as often in 1 and 2 Corinthians as in the rest of the New Testament, and may have been one of the slogans used in controversy in Corinth. Here it describes the misdirected enthusiasm which set followers of Paul, Apollos, and Peter against one another. The Greek is literally "do not boast in men." ItCL brings out the connection between this phrase and the following words: "do not boast of belonging to someone, for everything belongs to you." The rendering "belonging to someone" seems to fit in better with verse 22 than TEV's translation "what men can do." The reference seems to be that of belonging to someone as a follower or disciple.

The final sentence introduces a contrast rather than a logical result. Instead of being proud of being the disciple of some human being, the Corinthian Christians should realize that everything belongs to them. TEV's "Actually" is added to express this contrast. The change to a neuter pronoun (**all things**) is necessary because not only people but things are mentioned in the next verse. In some languages it may be necessary to refer separately to people and things. So one could restructure the final sentence of verse 21 and the first part of verse 22 as "Everyone belongs to you—Paul, Apollos, Peter—and everything is yours—the world, life and death . . . ."

---

[5] Héring (1949) thinks that "men" is the correct text here, but the evidence for this is slight, and there was always a tendency to make the quotation correspond to the Septuagint.

3.22	RSV	TEV

whether Paul or Apollos or Cephas or the world or life or death or the present or the future, all are yours;

Paul, Apollos, and Peter; this world, life and death, the present and the future—all these are yours,

Translators should notice before going any farther that there will be a second turn in Paul's thought in verse 23:

not "I belong to Paul . . ."
but "everything belongs to you"
nevertheless "you belong to Christ . . . ."

NEB solves this problem by making verse 22 a parenthesis, the end of which is marked by the repetition of "everything is yours."

TEV's translation reflects a more natural English way of grouping the series of nouns in the Greek, which are connected by a word which is literally "or" or "and" (TEV). The semicolon in TEV puts these nouns into two groups. Translators need to decide how their languages would naturally show these two main groups.

Most modern translations use "Peter" (TEV) instead of **Cephas** for the sake of consistency and to keep the reader from becoming confused. The original readers would have known that Cephas was the same person as Peter, but most modern readers are unaware of this fact.

Note that **the world** here has a good or at least neutral sense, not a bad sense as in verse 19.

There is no difference between "all things are yours" in verse 21 and **all are yours** in this verse. In some languages it may be more effective to repeat the same expression.

3.23	RSV	TEV

and you are Christ's; and Christ is God's.

and you belong to Christ, and Christ belongs to God.

The translation of this verse should not be difficult, once the translator has examined verses 21b-23 as a whole. TEV's "you belong to Christ, and Christ belongs to God" reflects better English style than RSV's rendering **you are Christ's; and Christ is God's.**

Chapter 4

Apostles of Christ

1 This is how one should regard us, as servants of Christ and stewards of the mysteries of God. 2 Moreover it is required of stewards that they be found trustworthy. 3 But with me it is a very small thing that I should be judged by you or by any human court. I do not even judge myself. 4 I am not aware of anything against myself, but I am not thereby acquitted. It is the Lord who judges me. 5 Therefore do not pronounce judgment before the time, before the Lord comes, who will bring to light the things now hidden in darkness and will disclose the purposes of the heart. Then every man will receive his commendation from God.

1 You should think of us as Christ's servants, who have been put in charge of God's secret truths. 2 The one thing required of such a servant is that he be faithful to his master. 3 Now, I am not at all concerned about being judged by you or by any human standard; I don't even pass judgment on myself. 4 My conscience is clear, but that does not prove that I am really innocent. The Lord is the one who passes judgment on me. 5 So you should not pass judgment on anyone before the right time comes. Final judgment must wait until the Lord comes; he will bring to light the dark secrets and expose the hidden purposes of people's minds. And then everyone will receive from God the praise he deserves.

In this section Paul returns to the theme of judgment, which he previously treated in 3.5-15 and now applies more specifically to his qualifications as an apostle (see 4.9). The paragraph is full of terms which refer to judgment and especially to qualifications for an official position. These terms are discussed in greater detail below.

The words "I have applied" in 4.6 almost explicitly state that 4.5 marks the end of a section.

The TEV section heading "Apostles of Christ" might in some languages indicate wrongly that the apostles merely belong to Christ rather than being servants of Christ. In such a case one may render this heading as "We are apostles who serve Christ," "God has called us to serve Christ," or "We are messengers sent by Christ."

This is how one should regard us, as servants of Christ and stewards of the mysteries of God.

You should think of us as Christ's servants, who have been put in charge of God's secret truths.

The Greek text begins with a word which means "thus," and this word is followed later in the sentence by a word meaning **as.** RSV and TEV translate only this second word. In some contexts these two words are often used in comparisons (see 3.15 and 9.26 [twice]), so that "thus" would refer only to the text that follows. However, most commentators and some translations take "thus" to refer instead (or also) to the preceding text. If this is so, the meaning would be "in these conditions" (Orr-Walther), "because these things are so" (Héring), or simply "therefore" (FrCL, JB) or "then" (Barrett). Otherwise the transition from 3.23 seems rather more abrupt than is usual in Paul's writings.

The Greek word for **regard** (TEV's "think") suggests reasoning or argument and is related to "thoughts" in 3.20 (see comments). It is used very frequently by Paul in 2 Corinthians and Romans, so it was not just a slogan of Paul's opponents in Corinth.

In this context, as in 4.6, **us** must mean Paul and his fellow evangelists, especially Apollos; Paul's readers are not included.

The word for **servants** is similar in meaning to that used in 3.5, but it also includes the idea of an assistant to someone in an official position. The phrase **servants of Christ** may also be rendered as "people who serve Christ." The word **steward** suggests this same official status. In biblical times the **steward** was often an estate manager who organized the work of other people. Sometimes he was a city official responsible, among other things, for conducting public worship. The Greek word for **steward** (*oikonomos*) is derived from *oikos*, the word for house or household (see 1 Tim 3.15). The word for "build on" (*epoikodomeō*) used in 3.10,12, 14 is also related to this word **steward.** TEV translates this word as "put in charge," because the word **steward** has a very narrow meaning in modern day English. Today this term usually refers to a person who attends to the needs of passengers on ships or trains, or it can refer to an official at a race track.

The mysteries of God: see the comments on 2.1,7. The wider context suggests that **the mysteries** was equivalent to the Christian message, especially its deeper implications which are understood only by the spiritually mature (see 2.6). Paul usually, though not in this section, speaks of the Christian mystery or mysteries as having been already revealed through Christ. Translators should therefore not take **servants of Christ and stewards of the mysteries** to mean that the apostles are responsible for keeping God's truths secret. On the contrary, they were to proclaim these secret truths.

In languages which do not use passives, this final clause may be rendered as "whom God has put in charge of his secret truths" or "whom God has given the responsibility of proclaiming his secret truths."

4.2 RSV	TEV
Moreover it is required of stewards that they be found trustworthy.	**The one thing required of such a servant is that he be faithful to his master.**

This verse is full of minor difficulties, though the general sense is fairly clear.

The first two Greek words, which RSV translates **Moreover,** are not found together anywhere else in the New Testament. Both are used separately as transitionals, and many commentators and translations understand them in this way. The UBS *Concise Greek-English Dictionary* gives the meaning "moreover, in this connection" for this verse. However, the first word by itself may mean either "here in this place" or "thus, as it is . . . ." If the more common meaning "here" is taken, Paul may already be implying the contrast between human and divine judgment which he makes explicit later on. This seems to make better sense; otherwise "thus" adds nothing to the sentence and is equivalent to the first word in verse 1. If the word means "here" in this verse, one may rephrase this passage as "Here (in this world) the one thing required of such . . . ." All translations, though, which we have consulted appear to choose the meaning "thus."

The second Greek word means **Moreover**, "as for the rest," or "in addition to." It marks a shift to another aspect of Paul's argument.

The text which is translated **required** is uncertain. Greek manuscripts vary between **it is required** and "you require," which may also be an imperative "require!" Most translations take the meaning as **it is required**. On the whole, the context suggests that at this point Paul is stating a basic principle rather than appealing to his readers. So **it is required** is a preferable rendering. Some translators will prefer to use an active verb here as Brc does: "the first quality that anyone looks for . . . ." If an active verb is used, its subject may be either singular ("anyone") or plural ("people"), with no difference in meaning. There is no suggestion of God requiring anything.

Luther's (Lu) translation has "all that is required . . . is that a man be found faithful." This is rather misleading; "all" is neither expressed nor implied in the text.

Of stewards translates a plural noun in Greek but refers to servants as a class, not to any particular servant. TEV's "servant" is thus a better rendering in modern English (see comment on verse 1).

In biblical Greek the verb **be found** sometimes refers to the result of an official inquiry. It thus can mean "be shown to be" or "prove to be," as for example in Romans 7.10; 1 Corinthians 15.15; 2 Corinthians 5.3. This may be the meaning here too.

TEV's "to his master" is not in the Greek but is added to show what kind of faithfulness is intended here. However, in some New Testament texts such as Hebrews 3.2,5, the word for **trustworthy** or "faithful" (TEV) suggests not only general "reliability" (Brc) but also effectiveness in a particular office. This would fit the present context well, the office being that of an apostle. One could then render this phrase as "that he be an effective worker" or "that he do his job in a trustworthy way."

4.3	RSV	TEV
	But with me it is a very small thing that I should be judged by you or by any human court. I do not even judge myself.	Now, I am not at all concerned about being judged by you or by any human standard; I don't even pass judgment on myself.

The phrase **But with me** brings out the suggestion of a contrast more clearly than TEV's "I." If we understand verse 2 correctly, verse 3 implies "Whatever happens here in earthly law courts, I am subject, not to this kind of judgment, but to the higher judgment of Christ." Paul states this explicitly later in the sentence, which in Greek runs to the end of verse 4. Verse 3 would then not be about Paul's feelings or his inward state of mind, as TEV's "concerned" might suggest. The verse is about Paul's real status as someone who is responsible to Christ, who appointed him as an apostle. It is possible, then, to translate this sentence as "As for me, whether you or any human court judge me, it is of no importance."

Verses 3-4 use a verb for "judge" (*anakrinō*) which comes from the root verb for "judge" (*krinō*) used in verse 5 (compare 2.14-15; 2 Cor 5.10). Among the possible meanings of *anakrinō* are (1) "cross-question" (Mft), (2) "pass judgment on" (NEB, NAB, JB), or more generally (3) "interrogate," "examine" (TNT). The immediate context (especially **human court**) suggests the latter general meaning of examining a witness or an accused person.

By any human court is literally "by a human day." "Day" was used in 3.13 to refer to the Judgment Day. This sentence may be restructured in a way similar to TEV as "that other people may judge me according to their standards." One could also combine this sentence with the one which precedes it; for example, "It is not important whether you or anyone else judges me."

The last few words of the verse move to a fresh aspect of Paul's theme. Many translations agree with TEV and RSV in using the word **even**, but the text does not necessarily mean that Paul considers his own conscience higher than that of any human court. This idea was common Stoic teaching in Paul's time. Since verse 4b expresses the main point that Christ's judgment is final, it is probably best to leave out **even** in this verse. FrCL has "nor do I judge myself." The word "myself" (TEV) is not emphatic as in "I did it myself," but is rather reflexive as in "I washed myself."

4.4 RSV	TEV
I am not aware of anything against myself, but I am not thereby acquitted. It is the Lord who judges me.	My conscience is clear, but that does not prove that I am really innocent. The Lord is the one who passes judgment on me.

This verse is linked to verse 3 by the weak connective "for." Verse 4a explains the previous statement "I do not even judge myself," and verse 4b is the positive counterpart of this negative statement.

RSV gives the literal meaning of the first part of this verse and makes good sense. TEV and other translations use "conscience" because the Greek word for "conscience" (*suneidēsis*) is related to the verb for "be aware of" (*sunoida*), just as "conscience" and "consciousness" are related in English. Translators need to remember that in the New Testament, the conscience usually has the negative function of signaling when something is wrong. Later ideas of conscience as an inner guiding light, or even something divine in humans, should not influence the translator. Perhaps a better translation is "I cannot think of anything that I have done wrong."

But I am not thereby acquitted: acquitted is literally "justified" or "declared innocent." Paul's thought is moving from the examination of people in court to the final verdict. In many places such as Romans 4.5, Paul uses this word in a deeper sense to refer to the event of being put right with God. In this verse, however, the context shows clearly that Paul is thinking for the moment of judgment on the human level.

The verb which is translated **judges** is again *anakrino* and probably still refers to the process of examination, but it is now examination being carried out by God. **The Lord** does not have **the** in Greek, and this may suggest the meaning "It is the one who is Lord who alone has the right to interrogate me."

4.5	RSV	TEV
	Therefore do not pronounce judgment before the time, before the Lord comes, who will bring to light the things now hidden in darkness and will disclose the purposes of the heart. Then every man will receive his commendation from God.	So you should not pass judgment on anyone before the right time comes. Final judgment must wait until the Lord comes; he will bring to light the dark secrets and expose the hidden purposes of people's minds. And then everyone will receive from God the praise he deserves.

Therefore indicates the conclusion of this part of Paul's argument; the conclusion is not a statement but a command (as in 3.21).

TEV is correct in supplying the word "anyone" in the first sentence. RSV's rendering is too vague. Although Paul is thinking mainly of himself and Apollos (verse 6), his thought has a wider range, as **all things** showed in 3.21-22, as well as his reference to wrong judgments in 3.18. Here, in contrast to verses 3-4, the verb for **pronounce judgment** is the simple form *krino*, referring not to an examination by a judge, but to the verdict at the end of the trial (as in Matt 7.1). Since Paul uses both *anakrino* and *krino* in verses 1-5, he probably intended a different meaning for each.

Before the time does not give the full sense of the Greek. TEV's "before the right time" is a better translation. The word for time in this verse refers to the right time, opportunity, or "psychological moment" for something to happen. In this context "the right time" is when **the Lord comes.**

The Lord, as in verse 4 and generally in Paul's writings, is Christ.

The things now hidden in darkness: RSV's **now** is not in the Greek, but the word **Then** in the final sentence shows that **now** is intended. **Then,** of course, refers to the future judgment. The clause **he will bring to light the things now hidden in darkness** may also be rendered as "he will bring the hidden things out of the darkness into light" or "he will bring the dark secrets out into the light."

Heart: in Hebrew thought, the heart was the seat of the intellect and will, much more than of the emotions. In this verse the stress is on a person's power of thought.

Every man is literally "each one" (see 1.12; 3.5,8,10,13). This term could be taken as referring only to Paul and Apollos, but Paul more likely is thinking ahead to the wider application in verses 6-8.

The difference between **commendation** here and "reward" in 3.14 is not as great as might at first appear. The nonmaterial "reward" is an expression of God's approval at the final judgment, and **commendation** in this context has the meaning "gives a favorable verdict."

From God is emphatic in the Greek, implying "not from men," as in Romans 2.29. Translators in many languages will need to use active rather than passive verbs in this verse; for example, "Then God will give to every person the praise which he deserves" or "Then God will praise each person as that person deserves."

6 I have applied all this to myself and Apollos for your benefit, brethren, that you may learn by us not to go beyond what is written, that none of you may be puffed up in favor of one against another. 7 For who sees anything different in you? What have you that you did not receive? If then you received it, why do you boast as if it were not a gift?

8 Already you are filled! Already you have become rich! Without us you have become kings! And would that you did reign, so that we might share the rule with you! 9 For I think that God has exhibited us apostles as last of all, like men sentenced to death; because we have become a spectacle to the world, to angels and to men. 10 We are fools for Christ's sake, but you are wise in Christ. We are weak, but you are strong. You are held in honor, but we in disrepute. 11 To the present hour we hunger and thirst, we are ill-clad and buffeted and homeless, 12 and we labor, working with our own hands. When reviled, we bless; when persecuted, we endure; 13 when slandered, we try to conciliate; we have become, and are now, as the refuse of the world, the offscouring of all things.

6 For your sake, my brothers, I have applied all this to Apollos and me, using the two of us as an example, so that you may learn what the saying means, "Observe the proper rules." None of you should be proud of one person and despise another. 7 Who made you superior to others? Didn't God give you everything you have? Well, then, how can you boast, as if what you have were not a gift?

8 Do you already have everything you need? Are you already rich? Have you become kings, even though we are not? Well, I wish you really were kings, so that we could be kings together with you. 9 For it seems to me that God has given the very last place to us apostles, like men condemned to die in public as a spectacle for the whole world of angels and of mankind. 10 For Christ's sake we are fools; but you are wise in union with Christ! We are weak, but you are strong! We are despised, but you are honored! 11 To this very moment we go hungry and thirsty; we are clothed in rags; we are beaten; we wander from place to place; 12 we wear ourselves out with hard work. When we are cursed, we bless; when we are persecuted, we endure; 13 when we are insulted, we answer back with kind words. We are no more than this world's garbage; we are the scum of the earth to this very moment!

In this section Paul returns to using an exclusive **we** where the readers are not included. Verse 6a suggests that **we** might mean only Paul and Apollos, but **us apostles** in verse 9 probably refers to other apostles also. There is no sufficient reason, then, for translating "we" as "I" here in this passage. Translators need to think carefully whether their language distinguishes between an exclusive "we" where the person being spoken to is not included, and an inclusive "we" where the hearer is included. Some languages even have a special pronoun for "we two," where the person being spoken to is excluded.

In this passage Paul is trying to persuade his readers to accept his right to give the often severe instructions which begin in chapter 5. Paul does this by a contrast between what some of the readers think their circumstances are and what Paul knows his own circumstances to be. In this contrast Paul uses rhetorical questions and irony very effectively. Before beginning their work on this passage, translators should consider how these special language devices can be best conveyed in their own languages. TEV shows how irony can be conveyed effectively in English.

One of the features which marks the beginning of a new paragraph here is the phrase **all this** (literally "these things") in verse 6. This phrase refers to the previous discussion. The word "this" in verse 14, probably referring to verses 6-13, also helps set this section as a new paragraph (see the detailed comments). The beginning of the section is also marked by the word **brethren** (TEV's "my brothers"). Here again this word means "fellow Christians," not literal family members (compare 1.10). The Greek text also begins with a word meaning "and" or "but," which usually shows a transition from one section to another. Verses 11-13 form an autobiographical subsection, the beginning and end of which are marked by the time phrases **to the present hour** (verse 11) and **now** (verse 13).

<u>4.6</u> RSV	TEV
I **have applied all this to myself and Apollos for your benefit, brethren, that you may learn by us not to go beyond what is written, that none of you may be puffed up in favor of one against another.**	For your sake, my brothers, I have applied all this to Apollos and me, using the two of us as an example, so that you may learn what the saying means, "Observe the proper rules." None of you should be proud of one person and despise another.

On the word **brethren** see the discussion in the introduction to this section. Paul does not specify here, as he did in 3.10-17, whether he is speaking to all the Corinthian Christians or only some of them. **None of you** may suggest the first.

Although **all this** clearly refers to something mentioned previously, commentators are not sure to what **all this** refers. Many translations and commentators think it refers to the figurative language about planting and building in 3.5-17. If so, RSV and TEV are right to translate **applied,** though the Greek does not have this meaning elsewhere in the New Testament.[1] Barrett translates: "I have . . . made these things seem to apply to Apollos and myself . . . ," the thought being "In all that I have said up to now, it may seem that I have been talking only about Apollos and myself; but what I have said can be applied more widely, namely to you readers." This would make good sense of the phrase **for your benefit,** which is emphatic in Greek because it comes at the end of a clause. Another suggested translation which is closer in meaning to TEV is "I have applied these figures of speech (referring to those used in chapter 3) to myself and Apollos . . . ."[2] TEV produces this same effect by putting the phrase at the beginning of the verse.

TEV's rendering "using the two of us as an example" brings out the full meaning of a phrase which literally means "in (or, by) us." The translation of "the two of us" does not add anything to the meaning, since the preceding words show that at this point Paul is speaking of Paul and Apollos alone.

---

[1] Arndt-Gingrich says "1 Cor 4:6 is more or less unique." In Philippians 3.21, the only other place in the New Testament where the active voice of the verb *metaschēmatizō* is used, it means "change (the form of)"; in 2 Corinthians 11.13-15 the middle voice is used with the meaning "disguise."

[2] M.D. Hooker, 1963, " 'Beyond the Things that are Written': An examination of 1 Corinthians 4.6," <u>New Testament Studies</u> 10.127-132.

TEV's construction ". . . me, using" will be difficult to translate in many languages. In such cases one may begin a new sentence after "me"; for example, ". . . me. I have used . . . ."

The next few words are so difficult to understand that some scholars have thought that they were not part of the original text. However, there is no manuscript evidence to back up their claim. These words are also not Paul's normal style, but it seems likely that he is quoting a current saying, as TEV indicates. The article in the Greek before the phrase "Not above (or, beyond) the things that are written" suggests that this phrase is such a quotation.

What is written renders a Greek phrase which may be translated literally as "the things that are written" (see 1.19). Paul may be thinking especially about parts of scripture he has already quoted in this letter. On the other hand he may be speaking generally, as TEV's "the proper rules" suggests. Other possible translations are "I wanted you to learn from our example what the proverb, 'Remain within the limits fixed by what is written,' means" (FrCL); ". . . what the principle, 'Not beyond the measure which God has set,' means" (GeCL). Others leave out any reference to **what is written** and say "Learn not to go beyond certain limits" (ItCL); "learn to 'keep within the rules,' as they say" (NEB); or more specifically, "Keep close to Scripture" (TNT).

The last part of the sentence **none of you may be puffed up . . .** may be linked either with the beginning of the verse ("I have applied this . . . so that no one may be puffed up") or with the middle ("so that you may learn . . . [and] so that no one may be puffed up"). The middle section of this verse seems to be a general statement which the last part of the verse develops and applies to the readers. RSV follows this ordering. TEV, though, puts the phrase **none of you may be puffed up** into a separate sentence.

The Greek verb translated **puffed up** refers basically to pride. It may also be rendered as "proud," "have a high heart," or "consider oneself to be important." This verb is also used in verses 18-19; 5.2; 8.1; 13.5, but appears nowhere else in the New Testament except in Colossians 2.18. It seems to have been a special temptation of the Corinthians, rather like the "boasting" of 1.29,31; 3.21; 4.7; 13.4. But in this verse it has the added element of self-deception (compare 3.18). Paul seems to be thinking at this point about two things: (1) the inflated idea which the Corinthian Christians, or some of them, had of themselves, and (2) their attachment to one leader over against another. The two matters were probably connected: people were proud of a party leader, and at the same time were proud of themselves. The language, though, is not clear at this point. In translation it is probably best to concentrate on (2), which fits the immediate context more closely. ItCL has "Do not become enthusiastic about one person by undervaluing another"; FrCL "None of you must become proud by taking sides for one man against another." There have been attempts to combine (1) and (2) in translation, but these have been usually clumsy; for example, "puffed up with rivalry" (Mft). The meaning in this verse is not simply that the Corinthian Christians value one leader more than another, but that they praise one leader in order to attack another.

The Greek for **none of you** and **another** is literally "the one" and "the other," but this does not mean that only two people are involved. It is referring to all those in the Corinthian church who were guilty of pride.

4.7 RSV	TEV
For who sees anything different in you? What have you that you did not receive? If then you received it, why do you boast as if it were not a gift?	Who made you superior to others? Didn't God give you everything you have? Well, then, how can you boast, as if what you have were not a gift?

You in this verse is singular in the Greek but refers to "any one of you." In fact, in verse 8 Paul returns to a plural pronoun with no change of meaning. In some languages it will be necessary to use a plural pronoun here.

In some languages the rhetorical questions in this verse will need to be translated as statements; for example, "No one made you superior to others! God gave you everything you have. . . ." See the comments on rhetorical questions on 1.13.

Who sees anything different in you? This first rhetorical question is unusual Greek; literally "for who distinguishes you?" The idea of "who distinguishes you from anyone else" is clearly implied. TEV's idea of being made "superior" to someone else is also possible here. The Greek verb is another compound of *krinō* "judge" and requires a human subject. The meaning is not "what is it in you which makes you different from anyone else?" but rather "who gives you a different status (makes you superior)?" The implied answer may be either (1) "no one" or (2) "not God." In favor of (2) is the fact that God is referred to implicitly later in the verse in the clause **that you did not receive** (TEV's "didn't God give you everything?"). It is also referred to explicitly in verse 9: "God has given . . . us apostles" (TEV). Another way to translate this first rhetorical question is "If there is anything different (or, superior) in you, it comes from God, not yourselves." However, in light of the fact that Paul seems to be battling the high opinion the Corinthians had of themselves, the following renderings are truer to the context: "You are not superior to anyone else," or even "No one has made you superior to others."

What have you that you did not receive? means "Everything you have, you received from someone else." This rhetorical question, in Greek as in RSV, avoids mentioning God directly, but it can only be from God that the gifts Paul mentions were "received." So in languages which do not use rhetorical questions, a translator could say here "God has given you everything that you have!" This rhetorical question, like the first one, refers both to the past, when the gifts were received, and to the present (TEV "everything you have").

TEV's "Well then" can be rendered as "If that is so," "In that case," or "Since that is true."

The phrase **why do you boast** can be expressed as an imperative; for example, "In that case, you should not boast as if what you have received were not a gift," or ". . . you should not boast as if what God has given you were not a gift," or "Since God has given you these things, you have no right to boast."

Boast refers to saying that one is better in some way than someone else. (See 1.29 for a further discussion on this word.)

The words "what you have" (TEV) are implicit in the text, and the phrase **not a gift** is literally "not receiving," but the context shows that it refers to the past. It is possible to render this as "as if what you have you did not receive as a gift."

RSV	TEV
Already you are filled! Already you have become rich! Without us you have become kings! And would that you did reign, so that we might share the rule with you!	Do you already have everything you need? Are you already rich? Have you become kings, even though we are not? Well, I wish you really were kings, so that we could be kings together with you.

Paul now returns to addressing the readers as a group, rather than addressing a typical individual within the Corinthian church.

In these first three sentences Paul is being ironic. RSV shows irony by making these sentences into statements rather than questions.

You are filled translates a verb which in nonfigurative language means "to have enough to eat (and drink)," as in Acts 27.38. The contrast with verse 11 ("we hunger and thirst") makes it possible that Paul really meant this here. Arndt-Gingrich, though, think the language is figurative, referring to spiritual food. TEV appears to agree. Translators will need to decide whether to think of this phrase as figurative or literal language. If it is decided to pick a literal meaning, one may say "Already you have received enough to eat and drink." The translator's choice will affect the understanding of **rich** in the second sentence. It is unlikely that this word has a literal meaning (see 1.26). In many languages which can use a word for **rich** both literally and figuratively, there will be no problem. If a translator feels that Paul is using this word in a figurative or spiritual sense, one can render this sentence as "You already have all the spiritual blessings, don't you?" or "Do you already have all the spiritual blessings?"

Without us (TEV's "even though we are not") may also mean "without our help," but the last part of the verse supports TEV's translation. This phrase also introduces the theme of a contrast between the apostles' hard life and the easy life which the Corinthian Christians expect to enjoy or think that they have attained.

The phrase **you have become kings** refers to a particular past event. **You did reign** in the next sentence has exactly the same construction in Greek. In certain languages there is no word which equals the concept of **king**. In such cases one may use a word for a high ruler such as a chief, and say "Do you already rule as chiefs, even though we do not?" or "You already rule as chiefs."

We and **you** in the last clause are emphasized, adding to the contrast. The final sentence of this verse may be restructured as "I wish you were really ruling so that we could rule together with you."

RSV	TEV
For I think that God has exhibited us apostles as last of all, like men sentenced to death; because we have become a spectacle to the world, to angels and to men.	For it seems to me that God has given the very last place to us apostles, like men condemned to die in public as a spectacle for the whole world of angels and of mankind.

For introduces the theme arising out of verse 8: the apostles are very far from living like kings.

TEV's "it seems to me" is a difficult expression. It may be better to follow RSV and say I think that or "I feel that."

We noted earlier, in verses 1-5, that Paul uses language relating to official appointments. The word which TEV translates as "given" is also used in the sense of an official appointment. Exhibited or "shown" gives a wrong meaning.

Last almost certainly means "last in rank," not "last in time." TEV's "the very last place" gives the meaning clearly. Perhaps the picture is that of a triumphal procession in which the apostles come at the end as captives "condemned to die in public," as TEV renders it. Or perhaps Paul is saying that the apostles seem to have the lowest rank in contrast to their real position as first in rank in the church (12.28 "in the first place apostles," TEV). Paul's language is still ironical. He means "If you look at the way we live, you would not think that we apostles are the most important among the church's leaders."

The appositional construction like men sentenced to death may be rendered as "like men (or, people) whom they have condemned to die."

A spectacle to the world: in this verse the word spectacle refers to the entertainment which takes place in a Roman theater. Paul may be thinking specifically of fights between gladiators and wild animals.

Angels are spiritual beings created by God to serve and worship him, and to be his messengers. Some of them, however, are evil. Paul implies here that Christians are given the special knowledge to know which are good and which are bad, and the authority to judge between them. See Hebrews 1; 1 Peter 1.12.

TEV is probably right in thinking that the world includes "angels" and "mankind." World is therefore used in a neutral sense as in 3.19, not in a bad sense as in 1.20. Men ("mankind"), of course, includes women.

The clause because we have become a spectacle to the . . . can be restructured as "for the whole world of angels and humans to look at (gaze upon)."

4.10   RSV   TEV

| We are fools for Christ's sake, but you are wise in Christ. We are weak, but you are strong. You are held in honor, but we in disrepute. | For Christ's sake we are fools; but you are wise in union with Christ! We are weak, but you are strong! We are despised, but you are honored! |

This verse consists of three contrasts following the pattern "we-you," "you-we." The purpose of this arrangement is probably to emphasize the fact that the apostles, not the readers, are the main subject of this section. However, in some languages it may be better style to follow TEV's example and make the third sentence follow the "we-you" pattern too.

For Christ's sake may be restructured as "because we belong to Christ" or "because we believe in Christ." The structure of the sentence suggests that there is little difference of meaning between for Christ's sake and in Christ. Paul certainly did not mean to contrast them here.

The language of this verse has some new features. The word for wise has not been used before (see 10.15; 2 Cor 11.19). Its meaning is very similar to the term used in 1.19-20, but it is less common. Perhaps it was not used as a slogan in the disputes at Corinth. The words for in disrepute and held in honor are also new in this letter. In honor is equivalent in meaning to "become kings" in verse 8. In disrepute (TEV's "despised") means simply "not honored." NEB's "in disgrace" is probably too strong for this context. These passive expressions may be rendered in the active voice; for example, "people honor you" and "people despise you."

4.11	RSV	TEV

To the present hour we hunger and thirst, we are ill-clad and buffeted and homeless,

To this very moment we go hungry and thirsty; we are clothed in rags; we are beaten; we wander from place to place;

As we noted in the introduction to this section, the Greek words translated as **To the present hour** and **now** in verse 13 make these verses a distinct sub-section. The Greek is longer and more emphatic here than in verse 13, but the meaning is the same. The apostle's state is described in verses 11-12a by seven expressions, the first six of which are simple verbs in the Greek joined by "and." TEV's expression "To this very moment" is good modern English.

Hunger and thirst should be understood literally, not like the phrase which occurs with **after righteousness** in Matthew 5.6. TEV's "go hungry and thirsty" shows that Paul is talking about a repeated condition. In languages which cannot equal the English expression "go thirsty" or "go hungry," one may say "we continually feel hungry and thirsty," or ". . . are hungry and thirsty," or "we often do not have enough to eat and drink."

The Greek word for **ill-clad** actually means "to be naked" but also has the wider meaning "not to be (properly) dressed." The latter meaning fits better with the context in this verse. TEV's "clothed in rags" is good modern English. However, translators should find a descriptive phrase in their own language which has the meaning of "dressed in worn out clothes."

Buffeted (TEV's "beaten") is a rare word in the Greek. In Mark 14.65 and Matthew 26.67, TEV translates this term as "slapped" (see also 1 Peter 2.20; the same verb is used figuratively in 2 Cor 12.7). The form of the word suggests hitting with the back of the hand[3] rather than with the fist or the palm. The important points here are that this was an insulting form of beating, and that it was done with the hand rather than with some kind of instrument. Translators in some languages will prefer to use active verbs here; for example, "people beat us" or "people slap us."

Homeless in the Greek implies primarily that the apostles lead an unsettled life, moving from place to place. TEV's rendering "wander from place to place" is therefore more accurate than that of RSV. Brc's "homeless vagrants" is a possible rendering.

4.12	RSV	TEV

and we labor, working with our own hands. When reviled, we bless; when persecuted, we endure;

we wear ourselves out with hard work. When we are cursed, we bless; when we are persecuted, we endure;

The first part of this verse, **we labor . . .** , concludes the list which Paul began in verse 11; the rest, from **When reviled,** begins another series of three contrasts which continue into verse 13.

---

[3] See Moulton-Howard-Turner (1919) 2.407.

The relation between the two expressions **we labor** and **working with our hands** is not certain. The second phrase may expand the first so that "work" and "labor" would mean the same. That is how most translations understand the words. For example, NEB has "we wear ourselves out working with our own hands." However, it is also possible that **labor** refers to Paul's work as an apostle, so that the full meaning would be "We work with our own hands while bearing all the burden of our work as apostles" (see for example 15.10; 16.16). Paul is no doubt thinking of his work as a tent-maker to support himself (see 9.6,12,15-18), but he suggests that other apostles also worked with their hands.

With our own hands is a literal translation of the Greek, but in some languages a literal translation would be impossible because it would suggest a contrast with "working with someone else's hands." In such a case the translator could use an expression referring to manual labor.

The three following contrasts have the form "being cursed, we bless," and so on. It is good to use a time reference to show the relation between each pair of verbs. RSV and TEV accomplish this with the word **When.** Another way of showing this time relationship is by saying "Although we are cursed, we bless." These verbs refer to repeated events, not to a single act of cursing or blessing.

The word which is translated **reviled** has the meaning of "abuse" or "insult." TEV's "curse" is perhaps too narrow in meaning.

Endure implies the object "persecution." In more colloquial English we can say "we put up with it" (so JB, Mft, AT).

The last part of this verse can be rendered as "When people insult us, we bless them; when they persecute us, we are able to endure this persecution."

4.13   RSV   TEV

when slandered, we try to conciliate;   when we are insulted, we answer back
we have become, and are now, as the   with kind words. We are no more than
refuse of the world, the offscouring of this world's garbage; we are the scum
all things.   of the earth to this very moment!

The first part of this verse ends the series of contrasts. **Slandered** means to speak in such a way as to damage someone's reputation. So a natural translation of **conciliate** would be "we say good things about other people" or "we speak kindly about other people." This sentence may also be rendered in the active voice; for example, "when people slander us, we speak kindly to them."

The key words in the rest of the verse are **refuse** and **offscouring.** These are strong and unusual terms, having very similar meanings. Most translations agree generally with TEV in using words that suggest something utterly despised which people throw out as garbage or refuse. This is the simplest and perhaps the most likely way of understanding the sentence. However, there is some evidence that both these words were sometimes used in speaking of Jewish or pagan sacrifices which were made to purify the worshiper who offered them. It is with this in mind that Barrett translates "We have become as it were the world's scapegoats; the scum of the earth," though the word is different from that used of the Old Testament scapegoat (Lev 16.20-28).

The context of **world** here suggests a bad meaning. **World** may refer to the universe generally, or, as more often when it has a bad meaning, it refers to the people in the world. Similarly, **all things** in the following phrase may be either masculine, referring to people, or neuter, referring to or including nonhuman things (see comments on 3.21). In this context human "society" (DuCL) or "humanity" (GeCL) may be truer to the meaning. Keeping this in mind, it is quite possible to render the latter section of this verse as "People of this world treat us as if we were mere garbage. They look upon us as if we were filthy scum." Other languages have even more expressive ways to render this. One may say, for example, "we are like the spitting pot (spittoon) in the king's palace" (ThCL).

RSV	**4.14-21**	TEV

14 I do not write this to make you ashamed, but to admonish you as my beloved children. 15 For though you have countless guides in Christ, you do not have many fathers. For I became your father in Christ Jesus through the gospel. 16 I urge you, then, be imitators of me. 17 Therefore I sent[g] to you Timothy, my beloved and faithful child in the Lord, to remind you of my ways in Christ, as I teach them everywhere in every church. 18 Some are arrogant, as though I were not coming to you. 19 But I will come to you soon, if the Lord wills, and I will find out not the talk of these arrogant people but their power. 20 For the kingdom of God does not consist in talk but in power. 21 What do you wish? Shall I come to you with a rod, or with love in a spirit of gentleness?

g Or *am sending*

14 I write this to you, not because I want to make you feel ashamed, but to instruct you as my own dear children. 15 For even if you have ten thousand guardians in your Christian life, you have only one father. For in your life in union with Christ Jesus I have become your father by bringing the Good News to you. 16 I beg you, then, to follow my example. 17 For this purpose I am sending to you Timothy, who is my own dear and faithful son in the Christian life. He will remind you of the principles which I follow in the new life in union with Christ Jesus and which I teach in all the churches everywhere.

18 Some of you have become proud because you have thought that I would not be coming to visit you. 19 If the Lord is willing, however, I will come to you soon, and then I will find out for myself the power which these proud people have, and not just what they say. 20 For the Kingdom of God is not a matter of words but of power. 21 Which do you prefer? Shall I come to you with a whip, or in a spirit of love and gentleness?

Practically all commentaries and translations see verses 14-21 as the end of what Barrett terms "the long opening section of the epistle." However, verse 21 is linked to the preceding section by the word **this** in verse 14, and is also linked less closely to what follows in chapter 5. It is not grammar or vocabulary which links it with chapter 5, but rather Paul's attitude to his readers. Verses 6-13 of this chapter have been full of irony, first about the readers and then about the apostles themselves. Paul is implicitly criticizing his readers, and this criticism becomes strong and explicit in chapter 5. The tone of the present section, by contrast, is first of all affectionate, especially verses 14-15. It becomes sterner in the following verses, but even there the criticism is addressed only to some of the readers (verse 18).

A general question in this passage is whether Paul is using mainly the language of a father or of a teacher. The difference between the roles of a father and of a teacher was perhaps less great in New Testament times than in a modern society in the West. Christians often used kinship terms to describe their relationship to one another (compare 2 Cor 6.13; Philemon 10), and though such terms were clearly used with an extended meaning, they were more than ordinary figures of speech. Even among Jews, a teacher of the Law was sometimes described as the father of his pupil, and both fathers and teachers sometimes called on their children or pupils to imitate them. Similarly, both a father and a teacher could use the "rod" of discipline (TEV). The word which TEV translates as "guardian" in verse 15 did not mean "teacher," so no contrast with "father" is suggested here. In translation it is perhaps safest to be guided by the explicit father-son language of verses 14-15. But we should also recognize that the father-son relationship included teaching and discipline.

4.14   RSV   TEV

I do not write this to make you ashamed, but to admonish you as my beloved children.

I write this to you, not because I want to make you feel ashamed, but to instruct you as my own dear children.

This refers mainly to the previous verses, but the present tense **I . . . write** leaves open the possibility that Paul is also thinking of the severe things which he will write, for example, in chapter 5. **I do not write this . . .** may be expanded to "I do not write these things to make you ashamed."

Make you ashamed: this phrase may also be rendered as "make you lose face" or "make black in the face."

The phrase **but to** may be expanded to "but in order to."

To admonish you (TEV's "instruct"): the verb in the Greek text is uncertain, with manuscripts varying between "instructing" and "I instruct." Most commentators prefer "instructing" because it makes a better contrast with "making ashamed" than with "I write" (TEV). The not-making-ashamed and the instructing are both results of Paul's writing. **Admonish** could also be rendered as "teach a lesson to" or "make you understand."

My beloved children: this phrase may be expressed as a simile; for example, "as though you were my own dear children" or "as though you were my children whom I love very much."

4.15   RSV   TEV

For though you have countless guides in Christ, you do not have many fathers. For I became your father in Christ Jesus through the gospel.

For even if you have ten thousand guardians in your Christian life, you have only one father. For in your life in union with Christ Jesus I have become your father by bringing the Good News to you.

The word **For** at the beginning of this sentence indicates that Paul is about to develop the theme which he has just announced, namely, that of the father-children relationship with his readers. The words **For though** introduce a condition which is not met: the readers do have **guides** or "guardians" (TEV) such as Apollos, but not "ten thousand" of them. The translator should either put in the equivalent of RSV's **countless** here or any large round number which gives the same meaning.

The Greek word for **guides** or "guardians" (TEV) is difficult to translate, because in modern societies there is no one who fulfills the same function as that of a "guardian" in ancient Greek and Roman society. A guardian was a slave who accompanied a child to school. In Galatians 3.24-25 Paul uses this same Greek word in comparing the Old Testament Law to a "guardian," but in this verse he is referring to other evangelists who came after him (see 3.6). The Law in Galatians 3.24 is a guardian "to Christ." Here in this verse the other evangelists are guardians **in Christ,** that is, for those who are already Christians. Here, the metaphor of a "guardian" is appropriate because it has to do with children by implication. It is obvious that Paul considers the readers to be like children, not yet mature Christians (see 3.1-2).

In Christ is the same Greek expression in both appearances in this verse. TEV translates it as "in your Christian life" in the first instance and "in your life in union with Christ" in the second, but the meaning is much the same. FrCL keeps the same meaning in the second place: "as far as your life in Jesus Christ is concerned, it is I who became your father by bringing you the Good News." Paul adds the phrases **in Christ Jesus** and **through the gospel** to help the readers to understand the bold claim **I became your father.**

A positive English rendering of RSV's **you do not have many fathers** is TEV's translation, "you have only one father." Either way of expressing this is natural in English. Translators need to find the most natural way in their languages to render this clause.

If the literal rendering of the clause **I became your father** gives the impression in the translator's language that there was a "spiritual mother" in Corinth too, it would be better to say, for example, "I became like a father to you."

4.16	RSV	TEV
	I urge you, then, be imitators of me.	**I beg you, then, to follow my example.**

As the word **then** shows, this verse brings to a conclusion Paul's brief appeal to his status as the readers' spiritual father. **I urge you** may also be translated as "I beg you" (TEV) or "I ask you very strongly." **Be imitators of me:** as children should imitate their father, or pupils imitate their teacher.

We do not know what Paul meant by the action of imitating him. Perhaps he was thinking most directly of the humiliations mentioned in verses 11-13, which contrasted with the proud claims of some of the Corinthian Christians. Paul similarly appeals to his own way of life as an example in 1 Thessalonians 2.1-9, an earlier letter; see also 1 Thessalonians 1.6. However, the reference to "my ways" in 1 Corinthians 4.17 is taken by some commentators to mean a rather fixed set of ethical rules; see the comments on 4.17. This is probably what Paul is referring to in this verse. The phrase **be imitators of me** may also be expressed as "that you follow my example" or ". . . the example which I have set for you."

Therefore I sent [g] to you Timothy, my beloved and faithful child in the Lord, to remind you of my ways in Christ, as I teach them everywhere in every church.

[g] Or am sending

For this purpose I am sending to you Timothy, who is my own dear and faithful son in the Christian life. He will remind you of the principles which I follow in the new life in union with Christ Jesus and which I teach in all the churches everywhere.

Therefore connects Paul's argument in this verse with the phrase "be imitators of me" in the previous verse. Paul is urging his readers to let Timothy "help you in following my way of life" or "my principles." Some manuscripts, followed by NEB, BJ (not JB), and TOB, add a word which makes the phrase more emphatic without otherwise changing its meaning. For example, NEB says "that is the very reason why . . . ." This particular Greek phrase is found nowhere else in Paul's writings. Scribes may have omitted it because they felt it added nothing to the meaning. Translators may want to use this phrase in order to make a stronger connection with verse 16.

I sent to you Timothy: the Greek is literally "I have sent . . . ." In letters, the past tense was often used in place of the present because the writer, so to speak, put himself in the position of the readers, for whom the events would be past when the letter was received. But translations and commentaries are divided about whether this past tense does in fact refer to a past event. Many translations like RSV use a past tense, but others such as TEV use the present tense. It is certain though, that if this verse and 16.10 are really part of the same letter (see the introduction, "Translating 1 Corinthians"), Timothy would still be with Paul and could scarcely have been sent to carry the letter to Corinth. Either he started his journey earlier, in which case the past tense must be used here; or he left at the time that the letter was sent, and traveled by a different route. After considering all the arguments, to use a past tense here seems preferable, but we cannot be certain. Translators will need to choose between a past or present tense here and put the alternate translation in a footnote.

My beloved and faithful child: Timothy was not Paul's real son. So in some languages it will be more natural to use a simile here; for example, "he is like my beloved and faithful son." **Faithful** should be understood as "faithful to me" rather than "faithful to Christ." As in verse 15, Paul recognizes that, although he is a spiritual father, such fatherhood is **in the Lord.** Paul is Timothy's spiritual father in a family of which Christ is the head. GeCL translates "As a Christian he is my dear son, and I can rely on him."

The clause **to remind you** may be expressed as "he will cause you to remember."

On the meaning of **my ways** (TEV's "the principles which I follow"), see comments on verse 16. The meaning in this verse could also be "the principles which I teach." If this meaning is correct, the last part of the verse would mean that Paul taught these principles, not only in Corinth, but everywhere he went. This meaning would fit the context, which is more concerned with Paul's teaching than with his behavior.

Some manuscripts, followed by RSV, NEB, JB, and perhaps others, omit "Jesus" after **Christ** (see TEV). There is no difference in meaning or even in emphasis, so translators should do what is most natural in their own languages.

Everywhere duplicates part of the meaning of **in every church.** The result in Greek is greater emphasis, but in some languages it may be necessary to lighten the style and say, for example, "which I teach the churches everywhere" or "which I teach believers everywhere." **Every church** in this context refers to local congregations, for example in Corinth, Philippi, and elsewhere.

The final section of this verse may be restructured as follows: "He will cause you to remember the principles that I follow as I live the new life in union with Christ Jesus. These are the principles which I teach to all groups of Christians everywhere."

4.18   RSV   TEV

Some are arrogant, as though I were not coming to you.   Some of you have become proud because you have thought that I would not be coming to visit you.

The firmer tone of this and the following verses prepares the way for the stern teaching of chapter 5 (see the introduction to this section).

Arrogant (literally "puffed up") is the word used in verses 6 and 19 of this chapter, but not, for example, in 1.29,31; 3.21. If there is any difference in meaning, it is that the verb used here emphasizes more strongly that these Corinthians have no good reason for being proud. The verb in 1.29, on the other hand, may be used in a good sense of "boasting in the Lord," and refers particularly to speaking or singing the praises of someone. Translators need to find a word here that shows clearly the unchristian pride or arrogance of the Corinthian Christians.

As though is literally "as if" (I were not coming to you).

This verse can be restructured as follows: "Some people among you think that I will not be coming to visit you, and so they have become proud."

4.19   RSV   TEV

But I will come to you soon, if the Lord wills, and I will find out not the talk of these arrogant people but their power.   If the Lord is willing, however, I will come to you soon, and then I will find out for myself the power which these proud people have, and not just what they say.

TEV changes the order of the first part of this verse and begins with the dependent clause "If the Lord is willing." This changes the emphasis slightly in English. The stress in the Greek, though, falls on the clause **I will come.** Translators need to find the most natural way of ordering these sentences in their languages.

The sentence **I will come to you soon** may be expanded as "I will come to visit you soon."

The clause **if the Lord wills** may be expressed as "If the Lord wants me to."

I will find out is literally "I will know." The verb implies "I will discover personally," but there is no suggestion that this knowledge will be kept secret. This sentence may also be translated as "It will become evident to me" or "I will know for sure."

For the contrast between **power** and **talk** (literally "word"), see verse 20; also 2.4,13; 2 Corinthians 10.5. 1 Corinthians 2.4 suggests that the **power** is that of the Holy Spirit—that Paul will test whether these people really do have the power of the Holy Spirit.

4.20	RSV	TEV

For the kingdom of God does not consist in talk but in power.	For the Kingdom of God is not a matter of words but of power.

Paul does not say much in his letters about God's **kingdom**. As in the Gospels, the word primarily means God's kingly rule, not a place or country in the sky. Almost always Paul writes of **the kingdom of God** as something which is coming in the future (compare verse 8). Paul seems to be referring to a saying used among Christians, as the word **For** suggests (compare Rom 14.17). One can restructure this verse as "God's rule is shown in the lives of people by what they do rather than by what they say."

4.21	RSV	TEV

What do you wish? Shall I come to you with a rod, or with love in a spirit of gentleness?	Which do you prefer? Shall I come to you with a whip, or in a spirit of love and gentleness?

This verse consists of two questions, the second of which expands or explains the first. These are rhetorical questions. Paul is making a last appeal to his readers before the severe teaching of chapter 5 begins. The initial phrase may be expressed as "Which would you like me to do?"

The word for **rod** is quite common in the Septuagint and elsewhere, with meanings ranging from "stick" generally, through the "staff" of a traveler or a shepherd, to the symbolic staff or "scepter" of a ruler. This is the only place where Paul uses this noun, so we must find its meaning almost entirely from the context of this verse. It is most unlikely that Paul thinks of a literal stick with which he is threatening to beat his converts. It is also most unlikely that he thinks of himself as a ruler. His authority is "in Christ" (verses 15,17), and he describes it as that of a father (verse 15) or a teacher (verse 17). Both fathers and teachers had the acknowledged right to correct their children or pupils, if necessary, by using force. This idea is difficult to convey in the setting of many modern societies. Paul's language also seems to have irony in it. Translators have found different ways of explaining or bringing out the meaning of this phrase. DuCL and NEB say "a rod in my hand"; Mft and Brc have "rod of discipline." Phps uses a verb instead of the noun: "ready to chastise you."

With love in a spirit of gentleness translates the Greek quite literally. **Spirit** here does not refer to the Holy Spirit. In contrast to the **rod** of discipline which Paul has mentioned in the previous sentence, he is here referring to treating the Christians in a loving way. A possible rendering is "or will I be able to display my love for you and treat you gently?" So the final part of the verse can be translated as "When I come to visit you, will it be necessary to punish you, or will I be able to display my love for you and treat you gently?"

The final part of this verse will be more normally expressed in certain languages as "When I come to visit you, shall I bring a whip, or shall I come and show a spirit of love and gentleness?"

Chapter 5

Immorality in the Church

1 It is actually reported that there is immorality among you, and of a kind that is not found even among pagans; for a man is living with his father's wife. 2 And you are arrogant! Ought you not rather to mourn? Let him who has done this be removed from among you.

3 For though absent in body I am present in spirit, and as if present, I have already pronounced judgment 4 in the name of the Lord Jesus on the man who has done such a thing. When you are assembled, and my spirit is present, with the power of our Lord Jesus, 5 you are to deliver this man to Satan for the destruction of the flesh, that his spirit may be saved in the day of the Lord Jesus *h*

6 Your boasting is not good. Do you not know that a little leaven leavens the whole lump? 7 Cleanse out the old leaven that you may be a new lump, as you really are unleavened. For Christ, our paschal lamb, has been sacrificed. 8 Let us, therefore, celebrate the festival, not with the old leaven, the leaven of malice and evil, but with the unleavened bread of sincerity and truth.

9 I wrote to you in my letter not to associate with immoral men; 10 not at all meaning the immoral of this world, or the greedy and robbers, or idolaters, since then you would need to go out of the world. 11 But rather I wrote *i* to you not to associate with any one who bears the name of brother if he is guilty of immorality or greed, or is an idolater, reviler, drunkard, or robber—not even to eat with such a one. 12 For what have I to do with judging outsiders? Is it not those inside

1 Now, it is actually being said that there is sexual immorality among you so terrible that not even the heathen would be guilty of it. I am told that a man is sleeping with his stepmother! 2 How, then, can you be proud? On the contrary, you should be filled with sadness, and the man who has done such a thing should be expelled from your fellowship. 3-4 And even though I am far away from you in body, still I am there with you in spirit; and as though I were there with you, I have in the name of our Lord Jesus already passed judgment on the man who has done this terrible thing. As you meet together, and I meet with you in my spirit, by the power of our Lord Jesus present with us, 5 you are to hand this man over to Satan for his body to be destroyed, so that his spirit may be saved in the Day of the Lord.

6 It is not right for you to be proud! You know the saying, "A little bit of yeast makes the whole batch of dough rise." 7 You must remove the old yeast of sin so that you will be entirely pure. Then you will be like a new batch of dough without any yeast, as indeed I know you actually are. For our Passover Festival is ready, now that Christ, our Passover lamb, has been sacrificed. 8 Let us celebrate our Passover, then, not with bread having the old yeast of sin and wickedness, but with the bread that has no yeast, the bread of purity and truth.

9 In the letter that I wrote you I told you not to associate with immoral people. 10 Now I did not mean pagans who are immoral or greedy or are thieves, or who worship idols. To avoid them you would have to get out of the

the church whom you are to judge? 13 God judges those outside. "Drive out the wicked person from among you."

^h Other ancient authorities omit *Jesus*
ⁱ Or *now I write*

world completely. 11 What I meant was that you should not associate with a person who calls himself a brother but is immoral or greedy or worships idols or is a slanderer or a drunkard or a thief. Don't even sit down to eat with such a person.

12-13 After all, it is none of my business to judge outsiders. God will judge them. But should you not judge the members of your own fellowship? As the scripture says, "Remove the evil man from your group."

All commentaries and translations which we have consulted make a clear break between chapters 4 and 5. The theme of 4 does not carry through into 5, and there is also no grammatical connection between the two chapters. However, as we have already said in our comments on chapter 4, the last section prepares the way for Paul's more specific teachings which begin in chapter 5.

The Corinthian Christians had raised some important questions which Paul wanted to answer. So in this section and the following ones he deals with these and other questions.

One could say that the whole of chapters 5—11 speak about different aspects of the theme of Christian freedom. See especially 6.12; 10.23.

Translators in certain languages may need to expand the TEV section heading "Immorality in the Church." For example, one may say "Paul condemns an immoral person in the Corinthian church" or "A Corinthian Christian is guilty of immorality."

5.1	RSV	TEV

It is actually reported that there is immorality among you, and of a kind that is not found even among pagans; for a man is living with his father's wife.

Now, it is actually being said that there is sexual immorality among you so terrible that not even the heathen would be guilty of it. I am told that a man is sleeping with his stepmother!

TEV adds "Now" to show that Paul is changing his theme.

Actually is the first word in the Greek text. It is not used elsewhere in the New Testament at the beginning of a sentence. In other places it has the meaning "(not) at all"; see Matthew 5.34; 1 Corinthians 15.29; and perhaps 6.7. Outside the New Testament this word usually means "everywhere," and several translations take this to be the meaning here, for instance FrCL, GeCL, ItCL. **Actually** fits the context better. However, no matter which meaning is taken, the translator should use an emphatic word or expression here.

It is . . . reported is literally "It is heard." We do not find this expression again in Paul's writings, but the same passive verb, in the past tense, is translated by TEV as "the news spread" in Mark 2.1. Translators may feel that it is more natural in their languages to replace "it is heard" by "people are saying" or "people have actually told me." Paul uses a passive verb in the Greek and thus avoids naming the person or persons who have given him this information. His reticence in naming his informants may indicate that he wanted to approach the matter of immorality gently. The phrase **It is actually reported** may be translated as "they have told me" or "they have actually told me."

The second part of the verse in the Greek repeats some of the words and information which are found in the first part. TEV, though, combines the two parts, and adds the word "terrible" for emphasis.

The word which RSV translates as **immorality** originally referred to dealings with prostitutes. But it could be used in the wider sense as in this verse. The last part of the sentence and the following verses show that Paul is talking about the immorality of only one person or couple in the church. So Brc translates this as "a case of sexual immorality." It is important that the translator carefully considers the range of words for "sexual immorality" which are available in his language. "Sexual immorality" is the main theme both in this verse and in verses 9-11.

The clause **there is immorality among you** may also be translated as "someone in your group has committed sexual immorality."

There is nothing in the Greek which corresponds literally to the TEV phrase "would be guilty of it." In fact, the Greek text is rather awkward. It says literally "and such sexual-immorality which not-even among the pagans, so-that a man have his father's wife." Many translations give the impression that pagans or heathen would not commit such sin. But the text probably means that the law and customs even of pagans would not allow it. Phps translates this as "immorality of a kind that even pagans condemn."

GeCL translates the phrase **the pagans** as "the peoples who do not know God's Law." The meaning is simply non-Jews. But one should avoid rendering this as, for example, "other peoples," since there were almost certainly non-Jews as well as Jews among the Christians in Corinth. However, in a wider sense one may translate this phrase as "people who do not worship the true God."

The last part of the verse contains two features in the Greek which a literal translation tends to miss. First, the tense of the verb **living with** ("have" in Greek) shows that this man was committing sexual immorality continually, not just once. This word can be rendered as "is sleeping with" (TEV) or "is living with." These are common English euphemisms or round-about ways of referring to sexual intercourse. Translators may need to find appropriate euphemisms for sexual intercourse in their own languages, unless it is all right to speak openly about sexual matters. Second, the Greek expression **father's wife** almost certainly means the man's stepmother, not his own mother. TEV has translated it in this way.

5.2	RSV	TEV

And you are arrogant! Ought you not rather to mourn? Let him who has done this be removed from among you. | How, then, can you be proud? On the contrary, you should be filled with sadness, and the man who has done such a thing should be expelled from your fellowship.

It is uncertain whether one should understand the three parts of this verse as rhetorical questions, exclamations, or statements. The following examples show the variety of possible translations of this verse. TNT says "And you remain arrogant. Why have you not rather mourned, so that he who did this thing would be expelled from your midst?" NEB has "And you can still be proud of yourselves! You ought to have gone into mourning; a man who has done such a deed should have been rooted out of your company."

The **And** with which the Greek sentence begins marks a contrast between the immorality of verse 1 and the boasting of verse 2a. Mft translates it as "And yet," while NEB has "And . . . still." TEV's use of the word "then" fulfills the same function.

The first **you** in the verse is emphatic.

Arrogant is literally "puffed up," as we have already noted in 4.16,18. The Greek suggests that Paul's readers have been in this proud state of mind for a long time.

Ought you not rather to mourn can be translated as "You should rather mourn" or "Really, you should mourn." Such a translation indicates what the reader's reaction should have been when they found out about this man's immorality. According to Jewish tradition, to go into mourning was not only an expression of sadness, nor was it limited to the time immediately after a death, but mourning also expressed horror and condemnation. The immoral person must be punished.

The last part of the verse, from **Let him who has done this . . .** , may be understood (a) as the result of the mourning; (b) as the purpose of the mourning; (c) as explaining "the nature of the mourning" (Orr and Walther); or (d) as an imperative.[1] Many translations choose (d) and express it either as a command or with the word "should" or some similar expression. One may say, for example, "expel the man . . . from your group" or "you should not associate anymore with the man who . . . ."

From among you is literally "out of your midst." TEV's "be expelled from your fellowship" is good modern-day English.

5.3-5. The structure and meaning of these verses are uncertain.[2] The problem is to know how the phrases **in the name** and **with the power of our Lord Jesus Christ** relate to the rest of the sentence. Conzelmann summarizes the main possible relations between various parts of this long sentence as follows:

1. "When you are assembled in the name . . . deliver (this man) with the power of our Lord Jesus."
2. "When you are assembled in the name . . . and with the power of the Lord Jesus."
3. "Deliver (this man) in the name . . . and with the power of our Lord Jesus."
4. Both "in the name . . ." and "with the power . . ." refer both to "assembled" and "deliver."
5. "Deliver (this man) in the name of the Lord Jesus, when you are assembled in (his) power."
6. "I have already pronounced judgment in the name of the Lord Jesus," and "when you are assembled with the power of our Lord Jesus."

RSV, TEV and most other translations have rendered this verse according to 6.

---

[1] See W.G. Morrice, 1972, "The Imperatival *Hina*," The Bible Translator 23.326-330, especially 328; also Barrett with further references.

[2] See J. Murphy-O'Connor, 1977, "1 Corinthians, V. 3-5," Revue Biblique 84.239-245.

RSV	TEV
For though absent in body I am present in spirit, and as if present, I have already pronounced judgment 4 in the name of the Lord Jesus on the man who has done such a thing. When you are assembled, and my spirit is present, with the power of our Lord Jesus,	And even though I am far away from you in body, still I am there with you in spirit; and as though I were there with you, I have in the name of our Lord Jesus already passed judgment on the man who has done this terrible thing. As you meet together, and I meet with you in my spirit, by the power of our Lord Jesus present with us,

See RSV for the division between verses 3 and 4. TEV has restructured the translation by placing "in the name of our Lord Jesus" earlier in the sentence, for the sake of style.

The text begins with an emphatic I. This probably contrasts with the emphatic you" of verse 2. It may also contrast with the judgment of the whole community with which verse 4 is concerned. The meaning in the second case would be "As far as I am concerned, I have already reached a decision, but the whole congregation must confirm and apply this."

The contrast **absent in body . . . present in spirit** recalls a similar passage in 4.18-19.

TEV's "far" is implicit in the Greek text and can be included by the translator if deemed necessary.

Spirit does not refer to the Holy Spirit or to a spiritual entity or separate personality in Paul's body, but refers to Paul's mind or thoughts. In most languages it will be helpful to render **I am present in spirit** as "I am present with you in my thoughts." Some languages, of course, have one word for both "heart" and "mind." Such a word would be meaningful in this verse.

The phrase **as if present** may also be rendered as "as though I were present in Corinth with you."

I have already pronounced judgment is literally "I have judged," but the tense of the Greek verb suggests that it is a judgment which still stands.

In the name of the Lord Jesus: KJV followed Greek manuscripts which have "our Lord Jesus Christ," but "Christ" is almost certainly not part of the original text. The word "our" (TEV) may not have been in the original text either, in which case the translation would be **the Lord Jesus,** as in RSV and GeCL. Most translations, though, agree with TEV. The UBS Greek text omits "Christ" and puts "our" in square brackets, indicating that this word may not be part of the text. **Our Lord Jesus** certainly translates the correct Greek text at the end of this verse.

Done translates a different Greek word from the one used in verse 2, but the meaning is the same.

As in verse 1, "terrible" in TEV is implied in the Greek text and may be added by translators if deemed necessary.

The clause **and my spirit is present** may be rendered as "I remember you in my heart."

With the power of our Lord Jesus may be expressed as "with the authority of our Lord Jesus."

It is possible to make the phrase **with the power of our Lord Jesus** relate only to **my spirit is present,** just as earlier in the sentence Paul speaks of having judged **in the name of the Lord Jesus.** However, it probably makes better sense to think of the assembled Corinthian Christians, Paul, and the power of Jesus all working together to condemn and punish the guilty man. **Power** here refers to Jesus' "authority" rather than to some supernatural power which Paul and the Corinthian Christians will manipulate. A possible translation model for the final part of this verse is "When you meet together, and I am meeting with you in my thoughts, through the authority of the Lord Jesus . . . ."

There is probably no difference in meaning between **in the name** and **with the power**.

5.5	RSV	TEV

<table>
<tr><td>

you are to deliver this man to Satan for the destruction of the flesh, that his spirit may be saved in the day of the Lord Jesus.[h]
</td><td>

you are to hand this man over to Satan for his body to be destroyed, so that his spirit may be saved in the Day of the Lord.
</td></tr>
</table>

[h] Other ancient authorities omit *Jesus*

The structure of the Greek sentence is loose, as we stated in the comments at the beginning of this section. But it seems best to link **deliver this man** with **I have already passed judgment**. **This man** is literally "such a man," but only one case is under consideration. The meaning, then, is "such a bad man," not "any such man" (compare 2 Cor 2.6-7).

Deliver . . . to is often used of people being handed over to evil powers (see Rom 1.24,26,28, where TEV has "given . . . over"). It is also used of someone being betrayed or handed over to his enemies (see 11.23, "betrayed," and compare Mark 14.42).

Satan may need a glossary note in some languages (compare 7.5; 2 Cor 2.11; 11.14; 12.7). ItCL's note is as follows: "Devil. In the New Testament, refers to the most direct enemy of God, the tempter and seducer of mankind. He is also called Beelzebul or Satan (Mark 3.22,23)." The present context shows that Paul is thinking of a spiritual power.[3]

Flesh (TEV's "body") is contrasted with **spirit** in this context. The thought is probably that the guilty man is condemned to physical death by being thrown out of the Christian fellowship (compare 11.30; Acts 5.1-11). The purpose of punishing him physically now, is that he may be spiritually saved when Christ returns in judgment (see 3.13). TEV has added "his" before "body," as it is implied in the text and is a more natural translation.

The clauses **for the destruction of his flesh, that his spirit . . .** may be restructured in the following way: "so that even though his body is destroyed, his spirit may be saved" or "so that even though Satan destroys his body, Jesus will save his spirit."

Day of the Lord Jesus: as in verse 4, many Greek manuscripts have "of our Lord Jesus Christ." The UBS Greek text, however, has "the Lord." This is probably what Paul wrote, and TEV has translated it this way. Some translators may need to render the phrase **day of the Lord Jesus** as "the day when our Lord

---

[3] The suggestion of Orr and Walther that "Satan" may refer to a human "public prosecutor" can scarcely be taken seriously and does not affect even their own translation.

returns" or "the day of the Lord's judgment," so as to avoid giving the impression that it is a day which belongs to the Lord. Translators should also avoid any phrase which might be understood as meaning "Sunday."

5.6	RSV	TEV
	Your boasting is not good. Do you not know that a little leaven leavens the whole lump?	It is not right for you to be proud! You know the saying, "A little bit of yeast makes the whole batch of dough rise."

Boasting: see the comment on 4.18.

Not good: the text also suggests the meaning "not pleasant (to listen to)."

Other ways of rendering **Your boasting is not good** are "You should not be proud" or "You have no reason to be proud."

Do you not know . . . ? or "Don't you know . . . ?" is a phrase which Paul often used in reminding his readers of what they had already been taught (see 3.16; 6.2,3,9,15,16,19). This rhetorical question is equivalent to a strong statement: "Surely you know . . . ," or "Surely you have heard what is said in the past," or "I am sure that you are familiar with the saying . . . ."

Some biblical metaphors or figures of speech may be changed if necessary in translation, but the metaphor of **leaven** or "yeast" (TEV) is so deeply rooted in Old Testament events and traditions that it must be kept here. If necessary the translator may have a footnote or a note in a glossary explaining this metaphor. A good example is the note on "yeast" in the TEV Word List. Paul refers to some of these Jewish traditions in verses 7 and 8. In this passsage, one aspect of the metaphor "yeast" suggests another aspect. In verses 6b, 7a, 7b, and 8, four different ideas are expressed with the language of "yeast" as the only link between them. Verse 6b, which may have been a proverb (compare Gal 5.9), contrasts the small amount of yeast with the much larger lump of dough which it causes to rise. The next verses go on to show that this effect is bad (contrast Matt 13.33 and Luke 13.20-21, which give a good meaning to the effect of yeast).

5.7	RSV	TEV
	Cleanse out the old leaven that you may be a new lump, as you really are unleavened. For Christ, our paschal lamb, has been sacrificed.	You must remove the old yeast of sin so that you will be entirely pure. Then you will be like a new batch of dough without any yeast, as indeed I know you actually are. For our Passover Festival is ready, now that Christ, our Passover lamb, has been sacrificed.

The expanded translation in the first sentence of TEV brings out the negative and positive aspects of the Greek word which RSV translates literally **cleanse out.**

The first part of this verse brings out the moral of verse 6b. Translators may link the two verses by adding "so"; for example, "So you must remove the old yeast." Paul uses language drawn from Exodus 13.7 and perhaps Exodus 12.3-21, which describes the basis of the Jewish Passover feast. The custom was (and still is) to clear out all yeast from Jewish houses before people celebrated the Passover. Paul is applying this custom to people's behavior, so TEV is right to add "of sin." TEV anticipates verse 8 in order to explain this language to non-Jewish readers of this translation. Translators may need to use a simile; for example, "take out the sin which is like old yeast."

The difference between the translation in RSV and TEV is that RSV translates the Greek metaphor literally, whereas TEV has done away with the metaphor and given the meaning through a simile. **Leaven** equals sin, and the phrase **Cleanse . . . that you may be a new lump** means "Cleanse yourselves from sin so that you may be pure." Paul is making a spiritual application here. As with modern English, many translators will find it difficult to maintain the metaphor here.

The clause **that you may be a new lump** may be expressed as "that you may become a people who are completely new." The word **new** translates a Greek word often used of "fresh" food. TEV has expanded the text to some extent to make its meaning clear, yet nothing has been added to the meaning of the Greek.

The word **For** before the clause **Christ, our paschal lamb . . .** introduces a different thought. GeCL makes this transition even clearer: "And so you are, since Christ our Passover lamb was sacrificed." The sacrifice of the lamb was central to Passover, as TEV's expanded translation shows. The verb **has been sacrificed** refers to a single event in the past, so a translation like NEB's "our Passover has begun . . ." is misleading. However, NEB brings out better than RSV or TEV the fact that "Christ" is emphatic in the Greek: ". . . the sacrifice is offered—Christ himself." Another possible translation is "Christ was sacrificed as our Passover lamb." The difference in meaning is slight.

5.8	RSV	TEV
	Let us, therefore, celebrate the festival, not with the old leaven, the leaven of malice and evil, but with the unleavened bread of sincerity and truth.	Let us celebrate our Passover, then, not with bread having the old yeast of sin and wickedness, but with the bread that has no yeast, the bread of purity and truth.

The Greek for **therefore** (TEV's "then"), as in 1.7; 3.7,21; 4.5, introduces the conclusion of this part of Paul's argument. Paul draws a moral and spiritual lesson from the fact that the Passover had to be celebrated by eating bread without leaven, or yeast.

Celebrate is a present tense in Greek as in English, but it should not be translated as "Let us keep on celebrating this feast." The verb refers to the celebration of any feast, but the context indicates that the reference is to the Passover.

TEV's "bread having" is implicit in the Greek text. The text is literally "not with old yeast nor with yeast of evil and wickedness." The second phrase explains the first. TEV is correct to combine these two phrases. The words **malice** and **evil** have very similar meanings here, thus TEV's rendering "sin and wickedness." Paul used two different words to make a good stylistic effect. Again Paul is using metaphors which in many languages need to be changed to similes. The bread with **the leaven of malice and evil** refers to lives full of **malice and evil**. The

unleavened bread of sincerity and truth refers to lives which are full of these virtues. The meaning of the word which is translated **sincerity** is given in 2 Corinthians 2.17, where it refers to sincerity in speaking. **Truth** may have the wider meaning of "dependability" or even "being worthy of trust" (honesty). "Speaking the truth" is more likely to be the meaning here. An alternative way of restructuring 5.8 is "When we celebrate our Passover, let us not do it with malice and evil, which are like bread made with yeast, but rather use sincerity and truthfulness, which are like unleavened bread."

5.9   RSV   TEV

I wrote to you in my letter not to associate with immoral men;	In the letter that I wrote you I told you not to associate with immoral people.

The Greek word for **I wrote** can mean either "I wrote" or "I am writing" (see the comments on "sent," 4.17). In this verse Paul's reference to another letter means that the verb **I wrote** must be a real past tense. **I wrote to you in my letter** is literally "I wrote to you in the letter." RSV expands this to **in my letter** to make the meaning clear. In some languages it may be necessary to say "in my earlier letter" or "in my first letter." **Wrote** implies the meaning "ordered" or "instructed," as TEV's rendering "I told you" shows. So it may be necessary to translate this sentence as "I instructed you in the letter which I wrote to you not . . . ."

Associate translates a rare word which is used only by Paul in the New Testament, although it occurs in other Greek literature. Another translation could be "have nothing to do with."

The Greek for **immoral men** (TEV's "immoral people") is related to the abstract noun for "sexual immorality" used in verse 1, and has a similar meaning here.

Men, of course, refers to people in general, including both men and women.

5.10   RSV   TEV

not at all meaning the immoral of this world, or the greedy and robbers, or idolaters, since then you would need to go out of the world.	Now I did not mean pagans who are immoral or greedy or are thieves, or who worship idols. To avoid them you would have to get out of the world completely.

Not at all translates an emphatic Greek negative expression. TEV's "not" is perhaps too weak. The following words make it clear that Paul was not recommending that the Corinthian Christians separate themselves from all evildoers, for this would be impossible. FrCL has "I was not thinking, in a general way, of all those who in this world are immoral"; JB says "I was not meaning to include all the people in the world who are sexually immoral."

Of this world is a literal translation of the Greek. TEV renders this phrase as "pagans." The meaning **world** here is probably rather different from that of **world** in **out of the world** later in this verse. In the phrase **of this world, world** has a bad sense (see comments on 1.20). **World** in the phrase **out of the world,** though, has the neutral meaning "universe." Translators need to decide whether they can use the same word in both places, thus keeping the play on words that is in the Greek. But if the meaning is distorted by using only one word, then it is necessary to use two words such as TEV has done.

The words following **immoral** contain one of many lists of vices which are found in the New Testament and other ancient Greek and Jewish writings. This list parallels the one in 1 Corinthians 6.9-10, and translators should check that their translation in these two passages is consistent.[4]

Immoral, as in verse 9, means "sexually immoral" and, like the following sins, includes both men and women.

Greedy means "wanting more than one has." This is an attitude so contrary to Christian love that Paul does not only link it with idolatry (as here), but also describes it as a form of idolatry (Col 3.5; compare Matt 6.24, where the language is different).

Robbers: the idea of taking someone else's property by force is the dominant one here.

TEV's "To avoid them" is implicit in the Greek. It may be added by translators to make the meaning clear.

5.11	RSV	TEV

But rather I wrote[i] to you not to associate with any one who bears the name of brother if he is guilty of immorality or greed, or is an idolater, reviler, drunkard, or robber—not even to eat with such a one.

What I meant was that you should not associate with a person who calls himself a brother but is immoral or greedy or worships idols or is a slanderer or a drunkard or a thief. Don't even sit down to eat with such a person.

[i] Or now I write

Commentators and translations disagree as to whether **rather I wrote** or "now I write" (RSV footnote) is meant here. We have explained the reason for this in the comments on 4.17 and also 5.9. A majority of modern translations take the verb to express a real past tense, referring as in verse 9 to Paul's earlier letter. But GeCL and NEB think it is present in meaning and refers to the letter Paul is writing now. There seems to be, however, a contrast between this verse and 9, and RSV's text weakens this contrast. Some translations, such as JB and AT, agree with RSV, but omit **rather** and **but.** The main argument against RSV's footnote is that if Paul intended a contrast between past and present letters, it is difficult to see why he did not make this plain by using the present tense here, as for example in 14.37; 2 Corinthians 13.10. If the translator follows RSV's text, **I wrote** must really mean "I meant to write." TEV and many other CLTs have rendered it in this way. It is probably the best way to translate this phrase. However, it is advisable to have a footnote similar to RSV's.

The phrase "What I meant was" (TEV) may also be rendered as "What I was referring to was" or "The meaning of the words which I wrote was."

---

[4] Lists of vices can be found in 1 Corinthians 6.9-10; 2 Corinthians 12.20-21; and elsewhere.

Name may mean not only "who calls himself" but "who is known as a believer in the Christian community."

Brother means "fellow Christian" and not a real family member.

One should keep Paul's order of items in the list of sins, although there is probably no significance to this ordering.

Reviler has a wider meaning than TEV's "slanderer." The Greek word refers to someone who speaks insultingly or abusively of others. **Drunkard** means someone who is habitually drunk.

Not even eat with such a one explains the earlier command in this verse **not to associate with . . . .** To share any meal, especially the Lord's Supper, was a more serious matter in New Testament times than in modern western-type societies (compare Gal 2.12).

5.12-13	RSV	TEV

For what have I to do with judging outsiders? Is it not those inside the church whom you are to judge? 13 God judges those outside. "Drive out the wicked person from among you."

After all, it is none of my business to judge outsiders. God will judge them. But should you not judge the members of your own fellowship? As the scripture says, "Remove the evil man from your group."

RSV gives the original order of the four short Greek sentences which make up these two verses. But TEV, like other CLTs, changes the order. As TEV shows, two strands of thought are involved. One is a development from the misunderstanding which verses 9-11 have tried to clear up: Christians are not concerned to judge non-Christians. The second reinforces the instructions with which most of chapter 5 is concerned: wrongdoers are not to be tolerated in the Christian community. In the text, Paul moves from the first strand of thought (verse 12a) to the second (verse 12b) and back again (verse 13a). He concludes the second part of the argument with an Old Testament quotation (verse 13b). The line of thought is clearer if these two strands are separated as TEV has done, so that emphasis still falls on verse 13b.

For (TEV's "After all") indicates a shift in Paul's thinking. He now draws a general principle from the previous discussion of how his earlier instructions had been misunderstood.

The verb **judge** is the simple form of *krino* (see 2.14 for a discussion of this verb and its compounds). In verse 13a it is uncertain whether Paul intended to write **God judges** or "God will judge" (TEV). The difference between the two Greek words is only one of accents, but the oldest manuscripts do not have these accents. Most translations agree with TEV; but ItCL, NEB, and JB, like RSV, have the present tense. This would suggest the meaning "it is not my function, but God's, to judge those outside."

Outsiders clearly means "those outside the church," or "people who are not Christians." There is nothing in the Greek to suggest a bad meaning (see Mark 4.11; Col 4.5; 1 Thes 4.12).

TEV understands **what have I to do with judging those outside** as the negative statement "It is none of my business . . . ." This interpretation is clearly the correct one. Verse 12b, the third sentence in TEV, can be understood in the same way; for example, "It is your business to judge (insiders)" or "It is . . . to judge your fellow Christians." However, Paul's question about yeast in verse 6b suggests that he is not giving new teaching here but reminding the readers of what they have already heard. Verse 12b may therefore be understood more easily as a real question, as in TEV.

The order of verse 13a (the second sentence in TEV) emphasizes **God,** as in the English "it is God who will judge them."

TEV makes it clear that the final words of the verse are a quotation by adding "As the scripture says." Paul's first readers would have realized immediately that this was scripture, but modern readers may not. So translators should add this phrase "As the scripture says." In some languages it may be necessary to say "as one reads in the Scriptures" or "as it is written in the Scriptures."

The words which Paul quotes come at the end of various sections of Deuteronomy in which sins similar to those mentioned by Paul are condemned; see Deuteronomy 13.5 (13.6 in the Septuagint); 17.7; 19.19; 22.24; 24.7. In these Old Testament passages **drive out** is a command using a singular verb, addressed to Israel corporately as if to an individual. In this verse the verb is plural, addressed to the church at Corinth. These words which were first addressed to Israel are now applied to the church, but this does not affect the translation. The **wicked person** in the Old Testament passage means "any evil person who commits this crime." Paul may be thinking of the particular evil man whom he discussed in verses 1-5, but in the light of verses 9-12 it is more likely that Paul now means "any such evil person."

Chapter 6

RSV   **6.1-11**   TEV

Lawsuits against Fellow Christians

1 When one of you has a grievance against a brother, does he dare go to law before the unrighteous instead of the saints? 2 Do you not know that the saints will judge the world? And if the world is to be judged by you, are you incompetent to try trivial cases? 3 Do you not know that we are to judge angels? How much more, matters pertaining to this life! 4 If then you have such cases, why do you lay them before those who are least esteemed by the church? 5 I say this to your shame. Can it be that there is no man among you wise enough to decide between members of the brotherhood, 6 but brother goes to law against brother, and that before unbelievers?

7 To have lawsuits at all with one another is defeat for you. Why not rather suffer wrong? Why not rather be defrauded? 8 But you yourselves wrong and defraud, and that even your own brethren.

9 Do you not know that the unrighteous will not inherit the kingdom of God? Do not be deceived; neither the immoral, nor idolaters, nor adulterers, nor sexual perverts, 10 nor thieves, nor the greedy, nor drunkards, nor revilers, nor robbers will inherit the kingdom of God. 11 And such were some of you. But you were washed, you were sanctified, you were justified in the name of the Lord Jesus Christ and in the Spirit of our God.

1 If one of you has a dispute with a fellow Christian, how dare he go before heathen judges instead of letting God's people settle the matter? 2 Don't you know that God's people will judge the world? Well, then, if you are to judge the world, aren't you capable of judging small matters? 3 Do you not know that we shall judge the angels? How much more, then, the things of this life! 4 If such matters come up, are you going to take them to be settled by people who have no standing in the church? 5 Shame on you! Surely there is at least one wise person in your fellowship who can settle a dispute between fellow Christians. 6 Instead, one Christian goes to court against another and lets unbelievers judge the case!

7 The very fact that you have legal disputes among yourselves shows that you have failed completely. Would it not be better for you to be wronged? Would it not be better for you to be robbed? 8 Instead, you yourselves wrong one another and rob one another, even your own brothers! 9 Surely you know that the wicked will not possess God's Kingdom. Do not fool yourselves; people who are immoral or who worship idols or are adulterers or homosexual perverts 10 or who steal or are greedy or are drunkards or who slander others or are thieves—none of these will possess God's Kingdom. 11 Some of you were like that. But you have been purified from sin; you have been dedicated to God; you have been put right with God by the Lord Jesus Christ and by the Spirit of our God.

There is no grammatical feature at the beginning of this section to link it with what precedes it. The last two verses of chapter 5 have reintroduced the

[106]

theme of judgment, and the list of vices in 6.9-10 overlaps with that in 5.10-11. However, as far as the structure of the text is concerned, there seems no doubt that 6.1 marks a new beginning.

Most translations end a paragraph or section after verse 11. CLTs which we have consulted agree with TEV in making another paragraph division after verse 6. RSV, Phps, and JB divide the text after verse 8. Orr and Walther begin a new section with **Do not be deceived** in verse 9b (compare 3.18). It is true that Paul moves from a legal to a theological understanding of righteousness at 9b, but this is a development within a theme rather than a completely new subject, so a new paragraph is not needed here. It seems, then, that translators may make a paragraph division after verse 6 and start a new section with verse 12.

This section raises some translation problems which we have met before, especially the translation of ironical language (see comments on 4.6-13) and of rhetorical questions (see comments on 1.13). "Brother" should be understood as "fellow Christian" throughout this section. It does not refer to actual family members.

The TEV section heading "Lawsuits against Fellow Christians" may be rendered as "Christians take fellow believers to court" or "Christians accuse fellow Christians in court."

6.1 RSV	TEV
When one of you has a grievance against a brother, does he dare go to law before the unrighteous instead of the saints?	If one of you has a dispute with a fellow Christian, how dare he go before heathen judges instead of letting God's people settle the matter?

The Greek for **grievance** (TEV's "dispute") is more general than in English. In some contexts it may mean a business transaction. Here, however, the context requires the meaning "legal dispute" or "lawsuit."

Against a brother is literally "against another," but the context indicates that "fellow Christian" (TEV) is the meaning here. One may also translate this as "another member of the church."

In Greek the word **dare** is emphatic because it appears at the beginning of the section. RSV and TEV put it later in the verse. In many languages it will be necessary to keep **dare** at the beginning of the verse as in Greek.

The phrase **does he dare** may be expressed as "what right has he," or one may change the rhetorical question to a statement and say "he has no right to."

The main difficulty in this verse is the translation of the words for **unrighteous** (TEV's "heathen") and **saints** (TEV's "God's people"), which Paul is obviously contrasting. **Saints** refers to the church, not to Israelites as in the Old Testament. It is possible to distinguish at least three elements of meaning in this word.[1] First is the ethnic aspect, referring to Christians as "God's people" as if they were a distinct race. Second is the ethical meaning, referring to Christians as belonging to God and thus holy. Third is the theological aspect, stressing that Christians are "washed," "sanctified," and "justified." TEV rightly suggests that

---

[1] Technically known as semantic components. See E.A. Nida (1975), especially chapter 2.

Paul's thought moves from the ethnic aspect in verses 1 and 6 to the ethical aspect in verses 7-10 and the theological aspect in verse 11.

The word **unrighteous** (Greek *adikon*) probably refers to pagans, people who do not worship the true God. In this context **unrighteous** does not mean "unjust" but "not justified." This and related words recur several times in this section: "suffer wrong" (verse 7, Greek *adikeisthe*), "wrong" (verse 8, Greek *adikeite*), and "sanctified" (verse 11, Greek *edikaiōthēte*) are all related. Paul uses them to bind his teaching together in this passage; but the effect will usually be difficult or impossible to reproduce in translation. In any case, what matters is that the meaning is coherent.

TEV adds the phrase "settle the matter" to bring out a meaning which is implicit in the text. One may also express this phrase as "judge the case."

6.2	RSV	TEV
	Do you not know that the saints will judge the world? And if the world is to be judged by you, are you incompetent to try trivial cases?	Don't you know that God's people will judge the world? Well, then, if you are to judge the world, aren't you capable of judging small matters?

The two halves of this verse are in the form of rhetorical questions. These questions are designed to show emphasis and not to elicit an answer, as we have already mentioned. So these questions may be translated as strong positive statements.

Do you not know: this rhetorical question is equivalent to a strong statement, "Surely you know," or "You have been taught that," or "I am certain that you are aware of the fact that" (see comments on 5.6). Here, and perhaps also in verse 3, Paul is referring to a teaching which his readers have already received.[2]

For a discussion of **saints** or "God's people" (TEV), see comments on verse 1.

Will judge, here and in verse 3, can be a present tense in the Greek, "judge," meaning "have the function of judging." But the context, especially the verb "will inherit" in verses 9-10, suggests a future event.

World probably has here its neutral sense of "universe," including angels (verse 3).

RSV's **And if** does not show the logical connection between these two rhetorical questions. TEV clearly shows this connection with "Well then, if . . . ." One could also render this as "So, if . . ." or "In that case, if . . . ."

In languages which do not use passives it will be necessary for the translator to render **if the world is to be judged by you** as "if you are to judge the world," as TEV has done.

Are you incompetent is literally "are you unworthy?" The Greek suggests not only "unqualified to judge" but also "not having the moral capacity for judging." A possible translation of this clause would be "Are you unqualified to judge small matters?" This rhetorical question could also be rendered as a statement; for example, "So then, if you are to judge the world, you are certainly qualified to judge small matters."

---

[2] The belief that God's people would share in the final judgment is mentioned in Daniel 7.22, and more clearly in Matthew 19.28.

Trivial cases: the same word for **cases** is used in verse 4. The term may mean either "lawsuits" or "law courts." Most commentaries and translations pick the first meaning. One could therefore render the final clause as "you are certainly qualified to judge trivial (small) lawsuits."

6.3   RSV   TEV

Do you not know that we are to judge angels? How much more, matters pertaining to this life!

Do you not know that we shall judge the angels? How much more, then, the things of this life!

Some translations understand the two halves of this verse as separate questions, whereas others consider that the verse is punctuated as a single question. Translations also vary according to whether the second half is taken as a question or an exclamation (see the punctuation note in the UBS Greek New Testament). These differing views really do not affect the translation. Translators must do what is most effective and natural in their own language.

The question **Do you not know . . . ?** has the same meaning as in verse 2.

We includes both Paul and his readers and means the same as "God's people" in verses 1-2, though in verse 1 Paul is referring more specifically to "God's people" in Corinth.

For **angels,** see comment on 4.9.

How much more in the second half of the verse introduces a type of argument that is often used in the Gospels (for example, Matt 6.26,30) and other parts of the New Testament (1 Cor 12.24; 2 Cor 3.9,11). The word translated **How much more** is not used elsewhere in the New Testament, but the meaning is clear. Other English equivalents would be "not to mention . . ." or "let alone . . . ."

Matters pertaining to this life is repeated in verse 4, though RSV omits the phrase there for stylistic purposes and says **If then you have such cases.** Paul does not suggest that **matters pertaining to this life** are wrong, but that they are far less important than sharing in the final judgment. A possible way of translating this final sentence is "If that is so, we should be even more capable of dealing with everyday matters."

6.4   RSV   TEV

If then you have such cases, why do you lay them before those who are least esteemed by the church?

If such matters come up, are you going to take them to be settled by people who have no standing in the church?

The first part of this verse, **If then you have such cases,** has the main function of linking this verse with verse 5. CLTs differ according to how much they condense this verse. ItCL begins a new paragraph and translates "When therefore you have to resolve questions of this kind . . . ." Another way to condense this verse is "Such questions should not be settled by people who have no standing in the church."

The rest of the verse, from the clause **why do you lay them before,** raises four related problems. The first and least important is that of punctuation. The clause can be taken as a question, a command, an exclamation, or a statement (see punctuation note in UBS Greek New Testament). This problem scarcely affects the meaning. For example, BJ's "You are going to take for judges people whom the church despises!" means practically the same as TOB's "you set up as judges people whom the church despises?" In some languages, however, it may be more natural to change this rhetorical question into a negative statement: "You really should not choose as judges people of no standing in the church."

The second problem is that of how to translate this clause if it is understood as a rhetorical question. The options are: "do you (take) . . . ?" (NAB, compare also TNT, TOB), "are you going to . . . ?" (TEV, AT), "how can you . . . ?" (NEB, Brc), and "why do you . . . ?" (RSV, ItCL, Phps). There is little difference in meaning among all of these. "How can . . . ?" probably brings out most clearly in English the fact that the question does not expect a real answer.

The third problem is that of deciding whether (1) Paul is talking about law cases in general, or (2) referring to a particular case. As often in his letters, Paul probably has one or more particular cases in mind, but draws general principles from them. Only JB, among the translations consulted, clearly chooses (2). It shows this choice by using the past tense: "when you have had cases of that kind, the people you appointed to try them were not even respected in the Church." The preceding words, **if then you have** certainly allow for (1) to be chosen by a translator. However, it seems clear from verses 1 and 6 that Paul is discussing a real situation, and thus (2) is a better choice.

The last and most difficult problem concerns the identity of the people **who are least esteemed by the church.** Are they the people who occupy "the very last place" within the church (4.9; contrast 12.28, where the same phrase "in the church" is used)? Or are they "outsiders" (5.12), the "heathen judges" of verse 1 (compare verse 6)? If they are these "heathen," then the phrase **who are least esteemed by the church** would mean "from the point of view of the church (they) are of no account" (Mft, compare JB).

The translator must consider the following arguments before deciding whether or not Paul is referring to Christians.

(a) The verb translated **lay . . . before** (TEV's "take . . . to be settled by") is literally "set up" or "appoint as judges." It is clear that Christians would have no power to appoint secular judges. However, Paul could be speaking loosely of Christians choosing to use the services of non-Christian courts.

(b) Barrett doubts whether Paul would have spoken of Christians as "people of no standing." He comments: "Every Christian 'counts for something' in the church." But in fact, Paul several times uses the verb translated here "count for nothing" in speaking of Christians' attitudes toward one another; see Romans 14.3,10 ("despise"); 1 Corinthians 16.11 ("despise"); 2 Corinthians 10.10 ("of no account"); Galatians 4.14 ("despise"); 1 Thessalonians 5.20 ("despise"). These references, however, do not prove that Paul is speaking about Christians in this verse. They merely provide evidence that he did sometimes speak about Christians in this way.

(c) The context, especially "heathen judges" in verse 1, suggests that Paul is summing up the previous argument rather than making a contrast or changing a theme.

(d) It has been suggested that the Christian community in Corinth had appointed such unworthy church members to decide their disputes that people had turned in despair to non-Christian judges. If this situation were true, verse 4 would be a statement referring to these poorly qualified Christians who had been appointed as judges. Verse 5 would then go on to suggest that the church could find someone better. This would make a good connection with what follows, but we do not know enough about the situation in Corinth to be sure.

Most modern translators suggest that the people **who are least esteemed by the church** are non-Christians; NEB, for example, has "outsiders." That means "people who have no standing to decide problems in the church because they are not members of it." Given all the evidence which we have presented, "non-Christians" is probably the correct meaning here.

Lay them before is literally "set up as judges," or less probably "submit to the judgment of." The choice partly depends on how the translator resolves the problem which we have discussed in paragraphs (a) through (d).

6.5   RSV   TEV

I say this to your shame. Can it be that there is no man among you wise enough to decide between members of the brotherhood,

Shame on you! Surely there is at least one wise person in your fellowship who can settle a dispute between fellow Christians.

There is no difficulty with the meaning of **I say this to your shame.** However, no translation which we have consulted makes it clear whether **this** refers to what Paul has just said, or to what he is about to say. Both are possible, since the general subject is the same. It is more likely, however, that this phrase should be linked with what follows. This linking is done in JB and BJ through punctuation. Paul is counterbalancing the emphatic verse 5b by a preliminary statement concerning the reason why he is about to express himself so strongly. One could paraphrase this sentence as follows: "Let me ask you a question which should make you ashamed. Has it really come to this, that there is not a single person among you who is 'wise' enough to settle a dispute between Christians?" If, as seems very likely, Christians in Corinth were always talking about "wisdom," Paul's question in this verse would indeed shame the readers by showing a contrast between their boasting and their real capabilities.

The clause which is translated **decide between members of the brotherhood** is ungrammatical in Greek. However, this clause is almost certainly a condensation of an idiom which means "settle a dispute between one brother and another."[3] The context requires this meaning here.

The punctuation problem in verses 5-6 is less important for the meaning than that in verse 4 (see footnote in UBS Greek text). The main choice is between exclamations and negative rhetorical questions which have the same effect. RSV uses a rhetorical question in 5 and a strong statement in 6. TEV punctuates verse 5 as a statement and verse 6 as an exclamation, but both verses have the effect of strong statements. Again, translators need to decide what is most natural and effective in their language.

6.6   RSV   TEV

but brother goes to law against brother, and that before unbelievers?

Instead, one Christian goes to court against another and lets unbelievers judge the case!

---

3 See G.M. Lee, 1968, "1 Corinthians vi.5," Expository Times 79.210.

RSV reflects an emphasis in the Greek which is weaker in TEV. The Greek is literally "brother against brother, and this before unbelievers." "And this" could be translated as "and even more than that," to bring out its full force. A similar phrase "and that even" is used at the end of verse 8. The phrase **and that before unbelievers** may be rendered as "and lets people who do not believe in Christ judge the case."

6.7	RSV	TEV

To have lawsuits at all with one another is defeat for you. Why not rather suffer wrong? Why not rather be defrauded?	The very fact that you have legal disputes among yourselves shows that you have failed completely. Would it not be better for you to be wronged? Would it not be better for you to be robbed?

The Greek text begins with a word which RSV does not translate. It usually means "already," but here the meaning is probably "really." TEV's rendering "The very fact" understands the word to be a logical expression, and this is more probable in the present context. The phrase "The very fact" also appears to include a translation of another Greek word which is enclosed in square brackets in the UBS Greek text. A few important manuscripts omit this word.

The Greek word translated **lawsuits** here is a different one from the word translated "grievance" in verse 1, but both probably refer to "disputes" (TEV).

At all: RSV seems to understand the Greek word meaning "completely" as going with the word **lawsuits** rather than the verb **defeat** or "fail." TEV's rendering "have failed completely" seems to be the more probable one.

The clause **to have lawsuits at all with one another** can also be rendered as "the fact that you take each other to court to settle your differences . . ." or "the fact that you try to settle your differences by going to court . . . ."

Is (TEV's "shows") can be rendered as "is good evidence of," "reveals," or "indicates."

Defeat: the Greek may suggest "failure" also (see TEV). "Failure" seems to suit the context better, since Paul has not mentioned any particular opponent.

One may translate the clause **is defeat for you** as "means that you are not living up to your Christian principles at all" or "you are not acting like Christians at all."

The rest of the verse consists of two rhetorical questions which are similar in meaning. The repetition **Why not rather** is emphatic in Greek, but it need not be kept in translation if it would produce a heavy sentence.

The second verb **defrauded** (TEV's "robbed") has some similarity in meaning to **suffer wrong,** but it is more specific.

Some translators may prefer to render these two rhetorical questions as statements. In that case one may say, for example, "It would be better for you to let other people wrong you. And it would be better for you to let other people take from you what is yours."

6.8	RSV	TEV

But you yourselves wrong and defraud, and that even your own brethren.

Instead, you yourselves wrong one another and rob one another, even your own brothers!

But marks a strong contrast with verse 7, as TEV's "Instead" shows.

The emphatic **you yourselves** stresses that the situation is the opposite of what it should be. Paul is stressing that instead of patiently enduring wrong and robbery, they are actively wronging and hurting each other. Languages will have differing ways of showing this emphatic quality. One can say "Instead, you turn around and . . . ."

Wrong and **defraud** represent the same Greek words as are used in 7b.

Even your own brethren: see the comments on verse 6. "Even fellow Christians" is a better translation in most languages, as Paul is not referring to actual family members.

6.9a	RSV	TEV

Do you not know that the unrighteous will not inherit the kingdom of God?

Surely you know that the wicked will not possess God's Kingdom.

Do you not know may also be expressed as "Surely you know" (TEV) or "I am certain that you know."

Unrighteous is the word which TEV translated as "heathen" in verse 1 (see the comments). However, the meaning has now broadened, so "wicked" (TEV) is a more accurate translation.

Inherit means "take possession of," as Israel took possession of the Promised Land (see Gen 15.7; Matt 5.5; 1 Peter 1.4). There is no thought here of "inheritance" from someone who has died. TEV's translation "possess" reflects the meaning of the Greek more accurately than RSV's rendering. The whole clause can be translated ". . . God will never give to the wicked the right to rule with him."

6.9b-10	RSV	TEV

Do not be deceived; neither the immoral, nor idolaters, nor adulterers, nor sexual perverts, 10 nor thieves, nor the greedy, nor drunkards, nor revilers, nor robbers will inherit the kingdom of God.

Do not fool yourselves; people who are immoral or who worship idols or are adulterers or homosexual perverts 10 or who steal or are greedy or are drunkards or who slander others or are thieves—none of these will possess God's Kingdom.

Do not be deceived: the Greek is different from 3.18 and means "Do not err," "Make no mistake." One could also say "You can be very sure of this." The function of this clause is to draw attention to the list of vices which follows. We discussed several of these vices in the comments on 5.10-11. A difficulty in translating this list is that of finding different expressions, especially in common language, for terms having almost the same meaning. To be sexually **immoral** needs a more general expression than **adulterers,** which refers to the violation of the marriage bond. **Sexual perverts** translates two Greek words which refer respectively to "the passive and active partners . . . in male homosexual relation" (Barrett). Translations generally combine these expressions, otherwise one would have to find technical expressions such as "catamites and sodomites" in English. Even "homosexual perverts" (TEV) is rather difficult language. GeCL has "relations with partners of their own sex"; TNT has "men who submit to or who practise homosexuality." Many languages can use roundabout ways of speaking about homosexual relations. Paul thought of the practice of homosexuality as a form of perversion. If the people for whom this passage is translated do not normally share Paul's attitude, it may be important to use a word meaning "pervert," to make Paul's meaning explicit.

The Greek word translated **robbers** is very close in meaning to **thieves,** but **robbers** refers to taking things violently.

Inherit the kingdom of God: see the last comment on verse 9a.

6.11	RSV	TEV
	And such were some of you. But you were washed, you were sanctified, you were justified in the name of the Lord Jesus Christ and in the Spirit of our God.	Some of you were like that. But you have been purified from sin; you have been dedicated to God; you have been put right with God by the Lord Jesus Christ and by the Spirit of our God.

And marks the climax of the argument of verses 9-10. In some languages this word may be effectively kept in translation. Compare Mark 1.28, where **And** at the beginning of the sentence marks the climax or conclusion of a narrative. Another way of rendering this expression and the following clause is "At one time some of you were like this."

The three following phrases are given emphasis in the Greek language by the repetition of "but" (see KJV). However, to repeat this word three times is not often natural in other languages. RSV repeats **you were** and TEV "you have been" to achieve a similar effect as that of the Greek text. These three clauses refer to different aspects, rather than successive stages, of what God has done for believers. A translation such as "you were purified, then dedicated, then put right with God" would be wrong.

You were washed is grammatically "you washed (yourself)" (similarly Mft), but the most likely meaning in this context is "you were washed" or "you have been washed."

TEV's translation "from sin" is implicit in the Greek, and the **washed** probably refers to baptism (compare Acts 22.16). NEB makes the reference to baptism clearer: "you have been through the purifying waters."

You were sanctified (literally "made holy") means "made to belong to" God or Christ; in other words, "God has claimed you for his own." It could also be translated as "you have become God's own people."

You were justified: this is the only place in 1-2 Corinthians where Paul uses this verb with its full theological meaning (see comments on 1 Cor 4.4), though he uses it often in Romans and Galatians. The meaning is that of being acquitted or declared innocent by God, and so placed in a right relationship with him. Brc has "you have entered into a new relationship with God." Paul's language, like that of this whole section, is legal, but the meaning of "justify" in nonfigurative language is close to that of "forgive." TEV's "put right with God" is a good translation in English.

In the name of the Lord Jesus Christ should not be understood as "on behalf of Jesus Christ." It is rather "by the power of the Lord Jesus Christ" and fits in well with the following phrase, **in the Spirit of our God.**

In some languages, to speak of **our God** implies that one owns God. To avoid this problem a translator may say "the God whom we serve."

Another translation model for the whole verse is "Some of you were like that. But the Lord Jesus Christ and the Spirit of our God have cleansed you from sin, dedicated you to God, and have put you right with God."

RSV	6.12-20	TEV

Use Your Bodies for God's Glory

12 "All things are lawful for me," but not all things are helpful. "All things are lawful for me," but I will not be enslaved by anything. 13 "Food is meant for the stomach and the stomach for food"—and God will destroy both one and the other. The body is not meant for immorality, but for the Lord, and the Lord for the body. 14 And God raised the Lord and will also raise us up by his power. 15 Do you not know that your bodies are members of Christ? Shall I therefore take the members of Christ and make them members of a prostitute? Never! 16 Do you not know that he who joins himself to a prostitute becomes one body with her? For, as it is written, "The two shall become one flesh." 17 But he who is united to the Lord becomes one spirit with him. 18 Shun immorality. Every other sin which a man commits is outside the body; but the immoral man sins against his own body. 19 Do you not know that your body is a temple of the Holy Spirit within you, which you have from God? You are not your own; 20 you were bought with a price. So glorify God in your body.

12 Someone will say, "I am allowed to do anything." Yes; but not everything is good for you. I could say that I am allowed to do anything, but I am not going to let anything make me its slave. 13 Someone else will say, "Food is for the stomach, and the stomach is for food." Yes; but God will put an end to both. The body is not to be used for sexual immorality, but to serve the Lord; and the Lord provides for the body. 14 God raised the Lord from death, and he will also raise us by his power.

15 You know that your bodies are parts of the body of Christ. Shall I take a part of Christ's body and make it part of the body of a prostitute? Impossible! 16 Or perhaps you don't know that the man who joins his body to a prostitute becomes physically one with her? The scripture says quite plainly, "The two will become one body." 17 But he who joins himself to the Lord becomes spiritually one with him.

18 Avoid immorality. Any other sin a man commits does not affect his body; but the man who is guilty of sexual immorality sins against his own body. 19 Don't you know that your body is the temple of the Holy Spirit, who lives in you and who was given to you by God? You do not belong to yourselves but to God; 20 he bought you for

a price. So use your bodies for God's glory.

Some commentators have thought that this section was originally part of a different letter. However, it seems best to think of it as a transition between (1) Paul's discussion of a specific case in chapter 5 and in 6.1-11, and (2) his answers to the Corinthians' questions which begin in chapter 7. In 6.9-11 he has already begun to broaden the perspective. The theme of holiness, especially in sexual relations, has been introduced in the preceding verses. There is, however, no grammatical link between this section and those which precede and follow it.

A major problem in translating this section is to decide when Paul is speaking about the whole church as the body of Christ, and when he is speaking of individual Christians. The key word here is **body**; it belongs to the same area of meaning as the words translated **stomach** (verse 13), **flesh** (verse 16b), and also **us** (verse 14). We will discuss the details below. The main point is that **body**, like **flesh** in this context, does not mean a part of human nature, contrasted, for example, with spirit and soul. Rather it refers to a person's whole being or nature.

The TEV section heading "Use Your Bodies for God's Glory" may be rendered as "You should use your bodies to bring glory to God" or ". . . to give honor to God."

6.12   RSV   TEV

"All things are lawful for me,"   Someone will say, "I am allowed
but not all things are helpful. "All   to do anything." Yes; but not every-
things are lawful for me," but I will not thing is good for you. I could say that I
be enslaved by anything.   am allowed to do anything, but I am not
                                         going to let anything make me its slave.

Commentators agree that the clause **All things are lawful to me** was a slogan used in Corinth at that time. It is repeated in 10.23, where the Greek is the same except that the phrase **for me** is omitted.

TEV adds the phrases "Someone will say" and "I could say" to show that these clauses in quotes are familiar to the Christians in Corinth. Translators in other languages may find it helpful to add these phrases too.

Are lawful for me: the Greek verb means "it is allowed" and therefore does not raise the question of who gives the permission. Clearly Paul is not thinking of the Old Testament Law. Probably the people who misused this saying thought that because the body did not matter, they could do anything they liked with it. **All things are lawful for me** may also be expressed as "It is permissible for me to do anything" or "There is no law against anything that I want to do."

TEV's rendering "Yes" is implicit in the Greek; it is added to strengthen the contrast expressed by "but." "For you" is also added by TEV. "For us" would be an alternative; for example, "but not all things are helpful (good) for us." Another possibility is "for my good." The last part of the verse **but I will not be enslaved by anything** explains **not all things are helpful.** The Greek word for **I** is emphatic and implies "I, for one," that is, Paul in contrast to some of his readers in Corinth. **Are helpful** can be rendered "are appropriate" or "are to one's advantage." The same Greek impersonal verb is used in 10.23; 2 Corinthians 8.10; and a related adjective is used in 1 Corinthians 12.7; 2 Corinthians 12.1.

Be enslaved by anything: the verb which is translated **be enslaved** is used twice in the active voice in 7.4, where it is translated "rule over." Underlying this verse and the following ones is the contrast between the false freedom of the slogan **All things are lawful for me** and true Christian freedom.

6.13	RSV	TEV

RSV	TEV
"Food is meant for the stomach and the stomach for food"—and God will destroy both one and the other. The body is not meant for immorality, but for the Lord, and the Lord for the body.	Someone else will say, "Food is for the stomach, and the stomach is for food." Yes; but God will put an end to both. The body is not to be used for sexual immorality, but to serve the Lord; and the Lord provides for the body.

This verse suggests that the Corinthians thought that the body had nothing to do with morals. Some translations take the first part of this verse to be another Corinthian slogan, or even part of the quotation in verse 11. FrCL and ItCL introduce it by "You also say." Barrett understands the whole of this sentence, including **God will destroy both,** to be a quotation; but translations which we consulted do not agree with Barrett. It seems better to see verses 12 and 13 as following the same pattern: first there is a quotation, then Paul's **but** or **and** introduces a comment. The sentence makes it quite clear that the **stomach** is thought of as the organ of digestion. However, it is often associated also with sex, as indirectly in this passage (see, for example, Sirach 23.6). The Greek makes it clear that the word **both** in **both one and the other** refers to **stomach** and **food.** The clause **God will destroy both one and the other** may be expressed as "God will destroy both of them."

TEV's "to be used" is implicit in the Greek. Many translators will find it helpful to use this phrase instead of RSV's **meant.** In languages which do not employ the passive, the phrase "not to be used" may be translated as "you should not use."

Immorality is the word used in 5.1. It clearly refers to "sexual immorality" (TEV) and is related to the word for a "prostitute" used in verses 15-16. In some languages it may be helpful to translate this clause as, for example, "the body should not be used for prostitutes." This would make a better contrast with **the Lord,** which refers to "Christ," as verse 14 makes clear. At this point in the argument, it seems likely that Paul is using **body** to mean the individual Christian.

The clause **but for the Lord** can be expressed as "but you should use your body to serve the Lord." It may be helpful to make the final clause a new sentence; for example, "It is the Lord who provides for the body."

6.14	RSV	TEV

RSV	TEV
And God raised the Lord and will also raise us up by his power.	God raised the Lord from death, and he will also raise us by his power.

The argument in this verse and the previous one is rather difficult to see until one realizes that **us** is now used in place of "the body" in verse 13. **Us** also includes the readers. Paul is teaching that our bodies do have importance, because God will raise them (us) as he raised Christ. There is also an implied contrast with verse 12b: God will destroy the "stomach," because it is only "a material organ which I use for a short time"; but he will raise us, that is, the body of believers. TEV does not show this contrast clearly. The Greek is more strictly "God both raised the Lord from death, and will also raise us by his power."

This verse may also be expressed as "God caused the Lord to come alive again, and he will use his power to cause us to come alive."

In the first paragraph we assumed that the future tense **will . . . raise us** is correct (compare 2 Cor 4.14). However, there is important manuscript evidence also for the present tense "raises" and the past tense "raised." All translations consulted, except BJ, choose the future tense as fitting in better with the argument. In chapter 15 the present tense is often used, but it is in the passive voice. Others may have changed to past tense to introduce a reference to baptism. However, it is also possible to argue that the past tense is more difficult, and therefore more likely to be what Paul originally wrote. Most people, however, agree with the UBS Greek text, RSV, and TEV in choosing the future tense **will . . . raise**. **Will . . . raise . . . up** translates a Greek compound (like the English "raise up") of the verb **raised** used in the first clause of this verse. GeCL restructures and expands the second half of the verse, "so his power will also awaken us to new life."

6.15   RSV   TEV

Do you not know that your bodies are   You know that your bodies are
members of Christ? Shall I therefore   parts of the body of Christ. Shall I take
take the members of Christ and make   a part of Christ's body and make it part
them members of a prostitute? Never!   of the body of a prostitute? Impossible!

The Greek for **Do you not know** in this verse and in verse 16 is the same (see comments on 3.16). However, the content of the two verses suggests that verse 15a contains traditional teaching which the Corinthians had already been given. Verse 16a, though, introduces new teaching which should be immediately obvious to the Corinthian Christians, especially in the light of the Old Testament quotation in verse 16b.

As elsewhere, Romans 11.16-24 for example, Paul's use of figurative language is a little confused. In this verse the bodies (plural) of Christians are described as parts or organs of the body of Christ. Later in 12.12-27 it is clear that Paul is describing individual Christians as parts or organs of the body of Christ, which is the church (see also Rom 12.5). The difference between this passage and chapter 12 is that Paul is not at present concerned with unity and diversity within the church, but rather with its purity. **Members of Christ** (TEV's "part of Christ's body") here as in chapter 12 means the church. Paul's point at the moment is that **the members** belong to Christ and must therefore be holy.

In the second half of the verse, as in verse 12b, Paul takes himself as an example. As in Romans 7.7-25, Paul writes **I** but includes other people in addition to himself. In some languages it may therefore be necessary to use an inclusive "we." The meaning is not very clear either in Greek or in English, but Paul explains himself in the next verse. The meaning of the Greek word translated **take** is usually "take away" (TNT, AT). Brc brings out the full meaning by translating "And am I then going to take the limbs which rightly belong to Christ and make them the limbs which belong to a prostitute?" **Shall I . . . take** is a rhetorical question which in many languages may be translated as a statement; for example, "I would never take . . . ."

The words **take** and **make** are really part of a single action or event, as in the English phrase "come and see."

The word **prostitute** is clearly feminine in the Greek text.

Never! translates a Greek phrase which is frequently used in the theological arguments of Romans and Galatians (see, for example, Rom 11.11; Gal 2.17), but it is not used elsewhere in 1-2 Corinthians. There is no reference to God here, although KJV has "God forbid." The phrase means literally "let (it) not be." One could also render it as "certainly not" or "that is impossible!"

6.16   RSV   TEV

Do you not know that he who joins himself to a prostitute becomes one body with her? For, as it is written, "The two shall become one flesh."

Or perhaps you don't know that the man who joins his body to a prostitute becomes physically one with her? The scripture says quite plainly, "The two will become one body."

Some manuscripts have "Or" (see TEV) at the beginning of this verse, while others omit it. In the UBS Greek text "or" is in square brackets. Scribes may have added it because of the influence of verses 2, 9, and 19, in order to smooth the transition from **Do you not know?** in verse 15 to the present verse. Many translations, including RSV, omit the word; whether they do this for textual or translational reasons is difficult to say.

TEV's "perhaps" is implied.

The rhetorical question **Do you not know?** is not a request for information, but Paul asks this question to emphasize his argument. One may translate this question as a statement; for example, "You ought to be aware of the fact that . . ." or "You should know that . . . ."

Joins himself here means "has sexual relations with" and may be translated this way in certain languages.

A prostitute is literally "the prostitute," meaning "any prostitute," just as "the body" in verse 13 probably meant "anyone's body."

Becomes one body is a literal translation of the Greek. TEV uses "physically one" to avoid repeating the word "body."

With her is not in the Greek but is required in English and other languages to fill out the meaning.

This verse ends with an exact quotation from the Septuagint of Genesis 2.24. The literal equivalent of **as it is written** is simply "for, says," meaning either "scripture says" (TEV) or "God says." "Scripture" is probably the meaning since God is not mentioned in the immediate context. In many languages one cannot talk about scripture "saying" or "speaking," but one may say, for example, "we read in the scriptures." TEV's "quite plainly" is implied.

The two may be rendered "the man and the woman."

RSV   TEV

But he who is united to the Lord be-   But he who joins himself to the Lord
comes one spirit with him.   becomes spiritually one with him.

The main contrast between this verse and verse 16 is probably not between
"physically" and "spiritually," as TEV and many other translations suggest, but
between a **prostitute** and **the Lord**. **One flesh** (body) and **one spirit** are not oppo-
sites, but different aspects of the same human reality. " 'One spirit,' now explains
what is the nature of this 'one body' " (Conzelmann).

One may render the phrase **becomes one spirit with him** as "one with him in
his heart."

6.18   RSV   TEV

Shun immorality. Every other sin which   Avoid immorality. Any other sin
a man commits is outside the body; but   a man commits does not affect his
the immoral man sins against his own   body; but the man who is guilty of
body.   sexual immorality sins against his own
                                            body.

Shun is literally "run away from" and may be translated this way in certain
languages. GeCL has "Avoid immorality at all costs!" Paul uses similar language
in 10.14: "shun the worship of idols." The meaning of **Shun** is the same in both
places. One could also say "Do not commit . . . at all" or "Have nothing to do
with . . . ."

For **immorality**, see comment on 5.1.

The word for **sin** is one which Paul uses only here and in Romans 3.25,
where he refers to "former sins." In Romans it may have its original meaning of
"the result of sin" rather than "the act of sinning." However, in this passage Paul
is clearly talking about sinful acts themselves.

A man means "a human being." Paul was clearly thinking of "males" in
verses 15-16, but in this verse and for the rest of this chapter he is referring to
both males and females (humans). So this phrase **every other sin which a man
commits** may be expressed as "all other sins which humans commit."

Is outside: GeCL expresses this as "does not soil." Another way of saying
this is "does not make dirty." ItCL translates in such a way as to show that **body**
means "person": "Any other sin which a man commits remains in a certain sense
external to him; but the man who gives himself to immorality fundamentally
destroys himself."

The clause **sins against his own body** may be translated as "commits sins
which hurt his own body."

6.19   RSV   TEV

Do you not know that your body is a   Don't you know that your body is the
temple of the Holy Spirit within you,   temple of the Holy Spirit, who lives in
which you have from God? You are not   you and who was given to you by God?
your own;   You do not belong to yourselves but to
                                            God;

This verse develops the thought of verse 17, especially the reference to "spirit," though at this point Paul is concerned, not with the human spirit, but with the Holy Spirit. **Do you not know** suggests that Paul is reminding his readers of previous teaching, though in this verse he is more concerned with individual members than with the church as a whole. For this reason the translation **within you** (TEV's "in you") is more probable than "among you." For other ways to translate **Do you not know,** see the comments on verses 2,3,9,16.

In some languages it will be necessary to render the clause **your body is a temple** as "your body is like a temple where the Holy Spirit lives."

Which you have from God may be expressed as "which God has given to you." These words refer to the Holy Spirit, as TEV shows.

The structure of the Greek sentence suggests that the clause **You are not your own** is connected with the first part of verse 19 rather than with verse 20a, as in RSV, TEV, and other translations. Several translations connect this clause with the beginning of verse 19 and agree with the UBS Greek text in making the whole verse a question; for example, "Do you not know . . . and that you are not your own?" (TNT). But other translations agree with TEV in thinking that the last part of verse 19 introduces a new thought which is explained in verse 20a. The Greek "and" before **You are not your own** may be understood in this way. AT restructures it in the following way: "Besides, you are not your own; you have been bought and paid for."

6.20   RSV   TEV

you were bought with a price. So   he bought you for a price. So use your
glorify God in your body.   bodies for God's glory.

You were bought may be expressed as "he bought you for a price" (TEV) or "he paid a price for you." The "he" here probably refers to the work of Christ, although it is impossible to be sure. Paul does not use "buy" figuratively anywhere else except in 7.23, where TEV again has "God bought you," although Christ has just been mentioned in 7.22. If the translator chooses to put "God" in the text, "Christ" may be given as an alternative in a footnote.

With a price probably does not mean "for a great price" (Vulgate). The meaning is more likely that the transaction has been completed: "God has bought and paid for you."

So introduces the conclusion; "Very well, then" (Barrett). The final sentence may be expressed as "Let each of you use his body to bring glory to God."

For **glorify,** see comment on "glorification" in 2.7.

Your body is emphasized in the Greek by its position at the end of the sentence. "Your bodies" (TEV) is more natural in English, since Paul is writing about individuals. In some other languages **your body** may be better, since each individual has one body. Translators should do what is natural in their own language.

All modern translations agree with RSV and TEV in omitting the words which KJV translated "and in your spirit, which are God's." The shorter Greek text which RSV and TEV follow represents "the decisive testimony of the earliest and best witnesses" (Metzger). Scribes who added the words "your spirit" failed to realize that **body** for Paul included the whole personality.

Chapter 7

Questions about Marriage

RSV

1 Now concerning the matters about which you wrote. It is well for a man not to touch a woman. 2 But because of the temptation to immorality, each man should have his own wife and each woman her own husband. 3 The husband should give to his wife her conjugal rights, and likewise the wife to her husband. 4 For the wife does not rule over her own body, but the husband does; likewise the husband does not rule over his own body, but the wife does. 5 Do not refuse one another except perhaps by agreement for a season, that you may devote yourselves to prayer; but then come together again, lest Satan tempt you through lack of self-control. 6 I say this by way of concession, not of command. 7 I wish that all were as I myself am. But each has his own special gift from God, one of one kind and one of another.

8 To the unmarried and the widows I say that it is well for them to remain single as I do. 9 But if they cannot exercise self-control, they should marry. For it is better to marry than to be aflame with passion.

10 To the married I give charge, not I but the Lord, that the wife should not separate from her husband 11 (but if she does, let her remain single or else be reconciled to her husband)—and that the husband should not divorce his wife.

12 To the rest I say, not the Lord, that if any brother has a wife who is an unbeliever, and she consents to live with him, he should not divorce her. 13 If any woman has a husband who is an unbeliever, and he consents to live with her, she should not divorce him. 14 For the unbelieving husband is consecrated through his wife, and the unbelieving wife is consecrated through

TEV

1 Now, to deal with the matters you wrote about.

A man does well not to marry.[e] 2 But because there is so much immorality, every man should have his own wife, and every woman should have her own husband. 3 A man should fulfill his duty as a husband, and a woman should fulfill her duty as a wife, and each should satisfy the other's needs. 4 A wife is not the master of her own body, but her husband is; in the same way a husband is not the master of his own body, but his wife is. 5 Do not deny yourselves to each other, unless you first agree to do so for a while in order to spend your time in prayer; but then resume normal marital relations. In this way you will be kept from giving in to Satan's temptation because of your lack of self-control.

6 I tell you this not as an order, but simply as a permission. 7 Actually I would prefer that all of you were as I am; but each one has a special gift from God, one person this gift, another one that gift.

8 Now, to the unmarried and to the widows I say that it would be better for you to continue to live alone as I do. 9 But if you cannot restrain your desires, go ahead and marry—it is better to marry than to burn with passion.

10 For married people I have a command which is not my own but the Lord's: a wife must not leave her husband; 11 but if she does, she must remain single or else be reconciled to her husband; and a husband must not divorce his wife.

12 To the others I say (I, myself, not the Lord): if a Christian man has a wife who is an unbeliever and she

her husband. Otherwise, your children would be unclean, but as it is they are holy. 15 But if the unbelieving partner desires to separate, let it be so; in such a case the brother or sister is not bound. For God has called us[l] to peace. 16 Wife, how do you know whether you will save your husband? Husband, how do you know whether you will save you wife?

[l] Other ancient authorities read *you*

agrees to go on living with him, he must not divorce her. 13 And if a Christian woman is married to a man who is an unbeliever and he agrees to go on living with her, she must not divorce him. 14 For the unbelieving husband is made acceptable to God by being united to his wife, and the unbelieving wife is made acceptable to God by being united to her Christian husband. If this were not so, their children would be like pagan children; but as it is, they are acceptable to God. 15 However, if the one who is not a believer wishes to leave the Christian partner, let it be so. In such cases the Christian partner, whether husband or wife, is free to act. God has called you to live in peace. 16 How can you be sure, Christian wife, that you will not save[f] your husband? Or how can you be sure, Christian husband, that you will not save[f] your wife?

[e] A man does well not to marry; *or* You say that a man does well not to marry.
[f] How can you be sure . . . that you will not save; *or* How do you know . . . that you will save.

In the previous sections Paul has said much about sexual immorality. The whole of chaper 7, apart from verses 17-24, is concerned more specifically with marriage and celibacy. Verse 1 states almost explicitly that this is the first of a series of questions which the Christians at Corinth had raised. **Now**, in this and similar contexts, indicates a change of theme. The word **concerning** was often used in the titles of Greek books to show what they were "about." The two words **now** and **concerning**, when they are used together, usually mark the beginning of a new section (see verse 25; 8.1; 12.1; 16.1).

The main difficulty in translating this section is that of identifying and finding equivalents for the euphemisms which Paul uses in referring to sexual matters. Languages differ in the directness with which they speak about sex. This section can serve as a good exercise for translators in deciding at what level of language they wish to translate, and what precisely they mean by "common language." Many languages have a wide variety of words and phrases which refer to sex. These range from technical words to the colloquial ones. The referential meaning of these terms will often be the same (that is, they will refer to the same things or events), but the emotive effect on the reader may be quite different.[1]

In this section three words for men and women are used:

(1) *Anthrōpos* (see 1.25): the most common meaning is "human being," and it should not be translated by a word referring only to a male adult unless the context requires it. In verse 1 of this section, the reference to sexual relations

---

[1] On this question, see Nida and Taber (1974), chapter 5.

with a woman does require that *anthrōpos* be translated "man," but this may not be the case in verses 7 and 26 (see the comment) and is certainly not so in verse 23.

(2) *Anēr* must mean adult male and may mean husband, if the context requires it. Throughout this chapter (verses 2-4,10,11,13,14,16,34,39) the meaning "husband" is required. The translation of verse 13, though, presents special problems (see comments), and "man" is sometimes used in RSV where *anēr* is not used in the Greek (for example, in verse 33).

(3) *Gunē* is the female counterpart of *anēr*. The meaning may be "woman" or "wife," depending on the context. In this chapter the meaning "wife" is required, except in verse 1.

7.1	RSV	TEV

Now concerning the matters about which you wrote. It is well for a man not to touch a woman.

Now, to deal with the matters you wrote about. A man does well not to marry.[e]

e A man does well not to marry; *or* You say that a man does well not to marry.

See the introduction to this section. TEV's "to deal with" is implied in the Greek. FrCL says "Let us pass now to the questions you asked me in your letter." One may also say "Now, I am going to speak about the matters which you wrote to me about."

It is well is literally "is good." However, "good" in this context does not mean "morally good" but "good for (someone)" in the sense of being to someone's advantage, as in Genesis 2.18, "It is not good that the man should be alone." One may also translate the phrase **It is well for a man** as "It is a good thing if a man . . ." or "If a man . . . he does a good thing."

Touch a woman is a Greek euphemism for "have sexual relations with a woman," whether one's wife or not (see the Septuagint of Gen 20.4,6; Prov 6.29). However, TEV's translation "marry" may be justified in this verse because sex outside of marriage is not being referred to here. The tense of the verb **touch** suggests a single act. **A woman** means "any woman." NEB's euphemism "to have nothing to do with women" is too general if one takes it literally. TNT's "not to have intercourse with a woman" is an explicit English way of saying this sentence. Other possible euphemisms are "live with a woman" or "stay and eat with a woman." Each language has it own special ways of referring to the act of sexual intercourse.

TEV has a footnote, "You say that a man does well not to marry," which suggests that Paul is quoting from a letter which the Corinthian Christians had sent to him earlier. Brc has "In regard to the point you make that . . . ." Orr and Walther translate the words as a question which might have been asked by the Corinthians: ". . . the matters about which you wrote: is it good . . . ?" Translators should take this suggestion seriously since Paul would be more likely to quote questions than statements from the Corinthians' letter. A possible translation is JB's rendering, "Yes, it is a good thing . . ." (also GeCL). This suggests that Paul is about to use words from the Corinthians' letter. Different languages have varying ways of indicating when a quotation is being made, quite apart from punctuation.

　　　　RSV　　　　　　　　　　　　TEV

But because of the temptation to
immorality, each man should have his
own wife and each woman her own
husband.

But because there is so much immorality, every man should have his own
wife, and every woman should have her
own husband.

The first few words of the Greek are literally "because of (sexual) immorality" (see comments on 5.1). Most translations have found it necessary to expand this phrase. **The temptation to** is implied in the Greek, as is TEV's rendering
"so much." Barrett brings out the meaning by translating "because cases of fornication occur." The word translated "fornication" or "immorality" is plural, implying more than one act. Brc has "In order to avoid illicit sexual relationships." The
difference in meaning between "in order to avoid immorality" and "because there
is so much immorality" is not great; the second translation implies the first.

Every man should have is literally a command using the third person singular, but this is misleading. Although Paul uses a grammatical imperative, he is
really not ordering anyone to do anything. The meaning is closer to FrCL's rendering, "it is better for each man to have . . . ." More precisely, Paul is not ordering the Corinthians to marry, but is saying that it may be necessary for men to
marry in order to avoid sexual immorality (compare verse 9). In this context the
word **have** does not mean "get married" but "be in a married state."

The Greek word translated as **own** is different in the two parts of the
verse. The two Greek words are used consistently in the New Testament in speaking respectively of husbands (Eph 5.28,33) and wives (1 Cor 14.35; Eph 5.22; Titus
2.5; 1 Peter 3.1,5). If there is any difference of meaning, the first expression
would mean "a wife who belongs to him," and the second "a husband who is hers
alone." The difference is so slight that all translations which we consulted have
ignored it. Far more important is the fact that Paul here, and especially in verses
3-4, says that husbands and wives are equally obligated to each other and therefore are not to have sexual relations with others.

7.3　　　　RSV　　　　　　　　　　　　TEV

The husband should give to his wife her
conjugal rights, and likewise the wife to
her husband.

A man should fulfill his duty as a husband, and a woman should fulfill her
duty as a wife, and each should satisfy
the other's needs.

As in verse 5, Paul uses a euphemism, **give to his wife her conjugal rights**,
to stress the fact that husband and wife ought normally to have sexual relations
with each other. In many languages it will seem strange to speak of sex within
marriage as a duty. Paul is not speaking in legal terms either, as RSV suggests.
ItCL has "the man should give himself to his own wife, and similarly the wife give
herself to her own husband." Translators should use a natural euphemism which
gives the meaning "husbands and wives should respect the sexual desires of each
other."

The husband, the wife means "any husband," "any wife."

The second half of verses 3 and 4 is introduced by a phrase meaning "but
similarly also," translated here as **likewise.** This phrase in Greek may slightly

emphasize the second half of the verse. In any case, the structure of the two verses excludes any suggestion that Paul is emphasizing the wife's duties more than those of the husband, or the other way around. The pattern is

verse 3a "the husband"   verse 3b "and also the wife"
verse 4a "the wife"   verse 4b "and also the husband"

Such a pattern is known as a chiasmus and is common in many languages. But in some languages it may be unnatural. If the translator changes the order, care should be taken to give equal emphasis to what is said about husbands and about wives. In some languages one may restructure this verse as follows: "Both the husband and wife should fulfill their conjugal duties to each other."

Should: see comments on verse 2. If people are married, they ought normally to have sexual relations with one another.

7.4   RSV   TEV

For the wife does not rule over her own | **A wife is not the master of her own**
body, but the husband does; likewise the | **body, but her husband is; in the same**
husband does not rule over his own | **way a husband is not the master of his**
body, but the wife does. | **own body, but his wife is.**

This verse states the principle on which verse 3 is based. **The wife** and **the husband** are emphasized by being placed at the beginning of each half of the sentence in Greek. In the same way **the husband** (TEV's "her husband") and **the wife** (TEV's "his wife") are emphasized by appearing at the end of the verse.

Does not rule over translates the same verb as that in 6.12 (see the comments); the idea is that of using authority. NEB has "The wife cannot claim her body as her own; it is her husband's. Equally, the husband cannot claim his body as his own; it is his wife's." Translators can also say "does not have the authority over" or "does not have the right over."

7.5   RSV   TEV

Do not refuse one another except | **Do not deny yourselves to each other,**
perhaps by agreement for a season, that | **unless you first agree to do so for a**
you may devote yourselves to prayer; | **while in order to spend your time in**
but then come together again, lest | **prayer; but then resume normal marital**
Satan tempt you through lack of self- | **relations. In this way you will be kept**
control. | **from giving in to Satan's temptation**
 | **because of your lack of self-control.**

This is the only verse in this section in which Paul gives a direct instruction, expressed by a second person imperative.

Refuse is the verb which in 6.7 was translated "defrauded." Here the meaning is to deprive the husband (or wife) of what in verse 3 was stated to be his (or her) right. Mft translates "Do not withhold sexual intercourse from one another." One may also say "you should not abstain from sexual intercourse with your married partner," or in languages which require the use of euphemism here, one can express this phrase as "you should not abstain from coming together" or ". . . not abstain from living and eating together."

Except translates an unusual Greek phrase which seems to suggest that Paul is speaking tentatively or even grudgingly (see verse 6). GeCL has "at most when you have agreed." One may also say "Unless perhaps you agree to deny yourselves to each other like this."

For a season (TEV's "for a while"): a general expression is needed here. JB's "for an agreed time" is too precise. The text states that the couple agree to abstain from intercourse for a while, but does not state that they agree on how long the time of abstinence should be. Brc's "for a limited period" brings out all that is implied in the text. One could also say "for a short time."

The rest of the verse consists of two clauses beginning with "in order that" in the Greek; literally "in order that you may devote yourselves to prayer and again be together, in order that Satan may not tempt you because of your lack of self-control." As this translation shows, there is no "and" between the two "in order that" clauses, so it is difficult to link them both directly to the main verb "come together." The construction which makes the best sense is also the one that is suggested by the order of the clauses: (1) "do not deny yourselves to one another, except . . . in order to devote yourselves to prayer"; (2) then "come together again so that Satan may not tempt you . . . ." In translation it may be necessary to express (1) and (2) in separate sentences. It will be helpful in many languages to add the information "after that" or "after that time" after the word **but**; for example, "but after that, you should come together again . . . ."

There are two more points which the translator should notice, even if he decides not to make them explicit in his translation. (1) The first "in order that" clause includes the instruction "come together again," and this means "in order to devote yourselves to prayer and then come together again." (2) Some translations, including RSV and TEV, understand the second "in order that" clause as equivalent to an imperative.

Devote yourselves includes the idea of having leisure for something, in this case, prayer. KJV has "fasting and prayer," but the first two words are almost certainly not part of the original text. The phrase **devote yourselves** may also be expressed as "give your time to."

Then come together again is a euphemism for "resume normal marital relations," as TEV shows. Translators need to find a common language expression to render this phrase.

The name **Satan** may need a glossary note in some languages (see comment on 5.5).

The last few words, literally "because of your lack-of-self-control," can be easily misunderstood if they are not translated dynamically and expanded to a certain extent. GeCL has "because the (sexual) drive in you is too strong," and FrCL says "otherwise you would risk no longer being able to control yourselves." A more simple way to translate this is "because you cannot continue to abstain from sexual relations" or "because you cannot continue to abstain from sleeping together."

7.6	RSV	TEV
	I say this by way of concession, not of command.	I tell you this not as an order, but simply as a permission.

The main problem of this verse is first of all to decide what the word **this** refers to, and secondly to translate the word clearly. Almost certainly, the **concession** (TEV's "permission") relates to the temporary abstinence from sexual relations. It does not relate to **coming together again** or to the whole of verses 2-5 (as if marriage itself were the **concession**). That it refers to "temporary abstinence from sexual relations" is confirmed by the tentative expression "except perhaps" of verse 5. **Concession** is the right word rather than "suggestion" (JB). This word is used in Sirach 3.13, where NEB translates "make allowances." "Permission" (TEV) is also an English equvialent.

There is a further question, whether the **concession** and the **command** come from Paul himself, from Christ, or from God. The sentence could be restructured "I say this because God has allowed me to say it, not because he has commanded me to do so." The language of this verse is very similar to that of 7.25, "I have no command from the Lord," so that verse 6 may imply that the **concession** and the **command** come from Christ. However, the immediate context suggests that Paul is speaking on his own authority. So translators should probably translate the verse in that way.

The phrase **by way of concession** may be expressed as "but I am permitting you to do this."

Translators must decide whether it is more natural and effective in their own language to express the negative side of the comparison first; for example, TEV's "not as an order" followed by the positive "as a permission." The Greek puts the positive first, as RSV's **by way of concession, not of command.**

7.7 RSV	TEV
I wish that all were as I myself am. But each has his own special gift from God, one of one kind and one of another.	Actually I would prefer that all of you were as I am; but each one has a special gift from God, one person this gift, another one that gift.

I wish is probably better than TEV's "I would prefer" or NEB's "I should like." A strong verb is required here—the equivalent of the English "I really would prefer," "I want," or "It would make my heart very happy."

In the Greek the transition from verse 6 is uncertain. Some manuscripts have "for," others "but." The word "but" which TEV translates as "actually" expresses a strong contrast, which is probably the case in this verse. Paul is indicating a change to a fresh aspect of the theme, or more precisely, he is returning in verse 7 to what he said in verse 1. In both verses he is speaking quite generally, so **all** includes both men and women. TEV's "of you" is not in the Greek text, but verse 7b shows that **all** must refer to Christians.

As I myself am implies "unmarried," as RSV and TEV make explicit in verse 8, where the Greek is the same. **As I . . . am** may also be expressed as "were in the same state as I am" or "were in the same condition . . . ."

The **but** which introduces the second half of the sentence is strong and means almost "nevertheless" or "however"; for example, "However, each one has . . . ."

Each can be rendered as "each person" or "each one of you."

Translators should consider how to express in their own language the double change of direction which is indicated by the words TEV translates "actually" and "but." Verse 7a echoes verse 1; verse 7b makes a transition between the previous discussion of marriage and the following advice to the unmarried and widows. The Greek, however, is too general to suggest that the phrase **of one kind** (TEV's "this gift") should be identified with marriage, and that **of another** (TEV's "that gift") be identified with celibacy. TEV shows the contrast quite clearly.

In languages which do not use the passive, the clause **each has his own special gift from God** may be expressed as "God gives a special ability to each one."

The final two clauses may be rendered "one person has this ability, and another one has a different ability."

7.8   RSV   TEV

**To the unmarried and the widows   Now, to the unmarried and to
I say that it is well for them to remain   the widows I say that it would be better
single as I do.   for you to continue to live alone as I do.**

TEV's "Now," as in verses 1 and 25, indicates that Paul is changing the theme.

Many translations, including RSV and TEV, put "I say" after the expressions **the unmarried** and **the widows** so as to emphasize them. In these expressions the definite article **the** probably implies "the unmarried and widows at Corinth (about whom you wrote)." **The unmarried** is masculine in the Greek but could refer to both men and women, and that is how all the translations we consulted understood this phrase. However, (1) **the widows** must be feminine, (2) biblical Greek does not use the related word for "widowers," and (3) throughout this passage Paul is careful to speak in a balanced way of men and women, wives and husbands. So it is possible to understand **the unmarried** to mean "men who are no longer married," that is widowers, rather than the meaning "those who have not been married." Some people have thought that Paul himself was a widower; if so, this would make the end of this verse even more meaningful. It could mean "it is good for them to remain in that state, as I do myself." If translators do not put "widowers" in the text, it can be included in a footnote.

I say may be emphasized by Paul. Later in verses 10, 12, and especially 25, he is certainly careful to distinguish between what he says on his own authority and what he says with the authority of Christ. Some translators may prefer to place the phrase **I say** at the beginning of the sentence; for example, "Now, I say to . . ." or "Now, I advise the . . . ."

It is well is literally "it is good," as in verse 1. The meaning is the same, but the comparative "better" (TEV), which is possible even in verse 1, is more likely in the present verse. This is confirmed by the comparative expression **better** in verse 9, which is an unrelated word in the Greek.

As in the following verses, the main verb in the Greek is in the third person, "that they remain . . . ." Since Paul says that he is about to speak **to** unmarried people, it is more logical to say "better for you . . ." (TEV) rather than **well for them . . . .**

Remain single is more literally "remain as I also," meaning "remain unmarried as I do myself."

        RSV   TEV

RSV	TEV
But if they cannot exercise self-control, they should marry. For it is better to marry than to be aflame with passion.	But if you cannot restrain your desires, go ahead and marry—it is better to marry than to burn with passion.

Almost all translations which we consulted add the word "cannot" or an equivalent expression. This is not in the Greek text, and since sexual immorality was certainly known within the church at Corinth (see 5.1; 7.2), a translation such as "if they are not living continently" (Barrett) gives the literal meaning. However, **cannot** is implied; they do not live continently because they cannot do so.

Should marry: the context makes it close in meaning to a direct command by Paul.

The verb **marry,** in Greek as in English, could be used with either men or women as its subject. The context shows that both are intended here.

In the second half of the sentence some manuscripts (not mentioned in the UBS Greek text) have the present tense, "to be in the married state," instead of the aorist, meaning "to get married." However, the manuscript evidence for the aorist is better. The difference in meaning between the two is probably not enough for an alternative translation to be given in a footnote.

Aflame: with passion is clearly implied by the context. Some commentators have thought that **aflame** referred to "burning in hell," but most modern commentators reject this interpretation.[2] One may also express **aflame with passion** as "to have sexual passion burning in you" or "to have hearts which burn with sexual passion." ThCL says "better than to have a heart hot with sexual passion." In some languages passion is said to "oppress" or "trouble."

        RSV   TEV

RSV	TEV
To the married I give charge, not I but the Lord, that the wife should not separate from her husband	For married people I have a command which is not my own but the Lord's: a wife must not leave her husband;

Married here certainly means "those who have been married and remain in the married state."

I give charge (TEV's "I have a command") is stronger than **I say** in verses 8 and 12. There is nothing in the verb **give charge** itself which would make it necessary to think that Paul is referring to a saying of Jesus, but the context strongly suggests that here Paul is quoting a teaching which is attributed to Jesus—in fact it is similar to that found in Mark 10.9,12. In this case and in verse 12, **the Lord** is Jesus during his earthly life.

The phrase **Not I but the Lord** is emphatic, even though it is an aside. The first half of the verse may be restructured as "This following command to the unmarried comes from the Lord, not from me: 'The wife should not separate from her husband.' "

---

[2] See M.L. Barre, 1974, "To marry or to burn: *pyrousthai* in I Cor. 7:9," Catholic Biblical Quarterly 36.193-202.

Should not separate is literally "let (her) not leave" (see comments on verse 2 for ways to translate third person imperatives). "Let" does not mean "allow," but represents a third person command in English, "she must not leave." Some scholars distinguish between: (1) temporary sexual abstinence, mentioned in verse 5; (2) separation, mentioned here, in verse 11a and in verse 15; and (3) divorce, mentioned in verses 11-13. In many modern societies divorce always involves a legal decision, and separation may require one too. However, in Jewish tradition and elsewhere in the Mediterranean world, this was not the case, so the distinction between (2) and (3) is not absolute. Even in the case of (1), it is mainly the phrase "for a season" which distinguishes it from (2) and (3). **Separate** and "divorce" (verse 11) are two different words in Greek. If these verses stood alone, they would suggest that Paul accepted the Jewish rule that a man could divorce (literally "let go," "send away") his wife, but a wife could not divorce her husband (this is still the case in Islamic countries). However, the following verses show that Paul, no doubt under the influence of Jesus' teaching, does not make this distinction. Perhaps a translator could express the phrase **should not separate from** in an idiomatic way; for example, "must not part ways with."

Her husband is literally "a man" or "a husband," but **her** is required in English both here and in the following verses (see the introduction to this section).

7.11   RSV   TEV

(but if she does, let her remain single or   but if she does, she must remain single
else be reconciled to her husband)—and   or else be reconciled to her husband;
that the husband should not divorce his   and a husband must not divorce his
wife.   wife.

The first half of this verse is an aside by Paul, so it has been put in round brackets (parentheses). The second half of the verse complements what Paul said in 10b.

The phrase **if she does** may be expressed as "if she does this" or "if she leaves her husband."

Remain single: the language is the same as that in verse 8. **Reconciled** is used elsewhere in the New Testament to refer to the restoration of good relations between God and men (for example, 2 Cor 5.18-20), but it is used here in the setting of human relationships.

In languages which do not use the passive, the phrase **be reconciled** may be rendered as "go back to" or "reconcile herself with."

7.12   RSV   TEV

   To the rest I say, not the Lord,   To the others I say (I, myself,
that if any brother has a wife who is an   not the Lord): if a Christian man has a
unbeliever, and she consents to live   wife who is an unbeliever and she
with him, he should not divorce her.   agrees to go on living with him, he must
                                            not divorce her.

It is grammatically possible to understand **the rest** (TEV's "others") as neuter, as in JB: "the rest is from me and not from the Lord." However, the context strongly suggests that Paul is speaking to a series of different groups: "the unmarried and the widows" (verse 8), "married" (verse 10), and **the rest** (verse 12). It is therefore necessary to decide who **the rest** are. This phrase is as vague in Greek as it is in English. But in the light of the following text, **the rest** probably refers to married couples of which one member has since become a Christian but not the other member. This situation was not covered by "the Lord's command."

The context shows plainly that **brother** means "a Christian man," the opposite of **an unbeliever**. The word for **unbeliever** does not refer in the New Testament to someone who is unfaithful in marriage. Here Paul is using it naturally, not insultingly, to mean a non-Christian.

The situations which Paul describes in verses 12-13 and 14-15 (as in verse 9) are probably real; the word **if** implies the meaning "as in the case."

Consents translates a compound verb meaning "is quite content." The words **consents** or "agrees" (TEV) in English imply a positive response to a suggestion made by someone else, but this is not implied in Greek.

The same verb **divorce** is used here and in verse 13.

7.13   RSV   TEV

If any woman has a husband who is an unbeliever, and he consents to live with her, she should not divorce him.

And if a Christian woman is married to a man who is an unbeliever and he agrees to go on living with her, she must not divorce him.

Commentators differ on whether to accept the text "If a woman" or "A woman who." The meaning, though, is almost the same. Paul was not referring to "a particular woman" but to **any woman**. He is talking about Christian women, so it is advisable to render this phrase as "if any Christian woman."

Has a husband will be a more natural rendering in many languages than "is married to a man."

7.14   RSV   TEV

For the unbelieving husband is consecrated through his wife, and the unbelieving wife is consecrated through her husband. Otherwise, your children would be unclean, but as it is they are holy.

For the unbelieving husband is made acceptable to God by being united to his wife, and the unbelieving wife is made acceptable to God by being united to her Christian husband. If this were not so, their children would be like pagan children; but as it is, they are acceptable to God.

Like verse 9b, this verse gives the basis for the previous statement in verse 13, as the word **for** indicates.[3] **Consecrated** is literally "sanctified" or "made holy." "Made acceptable to God" (TEV) is a clearer translation. FrCL translates "the unbelieving husband (or, wife) is near to God because of his union with his wife (or, her Christian husband)." Some scholars have thought that in this passage Paul uses the verb **consecrated** and the adjective **unclean** (TEV's "like pagan children") in a Jewish rather than a Christian way. This unusual sense is clear if it is remembered that the basic meaning of "holy" is "set apart to belong to God," and therefore "belonging to God's people" (see 1.2). The meaning here is then "I say this because a non-Christian husband is brought within God's people by being united to his wife, and an unbelieving wife is made part of God's people by her Christian husband."

Through her husband: the most probable text is "by the brother," but some Greek manuscripts have "by the husband." The same persons are referred to in either case, namely Christian husbands. As elsewhere in this passage **the husband/ wife** means "any husband/wife" and may be translated "a husband/wife" if he or she has not been mentioned before.

Many translators will prefer to restructure the first part of this verse with active verbs. One can say "For God treats the unbelieving husband as one of his own people because he has a Christian wife, and he treats the unbelieving wife as one of his own people because she has a Christian husband."

Otherwise, or "if this were not so" (TEV), contrasts with **but as it is** in the final clause. **But as it is** is a single word in Greek and may also mean "now." But here the word is used as a connective showing a logical relationship between the the two sentences.

Your children: TEV changes to the third person, "their children," to show that Paul is now referring only to the children of mixed marriages, not to all his readers' children.

Unclean or "pagan children" can be rendered as "children of people who do not worship the true God."

The phrase **but as it is** can be expressed as "but the fact is" or "but the truth is."

They are holy means the same as the word **consecrated** or "made acceptable" (TEV). One may say, for example, "God accepts them into his own family."

7.15

But if the unbelieving partner desires to separate, let it be so; in such a case the brother or sister is not bound. For God has called us[l] to peace. [l]Other ancient authorities read *you*	However, if the one who is not a believer wishes to leave the Christian partner, let it be so. In such cases the Christian partner, whether husband or wife, is free to act. God has called you to live in peace.

The first part of this verse contains a repetition in the Greek which RSV and TEV avoid because it would not be good English style: "But if the unbeliever separates, let him separate" (understood as ". . . separate from the Christian partner"). For a discussion on **separate** or "leave" (TEV), see the comments on verse 10.

Partner correctly shows that Paul is now referring to both husbands and wives, though "the unbeliever" is grammatically masculine. Later in the verse

---

[3] See J. Murphy-O'Connor. 1977, "Works without faith in I Cor., VII.17," Revue Biblique 84.349-361.

Paul goes back to speaking of men and women separately as **the brother and sister,** meaning in this context "a Christian husband or wife."

Desires to separate may be translated as "wishes to separate from" or "wishes to leave" (TEV).

The phrase **let it be so** can be rendered as "he should do so." But if a language has separate male and female third person pronouns like English, one may say "that person should do so," to indicate that both sexes are referred to.

Is not bound is literally "is not enslaved." A more positive rendering would be TEV's "is free to act." NEB expresses this as "is under no compulsion," and ItCL has "is free from the marriage bond." In some languages it may be necessary to complete the sentence by translating "is under no compulsion to stay with him (or her)."

The last part of the verse, **God has called us to peace,** becomes suddenly more general. **For** suggests that Paul introduces a new thought at this point, though the punctuation of the UBS Greek text does not require a new sentence.

There is good manuscript evidence for using **us** or "we" here, but translations generally agree with the UBS text in preferring "you" (plural; see TEV). It is also difficult to determine to whom "you" (TEV) refers. Brc understands "you" to mean the married people to whom Paul is writing. He paraphrases: "God meant marriage to be a perfect human relationship between two people." TNT, on the other hand, has "you believers," understanding "you" to refer to Christian partners in mixed marriages. This interpretation seems to suit the context better. The difficulty is not so much that unbelievers were unlikely to read Paul's letter, nor that Paul should commend peace with non-Christians (compare Heb 12.14), but that **called** can apply only to Christians.

The phrase **to peace** may be expressed as "be peaceful people" or "live peaceful lives." If we adopt the punctuation of the UBS Greek text, the last part of the verse is taken with what precedes it. In that case the meaning may be either (1) "However, let the partners stay together if possible, since God has called you to live in peace," or (2) "Let them separate without argument, for God has called you to live in peace." Of the two, (1) fits the Greek better and is adopted by NEB, TNT, and Phps.

7.16	RSV	TEV

Wife, how do you know whether you will save your husband? Husband, how do you know whether you will save you wife?

How can you be sure, Christian wife, that you will not save *f* your husband? Or how can you be sure, Christian husband, that you will not save *f* your wife?

f How can you be sure ... that you will not save; *or* How do you know ... that you will save.

Paul turns from addressing some of his readers generally to addressing an individual, a typical wife and husband. Translators must decide whether such a change is stylistically natural in their own languages. Of course, there is no difference in meaning.

Commentaries and translations give verse 16 almost opposite meanings, depending on whether they think this rhetorical question is expecting the answer "yes" or "no." TEV's footnote has the "pessimistic" understanding, where there is doubt. The positive statements of verse 14 and the end of verse 15 would naturally lead to an optimistic or hopeful understanding of verse 16.[4] The "optimistic" understanding of this verse is represented by TEV's "How can you be sure . . . that you will not save your husband?" NEB expresses it this way: "Think of it: as a wife you may be your husband's salvation; as a husband you may be your wife's salvation."

Wife may be rendered as "Christian wife" (TEV). Many languages will place this word at the beginning of the sentence as RSV does: "Christian wife, how can you . . . ?"

RSV   **7.17-24**   TEV

Live As God Called You

17 Only, let every one lead the life which the Lord has assigned to him, and in which God has called him. This is my rule in all the churches. 18 Was any one at the time of his call already circumcised? Let him not seek to remove the marks of circumcision. Was any one at the time of his call uncircumcised? Let him not seek circumcision. 19 For neither circumcision counts for anything nor uncircumcision, but keeping the commandments of God. 20 Every one should remain in the state in which he was called. 21 Were you a slave when called? Never mind. But if you can gain your freedom, avail yourself of the opportunity.[x] 22 For he who was called in the Lord as a slave is a freedman of the Lord. Likewise he who was free when called is a slave of Christ. 23 You were bought with a price; do not become slaves of men. 24 So, brethren, in whatever state each was called, there let him remain with God.

[x] Or *make use of your present condition instead*

17 Each one should go on living according to the Lord's gift to him, and as he was when God called him. This is the rule I teach in all the churches. 18 If a circumcised man has accepted God's call, he should not try to remove the marks of circumcision; if an uncircumcised man has accepted God's call, he should not get circumcised. 19 For whether or not a man is circumcised means nothing; what matters is to obey God's commandments. 20 Everyone should remain as he was when he accepted God's call. 21 Were you a slave when God called you? Well, never mind; but if you have a chance to become a free man, use it.[g] 22 For a slave who has been called by the Lord is the Lord's free man; in the same way a free man who has been called by Christ is his slave. 23 God bought you for a price; so do not become slaves of men. 24 My brothers, each one should remain in fellowship with God in the same condition that he was when he was called.

[g] but if you have a chance to become a free man, use it; *or* but even if you

_____

4 Conzelmann (page 124, note 48) claims, among other arguments for the pessimistic interpretation, that the translation "perhaps you will save your husband/wife" makes verse 17 unclear. It is difficult to see why this should be so, (a) because verse 17 belongs to a different section, and (b) because in any case an optimistic interpretation of verse 16 would broaden naturally into the advice "go on living as you were when God called you."

> have a chance to become a free man,
> choose rather to make the best of your
> condition as a slave.

These verses, with the possible exception of verse 17 (see comments), form a self-contained unit in which Paul turns from answering the Corinthian Christians' questions (see 7.1,25; 8.1) to repeat some teaching which he gives in **all the churches**. Paul's general theme concerns what it means to be called by God to be a Christian, and especially what this call implies for the outward condition in which different Christians were living at the time when God called them. The whole passage may be understood as an explanation or expansion of "God has called you to live in peace" (TEV, verse 15). The phrases **Never mind** and **avail yourself of the opportunity** (verse 21) fit in well with this line of thought. The rhetorical questions of verses 18 and 21 are equivalent to conditions (see the detailed comments).

The clauses and sentences of this passage are short. This is one of the signs that Paul may be engaged in dialogue or conversation with his readers (compare Rom 3.1-8), although the teaching in this section is not referring only to Corinthian Christians. Another sign in this passage is the repetition of identical thoughts (compare verses 20 and 24). Where two or more clauses and sentences overlap, in form and content, translators should pay special attention to the clauses and sentences which do not overlap or parallel each other.

The TEV section heading "Live as God Called You" may be rendered as "You must live as God wants you to" or "A true Christian life." Following GeCL, though, one may give this section the heading "Do not make unnecessary changes."

7.17 RSV	TEV
Only, let every one lead the life which the Lord has assigned to him, and in which God has called him. This is my rule in all the churches.	**Each one should go on living according to the Lord's gift to him, and as he was when God called him. This is the rule I teach in all the churches.**

The change from specific to general teaching is expressed clearly by ItCL: "with the exception of this case, the directive which I give in each community (that is, local church) is this . . . ."

The words translated **Only** are literally "If not." This is the only example in the New Testament of their being used at the beginning of a paragraph, or even a sentence; Galatians 1.7 "but I say this" (TEV) is the closest parallel. The meaning is given clearly by FrCL: "Except for this case," namely the possible separation mentioned in the first two parts of verse 15. **Every one** means, not only each of the partners in a mixed marriage, but also each of the readers.

Lead the life is literally "walk," "go in." "Walk" is a very common biblical expression for what English terms "a way of life." Some languages can translate this as "should continue walking one's life." However, in many languages the translator will need to change this metaphor to a more literal expression such as TEV's "go on living."

The clause **which the Lord has assigned to him** is literally "to each as the Lord divided," meaning "to each as the Lord gave him his share." The metaphor of **assigned** or "divided" goes back to the Old Testament idea of sharing out the Promised Land. Paul does not, as one might expect, use this verb in chapters 12 and 14 to refer to the sharing of spiritual gifts. He does use it, though, in 2 Corinthians 10.13 to speak of the sharing out of areas of work. The same idea of fixing boundaries is found in this passage. This phrase may also be expressed as "according to the ability which the Lord has given to him" or "making use of the ability which . . . ."

The Lord, as usual in Paul's writings, is Jesus, so it may be good to say "the Lord Jesus" here in order to bring out the difference from **God** in the following clause.

Commentators are uncertain about the tense of the verb translated as **assigned.** The UBS Greek text has the aorist tense, which indicates that God did this at a particular time in the past (as in 2 Cor 10.13).[5]

In which (TEV's "as he was") may be expanded slightly; for example, "and he should live his life as he was when God . . . ."

In which God has called him can be expanded to "when God called him to be a Christian" or ". . . to believe in Jesus."

This is my rule . . . : the Greek is literally "and this in all the churches I commanded" (TEV "teach"). This same verb is used in 11.34 where it is translated "give directions" (TEV "settle"). It may mean "set in order" but more probably has the meaning "command" or "lay down."

The context shows clearly that **churches** means "local Christian communities"; NEB and Brc have "congregations." In some languages it may be more natural to translate "This is the rule that I teach in all the other churches as well as yours."

7.18	RSV	TEV

Was any one at the time of his call already circumcised? Let him not seek to remove the marks of circumcision. Was any one at the time of his call uncircumcised? Let him not seek circumcision.

If a circumcised man has accepted God's call, he should not try to remove the marks of circumcision; if an uncircumcised man has accepted God's call, he should not get circumcised.

This verse contains two rhetorical questions which in some languages will need to be rendered as statements; for example, "Some of you were already circumcised at the time God called you" and "but some of you were already uncircumcised when God called you." TEV, however, turns these rhetorical questions into conditional sentences: "If a circumcised man has . . . " and "If an uncircumcised man . . . ." This is a natural way of expressing these rhetorical questions in English and some other languages.

---

[5] The aorist is the reading of most ancient manuscripts and appears to be followed by Mft and Brc. Most commentators, however, prefer the reading of a few generally reliable manuscripts which have the perfect tense, indicating a past event whose consequences reach into the present. Most translations, including RSV "has assigned" and NEB "the gift the Lord has granted," appear to agree, and this is the text of Nestle-Aland, 26th edition. Both are possible: throughout this passage, Paul uses the verb "to call" in both perfect (verses 15,17) and aorist (verses 18,20,21,22,24) tenses.

His call is literally "was called." Verse 17 states that this call comes from God. So languages which do not use the passive may render this phrase as "when you received God's call" or "at the time when God called you."

Circumcised will need a glossary note in translations which are intended for readers for whom the rite of circumcision has no religious meaning. See, for example, the TEV Word List. For such modern readers it is almost impossible to convey the full meaning in translations except by adding a lot of information. Paul means two things in this verse: (1) "if you were a Jew when God called you, do not renounce your heritage" (see Rom 9 5); and (2) "if you were circumcised when God called you, do not try to conceal the marks of circumcision" (see 1 Maccabees 1.15). Thus a glossary note will be necessary to bring out these meanings which the Jews, of course, would have understood naturally.

The phrase **marks of circumcision** may be rendered as "the scars caused by circumcision" or "the scars caused by the circumcision ceremony."

The second half of the verse, beginning with **Was anyone . . .**, complements the first. In the first half, **call** is the aorist tense; in the second, it is the perfect tense. Paul must have used this variation for reasons of style, so on both occasions this verb may be translated the same way in most languages.

7.19	RSV	TEV

For neither circumcision counts for anything nor uncircumcision, but keeping the commandments of God.

For whether or not a man is circumcised means nothing; what matters is to obey God's commandments.

For is not in the Greek text, even though generally Greek marks the connections between sentences more clearly than modern English does. But here, although it is clear that this verse gives the reason for Paul's instructions in verse 18, **For** is not expressed in the Greek. RSV and TEV are correct to put it in for understanding in modern English.

Modern translations restructure the Greek sentence to some extent. In the original, the repetition is effective style: "circumcision is nothing, and uncircumcision is nothing." In other languages, though, it may be more effective style to combine the two clauses. This will make the meaning of **counts for anything** (TEV's "means nothing") clearer. AT, for example, has "being circumcised or being uncircumcised does not make any difference." GeCL goes even further: "it is all the same to God whether anyone is circumcised or uncircumcised." One could also say "It is not important whether a man receives circumcision or not." Most versions agree with TEV in expanding the **but** into "what matters is . . ." or some equivalent phrase.

7.20	RSV	TEV

Every one should remain in the state in which he was called.

Everyone should remain as he was when he accepted God's call.

The function of this verse is to state more concisely and more generally the principle which Paul expressed in verse 17. In that verse Paul's thought was only beginning to move away from the question of marriage and divorce.

In Greek the text of this verse is literally "each in the calling (in) which he was called, in this let him remain." This kind of style is too heavy to translate word for word in most languages, so RSV and TEV restructure the verse. The Greek for "in the calling" here means, not the event in which God called the believer, but the condition or state in which the believer was living at the time when he or she was called. Verses 19 and 21 illustrate what is meant by the word **state.**

He was called: see the comment on verse 18 of this chapter.

<u>7.21</u>   RSV   TEV

Were you a slave when called? Never mind. But if you can gain your freedom, avail yourself of the opportunity.^{x}

^{x} Or *make use of your present condition instead*

Were you a slave when God called you? Well, never mind; but if you have a chance to become a free man, use it.^{g}

^{g} but if you have a chance to become a free man, use it; *or* but even if you have a chance to become a free man, choose rather to make the best of your condition as a slave.

The first clause can be translated as "If you were a slave when God called, never mind." **Never mind** is a colloquial English expression which means "don't worry" or "don't be concerned." This phrase may also be rendered as "don't let that bother your heart" or "don't be upset about it." The same Greek verb with the same meaning is used in Mark 12.14 and parallel Gospel passages, where TEV translates it as "pay no attention."

The meaning of verse 21b is not clear. The alternatives are given in (1) the TEV text, where "use it" means "use the chance to become a free man," and (2) the TEV footnote "but even if you have a chance to become a free man, choose rather to make the best of your condition as a slave." For convenience we will call (1) the "freedom translation" and (2) the "slavery translation." Scholars have long been divided between these two interpretations and still are. Among the modern translations which choose the "freedom translation" in their text are: TEV*, RSV, DuCL, FrCL, ItCL, NEB*, JB, Mft, Phps, and Brc (* indicates that the alternative is given in a footnote). Among the translations which choose the "slavery translation" are: GeCL, NAB, TNT, AT, BJ, and TOB. As often in Paul's letters, a problem like this arises because he leaves so much for the reader to understand; the text is literally "but if you (singular) can become free rather make use-of." The question is, make use of what? Your opportunity to become free, or your present state of slavery?

If the translator chooses the "freedom translation," **But** then becomes a very strong word which will introduce a contrast between (a) verse 21a and the rest of the passage (verses 17-24) which advises people to remain as they are, and (b) verse 21b which would then be an exception. One may say, for example, "but if you have the opportunity to actually become free, then use this opportunity." If the "slavery translation" (2) is chosen, the word **But** is used less strongly to introduce a straightforward contrast between the states of freedom and slavery: "but even if you have the opportunity to gain your freedom, you should choose rather to make the best of your condition as a slave."

There are three arguments which seem to point in the direction of the "freedom translation" as the more probable one.

First, the tense of the verbs **gain** and **avail . . . of** in the Greek is aorist, indicating a particular event. If the meaning had been "make use of your slavery," one would have expected a present imperative, as in verses 17 and 20, meaning "go on making use of your slavery." However, Paul's use of tenses in this passage is so uncertain that not much weight can be placed on this argument.

Second, in a somewhat similar passage, 9.12,15, Paul speaks about his not using the right to be paid for his work. The verb "use" (TEV) is the same as the one used here. If the meaning is the same, this is a further slight argument in favor of the "freedom translation."

Third, in 7.28 Paul makes a similar concession or exception to a general rule, although the language is not identical. He says "but if you marry."

In summary, it seems that the translator would be wise to choose the "freedom translation" rather than the "slavery translation."

7.22   RSV   TEV

For he who was called in the Lord as a   For a slave who has been called by the
slave is a freedman of the Lord. Like-   Lord is the Lord's free man; in the same
wise he who was free when called is a   way a free man who has been called by
slave of Christ.   Christ is his slave.

In most languages the word **For** can be omitted. It is in the Greek, but Paul is not speaking here about a consequence or result of verse 21. Rather he is introducing a series of further points which are related to the themes of Christian freedom and being a servant (or slave) of Christ.

In the Lord: it is more common for New Testament writers to speak of God, rather than of Christ, as calling people to faith. "In the Lord" and "in Christ" are favorite expressions of Paul to express the believer's unity with Christ. The immediate context of this verse suggests that the meaning is "called to belong to the Christian fellowship" or "called to be one with Christ" rather than "called by the Lord," that is, "by Christ."

The word which is translated **freedman** is not used elsewhere in the Greek Bible but is fairly common in Greek secular literature. It refers to a former slave who has been set free, not someone who has always been free like Paul himself (see Acts 22.28). This raises the question, by whom has he been set free? The use of **the Lord** here, and the mention of **Christ** later in the verse, strongly suggests that the meaning is "a slave whom Christ has freed." Similarly, in the second half of the verse, "someone who serves Christ" implies "a slave who belongs to Christ."

7.23   RSV   TEV

You were bought with a price; do not   God bought you for a price; so do not
become slaves of men.   become slaves of men.

The first part of this verse is almost identical with that in 6.20; see the comments. The present context makes it likely that the passive expression **you were bought** implies not "God bought you" (TEV) but "Christ bought you."

1 Corinthians 6.20 and Revelation 5.9 imply this interpretation too. There is no clear example in the New Testament of the Greek word for "buy" used figuratively with God as the subject. As in 6.20, the meaning here is "bought and paid for," not "bought at a high price."

Both the meaning and the translation of **do not become slaves of men** are clear, though it is less clear to what situation Paul is referring.[6]

7.24	RSV	TEV

So, brethren, in whatever state each was called, there let him remain with God.

My brothers, each one should remain in fellowship with God in the same condition that he was when he was called.

This verse is very similar to verse 20, and the differences, though significant, are not contrasts. Verse 24, apart from **brethren** and **with God**, is shorter than verse 20 in Greek because Paul does not repeat the emphatic expression "in the calling (in) which he was called."

Brethren refers to "fellow Christians," not to actual kin or family members.

Each may be rendered as "each one of you."

TEV's rendering "in fellowship" before **with God** is implied in the Greek. This phrase can also mean "in God's presence" or "in God's sight," as in 3.19. In any case, translators should add words here, if necessary, to make the meaning clear.

RSV	**7.25-40**	TEV

Questions about the Unmarried and the Widows

25 Now concerning the unmarried,[y] I have no command of the Lord, but I give my opinion as one who by the Lord's mercy is trustworthy. 26 I think that in view of the present[m] distress it is well for a person to remain as he is. 27 Are you bound to a wife? Do not seek to be free. Are you free from a wife? Do not seek marriage. 28 But if you marry, you do not sin, and if a girl[z] marries she does not sin. Yet those who marry will have worldly troubles, and I would spare you that. 29 I mean, brethren, the appointed time has grown very short; from now on, let those who have wives live as though they had none, 30 and those who mourn as though they were not mourning, and those who rejoice as though they were not

25 Now, concerning what you wrote about unmarried people: I do not have a command from the Lord, but I give my opinion as one who by the Lord's mercy is worthy of trust. 26 Considering the present distress, I think it is better for a man to stay as he is. 27 Do you have a wife? Then don't try to get rid of her. Are you unmarried? Then don't look for a wife. 28 But if you do marry, you haven't committed a sin; and if an unmarried woman marries, she hasn't committed a sin. But I would rather spare you the everyday troubles that married people will have.

29 What I mean, my brothers, is this: there is not much time left, and from now on married men should live as

---

[6] Perhaps Paul is briefly recalling the party struggles and false teaching discussed in chapters 1 and 2. Bultmann, quoted by Barrett, paraphrases: "Do not make yourselves dependent on the value judgements of men."

rejoicing, and those who buy as though they had no goods, 31 and those who deal with the world as though they had no dealings with it. For the form of this world is passing away.

32 I want you to be free from anxieties. The unmarried man is anxious about the affairs of the Lord, how to please the Lord; 33 but the married man is anxious about worldly affairs, how to please his wife, 34 and his interests are divided. And the unmarried woman or girl[y] is anxious about the affairs of the Lord, how to be holy in body and spirit; but the married woman is anxious about worldly affairs, how to please her husband. 35 I say this for your own benefit, not to lay any restraint upon you, but to promote good order and to secure your undivided devotion to the Lord.

36 If any one thinks that he is not behaving properly toward his betrothed,[z] if his passions are strong, and it has to be, let him do as he wishes: let them marry—it is no sin. 37 But whoever is firmly established in his heart, being under no necessity but having his desire under control, and has determined this in his heart, to keep her as his betrothed,[z] he will do well. 38 So that he who marries his betrothed[z] does well; and he who refrains from marriage will do better.

39 A wife is bound to her husband as long as he lives. If the husband dies, she is free to be married to whom she wishes, only in the Lord. 40 But in my judgment she is happier if she remains as she is. And I think that I have the Spirit of God.

[y] Greek *virgins*
[m] Or *impending*
[z] Greek *virgin*

though they were not married; 30 those who weep, as though they were not sad; those who laugh, as though they were not happy; those who buy, as though they did not own what they bought; 31 those who deal in material goods, as though they were not fully occupied with them. For this world, as it is now, will not last much longer.

32 I would like you to be free from worry. An unmarried man concerns himself with the Lord's work, because he is trying to please the Lord. 33 But a married man concerns himself with worldly matters, because he wants to please his wife; 34 and so he is pulled in two directions. An unmarried woman or a virgin concerns herself with the Lord's work, because she wants to be dedicated both in body and spirit; but a married woman concerns herself with worldly matters, because she wants to please her husband.

35 I am saying this because I want to help you. I am not trying to put restrictions on you. Instead, I want you to do what is right and proper, and to give yourselves completely to the Lord's service without any reservation.

36 In the case of an engaged couple who have decided not to marry: if the man feels that he is not acting properly toward the girl and if his passions are too strong and he feels that they ought to marry, then they should get married, as he wants to.[h] There is no sin in this. 37 But if a man, without being forced to do so, has firmly made up his mind not to marry,[i] and if he has his will under complete control and has already decided in his own mind what to do—then he does well not to marry the girl.[j] 38 So the man who marries[k] does well, but the one who doesn't marry[l] does even better.

39 A married woman is not free as long as her husband lives; but if her husband dies, then she is free to be married to any man she wishes, but only if he is a Christian. 40 She will be happier, however, if she stays as she is. That is my opinion, and I think that I too have God's Spirit.

[h] an engaged couple . . . as he wants to; *or* a man and his unmarried daughter: if he feels that he is not acting properly

toward her, and if she is at the right age to marry, then he should do as he wishes and let her get married.

i not to marry; *or* not to let his daughter get married.

j marry the girl; *or* let her get married.

k marries; *or* lets his daughter get married.

l doesn't marry; *or* doesn't let her get married.

The introductions to both 7.25 and 8.1 have the same wording: **Now concerning** (what you wrote). In each case this phrase is introducing new material, and this is a clear indication that 7.25-40 should be taken as a single section. However, its relation to the wider context and to its own internal structure is more difficult to grasp than one might expect. This problem is shown by the varied headings given to this passage: the UBS Greek text, on which TEV's heading is based, has "The Unmarried and Widows," although in TEV widows are mentioned only in verses 39-40; GeCL's heading is "Ready for the Lord," emphasizing verses 29-31; and Phps' heading is "In present circumstances it is really better not to marry." Another solution can be "Paul answers problems concerning unmarried people and widows."

Within the wider context, verses 25-40 may be seen as a return to the themes of sex and marriage. These themes have been interrupted by the more general teaching of verses 17-24. If one compares 7.1 and 7.25, it will be fairly evident that the Corinthian Christians had asked Paul two separate questions about these related matters of sex and marriage.

The internal structure of the passage may be seen as follows. Verse 25 introduces the subject of "virgins," and Paul follows this with advice about sex and marriage. This verse is echoed by verse 40, in which the words **in my judgment** bring this section to a neat conclusion. However, apart from passing references in verses 28-34, Paul says nothing about "virgins" until verse 36. So most of verses 25-35 may be a long diversion from the main theme. Verse 26 is more general than verse 25 and largely repeats the theme of verses 17-24.

Within verses 27-35 the structure is easier to see. In some places it even has a rhythmic form similar to poetry. In verse 27 Paul applies to married and unmarried people the principle which he stated in verse 26. Then in verse 28 (perhaps like verse 21) he allows an exception. Verses 29-31 form a single unit with its own solemn introduction: "the appointed time has grown very short." This brings in the theme of the "last days" and applies it to the situation of four or perhaps five groups of people. Then Paul draws a conclusion. Verses 32-34 are about the theme of anxiety or concern. First this theme is applied to unmarried and married men, then to unmarried and married women. Verse 35 is the conclusion of verses 26-35. In verses 36-38 Paul deals directly with the question of virgins, which he announced in verse 25. Then in verses 39-40a Paul turns to the situation of widows; and verse 40b is the general conclusion to the whole section. This complicated pattern may be summarized as follows:

TABLE 2

THE STRUCTURE OF 1 CORINTHIANS 7.25-40

25 virgins

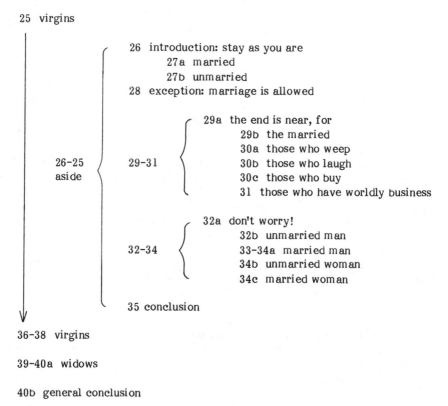

26 introduction: stay as you are
    27a married
    27b unmarried
28 exception: marriage is allowed

26-25
aside

29-31

  29a the end is near, for
    29b the married
    30a those who weep
    30b those who laugh
    30c those who buy
    31 those who have worldly business

32-34

  32a don't worry!
    32b unmarried man
    33-34a married man
    34b unmarried woman
    34c married woman

35 conclusion

36-38 virgins

39-40a widows

40b general conclusion

Apart from the problem of structure, the main general difficulty in translating this passage is that we do not have enough information about the situation in Corinth. So it is difficult to choose among various possible meanings of the text. This difficulty is particularly great in verses 36-38, as the TEV footnotes show.

7.25	RSV	TEV

Now concerning the unmarried,[y] I have no command of the Lord, but I give my opinion as one who by the Lord's mercy is trustworthy.

[y] Greek *virgins*

Now, concerning what you wrote about unmarried people: I do not have a command from the Lord, but I give my opinion as one who by the Lord's mercy is worthy of trust.

The word **concerning** may be rendered in many languages as "to answer the question about" or "I want to answer the question about."

Here and in 8.1, the words "what you wrote" (TEV) are implied in the Greek text. We can justify this addition by the clause "the matters which you wrote about" that appears in 7.1.

The word for **unmarried** in the Greek often refers to a "virgin." However, here it may possibly mean a woman who has never been married. But it may also refer to women who have been but are no longer married—that is, widows or divorced women. If either of these explanations is correct, "unmarried people" (TEV) is probably too general a translation in this verse. Verses 36-38, where Paul finally reaches the theme which he announces here, tend to confirm this conclusion.

Another aspect of the question is whether **unmarried** refers to just women, as is usually the case, to men as in Revelation 14.4, or to both men and women. In most places the use of feminine grammatical forms decides the question. For example, in verses 28, 34, and 36-38, Paul is certainly speaking of women only. In verse 25 the grammar is not clear, so some scholars have thought that men only are referred to. But the context makes this interpretation unlikely. If verses 26-35 are understood as an aside, as we have suggested in the introduction to this section and in Table 2, then **the unmarried** in verse 25 probably refers to women only. NAB, BJ, TOB retain the ambiguous word "virgins," AT thinks the reference is to "unmarried women," and Phps has the more specific "young unmarried women." For example, references to "girls" in verses 28 and 34 suggests very strongly that this is the case. However, since verses 27, 28, and 32-34 refer, in Paul's usual balanced way, to both men and women, he may be referring to both in verse 25 also. Other CLTs and TNT agree with TEV that the rendering should be "unmarried people."

In summation, it seems that the most likely meanings here are "people who have not had sexual experience" or "people who have not been married."

The word which is translated **command** is usually found in the New Testament in a set phrase meaning "by order." This **command** can be either from Christ, or sometimes it is from God; see 7.6; 2 Corinthians 8.8. There is nothing in the text itself which tells us whether such a **command** is thought of as coming from the teaching of Jesus while he was on earth, or by a revelation from the risen Christ. The clause **I have no command of the Lord** can be put in the active voice in many languages; for example, "The Lord did not give me any command" or "The Lord did not tell me what to do."

Trustworthy is literally "faithful." The Greek word does not mean simply "a believer," as it does in 2 Corinthians 6.15, but refers to someone who has been appointed to a responsible position, a trustworthy person.

7.26	RSV	TEV
	I think that in view of the present^m distress it is well for a person to remain as he is.	Considering the present distress, I think it is better for a man to stay as he is.

^{m} Or *impending*

In view of may be expressed as "when we consider" or "when we look at."

The phrase **the present distress** raises two questions: (1) Is the meaning "now" or "coming soon"? There is no text in the New Testament in which this Greek word must itself mean "imminent" (Mft) or "coming soon." However, words draw their meaning largely from contexts and from the situation to which they refer, so this question cannot be separated from the second one. (2) Is Paul referring to some personal problem or stress? Or is he referring to "a time of stress" which would affect, or was already affecting, the entire Christian community, or even the whole world as in verse 29? The word which is translated **distress** is commonly used in passages which speak about the end of time, and Paul may have been anticipating here the thought of verses 29-31, where he says "there is not much time left." He is probably thinking of the present "difficult situation" (ItCL) of Christians as a sign that the distress of the last days is already beginning. It may be necessary, then, for translators to expand this text slightly: "The difficult times (distress) have already begun. Therefore . . . ."

Well is literally "good"; see 7.1,8. The context implies that there is a comparison, as in the TEV rendering "better," and this seems to be the best translation.

Person: the following verse makes it clear that Paul is speaking exclusively to and about men for the moment. So TEV's rendering "man" is the correct one here.

The sentence **it is well . . . to remain as he is** may be restructured; for example, "if a man remains as he is, that will be better" or "if a man stays in his present condition, that will be better."

7.27-28a	RSV	TEV

Are you bound to a wife? Do not seek to be free. Are you free from a wife? Do not seek marriage. 28 But if you marry, you do not sin, and if a girl^z marries she does not sin.

Do you have a wife? Then don't try to get rid of her. Are you unmarried? Then don't look for a wife. 28 But if you do marry, you haven't committed a sin; and if an unmarried woman marries, she hasn't committed a sin.

^z Greek *virgin*

In these verses Paul returns to the style of verse 21. He addresses rhetorical questions to a single reader. This would be a typical married (verse 27a) or unmarried (verse 27b-28a) reader. It is possible in many languages to translate these rhetorical questions as conditional sentences; for example, "If you are married . . . ."

Do not seek to be free: the Greek verb means literally "loosen, untie," and can refer figuratively to loosening the marriage bond. Each language has special words referring to the act of terminating or loosing a marriage relationship.

Are you free from a wife? means "Are you in a state of freedom from the (marriage) bond?" It does not mean "Have you been divorced?"

Do not seek marriage may be translated as "Do not try to get married" or "You should remain single."

The verbs **you do not sin** and **does not sin** are past tenses in the Greek. Some translators can translate these past tenses by a present tense, or a future perfect tense "you will not have sinned." Some, however, can combine the two parts of the verse: "If, however, you do marry, it is no sin, either for you or the girl."

Girl: the context suggests that Paul is more concerned with her unmarried state than her lack of sexual experience (virginity) or her age. Therefore TEV's rendering "unmarried woman" is the better translation here.

7.28b	RSV	TEV

Yet those who marry will have worldly troubles, and I would spare you that.	But I would rather spare you the everyday troubles that married people will have.

The future tense **will have** and the phrase "from now on" in verse 29 suggest that the end is coming soon and the signs of its coming can already be seen (verse 26). However, the end has not come yet (compare 2 Thes 2.2). Therefore verse 28b should not be translated as a general statement that marriage brings trouble.

The Greek word for **troubles** is often used in describing the last days. ItCL expands the phrase **worldly troubles** to "because of family life"; NEB has more generally "in this bodily life"; TNT "in the world."

Spare may be expressed as "protect from" or "keep from."

7.29	RSV	TEV

I mean, brethren, the appointed time has grown very short; from now on, let those who have wives live as though they had none,	What I mean, my brothers, is this: there is not much time left, and from now on married men should live as though they were not married;

Brethren: see comment on verse 24.

I mean, brethren gives the impression in English that Paul is about to explain what he has just said. However, there are reasons to believe that Paul is introducing a new thought here: (1) The word **brethren** generally introduces a new paragraph. (2) Paul uses exactly the same expression **I mean, brethren** in 15.50 at the beginning of a new paragraph. (3) In both this verse and in 15.50 there is good reason to think that Paul is repeating a common Christian teaching, not anything new or peculiar to himself. The impact of the phrase **I mean, brethren** is therefore probably similar to Jesus' saying, "Truly, I tell you" (see Matt 5.18 and elsewhere). If this is so, AT's rendering "but this I do say, brothers," or GeCL's "For this you must know, brothers," gives the right effect. One may also say "I am sure that you know this, fellow Christians."

The appointed time has grown very short: the meaning may also be "the end time will come soon."

The meaning of the phrase translated **from now on** and its relation to the rest of the sentence are uncertain (see the punctuation note in the UBS Greek text). However, in Greek this phrase usually starts a new sentence and rarely ends one. Most translators and commentaries, therefore, agree with RSV and TEV's punctuation. Paul has just announced a general principle which the Corinthian Christians already know. Now he goes on to draw conclusions for readers in different situations. With this interpretation in mind, there are various ways to translate this phrase: "so," "since that is so," and "therefore." We could also link the two parts of the verse closely together: "The time we live in will not last long. While it lasts . . . ."

The sentence **let those who have wives live as though they had none** does not mean that married men should abandon their wives and lead a celibate life (see verse 27), or feel free to marry someone else. The words **as though** show that Paul feels that married men should carry on their married lives under the realization that they live in the end times, and that they have much more important things to deal with than the fact that they are married. The present world will soon end. TEV's translation "live as though they were not married" is clearer than RSV's.

7.30   RSV   TEV

| and those who mourn as though they were not mourning, and those who rejoice as though they were not rejoicing, and those who buy as though they had no goods, | those who weep, as though they were not sad; those who laugh, as though they were not happy; those who buy, as though they did not own what they bought; |

The words **mourn** and **rejoice** suggest the noisy expression of inner feelings. Therefore **mourning** refers to "weeping and wailing," not to silently shedding tears; **rejoice** probably means "making a joyful noise." Paul is possibly thinking that there is so little time left that such things as being married, mourning for someone who has died, or celebrating the birth of a child are simply unimportant. Thus he could tell his readers who have reason to weep that they should behave as though they were not sad.

The constructions in TEV, ". . . weep, as though," ". . . laugh, as though," are too abrupt in many languages. One may render these as ". . . weep, let them act (behave) as though," and so on.

The clause **as though they had no goods** can be translated as "as though they did not possess goods" or "as though the things that they have bought do not belong to them."

7.31   RSV   TEV

| and those who deal with the world as though they had no dealings with it. For the form of this world is passing away. | those who deal in material goods, as though they were not fully occupied with them. For this world, as it is now, will not last much longer. |

The form of this verse is the same as that of the previous clauses beginning with "those who have wives" in 29b. It can be understood as a summary of the previous statements, making a transition to the conclusion in verse 31b. The Greek is literally "and those who use the world as not making-full-use-of-it," with the second verb "making-full-use-of-it" being a compound of the first verb "use." RSV's more general rendering is probably more accurate than TEV's narrow one. Translators should try to use a stronger verb for the second one; for example, "did not use all their time for these things." But while attempting to render the idea of "making-full-use-of," translators should avoid such words as "misuse" or "exploit." These would be misleading.

The words **form** and **is passing away** are not used elsewhere by Paul. The Greek word for **form** usually applied to a person's outward appearance, and some translations choose this meaning here ("the figure of the world," BJ, TOB). However, Paul's statements elsewhere about the last days suggest that even if at this point Paul is quoting older teaching, he understands it to mean more than "this present world will change its form, but will still remain." Most translations agree with the thinking behind TEV's rendering "as it is now," but they express it in differing ways: "this world and all its affairs" (TNT), "the present world" (GeCL), "the whole frame of this world" (NEB), "the world as we know it" (JB), "the present phase of things" (Mft, similarly Phps), "this world in its present changing form" (Brc). Notice that TEV replaces RSV's positive expression **is passing away** by an equivalent negative expression "will not last much longer," which is clearer and more vivid English. Translators can study the variety of translations given above to decide how best to render this sentence in their own languages.

7.32	RSV	TEV
	I want you to be free from anxieties. The unmarried man is anxious about the affairs of the Lord, how to please the Lord;	I would like you to be free from worry. An unmarried man concerns himself with the Lord's work, because he is trying to please the Lord.

Verses 32-34 use a verb four times meaning "concern oneself" or "be anxious," and once a related adjective meaning "unconcerned" or "not worrying." The problem in translating these terms is that they seem to be used in a good sense when it is a question of **the affairs of the Lord,** and in a bad sense when referring to wives or husbands. Paul uses this word positively in 12.25 and Philippians 2.20, and negatively only in Philippians 4.6, where TEV has "don't worry about."

RSV's word **anxious,** which is used throughout the passage, is not the best English equivalent. On the other hand, it may be difficult to find a neutral term like TEV's "concerns," which is effective in English. In that case it is better to use different or even unrelated words than to distort the meaning.

In some languages it may be necessary in this passage to state explicitly that the married and unmarried people whom Paul refers to are Christians. One may say, for example, "the unmarried Christian man," and so on. One may also show in some way that Paul is not speaking of married and unmarried people in general. In this respect, one may say at the beginning of the second sentence, "Among Christians, an unmarried man . . . ."

The phrase **to be free from anxieties** may be expressed as "not to be worried at all" or "not to have any worries (anxieties) at all."

When we contrast this verse with verse 33, it is clear that **unmarried** is the correct translation, no matter what meaning is given in verse 8. Paul obviously means "unmarried man" here (TEV), because it is contrasted with unmarried woman in verse 33. "The unmarried man," like similar phrases in this passage, means "the (typical) unmarried Christian man," "any unmarried Christian man."

The affairs of the Lord is literally "the (things) of the Lord," so NEB and Brc translate "the Lord's business." GeCL combines this phrase with what follows, and translates "to live in a way pleasing to the Lord." Whichever translation is chosen, the translator should, if possible, make this phrase a contrasting parallel to the phrase "worldly affairs" in verses 33 and 34, as the Greek in those verses, "the affairs of the world," is very similar in form to **the affairs of the Lord.**

7.33 RSV TEV

RSV	TEV
but the married man is anxious about worldly affairs, how to please his wife,	But a married man concerns himself with worldly matters, because he wants to please his wife;

This verse parallels closely verse 32b and raises no new problems.

7.34 RSV TEV

RSV	TEV
and his interests are divided. And the unmarried woman or girl[z] is anxious about the affairs of the Lord, how to be holy in body and spirit; but the married woman is anxious about worldly affairs, how to please her husband. [z] Greek *virgin*	and so he is pulled in two directions. An unmarried woman or a virgin concerns herself with the Lord's work, because she wants to be dedicated both in body and spirit; but a married woman concerns herself with worldly matters, because she wants to please her husband.

Divided: the married man's effort is constantly divided between trying to please his wife and Christ. TEV's rendering "pulled in two directions" is implied in the context and is a vivid English way to describe this situation. One could also say "has two hearts (minds, livers)."

As the variants in the UBS Greek text show (see also Metzger), it is difficult to be certain of the wording and punctuation of the first part of this verse. Most of the variants can be explained as scribal attempts to cope with the difficulties mentioned in the next paragraphs.

The next part of the verse is quite ungrammatical in the Greek, as Barrett's translation shows: "the unmarried woman and the virgin is anxious . . . ." Translations and commentaries take this phrase in at least five different ways: (1) Paul is referring to one group, namely "the woman . . . when she is unmarried" (GeCL). If this is what Paul meant, it is difficult to know why he used two different expressions linked with "and." (2) The difference between the two expressions is primarily one of age: "an unmarried woman, whether an adult or a girl" (ItCL and others). (3) The **unmarried woman** means "widows," just as the unmarried in verse 8 means "widowers" (see comments). (4) The **girl** (virgin) refers to a group of women who have decided to remain unmarried; NEB "unmarried or celibate." This, however, does not seem to be the meaning of "virgin" elsewhere in this passage. (5) "The virgin—indeed, any unmarried woman" (NAB). If (5) is the meaning, it is difficult to see why Paul used the terms in the opposite order. All these translations, (1) through (5), are possible. Most modern translations, however, choose (2), but it may be worth putting (3) in a footnote.

Holy means "dedicated" (TEV; see the extensive comments on 1.2 which explain the conception of sanctified or "set apart").

In body and spirit: body and spirit are not being contrasted here; the phrase is equivalent to "in her whole being"; FrCL "in all she does and thinks." One can translate the whole clause **how to be holy in . . .** as "wants to dedicate her whole being to the Lord."

7.35	RSV	TEV

RSV	TEV
I say this for your own benefit, not to lay any restraint upon you, but to promote good order and to secure your undivided devotion to the Lord.	I am saying this because I want to help you. I am not trying to put restrictions on you. Instead, I want you to do what is right and proper, and to give yourselves completely to the Lord's service without any reservation.

This verse is a single sentence in Greek. The first part of the sentence suggests that Paul is giving advice which he feels is useful but not absolutely necessary to follow. He has not been speaking of matters which are clearly right or wrong, but of how he thinks Christians should best live in the short time before the last days. TEV's "I want to," "I am . . . trying," and "I want" help to bring out Paul's feelings more clearly than RSV's rather literal translation.

One may translate **I say this** as "I talk to you like this" or "I have said all these things to you . . . ."

Restraint: the image is that of putting a halter around the neck of a domestic animal (compare 2 Cor 1.24). This whole sentence **not to lay any restraint upon you** may be translated as "I am not trying to restrain you in any way" or "I am not . . . to put a restrictive burden on you."

There may be an implied contrast between **any restraint** and **undivided devotion.** In this case the implied meaning is "far from trying to restrict you, I want to help you serve the Lord without being restricted in any way."

To promote good order refers to decent behavior rather than to church discipline. Another way to render this sentence is "I want you to live in a right and proper way."

7.36-38

Verses 36-38 must be understood as being a single discourse unit. As the footnotes in TEV and some other translations show, these verses may be interpreted in various ways. The problems arise partly from the fact that Paul does not define the meaning of the word which is translated "any one" in verse 36. There are four main lines of interpretation which are set out in Table 3.

In (A) "any one" is the father of a daughter who is in danger of becoming too old for marriage. "Betrothed" is literally "virgin," and the Greek word can occasionally mean "daughter." The "control" in verse 37 would therefore be the power of a father to decide whom his daughter should marry. This explanation is followed in the footnotes in TEV, DuCL ("engaged daughter"), NEB, and TOB, and in the text of JB. The problems with this interpretation are as follows: (1) "Let them marry" in verse 36 seems to refer to the daughter's fiancé, who has not been mentioned before. (2) It is difficult to understand the words "it is no sin" (to him, the father). (3) It is difficult to see why Paul should praise the father for "a decision which costs him nothing" (Héring); and (4) the whole chapter deals with marriage relationships rather than the relationship between father and daughter.

TABLE 3

TRANSLATION POSSIBILITIES FOR
1 CORINTHIANS 7.36-38

But if any
- A father
- B spiritual bridegroom
- C brother-in-law
- D fiancé

thinks he is not behaving properly

toward his
- A unmarried daughter,
- B spiritual bride,
- C dead brother's young widow,
- D fiancée,

and
- A she
- B he?
- C she?
- D he (or she)

is
- A of (or past) marriageable age,
- B has strong sexual desires,
- C of (or past) marriageable age,
- D has strong sexual desires (or as A),

and it has to be, let

him do as he (she?) wishes: let
- A the daughter and her fiance
- B the spiritual bride and bridegroom
- C the man and his sister-in-law
- D the engaged couple

marry—it is no sin. 37 But whoever . . .
- A is under no outward
- B,D is under no inner
- C is under no outward

A constraint, but has the right to do as he wishes with his daughters,
B,D compulsion, but can keep his sexual desires under control,
C constraint, but has the right to do as he wishes with his sister-in-law,

and has determined this in his heart to keep her as she is, unmarried, he will do

well. 38 So that he who
- A gives his daughter in marriage
- B marries his spiritual bride
- C marries his sister-in-law
- D marries his fiancée

does well; and he who refrains from (A: giving his daughter in) marriage does better.

Explanation (B) is apparently followed by TEV text, FrCL, NEB, TNT, and Mft. It presupposes the existence of a custom whereby couples considered themselves as spiritually engaged or married to one another. There is no evidence, however, for such a custom in the first century.[7] We should note that the words "in the case of an engaged couple who have decided to marry" (TEV) are not in the text, though they are implied if a translator chooses interpretation (B). NEB has prepared for explanation (B) by translating "virgins" as "celibacy" in verse 25, and by referring to the "celibate women" in verse 34. However, it is by no means certain that these translations are correct ones. And in any case, in verse 36 Paul is turning to a different aspect of the Corinthian Christians' questions about marriage.

Explanation (C) supposes that Paul was here discussing a case in which the Old Testament rules given in Deuteronomy 25.2-10 had been applied to the church at Corinth.[8] These provided for a man to "inherit" the wife of his deceased brother. But verse 39 shows clearly that this custom was at least not compulsory in Christian circles.[9]

Explanation (D), which is followed by RSV, GeCL, ItCL, AT, Phps, and TOB, is probably the simplest. It assumes that Paul is speaking of a normal, engaged couple, not a couple "who have decided not to marry." This is generally the simplest and perhaps the most likely explanation; individual difficulties will be dealt with in the detailed comments. This is the explanation which is chosen by the majority of modern commentators. Translators, therefore, will not be wrong in choosing (D).

7.36	RSV	TEV

If any one thinks that he is not behaving properly toward his betrothed,[z] if his passions are strong, and it has to be, let him do as he wishes: let them marry—it is no sin.

[z] Greek *virgin*

In the case of an engaged couple who have decided not to marry: if the man feels that he is not acting properly toward the girl and if his passions are too strong and he feels that they ought to marry, then they should get married, as he wants to.[h] There is no sin in this.

[h] an engaged couple ... as he wants to; *or* a man and his unmarried daughter: if he feels that he is not acting properly toward her, and if she is at the right age to marry, then he should do as he wishes and let her get married.

---

[7] The Shepherd of Hermas, Vision 11, is sometimes quoted as evidence for this custom from the second century. It is, however, uncertain whether this custom existed in real life. In Vision 13 the same virgins are described as "holy spirits," and in Vision 15 they are given the names of virtues.

[8] J.M. Ford, 1963, "Levirate Marriage in St. Paul (1 Corinthians 7)," New Testament Studies 10.361-365.

[9] See Barrett, pp. 183-184.

The verse begins in Greek with words meaning "But if." suggesting that Paul is about to move to another question. He may be referring to a situation which has already arisen at Corinth, perhaps similar to that implied in verse 5, except that the couple in question in verses 36-38 are not yet married.

Thinks (TEV's "feels") involves a judgment or decision rather than emotion.

Not . . . properly is an adjective which is related to "good order" in verse 35. This phrase may be expressed as "acting in a way he should not" or "behaving in a wrong way toward."

His betrothed ("the girl," TEV) is literally "his virgin"—a rather strange expression, especially if a daughter is meant as in explanation (A) above. However, "his virgin" could mean "his sweetheart" or "his beloved."

The Greek does not tell us whether the subject of **are strong** is the **passions** of the man or of the woman. The problem is that in Greek an adjective is used which, if applied to a woman, commonly means that she is beyond the prime in age—namely that she is no longer young. However, the word may also be applied to a person, especially a man, who has strong sexual impulses. The situation is similar to that described in verse 9.

The thought of the last part of verse 36, **let them marry . . .** , is similar to that of verse 28a but is more fully developed.

The clause **it is no sin** is literally "(he) does not sin."

7.37   RSV   TEV

But whoever is firmly established in his heart, being under no necessity but having his desire under control, and has determined this in his heart, to keep her as his betrothed,^{z} he will do well.

^{z} Greek *virgin*

But if a man, without being forced to do so, has firmly made up his mind not to marry,^{i} and if he has his will under complete control and has already decided in his own mind what to do—then he does well not to marry the girl.^{j}

^{i} not to marry; *or* not to let his daughter get married.
^{j} marry the girl; *or* let her get married.

Paul's language here suggests that he is dealing with an actual case at Corinth. This impression is given more clearly here than in verse 36.

Firmly expresses the meaning of the Greek perfect tense of the verbal expression **established in his heart,** which refers to a state of being rather than to a single past event. The clause **firmly established in his heart** may be expressed as "has set his heart strongly."

Being under no necessity uses the word which was translated "distress" in verse 26, but there is no suggestion in this verse of events in the "last days." This phrase may also be rendered as "nobody is making him do it" or "without anything forcing (compelling) him."

The clause **having his desire completely under control** may be rendered as "but if he is able to control his desires (will) completely . . . ."

To keep her as his betrothed is literally "to go-on-keeping his own virgin," certainly implying that she will stay unmarried and still a virgin.

He will do well translates a Greek text which requires expansion in many languages, including English. **Well** is the adverb which corresponds to the adjective "good" in 5.6, and "well" in 7.1 and 7.8. An expanded translation such as TEV's "he does well not to marry the girl" will bring out the meaning clearly here.

7.38 RSV	TEV
So that he who marries his betrothed[z] does well; and he who refrains from marriage will do better. [z] Greek *virgin*	So the man who marries[k] does well, but the one who doesn't marry[l] does even better. [k] marries; *or* lets his daughter get married. [l] doesn't marry; *or* doesn't let her get married.

So introduces the conclusion of the previous argument.

The phrase **does well** may be expressed as "does a good thing." **Will do better** can be rendered as "does a much better thing."

7.39 RSV	TEV
A wife is bound to her husband as long as he lives. If the husband dies, she is free to be married to whom she wishes, only in the Lord.	A married woman is not free as long as her husband lives; but if her husband dies, then she is free to be married to any man she wishes, but only if he is a Christian.

Is bound is the verb which was used in verse 27, **Are you bound to a wife?** One may expand this phrase slightly; for example, "is not free to marry" or "is not allowed to remarry."

Dies is literally "falls asleep," which is a common New Testament metaphor for death, especially the death of Christians.

Only in the Lord: TEV and most other translations take this to mean that the other partner must be a Christian; thus TEV's rendering "but only if he is a Christian." This interpretation is almost certainly implied in the Greek, but the direct meaning of the phrase is more probably "only (it must be) as a Christian" or "within the Lord's fellowship" (NEB). A possible translation would be "it must be a Christian marriage."

7.40 RSV	TEV
But in my judgment she is happier if she remains as she is. And I think that I have the Spirit of God.	She will be happier, however, if she stays as she is. That is my opinion, and I think that I too have God's Spirit.

In my judgment: in this case TEV follows more closely than RSV the order of the Greek. This brings out better the contrast or distinction between "my opinion" and "God's Spirit."

The phrase **remains as she is** may be translated as "remains unmarried" or "doesn't get married."

Verse 40b is similar in language and thought to verse 25b and completes this section. **I** in the Greek is stressed, meaning rather "I too" as in TEV. This statement by Paul may allude to the claims of people in Corinth who "think" that they have special wisdom (3.18; 8.2) or special gifts from the Holy Spirit (14.37). Mft has "I suppose I have the Spirit of God as well as other people." However, TNT's "moreover I think I have God's Spirit" is certainly a possible translation. The difficulty arises because Paul is trying to do two things at the same time: (1) to indicate a slight contrast with the preceding words ("it is [only] my opinion, but . . ."), and (2) to introduce a new thought. However, TEV's translation is most likely the more correct one, but it could be restated in some languages as "I think that God's Spirit is guiding me."

Chapter 8

The Question about Food Offered to Idols

1 Now concerning food offered to idols: we know that "all of us possess knowledge." "Knowledge" puffs up, but love builds up. 2 If any one imagines that he knows something, he does not yet know as he ought to know. 3 But if one loves God, one is known by him.

4 Hence, as to the eating of food offered to idols, we know that "an idol has no real existence," and that "there is no God but one." 5 For although there may be so-called gods in heaven or on earth—as indeed there are many "gods" and many "lords"— 6 yet for us there is one God, the Father, from whom are all things and for whom we exist, and one Lord, Jesus Christ, through whom are all things and through whom we exist.

7 However, not all possess this knowledge. But some, through being hitherto accustomed to idols, eat food as really offered to an idol; and their conscience, being weak, is defiled. 8 Food will not commend us to God. We are no worse off if we do not eat, and no better off if we do. 9 Only take care lest this liberty of yours somehow become a stumbling block to the weak. 10 For if any one sees you, a man of knowledge, at table in an idol's temple, might he not be encouraged, if his conscience is weak, to eat food offered to idols? 11 And so by your knowledge this weak man is destroyed, the brother for whom Christ died. 12 Thus, sinning against your brethren and wounding their conscience when it is weak, you sin against Christ. 13 Therefore, if food is a cause of my brother's falling, I will never eat meat, lest I cause my brother to fall.

1 Now, concerning what you wrote about food offered to idols.

It is true, of course, that "all of us have knowledge," as they say. Such knowledge, however, puffs a person up with pride; but love builds up. 2 Whoever thinks he knows something really doesn't know as he ought to know. 3 But the person who loves God is known by him.

4 So then, about eating the food offered to idols: we know that an idol stands for something that does not really exist; we know that there is only the one God. 5 Even if there are so-called "gods," whether in heaven or on earth, and even though there are many of these "gods" and "lords," 6 yet there is for us only one God, the Father, who is the Creator of all things and for whom we live; and there is only one Lord, Jesus Christ, through whom all things were created and through whom we live.

7 But not everyone knows this truth. Some people have been so used to idols that to this day when they eat such food they still think of it as food that belongs to an idol; their conscience is weak, and they feel they are defiled by the food. 8 Food, however, will not improve our relation with God; we shall not lose anything if we do not eat, nor shall we gain anything if we do eat.

9 Be careful, however, not to let your freedom of action make those who are weak in the faith fall into sin. 10 Suppose a person whose conscience is weak in this matter sees you, who have so-called "knowledge," eating in the temple of an idol; will not this encourage him to eat food offered to idols? 11 And so this weak person, your

brother for whom Christ died, will perish because of your "knowledge"! 12 And in this way you will be sinning against Christ by sinning against your Christian brothers and wounding their weak conscience. 13 So then, if food makes my brother sin, I will never eat meat again, so as not to make my brother fall into sin.

The opening words of this chapter make it clear that Paul is beginning a new theme, that of **food offered to idols.** In the light of 7.1, where Paul talks about "the matters about which you wrote," the question in this chapter is almost certainly the next in a series of questions which were raised by the Corinthian Christians, and TEV's addition "what you wrote about" makes this fact clear. In the introduction to this Handbook we stated that we understand 1 Corinthians in its present form to be a single letter, not originally part of several letters. If this is so, Paul is now beginning to discuss the second (or third) question. The number of questions depends on whether 7.25-40 is considered a separate question or another aspect of Paul's previous discussion on marriage questions. Paul's answer to the next question does not begin until 12.1.

It is clear from the outline that Paul tends to deviate a great deal from the main points at issue while he is answering his correspondents' questions. We have noted this tendency in 7.26-35. In chapters 8-11 the theme of offering food to idols, announced in 8.1, is interrupted by chapter 9. In that chapter Paul returns to the question of his own authority as an apostle (see especially 3.10-15 and 4.1-13). In this chapter Paul's mention of the readers' **liberty** in 8.9 leads to a wider discussion of Paul's own rights and privileges as an apostle. In chapter 10 Paul returns to the theme of offerings to idols, but introduces a contrast with the Lord's Supper (10.16-17,21), a theme which Paul develops in 11.17-34. The latter passage, and still more 11.2-16, includes other instructions concerning Christian worship. Such instructions may constitute another deviation from what is probably the main theme of chapters 8-11; namely, the question about offerings to idols.

This somewhat complex structure probably arises for two related reasons: first, Paul, as a traveling evangelist, may have dictated the letter in very difficult circumstances; and second, he had a tendency to explore the wider implications of Christian faith and life while he was answering specific questions posed by his readers.

It is of practical importance for the translator to know the structure of chapters 8-10, for one must decide the wording of section headings and also where to divide the text into sections and paragraphs. The heading of chapter 8 in the UBS Greek text is "Food Offered to Idols," and this is closely followed by TEV. In fact, though, the problem is probably narrower, not referring to food in general (see comments on verse 1).

The difficulties in translating this chapter arise because we do not know enough about the situation at Corinth. So we cannot be sure when Paul is quoting from the Corinthian Christians' letter to him. Nor can we be sure when he is speaking in his own name, or quoting traditional Christian teaching. We discuss each example on its own merits in the detailed comments.

RSV	TEV
Now concerning food offered to idols: we know that "all of us possess knowledge." "Knowledge" puffs up, but love builds up.	Now, concerning what you wrote about food offered to idols. It is true, of course, that "all of us have knowledge," as they say. Such knowledge, however, puffs a person up with pride; but love builds up.

Now concerning may be expressed as "Now, I would like to speak about."

The construction **food offered** can be rendered as "food which people have offered." KJV's "things offered unto idols" is certainly too broad a translation. Modern translations, on the other hand, are divided between **food** (RSV, TEV, DuCL, NEB, JB, TNT) and "meat" (FrCL, GeCL, ItCL, BJ, TOB). The main reason for preferring "meat" is that the Greek clearly refers to something which had been killed before being offered to a deity. So offerings of cereals, for example, are excluded.

Another reason for a translator to avoid using the word **food** in this verse is that it would suggest that in verse 13 ("I will never eat meat") Paul's thought is narrowing. That is not the case. In fact, his thought is probably broadening (see comments on verse 13).

The phrase "meat offered to idols" is intended to have a negative sound. Pagans themselves, as distinct from Jews and Christians, would have spoken about "meat offered to sacred beings." Paul does this himself in 10.28, where he quotes what a pagan might say. But in this whole passage Paul is not concerning himself with taking part in pagan worship. Rather he is counseling against eating "meat" which has been sacrificed by someone else to a pagan God. Meat was commonly dedicated to pagan gods at the time the animal was killed.

TEV's clauses "It is true, of course," and "as they say," are implied in the Greek text. The quotation marks around "all of us possess knowledge" suggest, probably correctly, that Paul is here quoting a slogan which was currently used at Corinth. There is a problem knowing to whom the word **we** refers. This verse seems to contradict verse 7a, literally "but knowledge is not in all." The contradiction may be resolved in various ways: (a) By making verse 1 refer to some specific truth. ItCL has: "I know that we are full of knowledge about this argument" (namely, meat sacrificed to idols). (b) By making verse 7a specific: "all possess this truth," where "this" is understood or implicit in the Greek text. (c) By giving **knowledge** a different meaning in verses 1 and 7 (Héring). However, there is little in the wording of either verse to support any of explanations (a) through (c). It is therefore more likely either (d) that Paul is announcing a general principle in verse 1 and making a modification in verse 7a, or (e) that **all of us** in verse 1 refers to a smaller group than "all" (without "we") in verse 7. Explanation (e) is the simplest. The **we** of verse 1 may therefore be taken to refer to Paul and his readers who are considered "spiritually mature." This would imply that the **we** is somewhat emphasized, as it certainly is at the beginning of verse 6.

For detailed comments on the word **knowledge**, see 1.5. In some languages it may be difficult to translate **possess knowledge** literally, and it may be necessary to express the object of knowing. In such cases one may add some such phrase as "about this matter" (see ItCL quote above).

Puffs up: TEV adds "with pride," to bring out the meaning of this metaphor. A translator may also say "makes a person very proud" or "fills a person's heart with pride"; see also 4.6.

Builds up keeps the Greek metaphor. In some languages this metaphor may need to be replaced by some nonfigurative expression such as "strengthens."

8.2-3

In one Greek manuscript, which is supported by some other evidence, the text of these verses is different in three places. The difference is indicated in the following translation which is otherwise based on RSV: "if anyone imagines that he knows, he does not yet know as he ought to know. But if one loves, one is known."[1] The text followed by RSV and TEV is preferred.

8.2 RSV	TEV
If any one imagines that he knows something, he does not yet know as he ought to know.	**Whoever thinks he knows something really doesn't know as he ought to know.**

If any one: it is not necessary to suppose that the person(s) referred to are outside the group which Paul described as "all of us" in verse 1. Paul is here exploring more deeply what is meant by "knowledge."

This verse distinguishes between (a) the state of knowing something or having acquired a piece of knowledge (verse 2a), and (b) the event of acquiring knowledge (verse 2b). A possible translation is the following: "If a person thinks that he has attained to some degree of knowledge, he has not yet reached the stage when he has any knowledge at all in the real sense of the word."

8.3 RSV	TEV
But if one loves God, one is known by him.	**But the person who loves God is known by him.**

It is grammatically possible to understand the second part of this verse to mean "God is known by the person." However, in the light of 1 Corinthians 13.12, where the Greek is similar, and Galatians 4.9, which speaks explicitly of God knowing men, the correct translation is most certainly "God knows him" or "God knows that person."

---

[1] The omission of "by him" at the end of verse 3 is found in two other Greek manuscripts. It is tempting to accept this text as original, since it has the same general tone as verse 1, and scribes would naturally tend to make the text longer and more specific. However, the weight of evidence is so heavily on the side of the longer text that it is adopted by all translations and commentaries consulted. The opposite view is taken by Zuntz, pages 31-32.

　　　　RSV　　　　　　　　　　　　　　　TEV

Hence, as to the eating of food offered to idols, we know that "an idol has no real existence," and that "there is no God but one."

So then, about eating the food offered to idols: we know that an idol stands for something that does not really exist; we know that there is only the one God.

Paul restates the question of verse 1 in a more specific form, probably following the Corinthian Christians' own letter. He now discusses the act of eating meat offered to idols, rather than the question of meat offered to idols in general. Jews were strictly forbidden to eat such food, so the question is part of the wider issue of how far Christians should obey Jewish rules (see 7.18-19).

As to the eating can be expressed as "So then, I would like to speak about eating" or "So then, I would like to answer the question about eating."

Food offered: see the comment on 8.1.

We know: the **we** probably refers to the same group as that in verse 1, namely Paul and his readers (see the comments above).

Has no real existence: care should be taken not to translate this part of verse 4 in such a way as to conflict with verse 5, where Paul admits that other spiritual powers exist. FrCL's translation seems to be closer to the meaning than TEV's: "we know that an idol represents nothing real in the world." NEB makes explicit, by use of quotation marks, that the sentences "a false god has no existence in the real world. There is no god but one" are a saying used by the Corinthians or a saying which was current at Corinth. This may be correct.

The clause **there is no God but one** may be translated as "only one true God exists" or "there is no other god beside the real God." This was, of course, fundamental to Jewish faith; see Deuteronomy 6.4.

　　　　RSV　　　　　　　　　　　　　　　TEV

For although there may be so-called gods in heaven or on earth—as indeed there are many "gods" and many "lords"—

Even if there are so-called "gods," whether in heaven or on earth, and even though there are many of these "gods" and "lords,"

In this verse Paul is certainly speaking in his own name, perhaps showing that he understands the "weaker brethren" (see verses 7-13) who cannot speak so confidently as the Corinthians who are quoted in verse 4b. In English, TEV's "so-called 'gods' " strongly suggests that these gods are not rightly so called. The Greek, though, may mean simply "even if there are beings which people call gods . . . ." If the translator adopts a rendering like this, it should not be necessary to enclose "gods" and "lords" in quotation marks. **Lords** refers to nonhuman beings which the Greeks and others in the ancient world considered to be ruling in the area between heaven and earth. Possible renderings are "spiritual rulers" or "powerful spiritual beings."

The **gods** and **lords** were supernatural beings whom the Greeks considered to inhabit the region between heaven and earth. Paul's argument, though, is that even if such beings exist, God is supreme in the universe.

The first half of this verse may be restructured as follows: "Some people say that there are gods who live in the heaven and earth. Even though there are many of these so-called gods . . . ."

yet for us there is one God, the Father, from whom are all things and for whom we exist, and one Lord, Jesus Christ, through whom are all things and through whom we exist.	yet there is for us only one God, the Father, who is the Creator of all things and for whom we live; and there is only one Lord, Jesus Christ, through whom all things were created and through whom we live.

Comparison between verses 5 and 6 shows that emphasis in verse 6 must fall on **for us**, which has no counterpart in verse 5. "Only" is added by TEV to give appropriate emphasis to **one**.

RSV and TEV are right to translate the Greek rather literally, for the stress is on **one God** rather than on **Father**. The context also suggests that here **Father** means much the same as "the Creator" (TEV) and does not have the specifically Christian meaning of "Father of our Lord Jesus Christ."

The difference of prepositions in **for whom** and **through whom** is also in the Greek text. God has made us "through" or "by means of" Christ, and he has made us for himself. For the thought of verse 6a, see Deuteronomy 10.17.

Verse 6b **and one Lord . . .** may be a quotation from a very early Christian confession. One can translate this as "and we believe that there is only one Lord . . . ." **Lord, Jesus Christ through whom are all things . . .** will need to be rendered in many languages as: "Lord, Jesus Christ, through whom God created all things."

The clause **through whom we exist** may be rendered in an idiomatic way; for example, "all we Christians walk our lives through (dependent on) him." Or one may begin a new sentence at this point; for example, "He enables all us Christians to live our lives."

Verses 5-6 form a single sentence in Greek, as in RSV and TEV. Other translations find it more natural to divide the sentence; for example, ItCL:

> It is true that people speak about certain divinities in heaven and in earth; and indeed there are many of these "gods" and "lords." For us, however, there is only one God and Father. He has created all things, and it is by him that we live. And there is one Lord, Jesus Christ, by means of whom all things exist. And we live by means of him.

However, not all possess this knowledge. But some, through being hitherto accustomed to idols, eat food as really offered to an idol; and their conscience, being weak, is defiled.	But not everyone knows this truth. Some people have been so used to idols that to this day when they eat such food they still think of it as food that belongs to an idol; their conscience is weak, and they feel they are defiled by the food.

From here to verse 13, as the paragraph division in the UBS Greek text suggests, Paul turns to another aspect of the same question, that of the "weaker brethren." These are the less mature Christians for whom idols still have some real existence.

This before **knowledge** is implied. The meaning is "not everyone has this mature kind of knowledge of which we have been speaking."

Both the text and the meaning of the words translated **some . . . to idols** are uncertain. The UBS Greek text is literally "but some in the custom until now of the idol as meat-offered-to idols eat." Instead of "custom" many manuscripts have "conscience," which is a similar word in Greek. But this text is almost certainly influenced by the fact that **conscience** occurs later in the verse. "Custom" is the most likely word here. It is clear that **an idol** refers to idols in general, not to a particular idol. Some translations spell out in greater detail what is meant by **being . . . accustomed to idols,** either "idolatry" (NEB), or more generally "the old ideas" (GeCL). The danger of the translation "idolatry" is that it might wrongly suggest that these Christians were still taking part in the worship of idols. A possible translation is, then, "Some people have been so used in the past to worshiping idols, that to this day . . . ." "To this day" refers, not directly to eating meat sacrificed to idols, but to being used to a former way of thinking about idols.

The sentence **their conscience, being weak, is defiled** may be translated "because their conscience is weak, they feel that they are defiled . . . ."

Paul uses the word **conscience** frequently in this letter; see also 8.10,12; 10.25,27; 2 Corinthians 1.12; 4.2; 5.11. Its original meaning was "consciousness." It is especially used of a bad conscience, that its, the consciousness of having done something wrong. In this verse the meaning **conscience** and "consciousness" are combined, as TEV's addition of the words "they feel" shows. Many languages must express the idea of **conscience** with a phrase. In such cases one may say, for example, "their ability to discern between right and wrong is weak, and they feel . . ." or "they have difficulty deciding between what is right and wrong, and they feel . . . ."

8.8	RSV	TEV

Food will not commend us to God. We are no worse off if we do not eat, and no better off if we do.

Food, however, will not improve our relation with God; we shall not lose anything if we do not eat, nor shall we gain anything if we do eat.

The word for **Food** is quite general, referring to anything that is eaten.

Will not commend us to God: the image is that of making someone able to stand upright, as in the presence of the king. This clause may be rendered as "will not make us have a better relationship with God" or "will not cause God to accept us more than he did before."

No worse off and **no better off** are nonfigurative translations of the Greek, which carries on the reference to feeding: "We neither go without anything if we do not eat, nor do we have plenty if we eat."

RSV   TEV

Only take care lest this liberty of yours   Be careful, however, not to let
somehow become a stumbling block to   your freedom of action make those who
the weak.   are weak in the faith fall into sin.

The language of this verse is hesitant: "But be careful lest perhaps this
power of yours . . . ."

The word translated **liberty** may mean "power," "authority," or even
"rights." It is a theme which becomes important in chapter 9, where Paul discusses his own rights as an apostle.

The weak are Christians, as the context makes plain. One may also translate this phrase as "fellow Christians whose faith is weak."

The word for **stumbling block** is sometimes used to describe the result
which teaching about Jesus has on those who do not accept it (Rom 9.32-33;
1 Peter 2.8). Essentially, though, it means the same as another word for "stumbling block" used in 1 Corinthians 1.23 (see the comments). The reference was
originally to the Old Testament law against making a blind man stumble by putting
some object in his path. However, this language was widely used in the New
Testament with the wider sense of making someone "fall into sin" (for example,
Matt 18.6) or bringing about someone's spiritual destruction (see verse 11). Some
languages cannot speak of "falling into sin." In such cases one may say "sin by
eating such food."

8.10   RSV   TEV

For if any one sees you, a man of   Suppose a person whose conscience is
knowledge, at table in an idol's temple,   weak in this matter sees you, who have
might he not be encouraged, if his   so-called "knowledge," eating in the
conscience is weak, to eat food offered   temple of an idol; will not this encour-
to idols?   age him to eat food offered to idols?

The two main problems in understanding this verse are related. (a) Some
early manuscripts omit **you,** giving the meaning ". . . sees someone who has knowledge . . . ." The UBS Greek text has **you.** (b) The word which is translated **encouraged** is used elsewhere by Paul in the good sense of "building up," as in verse
1, but here it has a bad meaning.

We can resolve both these difficulties if we suppose that in this verse Paul
is presenting the point of view of someone at Corinth, perhaps expressed in a
letter from the Christians there. The meaning would then be " 'But,' you say, 'if
anyone sees someone who has knowledge eating in an idol's temple, will his weak
conscience not be strengthened, so that he can eat meat offered to idols?' "

There are two slight difficulties in this explanation which commentators
generally have overlooked: (a) The conjunction which connects verse 10 with 9
means "for," not "but," and this word often has a weak and rather general sense.
(b) As in verse 7, one might have expected Paul to use the pagan word for "meat"
offered to divinities (compare 10.28). However, the writers of the letter from
Corinth were Christians like Paul himself, and therefore would use a term which
expressed the negative Christian view of other gods.

If the translator rejects the explanation given in the last two paragraphs and adopts the longer text, which has **sees you,** "encourage" is probably the best translation of the verb for "build up."

The word translated **at table** literally means "reclining." This was the normal position at table in the Roman world. Modern day translators will need to think of their own customs for eating. In many languages the word for "eat" will probably be the best equivalent.

The clause **might he not be encouraged** will need to be slightly changed in certain languages. One may say, for example, "This will encourage him . . . , won't it?"

The Greek has "the" before **food offered to idols,** indicating that Paul has already mentioned the food or meat in question.

8.11	RSV	TEV
	And so by your knowledge this weak man is destroyed, the brother for whom Christ died.	And so this weak person, your brother for whom Christ died, will perish because of your "knowledge"!

And so is literally "for," carrying on the thought of verse 10 as a whole rather than stating the direct result of verse 10b.

Your before **knowledge** is strongly emphasized in the Greek text. One can translate this as "this knowledge of yours."

This weak man may be expressed as "this Christian with small faith" or "this person who believes in Christ weakly."

It is better to keep the phrase **the brother for whom Christ died** at the end of the verse, as in RSV, in order to emphasize it. This phrase also stands as a new idea in this context. GeCL brings this point out by keeping the original order, but by dividing the sentence, making the second part "and yet he is your brother for whom Christ died."

Brother, of course, means "fellow Christian" as in 1.1 and many other places.

8.12	RSV	TEV
	Thus, sinning against your brethren and wounding their conscience when it is weak, you sin against Christ.	And in this way you will be sinning against Christ by sinning against your Christian brothers and wounding their weak conscience.

Sinning, a present tense in the Greek, is expressed as future in TEV in order to remind readers that since verse 10 ("Suppose") Paul has been claiming that he is discussing a hypothetical or imaginary case, not a real one.

Wounding their conscience when it is weak does not mean that there are some times when a person's conscience is weak, and other times when the same person's conscience may be strong. TEV's more literal translation, "wounding their weak conscience," is closer to the meaning of the Greek. In some languages it may not be natural to speak of wounding someone's conscience, and a more general expression may be better, such as "hurting their weak conscience" or "doing harm to their weak conscience." For the meaning of the Greek word translated "conscience," see comments on verse 7.

In this verse, as in verse 11, a translator needs to find a way of emphasizing the words **you sin against Christ.** TEV has lost this emphasis by rearranging the sentence to produce a more flowing English style. One may maintain this emphasis by restructuring the verse slightly as follows: "When you commit sin against your fellow Christians and damage their consciences like this, you actually sin against Christ."

In this verse, in contrast to verse 11, **you** is plural, but there is no difference in meaning, since "brother" in verse 11 means "any fellow Christian."

<table>
<tr><td>8.13</td><td>RSV</td><td>TEV</td></tr>
</table>

RSV	TEV
Therefore, if food is a cause of my brother's falling, I will never eat meat, lest I cause my brother to fall.	**So then, if food makes my brother sin, I will never eat meat again, so as not to make my brother fall into sin.**

This verse appears to introduce a more general thought, since it refers to **meat** in general, not specifically to meat offered to idols. The two words are not related in Greek. It is true that the general word for **food** has already been used in verse 8. In Romans 14.2,21 Paul refers to Christians whose conscience forbade them to eat any meat at all. So it is possible that there were similar people in the church in Corinth. Some Christians may have refused to eat any meat in order to be sure of not eating meat which had been dedicated to idols.

The words **my brother's falling** and **my brother to fall** continue the image of destroying someone by making him stumble (compare verse 9).

Chapter 9

All translators, especially those working in languages which distinguish between an inclusive and an exclusive "we," should consider carefully Paul's use of personal pronouns throughout this chapter. In one or two verses in which Paul either uses illustrations from other walks of life (verses 7,13,24-25a) or applies these illustrations (verse 14), he employs the third person. Occasionally, especially in verses 13a and 24, he addresses the readers directly in the second person. In most of chapter 9, however, he uses the first person, either singular (verses 1-3,6,8,15-23,26-27) or plural (verses 4-5,10-11,25b). In verse 6 Paul explicitly states that the "we" refers to himself and Barnabas. This verse is so closely connected in thought, grammar, and style with verses 4-5 that it is reasonable to suppose that the "we" of verses 4-5 also excludes the readers. However, since verse 5 distinguishes between "we" and "the other apostles and the brothers of the Lord and Cephas," TEV, GeCL, and NEB think that in these verses Paul's "we" really means "I." Many translations, including RSV, DuCL, ItCL, JB, and TNT disagree, keeping the "we" in translation.

In verse 8 he clearly uses "I." However, in verse 10 all translations which we have consulted think that Paul is including other unnamed evangelists as well as himself, and all these translations have "we," "us," or "our." This verse is closely linked with verse 11. Paul is probably speaking in verse 10 of other evangelists, rather than applying the quotation in verse 9 to the general situation of Christians. The thought is similar to that of verse 14, where Paul refers to evangelists in the third person. On the other hand, the "we" of verse 25 occurs in a context which, as chapter 10 confirms, refers no longer to evangelists only, but to Christians in general, so it is an inclusive "we."

In the light of verses 10-12a, all translators except GeCL take the "we" in 12b to be an exclusive plural which refers to Paul and the other evangelists. GeCL notes that the thought of verse 12b is partly summarized in verse 15, which uses the first person singular. So GeCL uses the singular "I" in 12b, as in verses 10-12a also. However, the change in thought in verse 12b does not appear to involve a reference to different people. In the light of verse 6 it is probably better to use an exclusive "we" in verse 12b also.

In conclusion, therefore, we can say that there is no pure evidence that Paul uses "we" to mean "I" in this chapter. Nor can we be sure that, as Paul's thought moves backward and forward between himself and his fellow evangelists, he uses personal pronouns and related verb forms very carefully.

RSV	9.1-12a	TEV

Rights and Duties of an Apostle

1 Am I not free? Am I not an apostle? Have I not seen Jesus our

1 Am I not a free man? Am I not an apostle? Haven't I seen Jesus

Lord? Are not you my workmanship in the Lord? 2 If to others I am not an apostle, at least I am to you; for you are the seal of my apostleship in the Lord.

3 This is my defense to those who would examine me. 4 Do we not have the right to our food and drink? 5 Do we not have the right to be accompanied by a wife,[n] as the other apostles and the brothers of the Lord and Cephas? 6 Or is it only Barnabas and I who have no right to refrain from working for a living? 7 Who serves as a soldier at his own expense? Who plants a vineyard without eating any of its fruit? Who tends a flock without getting some of the milk?

8 Do I say this on human authority? Does not the law say the same? 9 For it is written in the law of Moses, "You shall not muzzle an ox when it is treading out the grain." Is it for oxen that God is concerned? 10 Does he not speak entirely for our sake? It was written for our sake, because the plowman should plow in hope and the thresher thresh in hope of a share in the crop. 11 If we have sown spiritual good among you, is it too much if we reap your material benefits? 12 If others share this rightful claim upon you, do not we still more?

[n]Greek *a sister as wife*

our Lord? And aren't you the result of my work for the Lord? 2 Even if others do not accept me as an apostle, surely you do! Because your life in union with the Lord you yourselves are proof of the fact that I am an apostle.

3 When people criticize me, this is how I defend myself: 4 Don't I have the right to to be given food and drink for my work? 5 Don't I have the right to follow the example of the other apostles and the Lord's brothers and Peter, by taking a Christian wife with me on my trips? 6 Or are Barnabas and I the only ones who have to work for our living? 7 What soldier ever has to pay his own expenses in the army? What farmer does not eat the grapes from his own vineyard? What shepherd does not use the milk from his own sheep?

8 I don't have to limit myself to these everyday examples, because the Law says the same thing. 9 We read in the Law of Moses, "Do not muzzle an ox when you are using it to thresh grain." Now, is God concerned about oxen? 10 Didn't he really mean us when he said that? Of course that was written for us. The man who plows and the man who reaps should do their work in the hope of getting a share of the crop. 11 We have sown spiritual seed among you. Is it too much if we reap material benefits from you? 12 If others have the right to expect this from you, don't we have an even greater right?

We discussed the relation of chapter 9 to chapters 8 and 10 in the introduction to chapter 8. We have divided the chapter in the middle of verse 12 partly for convenience, and partly because it is at this point that Paul seems to turn away from the theme of the rights and duties of an apostle. The TEV section heading is in this respect better than that of the UBS Greek text, which has simply "The Rights of an Apostle."

The difference of theme between the two parts of chapter 9 seem to correspond in a broad way to a change in style. Verses 1-12a are dominated by a series of rhetorical questions (no less than 15 of them, according to the UBS Greek text). In the rest of the chapter (verses 13, 18, and 24), rhetorical questions are no more frequent than usual in Paul's writings. On the problem of translating rhetorical questions in general, see comments on 1.13. Most of the questions in this section are negative in form and are thus equivalent to strong positive statements. In verses 6, 7, 10, and 11, they are positive in form and thus expect the answer "No." At one or two points, which we mention in the detailed comments below, it is not certain whether a statement or a question is intended. Where there are questions in these verses, they are directed toward the readers rather than to express any doubt in Paul's mind.

Verse 4 establishes a verbal link with 8.9 by repeating the Greek word translated "right" in this verse and "liberty" in 8.9. The same word is repeated in verses 12a and 12b, and links the two parts of chapter 9. As the example of TEV shows, this verbal link does not mean that in all languages the Greek word must be translated in these four places in the same way. We discuss its meaning in comments on the individual verses.

A further possible link between 9.4 and the theme of chapter 8 is mentioned in the comments on verse 4.

9.1	RSV	TEV

Am I not free? Am I not an apostle?   Have I not seen Jesus our Lord? Are not you my workmanship in the Lord?

Am I not a free man? Am I not an apostle?   Haven't I seen Jesus our Lord? And aren't you the result of my work for the Lord?

Free: what Paul means by this word is decided by the context. (1) The preceding verses suggest that it means "free to eat and drink what I like" (see the comments on verse 4). (2) Verses 5-12a and possibly verse 4 refer to the apostles' rights over the congregations they served. So **free** in verse 1 may therefore mean "free from the obligation to work for my living." Alternative (2) seems to be the more likely meaning. The rhetorical question **Am I not free?** can be rendered by the statement "I am a free man!" In fact all the questions in this verse may be rendered as statements in languages which do not use rhetorical questions.

TEV's "the result of" is implicit; compare 3.13, where TEV rightly adds "the quality of" before "each man's work." See also 2 Corinthians 3.2-3. Paul is not speaking here of his work as an apostle in itself, but of its result in the founding of a Christian community in Corinth.

In the Lord means in this context "by the Lord working through me" (Héring). **My workmanship in the Lord** may be rendered as in TEV, "the result of my work for the Lord," or "the result of the Lord working through me."

9.2	RSV	TEV

If to others I am not an apostle, at least I am to you; for you are the seal of my apostleship in the Lord.

Even if others do not accept me as an apostle, surely you do! Because of your life in union with the Lord you yourselves are proof of the fact that I am an apostle.

Emphasis in this verse falls on the words **to others** and **to you.** Paul is not thinking objectively about who is or is not really an apostle, but about whether or not the Christians at Corinth have accepted him as an apostle. The contrast between **others** and **you** suggests that the **others** are outside the Christian community at Corinth, or at least outside the group to which Paul is writing. They are probably the same as those "who would examine" Paul in verse 3. The clause **If to others I am not an apostle** can be rendered as "Even if others do not recognize that I am an apostle" or ". . . do not recognize that I am a messenger from Jesus Christ." **At least I am to you** may be phrased as "I am sure that you recognize that I am an apostle."

The second part of verse 2, from **for you are the seal . . .**, can be analyzed grammatically in various ways. It is clear that **seal** or "proof" (TEV) means evidence or confirmation that Paul is a real apostle. The problem arises with the last four words, literally "you are in the Lord," which are the same as the end of verse 1. If they are understood here also as "through the Lord," the meaning would be "you are my proof of my work as an apostle for the Lord." Brc translates "the fact that you are Christians is the seal which guarantees that I genuinely am an apostle." Translations which follow the order of the Greek, such as RSV, link **in the Lord** with **apostleship**. The parallel with verse 1 is an argument in favor of RSV's rendering, but it is impossible for us to be certain. A possible rephrasing of this sentence is "The fact that you yourselves live in union with the Lord proves that I am an apostle."

9.3   RSV   TEV

This is my defense to those who would examine me.	**When people criticize me, this is how I defend myself:**

The two key words of this verse, **defense** and **examine**, are taken from the language of the law courts. See also the comments on 2.4. Phps starts a new paragraph with verse 4, taking Paul's "defense" to consist of verses 1-3. This makes excellent sense.[1] In this case, the evidence in Paul's defense will not be his own argument but the fact of the existence of the church at Corinth. However, the word **This** occurs at the end of the Greek sentence. This fact is generally taken to suggest that **This** refers to what follows (see TEV), and that is probably the better way to translate this verse.

Most commentaries and translations which we have consulted understand verse 3 to refer to what follows, as TEV's colon shows. Verses 4-12a may not sound like a defense when they are read by themselves, but they do when they are seen in the light of verses 12b-27. Another way to phrase this verse is "I use the following things to defend myself when people criticize me."

9.4   RSV   TEV

Do we not have the right to our food and drink?	**Don't I have the right to to be given food and drink for my work?**

In verses 1-3 Paul has used singular forms corresponding to "I" and "me." In verses 4 and 5 he uses the plural forms **we** and **our**. Verse 6 speaks explicitly of "Barnabas and I" (singular), followed, of course, by a plural verb. The change from singular to plural at the beginning of verse 4 may be intended to prepare the way

---

[1] This arrangement is also defended by K. Nickel, 1974, "A parenthetical apologia: 1 Corinthians 9: 1-3," Currents in Theology and Mission 1.68-70. Compare the Spanish interconfessional translation, *La Biblia interconfesional: Nuevo Testamento.*

for reference to other apostles as well as Paul. So the translation **we** should be used here.

If we understand this verse in the light of what Paul said in chapter 8, particularly 8.13, it will mean "Do we not have the right to eat and drink whatever we like?" But if verse 4 is understood in the light of the following verses, it is more likely to mean "Do we not have the right to eat and drink free of charge?" Many translations such as RSV leave this question open and general. Those which make a choice agree with TEV. Mft, for example, says "Have we no right to eat and drink at the expense of the churches?" FrCL says "Do I not have the right to receive food and drink for my work?"

The phrases **right to** or "right to be given" (TEV) may be rephrased as "right to receive."

In certain languages **food and drink** may be translated more generally as "food."

It seems that the translator is justified in making explicit the expression "for my work" (TEV). It may be rendered as "for the work that I have done." In some languages this rhetorical question may be rendered as a statement: "We have the right to receive food and drink for our work."

9.5	RSV	TEV
	Do we not have the right to be accompanied by a wife,[n] as the other apostles and the brothers of the Lord and Cephas?	Don't I have the right to follow the example of the other apostles and the Lord's brothers and Peter, by taking a Christian wife with me on my trips?

[n] Greek *a sister as wife*

This rhetorical question is similar in form to that in verse 4. The translations **wife** or "sister as wife" (RSV footnote) are too literal, for in many cultures the word "sister" would be misunderstood. Therefore TEV's translation "Christian wife" is preferable.[2]

The language of the first half of the Greek sentence is condensed. This is typical of Paul's writing. He expresses two thoughts: (a) "Do I not have the right to marry on condition that my wife is a Christian?" and (b) "Do I not have the right to take my wife with me on my travels?"

The other apostles probably means "other than myself." There is no doubt that Paul included Peter among the apostles, and this verse suggests that Paul also considered that the brothers of Jesus were apostles.

Here **brothers** means literally men who have at least the same father (contrast 1.1, for example).

As in 1.12, it is better to translate **Cephas** as "Peter" (TEV).

In many languages this verse will need to be considerably restructured as TEV has done. Another way to render it is "Since the other apostles and the Lord's brothers and Peter take their wives with them when they travel, I have this right too."

---

[2] Some manuscripts omit the word for "sister," possibly correctly. See J.B. Bauer, 1959, "Uxores circumducere (1 Kor 9.5)," Biblische Zeitschrift 3.94-102. The UBS text includes it.

RSV   TEV

Or is it only Barnabas and I who have no   Or are Barnabas and I the only ones who
right to refrain from working for a   have to work for our living?
living?

The first word of this verse, **Or,** suggests that the verse offers an alternative to verses 4 and 5. This supports the view that these two verses are also
concerned with the support of the apostles and their families by the churches.
    Is it only Barnabas and I is literally "only (singular) I and Barnabas." But
Paul's grammar is not always strictly correct (see comments on 7.34). It is possible to translate the first part of this verse as "or are Barnabas and I the only
apostles who . . . ."
    The phrase **working for a living** may be expressed also as "have to earn
money by working."

9.7   RSV   TEV

Who serves as a soldier at his own   What soldier ever has to pay his own
expense? Who plants a vineyard with-   expenses in the army? What farmer
out eating any of its fruit? Who tends a   does not eat the grapes from his own
flock without getting some of the milk?   vineyard? What shepherd does not use
                                        the milk from his own sheep?

An apostle has a right to be supported by the churches. Paul illustrates this
right by comparisons with various kinds of secular work. The form of each part of
the verse is generally similar to the others, though the second and third resemble
one another more closely than the first and are linked by "or" in Greek.
    In the first part of the verse, the word translated **expense** in New Testa-
ment times generally meant "wages"; but in this context the idea of "expenses" is
preferable.
    The second part of the sentence does not explicitly use the words "farmer"
or "his own" (TEV), nor does the third part speak explicitly about the owner of a
flock of sheep. Paul is more likely thinking of a farm worker and a shepherd, that
is, people employed by someone else, as RSV seems to understand this verse. Such
an interpretation would make a better parallel to 7a: **Who serves as a soldier at his
own expense?** FrCL brings out this possibility: "Did you ever hear of a soldier
serving in the army at his own expense? or a man not eating the grapes from the
vineyard he has planted? or a shepherd not taking milk from the flock he is looking
after?"
    The word translated **getting** (TEV's "use") is literally "eat." Paul may be
including the thought of eating solid products made from milk, but this is not
clearly expressed. Therefore a more general word such as "use" is preferable in
translation.
    Some Greek manuscripts omit the "or" which links the second and third
questions in this verse. It is part of the UBS Greek text but may be omitted in
translation, as in RSV and TEV, if it is not good style.
    In many languages translators will prefer to translate the three rhetorical
questions in this verse as statements. For example, the first question may be
rendered as "A soldier never has to pay his own expenses."

The expressions **Who serves as a soldier**, **Who plants a vineyard**, and **Who tends the flock** are difficult to translate in some languages. In such cases one may say "Does any soldier . . ." and so on.

9.8	RSV	TEV

Do I say this on human author-ity? Does not the law say the same?

I don't have to limit myself to these everyday examples, because the Law says the same thing.

This verse forms a transition between the everyday examples of verse 7 and the argument from scripture in verse 9.

It is difficult to know where to place the question marks in this verse (see punctuation notes in the UBS Greek text). Most translations take the second half of the verse to be a rhetorical question, since it is introduced by "or" in the Greek, a word which commonly introduces rhetorical questions.

It is not certain whether the first sentence is a rhetorical question or not.[3] TEV, however, translates both parts of the verse as statements. Translators may do well to follow TEV's lead here.

The words which RSV translates **on human authority** mean "in a human way," "from a human standpoint." TEV's "everyday examples" and ItCL's "examples from human experience" help to make a good contrast with **the law** in the second half of the verse. The **law** refers to the five books of the Law in the Old Testament, so TEV capitalizes "the Law." Some translations which do not use capitalization may need to say "law written by Moses."

Some languages cannot talk about the Law as "speaking" or "saying." In such cases the translator can say "The same thing is written in the Law" or "You can find the same thing in the book of God's Law."

Although the two Greek verbs which RSV translates **say** are different, they are probably used for variety with no difference in meaning.

9.9	RSV	TEV

For it is written in the law of Moses, "You shall not muzzle an ox when it is treading out the grain." Is it for oxen that God is concerned?

We read in the Law of Moses, "Do not muzzle an ox when you are using it to thresh grain." Now, is God concerned about oxen?

For, which TEV omits, introduces the quotation for which verse 8b has laid the basis. A translator may put in such a connective to show the relationship between 8b and the quotation in verse 9.

Some languages may need to restructure **it is written in the law of Moses** to "the Law which Moses wrote" or "the Law handed on by Moses." The whole phrase may also be rendered in a way similar to that found in TEV: "We read in the Law which Moses wrote." In any case, the translator must take care not to give the impression that Moses made the Law on his own authority.

---

3 By New Testament times it is impossible to draw any firm conclusion from the fact that different Greek negatives are used in the two halves of the verse. See Moulton-Howard-Turner Vol. 3, pages 281-283.

This quotation is taken from Deuteronomy 25.4. The same verse is quoted more accurately but with little difference of meaning in 1 Timothy 5.18. Paul is quoting an Old Testament verse which describes a Hebrew cultural event, the use of an ox to thresh the grain. In many languages it will be helpful to use as generic a translation as possible, if animals in particular cultures do not thresh the grain by treading on it. In such cases a translation like TEV's "when you are using it to thresh grain" will be satisfactory. However, in some cultures where a completely different method is employed for threshing grain, a cultural note will be helpful. In any case, Paul is using this Old Testament verse almost as a parable to explain a principle relating to humans (see verse 10).

It will be helpful for a translator to use an expression similar to TEV's "Now" to begin the second part of the verse. The expressions "In this example" or "In this case" can also be used. Such an addition will help to explain what Paul means by the word **concerned**. He does not mean that God is not in any way responsible for animals, but that in the verse which he has quoted, God is more **concerned** for us, as he explains in verse 10. The translator as such is not concerned with the question of whether Paul understands the Old Testament text and the intention of its writer correctly. There is no basis for such translations as "is God primarily (or, only) concerned about oxen?" But see comments on verse 10.

9.10	RSV	TEV

Does he not speak entirely for our sake? It was written for our sake, because the plowman should plow in hope and the thresher thresh in hope of a share in the crop.

Didn't he really mean us when he said that? Of course that was written for us. The man who plows and the man who reaps should do their work in the hope of getting a share of the crop.

The last part of verse 9 and the first part of verse 10 are closely linked and complementary, joined in the Greek by the word "or." The difficulty with verse 10a is that Paul says "Or does he speak entirely for our sakes?" rather than "Or does he not speak entirely for our sakes?" There is therefore no direct basis in the Greek text for TEV's negative question, "Didn't he . . . ?" NEB's "Or is the reference clearly to ourselves?" is closer in meaning; similarly RSV's **entirely**.

The relation between the rest of verse 10 and the first sentence is uncertain. The meaning may be either (a) "it was written for our sake in order that the plowman should plow in hope . . ." or (b) "for it was written for our sake that the plowman should plow in hope . . . ." In the first case the words about the plowman and the thresher are a commentary on the text just quoted. In the second case Paul is making a quotation from a source outside the Bible. Most translations which we consulted, including RSV and TEV, prefer (a).

In the crop is implied in the Greek and should be introduced in most languages.

9.11	RSV	TEV

If we have sown spiritual good among you, is it too much if we reap your material benefits?

We have sown spiritual seed among you. Is it too much if we reap material benefits from you?

At this point in Paul's argument, **we** probably means not only Paul and Barnabas, as in verse 6, but the apostles or evangelists generally. In any case, Paul is excluding his readers.

This rhetorical question may be restructured as follows: "We have sown spiritual seed among you, therefore it is not too much to expect that we should harvest material benefits from you." The **spiritual good,** literally "spiritual things," is essentially the Christian message. The phrase **sown spiritual good among you** may also be rendered as "sown good things in your hearts" or "sown spiritual things in your hearts."

The phrase **is it too much** may be translated as "is it unfair to" or "is it an unfair thing to."

The **material benefits,** literally "the fleshly things," are material support for evangelists and their families, as verses 4-7 make clear. Verse 11 slightly changes the agricultural language of verse 10. In some languages and cultures it may be preferable to use nonfigurative expressions, where **reap,** "harvest," or similar metaphors would not be naturally used in this way. One may say "If we have placed spiritual things in your hearts, is it too much to expect you to give us material benefits in return?"

9.12a   RSV   TEV

If others share this rightful claim upon   **If others have the right to expect this**
you, do not we still more?   **from you, don't we have an even**
                                                greater right?

A literal translation of this verse would be "If others share (as at the end of verse 10) this right (as in verses 4 and 5) over you, do we not more?" The meaning may be that other people, perhaps other evangelists, claim to share with Paul the right to be supported by the church. However, the verb for **share** more commonly has as its object something more concrete than a "right" (TEV). More probably, Paul means that other evangelists claim the right to a share in the Corinthian Christians' possessions. This meaning would fit the context excellently, as Phps shows: "and if there are others with the right to have these (material) things from you, have not we an even greater right?"

Verse 12a concludes the defense which Paul announced in verse 3. Verses 4-12a have been Paul's way of saying "I have the right as an apostle to have the churches support me." The theme of the second part of Paul's defense is announced in verse 12b.

                RSV   **9.12b-18**   TEV

12b Nevertheless, we have not
made use of this right, but we endure
anything rather than put an obstacle in
the way of the gospel of Christ. 13 Do
you not know that those who are employed in the temple service get their
food from the temple, and those
who serve at the altar share in the
sacrificial offerings? 14 In the same

12b But we haven't made use of
this right. Instead, we have endured
everything in order not to put any
obstacle in the way of the Good News
about Christ. 13 Surely you know that
the men who work in the Temple get
their food from the Temple and that
those who offer the sacrifices on the
altar get a share of the sacrifices.

way, the Lord commanded that those who proclaim the gospel should get their living by the gospel.

15 But I have made no use of any of these rights, nor am I writing this to secure any such provision. For I would rather die than have any one deprive me of my ground for boasting. 16 For if I preach the gospel, that gives me no ground for boasting. For necessity is laid upon me. Woe to me if I do not preach the gospel! 17 For if I do this of my own will, I have a reward; but if not of my own will, I am entrusted with a commission. 18 What then is my reward? Just this: that in my preaching I may make the gospel free of charge, not making full use of my right in the gospel.

14 In the same way, the Lord has ordered that those who preach the gospel should get their living from it.

15 But I haven't made use of any of these rights, nor am I writing this now in order to claim such rights for myself. I would rather die first! Nobody is going to turn my rightful boast into empty words! 16 I have no right to boast just because I preach the gospel. After all, I am under orders to do so. And how terrible it would be for me if I did not preach the gospel! 17 If I did my work as a matter of free choice, then I could expect to be paid; but I do it as a matter of duty, because God has entrusted me with this task. 18 What pay do I get, then? It is the privilege of preaching the Good News without charging for it, without claiming my rights in my work for the gospel.

Generally speaking, from this point on Paul turns to the second aspect of his "defense" (see verse 3), namely, the fact that he does not use his right to be financially supported by the churches. However, the break with verses 4-12a is not complete. Not only does he continue to refer to his **right** (see also verse 18), but verses 13-14 really belong to the first stage of the argument. In these verses Paul argues that, like other evangelists, he has the inescapable duty of preaching the gospel; but he is proud of doing something extra as well. This "extra" is that he does not claim the support to which he is entitled from the churches. In other words Paul is attempting to prove that he is an apostle like anyone else, even though he does not use his right to receive material help from the Corinthian Christians.

9.12b   RSV   TEV

Nevertheless, we have not made use of this right, but we endure anything rather than put an obstacle in the way of the gospel of Christ.

But we haven't made use of this right. Instead, we have endured everything in order not to put any obstacle in the way of the Good News about Christ.

We: see verse 4 for a discussion on the use of plural pronouns in this chapter.

We have not made use of this right may be rendered as "But we haven't tried to gain material benefits from you as is our right," or "We have the right to expect material benefits from you, but we haven't used this right." Concerning Paul's **right,** see comments on 8.9; 9.4.

Anything (Greek "all things") is explained by 4.10-13.

The phrase **rather than put** is too complicated for some languages. This may be rendered as "so that we might not put . . . ."

The word translated **obstacle** is not used elsewhere in the Greek Bible, but a related verb is used with the same sense in Romans 15.22; Galatians 5.7; and 1 Thessalonians 2.18. Paul may have preached the gospel without charge in order that no one should misunderstand his motives when he collected money on behalf of Christians in Judea (see 1 Cor 16.1-4).

The gospel of Christ means "the Good News about Christ" (TEV) rather than "the Good News told by Christ."

The phrase **put an obstacle in the way of the gospel of Christ** may be translated as "do anything which will prevent the Good News about Christ from being preached" or "do anything which will prevent people from preaching the Good News about Christ."

9.13 RSV	TEV
Do you not know that those who are employed in the temple service get their food from the temple, and those who serve at the altar share in the sacrificial offerings?	Surely you know that the men who work in the Temple get their food from the Temple and that those who offer the sacrifices on the altar get a share of the sacrifices.

Do you not know may be translated as "I am sure that you know" or "I am certain that you are aware of the fact that."

After the words **Do you not know** (see also 3.16), there follow two clauses which closely parallel each other in Greek and are not linked by any conjunction such as RSV's **and.** This suggests that the two clauses have almost the same meaning. Some scholars think that Paul is referring to priests in the first half of the verse, and Levites in the second. However, at least some of the Old Testament passages which form the background to this verse do not distinguish clearly between priests and Levites (see Num 18.5 and Deut 18.1). It is more likely that Paul says the same thing twice to give greater emphasis. As always in such cases, translators should ask themselves whether such repetition will be good style in their own languages. If not, they should find other ways of conveying emphasis. For example, if the translator judges that Paul is referring to the same people in both cases, it is possible to translate **and those who serve at the altar** as "and when they offer sacrifices . . . they get their share of the sacrifices."

RSV, TEV, and many other translations use the word **temple** twice. The same Greek word is used in both places, but the first time it is plural, literally "the holy things." Some translations make a slight difference in meaning; for example, NEB uses "temple service" and "temple offerings." TNT and Mft have "temple rites" and "temple." It is possible that Paul is thinking particularly of Numbers 18.5, which mentions first the "Holy Place" and then the "altar" (TEV). If this is so, the "holy things" will refer to things used in Temple ritual, and the second reference will be to the Temple itself. RSV's translation is then more correct than TEV's.

The word translated **serve** was used more generally in Greek to mean "to concern oneself with," "to be engaged in." However, it was sometimes used in religious texts, and in this case in the context of **the altar,** so TEV's translation "offer the sacrifices" can be justified.

In the same way, the Lord commanded that those who proclaim the gospel should get their living by the gospel.	In the same way, the Lord has ordered that those who preach the gospel should get their living from it.

This verse appears to refer to the saying of Jesus which is recorded in Matthew 10.10 and Luke 10.7, and is quoted in 1 Timothy 5.18 alongside an Old Testament text (see also Gal 6.6). The sentence does not mean that Jesus gave an order directly to teachers of the gospel, but that he gave instructions concerning how these teachers should support themselves. The Greek has simply "live," but both RSV and TEV correctly expand this to **get their living.** The meaning is determined both by the immediate context and by "get their food" in verse 13. The final phrase **should get their living by the gospel** may also be rendered as "should support themselves from preaching the Good News."

9.15   RSV   TEV

But I have made no use of any of these rights, nor am I writing this to secure any such provision. For I would rather die than have any one deprive me of my ground for boasting.	But I haven't made use of any of these rights, nor am I writing this now in order to claim such rights for myself. I would rather die first! Nobody is going to turn my rightful boast into empty words!

The first words repeat the opening sentence of verse 12b, but Paul is once more speaking in his name alone.

Made . . . use of: this is the same verb which Paul used in 12b.

Rights is implicit in the Greek text, though it is expressed in verse 12. In this verse the Greek has simply "none of these things."

Nor am I writing: the Greek is literally "neither have I written," but this does not mean that Paul is referring to an earlier letter. It was normal in Greek to refer in the past tense to a letter (in this case 1 Corinthians) which, from the reader's point of view, would have been written in the past. The natural English equivalent is "I am writing," and TEV emphasizes this fact by adding "now." However, translators should carefully consider how they use verb tenses and other grammatical devices in letter writing. These may be quite different from English.

This is literally "these things," probably meaning not the whole letter, but the argument of chapter 9.

The phrase **to secure any such provision** is more tactful than TEV's "in order to claim such rights myself." RSV's rendering reflects the Greek more closely. Barrett's translation, "in order that in my case things may be done in this way," gives the flavor of the Greek but expands it a little. All three of these translations are possible, though TEV and Barrett have better English style.

The rest of the second sentence is violently broken off.[4] It is literally "for it is good for me rather to die than—no one will empty my boasting." Some manuscripts and almost all translations attempt to make the break less abrupt in some

---

[4] See R.L. Omanson, 1983, "Some comments about style and meaning, 1 Corinthians 9.15 and 7.10," The Bible Translator 34.135-139.

way. Such broken sentences probably reflect Paul's great emotion and are quite common in his writings.

In the literal translation above there is a great deal of overlap between "good" and "rather," and these may be combined. The clause **I would rather die** may be expressed as "It would be better for me to die than do this." **Any one** does not refer to any particular person or group. And Paul is not suggesting that anyone was trying to make him accept payment.

Deprive me of my ground for boasting can be translated as "take away my reason for boasting." This is almost the last time in the letter that Paul develops the theme of boasting, expressed as a contrast between the Corinthians' wrong boasting (5.6) and the right kind of "boasting" in the Lord (1.31). In the present context this theme is closely linked with the idea of reward mentioned in verses 17-18 (see the comments on 12b). From a human point of view Paul has a right to boast, for he has not accepted payment for his work as an apostle.

9.16	RSV	TEV

For if I preach the gospel, that gives me no ground for boasting. For necessity is laid upon me. Woe to me if I do not preach the gospel!	I have no right to boast just because I preach the gospel. After all, I am under orders to do so. And how terrible it would be for me if I did not preach the gospel!

If we consider Paul's general theme in this chapter, the first part of this verse implies "It is not the fact I am preaching the gospel which in itself gives me reason for boasting." The rest of the verse then explains that to preach the gospel is an obligation, not a matter of free choice.

The first **For** may be expanded to "The truth is" or "Truly."

For **ground of boasting**, see comments on verse 15.

The clause **For necessity is laid upon me** may be rendered as "God has commanded me to do so."

Is laid refers by implication to the action of God in calling Paul to be an apostle (see 1.1).

Woe to me is more than an interjection expressing sorrow; it refers implicitly to future judgment. In that case one can translate this as "How terrible it will be for me." Paul does not use this expression elsewhere, but the translator may compare, for example, Matthew 23.13-23; Luke 6.24-26; and Revelation 18.10-19.

9.17-18	RSV	TEV

For if I do this of my own will, I have a reward; but if not of my own will, I am entrusted with a commission. 18 What then is my reward? Just this: that in my preaching I may make the gospel free of charge, not making full use of my right in the gospel.	If I did my work as a matter of free choice, then I could expect to be paid; but I do it as a matter of duty, because God has entrusted me with this task. 18 What pay do I get, then? It is the privilege of preaching the Good News without charging for it, without claiming my rights in my work for the gospel.

The UBS Greek text, followed by all translations we have consulted, puts a period (.) at the end of verse 17, dividing the verse into two halves. Its structure is as follows: "For if I do this voluntarily, I have a reward; but if (I do it) involuntarily, I have been entrusted with a commission." The difficulty with this structure is that the words **For** and **but**, and especially the related words translated **of my own will** and **not of my own will**, lead the reader to expect a contrast in the last part of each line. However, no contrast is clearly expressed. We can resolve this problem if the first part of verse 18 is linked with verse 17, giving the following structures:

"for if I do this voluntarily   I have a reward

but if involuntarily I receive
a commission from God,   what then is my reward?"

This interpretation is the basis for Phps' translation: "If I do this work because I choose to do so, then I am entitled to a reward. But if it is no choice of mine, but a sacred responsibility put on me, what can I expect in the way of reward?" Phps' translation makes good sense in this context. TEV's rendering is quite similar.

Have a reward may be rendered as "to receive wages."

I am entrusted with a commission means here "God has appointed me to a position of responsibility." The meaning of **entrusted** is similar to that of "faithful" in 1.9 and "trustworthy" in 4.2.

Reward in verse 18 is the more general meaning preferred by many translators. This word makes good sense in the present context. Paul does receive a reward, but of a kind different from financial support. The word translated **reward** sometimes has the more specific meaning of "something extra."

Make . . . free of charge can be rendered as "preach the gospel without asking for any money."

Not making full use of my right can be translated as "I do not claim my rights" or "I do not insist on receiving my rights." **My right** probably refers, not to Paul's general authority as an apostle, but more specifically to his right to be supported by the churches.

In the gospel is too literal. "In preaching the gospel" is a preferable rendering.

RSV	9.19-27	TEV

19 For though I am free from all men, I have made myself a slave to all, that I might win the more. 20 To the Jews I became as a Jew, in order to win Jews; to those under the law I became as one under the law—though not being myself under the law—that I might win those under the law. 21 To those outside the law I became as one outside the law—not being without law toward God but under the law of Christ—that I might win those outside the law. 22 To the weak I became weak, that I might

19 I am a free man, nobody's slave; but I make myself everybody's slave in order to win as many people as possible. 20 While working with the Jews, I live like a Jew in order to win them; and even though I myself am not subject to the Law of Moses, I live as though I were when working with those who are, in order to win them. 21 In the same way, when working with Gentiles, I live like a Gentile, outside the Jewish Law, in order to win Gentiles. This does not mean that I don't

win the weak. I have become all things to all men, that I might by all means save some. 23 I do it all for the sake of the gospel, that I may share in its blessings.

24 Do you not know that in a race all the runners compete, but only one receives the prize? So run that you may obtain it. 25 Every athlete exercises self-control in all things. They do it to receive a perishable wreath, but we an imperishable. 26 Well, I do not run aimlessly, I do not box as one beating the air; 27 but I pommel my body and subdue it, lest after preaching to others I myself should be disqualified.

obey God's law; I am really under Christ's law. 22 Among the weak in faith I become weak like one of them, in order to win them. So I become all things to all men, that I may save some of them by whatever means are possible.

23 All this I do for the gospel's sake, in order to share in its blessings. 24 Surely you know that many runners take part in a race, but only one of them wins the prize. Run, then, in such a way as to win the prize. 25 Every athlete in training submits to strict discipline, in order to be crowned with a wreath that will not last; but we do it for one that will last forever. 26 That is why I run straight for the finish line; that is why I am like a boxer who does not waste his punches. 27 I harden my body with blows and bring it under complete control, to keep myself from being disqualified after having called others to the contest.

Verses 20-22 form a single sentence in Greek. It will probably be necessary to divide it in translation. The general structure of the Greek sentence is as follows: verse 20 consists of two halves which mean essentially the same thing, apart from the parenthetic statement **though not being myself under the law;** verse 21 and the first part of verse 22, as far as **that I might win the weak,** also consists of two parts meaning essentially the same thing. Verses 20-21 refer to non-Jews. The last part of verse 22 rounds off the passage and partly repeats what was said in verse 19. **The gospel** also echoes the end of verse 19. As often, Paul emphasizes his argument by repeating thoughts.

9.19   RSV   TEV

For though I am free from all men, I have made myself a slave to all, that I might win the more.

I am a free man, nobody's slave; but I make myself everybody's slave in order to win as many people as possible.

The words **For** and **free** indicate a connection with verse 4 (see the comments). From this point to the end of the chapter, Paul links together the two main aspects of his defense covered in verses 4-12a and 12b-18.

I am free from all men: men is implicit in the Greek. Other CLTs agree with TEV in giving the meaning in two contrasting statements. Another possibility is to express **free from all** negatively, as for example in TNT, "Although I am no man's slave . . . ," contrasting with the following words, "I have made myself every man's slave." This is no doubt what Paul meant.

The word **all,** corresponding to TEV's "nobody," may mean either "all people" or "all things." However, the context shows that Paul is talking about people.

The exact meaning of **win** is uncertain. The meaning "to win as Christians," suggested by Barrett, fits verses 20 and 21 later in this chapter, where Paul talks about "winning Jews" and winning "those under the law." But if we applied this meaning to verse 22 also, the "weak" ("weak in faith") would have a more general meaning than that in 8.7-17. **Win** could also mean "to make and keep people as Christians to the end," and this would fit in well with chapter 10. It is probably better to leave this phrase ambiguous, as RSV and TEV have done.

The more should probably be rendered "as many people as possible," as in TEV.

<table>
<tr><td>9.20</td><td>RSV</td><td>TEV</td></tr>
</table>

RSV	TEV
To the Jews I became as a Jew, in order to win Jews; to those under the law I became as one under the law—though not being myself under the law—that I might win those under the law.	While working with the Jews, I live like a Jew in order to win them; and even though I myself am not subject to the Law of Moses, I live as though I were when working with those who are, in order to win them.

I became as a Jew: some commentators think that Paul is referring to a single event, perhaps the one recorded in Acts 21.23-36, where Paul and his friends go into the Temple to perform a purification ceremony.

The Jews: a definite article is rare in Paul's writings, and the verb **I became** usually refers to a single past event. However, it is probable that Paul is writing more generally. In that case, TEV's "I live like a Jew" is a preferable English translation and will make the meaning clear in many languages. The present context shows that Paul is thinking of the Jews as a religious group rather than simply as a race. This fact is confirmed by verse 2, where TEV is right to specify that the Law is "the Law of Moses." This is not explicit in the text here, but in verse 9 Paul has mentioned "the law of Moses."

Many Greek manuscripts omit the whole phrase translated **though not being myself under the law,** but there is so much repetition in the Greek text that it would be easy for a scribe's eye to jump from one occurrence of the phrase **under the law** to another.

Some translators may prefer to translate **under the law** as "required to follow (obey) the law."

The final clauses, from **to those under the law,** can be restructured to "I live as though I were required to obey the Law when I work with people who follow that Law, in order to win them to Christ."

<table>
<tr><td>9.21</td><td>RSV</td><td>TEV</td></tr>
</table>

RSV	TEV
To those outside the law I became as one outside the law—not being without law toward God but under the law of Christ—that I might win those outside the law.	In the same way, when working with Gentiles, I live like a Gentile, outside the Jewish Law, in order to win Gentiles. This does not mean that I don't obey God's law; I am really under Christ's law.

Those outside the law means "outside the scope of the Jewish law" rather than not having any law at all. TEV translates this as "Gentiles," and in most languages this is a good rendering.

RSV follows the structure of the Greek text quite literally, leaving the clauses **not being without law . . . the law of Christ** as an aside by Paul. TEV, however, changes the ordering of the sentences. It puts the first part of the verse and the last sentence together into one sentence. This is done to bring out the meaning more clearly. The aside by Paul is then placed at the end of the verse to show that Paul is emphasizing it.

As in verse 20, **I became** should be rendered as "I live" (TEV). It was not just one event in the past, but Paul did this whenever circumstances required it.

I became as one outside the law may be expressed as "I live outside the Jewish Law like a Gentile does" or "I live like a Gentile who does not follow the Jewish Law."

The sentence **not being without law toward God but under the law of Christ** is probably more difficult to interpret than to translate. It is not certain, though, to what Paul refers. There are two main possibilities. (a) The main contrast is between God and Christ, which, though unusual in Paul's writings, is not impossible. (b) Paul contrasts his being completely outside the scope of the Law and yet being subject to law. Most translations choose (a), where Paul throws emphasis toward Christ. An alternative translation would be "it is not that I am outside the scope of God's law; on the contrary, I do live under Christ's law." (Compare Gal 6.2 for a similar thought.)

A sample translation of this verse is as follows:

> In the same way, when I work with Gentiles, I live like a Gentile, not following the Jewish Law. I do this in order to win Gentiles to Christ. This does not mean, however, that I live outside the scope of God's law; on the contrary, I really do follow Christ's law.

9.22 RSV	TEV
To the weak I became weak, that I might win the weak. I have become all things to all men, that I might by all means save some.	**Among the weak in faith I become weak like one of them, in order to win them. So I become all things to all men, that I may save some of them by whatever means are possible.**

In our general comment on verses 20-22 we stated that the first part of verse 22 is close in meaning to verse 21. Paul has already spoken of himself in 2.3 and 4.10 as being weak. Then in 8.7-13 he speaks of weak Christians who had come out of a pagan background. If the **weak** in this chapter are the group discussed in 8.7-13, it is correct to refer to them as "weak in faith" as TEV does. TEV also adds "like one of them," to avoid the suggestion that Paul himself was "weak in faith." In most languages the word **weak** will need to be modified in some way to show the kind of weakness about which Paul is speaking. If possible, the same word for **weak** should be used in both halves of the first sentence, even if this makes the translation more literal than TEV.

Also in the first part of the verse, the word **To** will need to be expanded in translation; for example, "When I am among . . . ." The phrase **weak** or "weak in faith" can be rendered more meaningfully as "people who do not believe in Jesus strongly" or "people whose faith in Jesus is weak."

The second part of the verse sums up the thought of verses 20-22a.

The words **I became** occur twice in this verse. Although the tense in Greek seems to refer to a particular point in the past, the probable meaning is more general: "I become" (TEV) or "I have become and I remain."

The phrase **by all means** may be rendered as "by using every way that I possibly can."

It should be noted that Paul does not use the word "as" (TEV's "like") in this verse as he did in verses 20 and 21. In this verse Paul means that he really has "become weak" (TEV).

9.23   RSV   TEV

I do it all for the sake of the gospel,   **All this I do for the gospel's**
that I may share in its blessings.   **sake, in order to share in its blessings.**

Most translations, except TEV, understand this verse as summing up the previous passage rather than introducing the following section. If translators understand **it** to refer to the content of the previous verses, they should expand the beginning of the verse slightly; for example, "I do all the things I have mentioned because I want the gospel to go forward . . ." or "I do all these things to help the Good News about Jesus to spread."

There is a good reason, though, why TEV links this verse with the following section. The last few words have the theme of sharing or participating in the benefits of the Christian message. Paul prepares for this thought in verses 24-25, and develops the theme more carefully in verses 26-27.

If the translator follows TEV and feels that **it all** points forward, then one may render this verse in the following way: "I do the following things to help the Good News about Jesus spread, so that I will receive a share in the benefits from its message."

In any case, the translator will need to show clearly whether **it all** points backward or points forward.

9.24   RSV   TEV

Do you not know that in a race   Surely you know that many runners take
all the runners compete, but only one   part in a race, but only one of them
receives the prize? So run that you   wins the prize. Run, then, in such a
may obtain it.   way as to win the prize.

As in 3.16 and 9.13, **Do you not know** may be expressed as "I am sure that you know" or "I am sure that you are aware of the fact that." In this verse the above phrase does not introduce traditional Christian teaching but a generally known fact. The Greek of the words following this phrase is literally "those running in a race all run, but one receives the prize." Most translations expand this considerably. "Surely you know" (TEV) should link with the statement **but only one receives the prize.** Another way of expressing the first part of the verse is to combine the first two clauses: "I am sure that you know that only one runner in a race receives the prize."

Paul is not saying that only one Christian will persevere to the end, but that not all are certain to do so.

So run can be translated as "You should run" or "So you must run."

9.25   RSV   TEV

Every athlete exercises self-control in all things. They do it to receive a perishable wreath, but we an imperishable.	**Every athlete in training submits to strict discipline, in order to be crowned with a wreath that will not last; but we do it for one that will last forever.**

The first part of this verse echoes verse 24a, but the second part turns aside from the main thought. **Athlete** translates a Greek word which is more general than "runner" in verse 24 and prepares the way for an illustration about boxing in verse 26b.

Exercises self-control is the same verb used in 7.9 concerning self-control in sexual matters, but in this verse there is no special reference to sexual self-discipline. A phrase such as "disciplines himself very carefully" will be a good translation here.

The word translated **wreath** can also mean "crown." TEV brings this meaning out by adding the verb "crowned" where the Greek only has "will receive." This word has been added because wreaths in many English speaking countries are associated more with funerals than with running competitions. In other parts of the modern world they are placed around the neck, rather than on the head as in Greek custom. The context makes it clear that the text is referring to the prize which a successful athlete receives, not the crown of some ruler.

In Paul's time, winners of the Isthmian games, held near Corinth, were given a wreath of pine. But in earlier times more perishable materials had been used, and this is the point of Paul's illustration.

The phrase **but we an imperishable** will be too abrupt in many languages. Possible translations are "but we do our work to win an imperishable wreath" or "but we run our race to receive a prize which will never fade."

9.26   RSV   TEV

Well, I do not run aimlessly, I do not box as one beating the air;	**That is why I run straight for the finish line; that is why I am like a boxer who does not waste his punches.**

The word translated **Well** (TEV's "That is why") introduces a conclusion which is based on a previous statement.

I is emphasized, not in contrast with anyone else, but to show that Paul is about to apply to himself the illustrations used in verses 24-25.

In some languages it will be good to render **I do not run aimlessly** as a positive statement, "I run straight for the finish line," as TEV has done.

The second half of the verse introduces a new sport, boxing. Inexperienced boxers were said to "beat the air." TEV's restructuring, "does not waste his punches," is a good modern English equivalent of the Greek. Translators need to use an expression which boxers in their own culture employ.

but I pommel my body and subdue it, lest after preaching to others I myself should be disqualified.	I harden my body with blows and bring it under complete control, to keep myself from being disqualified after having called others to the contest.

If in the previous verse the translator used a positive statement for the sentence "I do not run aimlessly," the word **but** will not be necessary to begin this verse.

TEV expands **pommel** to "harden with blows." One may also say "I hit my body to make it hard (tough)."

Body here, as elsewhere, means human nature as a whole, in its weakness, not the literal body. Paul is using a physical metaphor to refer, not only to fasting, scourging, and similar practices, but also to discipline of his complete being.

Lest after (TEV's "to keep myself from being") is literally "in-order-that perhaps not." Both the Greek and the sentence as a whole show that Paul is speaking about a possible situation which is not yet a reality.

After preaching can be rendered as "after I have preached." **Preaching** is used by Paul in its normal Christian meaning of "proclaim the gospel." So RSV's translation is probably better than TEV's less general "after having called others to the contest." NEB, TNT, and even FrCL agree with RSV.[5]

Disqualified (compare 2 Cor 13.5-7) clearly refers to athletic competitions. In languages which do not normally use the passive voice it will help to render **should be disqualified** as "so that God will not disqualify me."

The final sentence of this verse can be translated as "So that God will not disqualify me after I have preached to others" or "So that after I have preached to others, God does not disqualify me."

---

5 FrCL more often agrees with TEV than do GeCL and ItCL.

Chapter 10

Warnings against Idols

RSV

1 I want you to know, brethren, that our fathers were all under the cloud, and all passed through the sea, 2 and all were baptized into Moses in the cloud and in the sea, 3 and all ate the same supernatural[o] food 4 and all drank the same supernatural[o] drink. For they drank from the supernatural[o] Rock which followed them, and the Rock was Christ. 5 Nevertheless with most of them God was not pleased; for they were overthrown in the wilderness.

6 Now these things are warnings for us, not to desire evil as they did. 7 Do not be idolaters as some of them were; as it is written, "The people sat down to eat and drink and rose up to dance." 8 We must not indulge in immorality as some of them did, and twenty-three thousand fell in a single day. 9 We must not put the Lord[p] to the test, as some of them did and were destroyed by serpents; 10 nor grumble, as some of them did and were destroyed by the Destroyer. 11 Now these things happened to them as a warning, but they were written down for our instruction, upon whom the end of the ages has come. 12 Therefore let any one who thinks that he stands take heed lest he fall. 13 No temptation has overtaken you that is not common to man. God is faithful, and he will not let you be tempted beyond your strength, but with the temptation will also provide the way of escape, that you may be able to endure it.

[o] Greek *spiritual*
[p] Other ancient authorities read *Christ*

TEV

1 I want you to remember, my brothers, what happened to our ancestors who followed Moses. They were all under the protection of the cloud, and all passed safely through the Red Sea. 2 In the cloud and in the sea they were all baptized as followers of Moses. 3 All ate the same spiritual bread 4 and drank the same spiritual drink. They drank from the spiritual rock that went with them; and that rock was Christ himself. 5 But even then God was not pleased with most of them, and so their dead bodies were scattered over the desert.

6 Now, all of this is an example for us, to warn us not to desire evil things, as they did, 7 nor to worship idols, as some of them did. As the scripture says, "The people sat down to a feast which turned into an orgy of drinking and sex." 8 We must not be guilty of sexual immorality, as some of them were—and in one day twenty-three thousand of them fell dead. 9 We must not put the Lord[m] to the test, as some of them did—and they were killed by snakes. 10 We must not complain, as some of them did—and they were destroyed by the Angel of Death.

11 All these things happened to them as examples for others, and they were written down as a warning for us. For we live at a time when the end is about to come. 12 Whoever thinks he is standing firm had better be careful that he does not fall. 13 Every test that you have experienced is the kind that normally comes to people. But God keeps his promise, and he will not allow you to be tested beyond your power to remain firm; at the time you are put to the test, he will give you the strength to

endure it, and so provide you with a way out.

m the Lord; *some manuscripts have* Christ.

These verses form a transition between what Paul has just said in 9.24-27 about the danger of failing in the Christian life, and the contrast between idolatry and the Lord's Supper in 10.14-22. Most translations and commentaries begin a new paragraph or section at verse 14.

Two general problems are likely to arise in translating this passage. First, it is full of allusions to the Old Testament, in addition to the quotation in verse 7. Not many translators can expect their own readers to have such a detailed knowledge of the Old Testament as Paul and the first readers of this letter had. Translators can supply some of the information in the form of references, as in RSV and TEV. At certain points the translation itself may be somewhat expanded, as for example when TEV translates **the sea** into "the Red Sea." However, the translator must always be careful not to make the text sound as if it were written in some time, place, or culture other than that of the first century.

Secondly, this passage has a well-defined structure, and gains its stylistic effect by the use of repetition and other rhetorical devices.

The general structure, which should be kept as much as possible in translation, is as follows:

I.   Introduction—verse 1a.
II. Positive aspects.
   A.   Four positive examples from the Old Testament—verses 1b-4a—the last example being expanded in verse 4b.
   B.   Conclusions drawn from the positive examples—verse 5.
   C.   Application to the readers—verse 6a.
III. Negative Aspects.
   A.   Five negative Old Testament examples—verses 6b-10.
   B.   Application to the readers—verses 11-13.

The word **all** is repeated five times in verses 1-4, giving great emphasis to the fact that all the people of Israel shared God's protection and blessings during the exodus and the following years of wandering in the desert. **All** contrasts with **most of them** in verse 5 and with **some of them,** which is repeated four times in verses 7-10.

The TEV section heading "Warnings against Idols" may be rendered as "Paul teaches Christians about idols" or "Christians should avoid worshiping idols."

10.1	RSV	TEV
	I want you to know, brethren, that our fathers were all under the cloud, and all passed through the sea,	I want you to remember, my brothers, what happened to our ancestors who followed Moses. They were all under the protection of the cloud, and all passed safely through the Red Sea.

RSV, TEV, and many other translations use a positive expression such as "I want you to know (remember)" to translate the Greek double negative, "I do not want you not to know." The translations "remember" (TEV) or "remind" are better than **know** because most if not all of Paul's readers certainly knew the Old Testament stories to which he refers. What Paul is saying is that he wants to make sure that they understand the inner meaning in these stories. Paul often uses the expression "I want you to remember" (TEV) when introducing teaching which he considers important enough to repeat (compare 12.1; 2 Cor 1.8; also Rom 1.13; 11.25; 1 Thes 4.13).

Brethren, here as elsewhere, should normally be translated as "fellow Christians" or "fellow believers." It does not refer to actual family members.

Fathers here has the meaning "ancestors" as in TEV. The following words show that Paul is not referring to the patriarchs only, but also to the whole people of Israel at the time of their liberation from Egypt.

Our before **fathers** is expressed in the Greek text, no doubt because Paul considers that all his readers, whether Jews or Gentiles by race, share as Christians in the heritage of Israel. Contrast Hebrews 1.1, where the Greek simply has "to the fathers."

Under the cloud can be expanded to "under the protection of the cloud" (TEV). Paul's language recalls Psalm 105.39, which speaks of "a cloud for a covering."

The cloud: the definite article **the** in English would normally indicate that the **cloud** was information known to both Paul and his readers. They would know which particular cloud he was talking about. NEB and Brc expand this phrase to "the pillar of cloud"; JB translates "our fathers were all guided by a cloud above them." This helps modern readers to know which cloud is spoken about. It will be helpful in many languages to avoid the passive voice here and say, for example, "the pillar of cloud protected all of them."

It will be helpful to translate the word **sea** as "Red Sea" (see TEV) in order to help modern readers identify this body of water."[1]

and all were baptized into Moses in the cloud and in the sea, | **In the cloud and in the sea they were all baptized as followers of Moses.**

This verse draws another lesson from the two incidents in Israel's history mentioned in verse 1.

In some Greek manuscripts the verb translated **were baptized** is in the middle voice, meaning "baptized themselves" or "got themselves baptized." However, the UBS Greek text maintains the passive voice, and it is translated that way in almost all versions.

For a discussion of **the cloud,** see comments on verse 1.

---

[1] Translators must decide as a matter of general principle how to translate "Red Sea" throughout the Bible. GeCL, like other CLTs, has "Red Sea" here, as in the Greek, but "Reed Sea," as in the Hebrew, in Exodus 10.19 and generally in the Old Testament. See note in TEV Word List. It is important to use the same name throughout the Bible. This should normally be the Old Testament form, but if a different form is current in the receptor language, this should be used everywhere.

If translators have "Red Sea" in verse 1, the reference in verse 2 may be translated as "sea," following RSV and TEV's example.

The expression **into Moses** may have been invented by Paul on the analogy of baptism "into Christ" (Rom 6.3). Most modern translations add something to bring out the full meaning: TEV has "followers of Moses"; FrCL renders it as "by being united with Moses." The probable meaning is "communion with Moses" or "united" with him in the experience of the exodus.

Perhaps verses 1 and 2 may be combined in the following way:

> I want you to remember, fellow Christians, that our ancestors
> all had the experience of being protected by the pillar of cloud
> in the desert, and of crossing through the Red Sea with dry
> feet. They were all, so to speak, baptized in union with Moses
> by these experiences.

10.3-4a	RSV	TEV

and all ate the same supernatural[o] food 4 and all drank the same supernatural[o] drink.

All ate the same spiritual bread 4 and drank the same spiritual drink.

[o] Greek *spiritual*

These two clauses are closely parallel. In the light of verses 16-17, it is very likely that Paul is thinking of the Lord's Supper.

The words **the same** occur twice and imply that the ancestors ate and drank the same food and drink as one another. The context does not support the interpretation "the same as Christians eat and drink in the Lord's Supper."

The meaning of the word translated **supernatural** (TEV's "spiritual") is uncertain. Several translations and commentators, including NEB, Mft, AT, and Brc, translate "supernatural" as RSV does, implying that God's Spirit was active in giving the food and water. This is certainly a major part of the meaning. However, Paul may also be looking ahead to the "spiritual," that is, Christian interpretation of the story which he will give in verse 4b. GeCL translates "divine rock." The problem with the word "spiritual" is that in most languages it is a "church" word used only by Christians. It is therefore better to use expressions such as **supernatural,** "divine," "heavenly," "by the power of God," and so on.

Paul's reference in verse 3, as in 3.2, is not only to bread, but to any kind of solid food. Thus RSV's translation is preferable to TEV's.

10.4b	RSV	TEV

For they drank from the supernatural[o] Rock which followed them, and the Rock was Christ.

They drank from the spiritual rock that went with them; and that rock was Christ himself.

[o] Greek *spiritual*

Translators should read general commentaries on these two clauses, for they help us to see Paul's understanding of the Old Testament in the light of the coming of Christ. Even before Paul's time, Jews understood the different Old Testament stories about Moses' striking the rock (Exo 17.1-7; Num 20.2-17) to mean that the same rock followed the Israelites in their travels. The last part of this verse, **and the Rock was Christ**, contains Paul's interpretation of this tradition.

For can be omitted in translation, for this verse merely expands 4a rather than drawing a logical conclusion from it.

Them after **followed** is clearly implied in the Greek, which is literally "from the following spiritual rock." In some languages it may be necessary to expand the text a little; for example, "they drank water flowing from a supernatural rock."

The last clause **and the Rock was Christ** is short and emphatic. Most translators should render it this way. It does not contrast with what precedes. Paul is drawing his own conclusion from it.

All translations which we consulted translate **Christ** as a proper name. TEV's "himself" is implied and can be added in translation for emphasis.

A sample translation of verses 3 and 4 may be as follows: "all of them ate the same food which God gave by his power, and drank the water which God caused to flow from the rock which accompanied them. That Rock was Christ himself."

10.5   RSV   TEV

Nevertheless with most of them God was not pleased; for they were overthrown in the wilderness.	**But even then God was not pleased with most of them, and so their dead bodies were scattered over the desert.**

This verse contrasts emphatically with verses 1b-4. as **Nevertheless** (TEV's "But even then") shows. **Nevertheless** may be expanded to "Even after all this."

Most of them refers to the group which is translated **some of them** in verses 7-10. Verse 8 states that it was a large group. The present verse, like verses 1-4, is still concerned with "our ancestors," and thus it may be helpful to repeat this phrase. For example, "Even after all this, God was not pleased with most of our ancestors."

God was not pleased may be translated as "God was angry with."[2]

The second half of the verse, beginning with **for** (TEV's "and so"), describes the result of God's rejection, or the evidence for it. Perhaps the word **for** could be translated as "as is shown by the fact" or "the result was that."

The verb translated **were overthrown** occurs only here in the New Testament and clearly echoes Numbers 14.16.

Overthrown: the meaning of the Greek is literally "lay low" and is very close to "fell" in Hebrews 3.17, echoing Numbers 14.29. Both verbs imply "were killed," and it will be necessary to make this clear, as TEV does by expanding **they** to "their dead bodies."

---

[2] This phrase is possibly a euphemism for "God rejected" or even "God destroyed," as the rest of the verse implies. Compare the loose quotation of Habbakuk 2.3-4 in Hebrews 10.37-38, and Hebrews' conclusion in verse 39.

The Old Testament passage indicates that they were killed by God, and in some languages it may be better to say so: "and so he (God) scattered their dead bodies over the desert" or ". . . God killed them and scattered their bodies over the desert."

Now these things are warnings for us, not to desire evil as they did.	Now, all of this is an example for us, to warn us not to desire evil things, as they did,

Now indicates that Paul is moving on to a new point, though one which is closely related to the examples of the previous verses. This verse draws a moral from the series of Old Testament examples in 1-5. It is therefore similar to verse 11, which draws a moral from the second series of Old Testament examples. Translators should consider the two verses together.

These, literally "these things," refers to the Old Testament examples given in verses 1-5, and especially to the fact that many of the Israelites died in the desert. This may be why TEV changes the plural **warnings** into the singular "an example . . . to warn us." Most translations, however, keep a plural, "these events."

The reason for TEV's double translation, "an example . . . to warn us," is that two elements of meaning are combined in the Greek word which is literally "type": "these things are types for us." The word can certainly mean "example," though more commonly a "good example" than a bad one. The following words, **not to desire evil as they did,** support the translation **warnings.** However, the wider context, particularly the use of "supernatural" ("spiritual") three times in verses 3-4 and also in verse 11, may suggest that God intended to set up a similarity between events at the time of the exodus and the events in Paul's time. For this reason NEB translates "These events happened as symbols," and in verse 11 has "All these things that happened to them were symbolic." Brc has "symbolic warnings." A translator would therefore be justified to render this sentence in a similar way; for example, "Now, all these things happened as symbolic examples to warn us . . . ."

The point of the illustration in this verse is that Paul wants his readers to be like the group of Israelites who pleased God, rather than the ones who were destroyed. Verses 11-13 will make this fact clear.

The latter part of this verse sounds weak in most translations. Paul used an unusual word for "desirers of evil," echoing Numbers 11.34 which has "craving." Mft brings this meaning out by translating "to keep us from *craving* for evil as *they craved.*" His italics indicate a reference to the Old Testament. Translators may use "crave" or "desire very strongly," or similar words.

They before **did** is emphatic, meaning "those people," namely the ancestors of the exodus generation.

Do not be idolaters as some of them were; as it is written, "The people sat	nor to worship idols, as some of them did. As the scripture says, "The people

down to eat and drink and rose up to   sat down to a feast which turned into
dance."   an orgy of drinking and sex."

This verse refers to the making of the golden calf in Exodus 32.1-6. Verse
7a has a strong link to Exodus 32.6a, which says "And they rose up early on the
morrow, and offered burnt offerings and brought peace offerings."

TEV's translation of the quotation from Exodus 32.6b is a vivid paraphrase,
the meaning of which may be implied in the Greek but is not expressed. Exodus
32.19 refers back to this as dancing rather than as "sex." Paul treats "sex" in the
following verse. The Greek verb which RSV translates **dance** means "play" or
"amuse oneself." FrCL "amuse themselves"; NEB has "revel." Other CLTs, also
TNT and AT, translate "dance."[3] **Dance** is probably the safer rendering. Paul's
main point is that the feast and the dancing took place, in effect, to honor a pagan
god.

The phrase **Do not be idolaters** will need to be slightly expanded in some
languages to "Nor should we worship idols."

For a discussion on **it is written,** see the comments on 9.9.

10.8   RSV   TEV

We must not indulge in immorality as   We must not be guilty of sexual im-
some of them did, and twenty-three   morality, as some of them were—and in
thousand fell in a single day.   one day twenty-three thousand of them
                                        fell dead.

We must not: we includes both Paul and his readers; but see the first comment on verse 10.

Indulge in immorality translates a single verb in the text. It was discussed
in the comments on 6.18, where Paul says "Shun immorality." The reference in
this verse is to Numbers 25.1,9, but the translation should not be harmonized to
read "twenty-four thousand." All translations which we have consulted understand
the reference to be to "sexual immorality."

And before **twenty-three thousand** probably means "with the result that."

The idea of "dead" (TEV) after **fell** is strongly implied, as in verse 5. Many
translators will prefer to say just "died in a single day."

10.9   RSV   TEV

We must not put the Lord^P to the test,   We must not put the Lord^m to the test,
as some of them did and were destroyed as some of them did—and they were
by serpents;   killed by snakes.

^{P} Other ancient authorities read *Christ* ^{m} the Lord; *some manuscripts have*
                                        Christ.

---

3 However, dancing and sex are connected in many cultures. The Greek
word used here for "dance" refers in the Septuagint of Genesis 26.8 to Isaac
"fondling his wife" (Isaac and Rebecca making love), but in Genesis 21.9 it has the
wider meaning of children "playing," or it may refer to homosexual contacts.

This verse refers to Numbers 21.5-6; compare Psalm 78.18.

The third edition of the UBS Greek text has "Christ" instead of "Lord," as in the footnotes in TEV and NEB, as well as in KJV. Many manuscripts have "the Lord." RSV and TEV texts, and most translations, follow these manuscripts. Some translations such as GeCL, ItCL, Phps, and Brc interpret "the Lord" as "God." Metzger comments that "the reading that best explains the origin of the other is *Christon* (Christ)"; compare verse 4. If translators choose **the Lord** as the text, there should be a footnote similar to the one in RSV or TEV, showing the other choice.

Commentators are uncertain as to the exact meaning of Paul's references to tempting **the Lord** or putting him **to the test**. The verb **put . . . to the test** is not used in Numbers 21.5-6, but in Psalm 78.18-19 it seems to mean "doing an experiment to see whether God would perform a miracle." In the present verse Brc probably brings out the full meaning in his translation, "nor must we try to see how far we can go with God and get away with it." This can also be phrased as "nor must we try to see how much we can sin before God punishes us."

And can be translated as "with the result that," as in verse 8.

Serpents is literally "the serpents," that is, the serpents in the story which Paul expects that his readers will know well. Modern readers may not know this story so well, so RSV and TEV omit "the." See comments on verse 1 concerning the use of the definite article with **sea**.

10.10	RSV	TEV

nor grumble, as some of them did and were destroyed by the Destroyer.	We must not complain, as some of them did—and they were destroyed by the Angel of Death.

This verse seems to refer to the narrative in Numbers 16.41-50.

The form of this verse is rather different from that of verses 8 and 9. A different word for **as** is used. Also, according to the most probable Greek text, Paul changes from the first person plural, "we must not," to the second person plural imperative, "do not." Many Greek manuscripts level out this difference and use "we" throughout, as does TEV. RSV uses neither, perhaps avoiding a decision. GeCL uses "you" throughout verses 8 and 9, but there is no manuscript basis for this. Most translations keep the change of person and are probably correct.

As in other places, no attempt should be made to harmonize this verse with Numbers 16.41, which says that not only some of the people, but "the whole community," complained.

Grumble usually refers to a repeated voicing of one's extreme displeasure. In this context a more general term is needed that will cover any kind of grumbling. The modern English word "complain" does not seem to carry this component of repetitiveness. Some languages have special words which almost sound like the act of grumbling and can be used effectively here.

And: see the discussion in verses 8 and 9.

The Destroyer: in the Old Testament the Israelites are frequently said to have grumbled against Moses and thereby against God. But here the word **the Destroyer** is not found elsewhere in the Greek Bible. This suggests that Paul is thinking of a summary of Numbers 16 in Wisdom 18.20-25, where in verses 22 and

25 a related word is used. Less probable is a reference to Exodus 12.23 (compare Heb 11.28), since in that passage the Destroyer attacks only the Egyptians. Most CLTs, also TNT, Mft, AT, Phps, and Brc, think that Paul is referring in this verse to a distinct "Angel of Death." In Exodus 12.23 the Destroyer is distinguished from "the Lord" (that is, God), but this is probably not so in 1 Corinthians, in Wisdom 18.20-25, and certainly not in Numbers 16.45. In some languages it may be necessary to turn the passive verb into an active form: "The Angel of Death destroyed them."

10.11	RSV	TEV

Now these things happened to them as a warning, but they were written down for our instruction, upon whom the end of the ages has come.

All these things happened to them as examples for others, and they were written down as a warning for us. For we live at a time when the end is about to come.

Compare the comments on verse 6. Many Greek manuscripts, followed by TEV, GeCL, NEB, JB, TNT, have "all" before **these things**. The UBS Greek text, though, has merely "these things." This text is followed by many translations; for example, Brc, "what happened to them."

The word translated **as a warning** (TEV's "examples") is an adverb related to "types" in verse 6. NEB again has "symbolic."

To them: the Greek is literally "those people." It means "other people than ourselves," not "other people than the Israelites mentioned in earlier verses." Some translators may want to repeat "our ancestors" here, or say "the Israelites."

The phrase **they were written down** can be translated "people wrote all these events down."

For our instruction is a little ambiguous. "As a warning to us" (TEV) or "in order to warn us" gives the meaning more clearly.

End is literally "ends" in the Greek. RSV and other translations are probably correct in assuming that copyists were influenced by the plural **ages** and thus wrote "ends." The meaning is most probably **end**. ItCL has a good translation, "We are living in a time close to the end."

10.12	RSV	TEV

Therefore let any one who thinks that he stands take heed lest he fall.

Whoever thinks he is standing firm had better be careful that he does not fall.

Any one: Paul is not thinking of any particular individual here, but rather "any Christian."

GeCL restructures this verse to give another imperative like "we must" in other verses. It says "so be careful: anyone who thinks that he is standing firm should take care that he does not fall."

TEV correctly adds "firm" to bring out the meaning of **stands**.

As in verse 7, **fall** does not mean simply to stumble, but rather to fall in such a way as to be destroyed.

RSV	TEV
No temptation has overtaken you that is not common to man. God is faithful, and he will not let you be tempted beyond your strength, but with the temptation will also provide the way of escape, that you may be able to endure it.	Every test that you have experienced is the kind that normally comes to people. But God keeps his promise, and he will not allow you to be tested beyond your power to remain firm; at the time you are put to the test, he will give you the strength to endure it, and so provide you with a way out.

The first sentence in this verse is literally "no test has taken you except a human one." RSV's translation is too literal and obscures the meaning. TEV has tried to clear up the meaning by expanding the text somewhat. "Test" is a better translation than **temptation,** since the rest of the verse, like verse 9, refers to the activity of God. Another possible restructuring of this first sentence is as follows: "Whenever you are tested, you should remember that other people have been tested like this too."

God is faithful is the phrase which occurred in 1.9. There it was translated by TEV as "God keeps his promises." The same phrase is used in 2 Corinthians 1.18. TEV's "God keeps his promise" seems appropriate in this context. In languages in which the passive is unnatural, the clause **he will not let you be tempted beyond your strength** may be rendered as "God will not allow anyone to test you beyond what you can bear." This probably refers to not only inner moral temptations, but the pressure of persecution from outside also.

The final two clauses are ordered differently in RSV and TEV. RSV considers that there is a means and purpose relationship between the clauses. However, this involves what seems to be a logical inconsistency, unless it means that a believer is able to endure the test (temptation) because he is sure that God will bring the test to an end. TEV understands "the final genitive phrase 'be able to endure' as a genitive of definition and not of result, which means that 'the way out' is the ability to endure the test."[4] NEB supports this view: "but when the test comes he will at the same time provide a way out, by enabling you to sustain it." The translator will need to weigh all the evidence and make a choice between the two possibilities.

The way of escape probably means "the appropiate way out."

RSV	TEV
14 Therefore, my beloved, shun the worship of idols. 15 I speak as to sensible men; judge for yourselves what I say. 16 The cup of blessing which we bless, is it not a participation[q] in the blood of Christ? The bread which we break, is it not a participation[q] in the	14 So then, my dear friends, keep away from the worship of idols. 15 I speak to you as sensible people; judge for yourselves what I say. 16 The cup we use in the Lord's Supper and for which we give thanks to God: when we drink from it, we are sharing in the

---

4 Robert G. Bratcher, *A Translator's Guide to Paul's First Letter to the Corinthians*, page 95.

body of Christ? 17 Because there is one bread, we who are many are one body, for we all partake of the one bread. 18 Consider the people of Israel;[a] are not those who eat the sacrifices partners in the altar? 19 What do I imply then? That food offered to idols is anything, or that an idol is anything? 20 No, I imply that what pagans sacrifice they offer to demons and not to God. I do not want you to be partners with demons. 21 You cannot drink the cup of the Lord and the cup of demons. You cannot partake of the table of the Lord and the table of demons. 22 Shall we provoke the Lord to jealousy? Are we stronger than he?

[q] Or communion
[a] Greek Israel according to the flesh

blood of Christ. And the bread we break: when we eat it, we are sharing in the body of Christ. 17 Because there is the one loaf of bread, all of us, though many, are one body, for we all share the same loaf.

18 Consider the people of Israel; those who eat what is offered in sacrifice share in the altar's service to God. 19 Do I imply, then, that an idol or the food offered to it really amounts to anything? 20 No! What I am saying is that what is sacrificed on pagan altars is offered to demons, not to God. And I do not want you to be partners with demons. 21 You cannot drink from the Lord's cup and also from the cup of demons; you cannot eat at the Lord's table and also at the table of demons. 22 Or do we want to make the Lord jealous? Do we think that we are stronger than he?

The general translation problems in this section have been discussed in the introduction to verses 1-13. On rhetorical questions, see particularly the comments on 1.13 and 9.1-12.

The paragraph begins with the conjunction **Therefore,** which brings Paul's previous argument to a conclusion and gives some practical teaching: **shun the worship of idols.** Commentators differ in the relations they see between this paragraph and earlier passages. References to idolatry and to pagan worship point back to verse 7, and more generally to chapter 8. In 10.19 Paul appears to reply to a possible objection that his argument here would contradict what he said in 8.4-6.

This paragraph also points forward. The theme of the Lord's Supper is introduced and points to the fuller account in 11.20-30. When Paul answers the Corinthian Christians' questions about diet, Paul is led to speak about the central acts of Christian worship and related matters which go far beyond the original question. It is, therefore, difficult to find a main theme. Nor is it necessary to do so in order to make a clear and understandable translation. What is necessary, here as elsewhere in the epistle, is that the translator is alert for themes which echo other parts of the epistle. These will be mentioned in the detailed comments.

10.14   RSV   TEV

Therefore, my beloved, shun the worship of idols.

So then, my dear friends, keep away from the worship of idols.

Therefore: Barrett translates this word as "the conclusion of this . . . is." Translators need to find a strong conjunction in their language which shows that Paul is now applying the previous argument.

My beloved means "fellow Christians." One can translate this as "my dear fellow Christians." TEV's "my dear friends" is also possible. This is a variation from Paul's more common phrase "my brothers." Compare Philippians 2.12.

Shun means literally "flee," or "run away." Some translators may prefer to avoid a metaphor here and say, for example, "do not worship idols at all." The connection between this verse and 6.18 is close, not only in language but also in thought. Already in the Old Testament sexual immorality and unfaithfulness to God were closely connected; see the comments on verse 8.

In Greek **the worship of idols** has the definite article, but this does not seem to be significant. Compare the comments on "cloud" and "sea" in verse 1.

10.15	RSV	TEV

I speak as to sensible men; judge for yourselves what I say.	I speak to you as sensible people; judge for yourselves what I say.

Commentators differ on whether Paul is being ironical or not in the first part of this verse. The word translated **sensible** here is the same as the word translated "wise" in 4.10. In 4.10 Paul is obviously ironical, even bitter. However, if the present passage is read by itself, there seems little or no indication of irony here. If this is so, verse 15a should be translated "by the way I speak, I am treating you as people who are in fact sensible" or "I am speaking to you because I know that you are sensible people." In both RSV and TEV the present tense **I speak** is used. However, Paul is thinking of what he is about to say, and in some languages it may be necessary to make this clear by using a future tense.

In verse 15b **for** is implied, and **yourselves** is emphatic. The meaning is "don't take my word for it, but come to your own conclusions."

10.16	RSV	TEV

The cup of blessing which we bless, is it not a participation^q in the blood of Christ? The bread which we break, is it not a participation^q in the body of Christ?	The cup we use in the Lord's Supper and for which we give thanks to God: when we drink from it, we are sharing in the blood of Christ. And the bread we break: when we eat it, we are sharing in the body of Christ.

^{q} Or *communion*

The two halves of this verse are similar in construction, though the first half is made more complicated by the clause **which we bless.** The difficulties of translating this verse are shown by the fact that both RSV and TEV use many more words than are in the Greek.

These two sentences are rhetorical questions. Translators in many languages will need to translate them as statements, as TEV has done.

In 16a **The cup** (with the article **The**) suggests, as in verse 1, that Paul's reader already knows which cup he is referring to. The reference is to a common practice in the church. The situation is, however, complicated by the fact that in Jewish meals, especially the Passover, the phrase "cup of blessing" was also used.

The **we** is not emphasized. It almost certainly refers to Christians in general, but without implying any contrast between Christians and Jews (compare verse 18).

In a Jewish setting the phrase **The cup of blessing** would mean "the cup over which a prayer of blessing is spoken," and to bless a material object would mean "to give thanks to God for it." So translators would be wise to adopt a translation similar to that of TEV, "the cup we use in the Lord's Supper and for which we give thanks to God" or "the cup we use in the Lord's Supper, over which we say a prayer of thanksgiving to God."

The difference between **participation** (RSV text) and "communion" (RSV footnote) is that **participation** means "sharing" with one another, while "communion" focuses on the relation between the believer and Christ, which is certainly also involved. The following verses suggest that Paul is thinking mainly about the union of Christians with one another. However, the idea of **participation** is also required by the reference to Christ's blood and body. Perhaps one could combine these ideas as Barrett does: "a common participation in the body of Christ"; GeCL translates more fully: "Think of the communion cup over which we speak the prayer of thanksgiving. Does it not enable us to share in the blood that Christ poured out for us?"

Blood here should be translated literally, since the comparison is between two liquids. Similarly, in 16b it is probably best to keep the literal translation of **body.**

10.17   RSV   TEV

Because there is one bread, we who are many are one body, for we all partake of the one bread.

Because there is the one loaf of bread, all of us, though many, are one body, for we all share the same loaf.

Here Paul moves from rhetorical questions to a direct statement, perhaps indicating that he is moving from teaching which the Corinthians already know to newer teaching.

The present tense **is** suggests that Paul is thinking here, as in chapter 11, not of the last supper of Jesus himself with his disciples, but of the Lord's Supper as people practiced it in the church of Paul's time.

Bread: TEV adds "loaf" to indicate that a single loaf is broken in the communion service, not just that those taking part eat the same type of food.

We who are many may be expressed as "all of us, though many" (TEV) or "all of us, no matter how many we are."

For **one body,** see introduction to 12.12-31a. Here Paul is saying that as Christians share the Lord's Supper, they become in every way one with each other and with Christ.

10.18   RSV   TEV

Consider the people of Israel;[a] are not those who eat the sacrifices partners in the altar?

Consider the people of Israel; those who eat what is offered in sacrifice share in the altar's service to God.

[a] Greek *Israel according to the flesh*

Consider is the verb which was translated "take heed" in verse 12, but the context gives a quite different meaning. Here no warning is involved; Paul is just asking the readers to give special attention.

The people of Israel is literally "Israel according to the flesh" but has no unfavorable meaning here. Paul adds the words "according to the flesh" because he thought of the church as fulfilling God's promises to Israel, and therefore as being, in a sense, the true or spiritual Israel. So he needed an expression, here as in Romans 9.4, to speak of non-Christian Jews. Today there is little danger of confusing Israel with the church. For this reason RSV and TEV omit the words "according to the flesh." Modern translators could render this as "the Jewish people," as DuCL has done. Brc has "Look at actual Jewish practice and belief."

The second part of the verse, from **those who eat . . .**, begins a series of rhetorical questions. There are four of them, according to the UBS Greek text and the punctuation. RSV translates the first as a question and TEV renders it as a statement. As in verse 16, Paul is appealing to well-known facts and common beliefs. The sentence is concise and may need to be expanded in translation. For example, "those who eat the sacrifices share with one another in the sacrifice to God made on the altar." When an animal was sacrificed by the Hebrews to God, part of it was burned on the altar, and part of it was eaten by the people who were performing this act of worship. The underlying thought, then, is that by sharing in the sacrificial meal, Jewish worshipers enter into a relationship with God which also unites them with one another. Paul's readers would know, of course, that although some sacrifices had to be burnt whole, there were others which priests, Levites, and even ordinary people could share by eating part of the flesh (see Lev 10.12-15; Deut 18.1-4).

10.19	RSV	TEV

What do I imply then? That food offered to idols is anything, or that an idol is anything?

Do I imply, then, that an idol or the food offered to it really amounts to anything?

This verse marks a sharp break in Paul's thought. He may have been thinking more quickly than his secretary could write. The implied connection with verse 18 may be as follows: "Someone may say that my argument proves too much, since it could apply not only to Jewish, but also to pagan ceremonies. After all, it is idolatry, not Judaism, with which the Corinthians are concerned."

The UBS Greek text punctuates the verse as three questions. The last two questions, "Is food offered to idols anything?" and "Is an idol anything?" are very similar in form and meaning. A few important manuscripts omit the last question, probably by accident.

Do I imply then may be translated as "Do I really mean" or "Do you understand what I am talking about? I mean that . . . ."

The meaning of the verse is best defined by comparing it with 8.4-6, where it is clear that Paul is denying, not the existence of other spiritual powers, but their claims on Christians' loyalty and worship.

Is anything is literally "to be something." In some places in the New Testament this means, not "to exist," but "to be important." See, for example, Galatians 2.6, where TEV translates "to be the leaders." Translators and commentators are divided about whether the words have the same meaning here. Brc takes the meaning "to exist," and translates "What is my argument? That a thing offered to an idol has any real existence? Or that an idol itself has any real existence?" On the other hand, several CLTs express in different ways the thought that although idols may exist, they are not significant for Christians. DuCL has "that an idol or food offered to an idol has any significance?"; FrCL ". . . has any value?"; GeCL "Do I mean by that that there is anything special about sacrificial flesh? Or that the idol to whom the sacrifice is made has any significance for us?"; ItCL "I do not mean by that that the sacrifice offered to the idol has any value or that the idol is of any importance." On the whole it seems better for translators to render this passage in a similar way to these other CLTs.

<table>
<tr><td>10.20</td><td>RSV</td><td>TEV</td></tr>
</table>

10.20　　　RSV	TEV
No, I imply that what pagans sacrifice they offer to demons and not to God. I do not want you to be partners with demons.	No! What I am saying is that what is sacrificed on pagan altars is offered to demons, not to God. And I do not want you to be partners with demons.

Verse 19 looks back at the previous argument, including 8.4-5, while verse 20 introduces a new thought. Both the contrast with verse 19 and Paul's change of direction are well produced by TEV's "No! What I am saying is . . . ."

What pagans sacrifice is literally "what they sacrifice." It will be helpful for a translator to expand this clause as TEV has done, in order to show where the sacrificing occurred: "what pagans sacrifice on altars."

The verb which is translated **sacrifice** is the same as that translated **offer;** RSV and TEV have variety for reason of style. This verb often applies to the killing of animals for sacrifice, and is therefore narrower in meaning than the English "to sacrifice."

The square brackets in the UBS Greek text around the word translated **offer** indicate that there is some doubt about its position in the text, but there is no question that it belongs there at some point.

NEB and JB make explicit the fact that Paul is here using the language of Deuteronomy 32.17. However, he employs a present tense, **they offer,** rather than the past tense, "they offered." Other than that, the quotation is the same. JB shows this point by italicising the quoted words, while NEB marks the quotation more emphatically by translating "the sacrifice the heathens offer are offered (in the words of scripture) to demons and to that which is not God."

The word **demons** could refer to a good spirit in secular Greek, but not in Paul's usage. Phps' rendering, "evil spiritual powers," is therefore correct and accurate.

The **and** in **and not to God** is natural in Greek, but not good English style. TEV leaves it out. Many other languages can do the same.

10.21　　　RSV	TEV
You cannot drink the cup of the Lord and the cup of demons. You cannot partake of the table of the Lord and the table of demons.	You cannot drink from the Lord's cup and also from the cup of demons; you cannot eat at the Lord's table and also at the table of demons.

There is no connective word in the Greek to connect this verse with verse 20, but there is great similarity, both of language and thought, between this verse and verse 16.

The Lord, as usual, means Christ.

The cup of the Lord means "the cup which the Lord gives," or more generally "the cup used in the Lord's Supper."

Drink the cup is unnatural English. The meaning is clearly "drink (wine) from the cup."

TEV adds "also" to bring out the full meaning of **and;** FrCL translates "You cannot drink at the same time from the Lord's cup and the cup of evil spirits."

The meaning of verse 21b, from **You cannot partake,** can best be understood in the light of verse 18b, "are not those who eat the sacrifices partners in the food" (see the comments). The meaning is "You cannot share in meals at the Lord's table and at the same time eat meals at the table of demons."

The cup of demons may mean "the cup which demons give," which would make a good parallel to "the cup which the Lord gives." It may also mean, more generally, "the cup which is used in ceremonies dedicated to demons." This parallels "the cup used in the Lord's Supper." This second translation probably fits the context more closely.

10.22   RSV   TEV

Shall we provoke the Lord to jealousy?   **Or do we want to make the Lord jealous? Do we think that we are stronger than he?**

Are we stronger than he?

Paul completes his argument with two more rhetorical questions. The first can be expressed as a statement, "If you do this, it can only be because you are trying to arouse Christ's (the Lord's) righteous anger."

Provoke the Lord to jealousy is a common translation of a verb which in Deuteronomy 32.16 is used to express the thought of making God angry, provoking him, or making him bitter or jealous. Jealousy in such a context implies resentment against those who do not give God the total loyalty which they have promised in the covenant. It is stronger than mere "envy" of another individual. NEB has "Can we defy the Lord?" We can expand NEB a little to "Are we to provoke the Lord without his punishing us?"

The verb translated **provoke . . . to jealousy** may be understood as a future indicative, "shall we . . . ?" or as a present subjunctive, "are we to . . . ?" There is little difference in meaning. Since the following verb is in the present tense, the present subjunctive is slightly more likely.

In verse 22b TEV rightly adds "Do we think that" to bring out the meaning "do we think that we are strong enough to defy the Lord without being punished?"

RSV   **10.23—11.1**   TEV

23 "All things are lawful," but not all things are helpful. "All things are lawful," but not all things build up. 24 Let no one seek his own good, but the good of his neighbor. 25 Eat whatever is sold in the meat market without raising any question on the ground of conscience. 26 For "the earth is the Lord's, and everything in it." 27 If one of the unbelievers invites you to dinner and you are disposed to go, eat whatever is set before you without raising any question on the ground of conscience. 28 (But if some one says to you, "This has been offered in sacrifice," then out of consideration for the man who informed you, and for conscience' sake— 29 I mean his conscience, not yours—do not eat it.) For why should my liberty be determined by another man's scruples? 30 If I partake with thankfulness, why am I denounced because of that for which I give thanks?

31 So, whether you eat or drink, or whatever you do, do all to the glory of God. 32 Give no offense to Jews or to Greeks or to the church of God, 33 just as I try to please all men in everything I do, not seeking my own advantage, but that of many, that they may be saved. 11 1 Be imitators of me, as I am of Christ.

23 "We are allowed to do anything," so they say. That is true, but not everything is good. "We are allowed to do anything"—but not everything is helpful. 24 No one should be looking out for his own interests, but for the interests of others.

25 You are free to eat anything sold in the meat market, without asking any questions because of your conscience. 26 For, as the scripture says, "The earth and everything in it belong to the Lord."

27 If an unbeliever invites you to a meal and you decide to go, eat what is set before you, without asking any questions because of your conscience. 28 But if someone tells you, "This food was offered to idols," then do not eat that food, for the sake of the one who told you and for conscience' sake— 29 that is, not your own conscience, but the other person's conscience.

"Well, then," someone asks, "why should my freedom to act be limited by another person's conscience? 30 If I thank God for my food, why should anyone criticize me about food for which I give thanks?"

31 Well, whatever you do, whether you eat or drink, do it all for God's glory. 32 Live in such a way as to cause no trouble either to Jews or Gentiles or to the church of God. 33 Just do as I do; I try to please everyone in all that I do, not thinking of my own good, but of the good of all, so that they might be saved. 11 1 Imitate me, then, just as I imitate Christ.

There is no grammatical connection between the beginning of this section and the preceding verses. For this and other reasons, some scholars have thought that it originally followed chapter 8, and that 9.1—10.22 belonged to a different letter. Other scholars think that this passage is connected both with the subject which Paul began to discuss in chapter 8, and also with the discussion of idol worship, particularly pagan sacrificed meals, in 10.14-22.

Most modern commentators and translations begin a new section after 11.1, not at the end of chapter 10. The subsection 10.31--11.1 forms a conclusion to the whole of chapters 8—10.

Some of the problems which we discuss in this section are very much problems of interpretation. We could solve them if we knew more about the situation to which the text refers. Translators therefore should consult general commentaries, as well as this Handbook.

	RSV	TEV

"All things are lawful," but not all things are helpful. "All things are lawful," but not all things build up.

"We are allowed to do anything," so they say. That is true, but not everything is good. "We are allowed to do anything"—but not everything is helpful.

Most modern translations put quotation marks around the phrase **All things are lawful** to indicate that it was probably a saying used in Corinth. A similar saying was quoted in 6.12, with an additional word in the Greek which RSV translates "for me." The first sentence, then, may be translated as "There is a saying which says, 'We . . .'" or "Some people say, 'We . . .'" or "You say 'We . . . .'" Here "We" (TEV) is implicit and may be added in translation to make the meaning clearer. The Greek does not explicitly refer to law, though this Greek word translated **lawful** is often used where Jewish rules and regulations are involved (see, for example, Mark 6.18; 10.2). The verb means "it is permitted" or ". . . is proper."

If we understand Paul to be quoting a current saying in Corinth, it may be necessary in translation to state by whom the saying is spoken. TEV has the impersonal "they," and FrCL has "certain (people)." It is also possible to have "You say . . . ." Such a translation can be justified by Paul's use of an indirect imperative "Let no one" in verse 24, and a direct imperative "You are free to eat" in verse 25 (see the comments on these verses).

On **not all things are helpful**, see comments on 6.12.

The second half of the verse closely parallels the first. However, **build up** (TEV "is helpful") in this second half probably refers to the act of strengthening the Christian community as a whole. Paul uses here the common metaphor of constructing a building to mean adding strength to the common life of the church. Compare 8.1,10 where the same word is used in a similar sense. So GeCL translates this as "but not everything helps the (Christian) community."

	RSV	TEV

Let no one seek his own good, but the good of his neighbor.

No one should be looking out for his own interests, but for the interests of others.

Third person imperatives such as **Let no one seek** are not very common in modern English, so TEV changes the construction into a statement using "should," in the sense of "ought to." Paul is here giving general advice; there is nothing in the language to suggest that he is referring to a particular person. For this reason, although **his own** and **his neighbor** are in the singular in the Greek, TEV is right in English to translate **neighbor** as "others," since more than one person is implicit here.

In some languages it will be helpful to translate this verse in the following way: "You should work for the interests of others rather than your own interests."

10.25	RSV	TEV

Eat whatever is sold in the meat market without raising any question on the ground of conscience.	You are free to eat anything sold in the meat market, without asking any questions because of your conscience.

The context, especially verse 28 and 8.10 (see the comments), suggests that Paul is specially concerned with **meat** offered to idols, but the Greek word could refer more generally to a market in which fish and possibly other types of food were sold. Thus, although NEB, TNT, and JB have a similar translation to that of RSV and TEV, other CLTs have "markets." **The** before **market** is not in the Greek, but it is most natural to assume that Paul was referring to the food market at Corinth.

The verb for **raising any question** is the same as that translated "discerned" in 2.14 and "judges" in 2.15. See the comments on 2.14, as the meaning in the present verse is rather different. Here the "examining" or "judging" is done by asking questions. Paul's advice here contrasts with the Jewish practice of asking carefully whether food was kosher (ritually pure) or not.

TEV's rendering "because of your conscience" is better English than **on the ground of conscience.** "Your" is implied, of course.

Conscience: this word may be rendered as "the mind (heart) which judges good and evil." A troubled conscience may need a phrase such as "having two hearts" or "having a troubled heart." Another possible model for translating this verse is "It is all right for you (or, You may) eat anthing which they sell in the meat market. Eating such meat should not trouble your heart."

10.26	RSV	TEV

For "the earth is the Lord's, and everything in it."	For, as the scripture says, "The earth and everything in it belong to the Lord."

The conjunction **For** has a double function. It indicates both that the verse is a quotation (Psa 24.1) and that the quotation is intended to give a reason for the statement in verse 25. TEV is therefore right to add "as the scripture says," though these words are not in the text. In languages which cannot talk about Scriptures "saying" or "speaking," one may render this as "It is written in the Scriptures that . . . ."

The Lord in the psalm undoubtedly means God, but it is possible that, here as elsewhere, Paul understood the psalm to refer to Christ. In any case, in the quotation **the Lord's** is emphasized; FrCL translates "It is to the Lord that the earth . . . belongs."

10.27	RSV	TEV

If one of the unbelievers invites you to dinner and you are disposed to go, eat whatever is set before you without raising any question on the ground of conscience.	If an unbeliever invites you to a meal and you decide to go, eat what is set before you, without asking any questions because of your conscience.

If: Christians very probably received such invitations in Corinth.

One of the unbelievers: (see comments on 6.6; 7.12-15). Paul means "those who do not believe in Christ," or perhaps more narrowly "pagans," excluding Jews. The word is not used here as an insult. Paul is merely stating a fact.

To dinner is not in the text but is clearly implied by verse 27b.

You are disposed is literally "you want," but this can be misunderstood as suggesting that the Corinthian Christians did not go to such meals. This is not Paul's intention.

It will be unnatural in some languages to put the two verbs **go, eat** together like this. In such a case, one may say "go, you should eat."

Whatever is set before you may be rephrased as "the food that they give to you" or "whatever they put on the table."

For **without raising . . . of conscience**, see comments on verse 25.

10.28-29a   RSV   TEV

RSV	TEV
(But if some one says to you, "This has been offered in sacrifice," then out of consideration for the man who informed you, and for conscience' sake— 29 I mean his conscience, not yours—do not eat it.)	But if someone tells you, "This food was offered to idols," then do not eat that food, for the sake of the one who told you and for conscience' sake— 29 that is, not your own conscience, but the other person's conscience.

The relation between these sentences and the context is uncertain. The simplest solution is that of RSV and Brc, which is to put these sentences in parentheses, thus allowing verse 29b to follow on naturally from verse 27. The difficulty is that Paul returns to the theme of verses 28-29a in verses 31-32. Other modern translations begin a new paragraph at verse 29b. The main theme in this passage is Christian freedom, which Paul discusses more thoroughly in chapter 9. In verses 28-29a, though, Paul is willing to allow a certain limitation in the use of Christian freedom.

Commentators discuss whether **some one** and **the man who informed you** refer to the same individual as the person designated by **his conscience** in 29a. Most probably they do, but **some one** is quite general and should not be made specific in translation.

Some manuscripts have the Greek word meaning "offered to idols" (TEV) which Paul more commonly used. However, the UBS Greek text has "offered in sacrifice." RSV has followed this text. Paul uses the word which a pagan would naturally choose. So the more likely translation is **offered in sacrifice.** If the context is not sufficiently clear, it may be necessary in some languages to be explicit and say "offered to idols as a sacrifice."

The man who informed you and **for conscience' sake** are closely connected in the Greek. It is possible without loss of meaning to translate "do not eat it, not because of your conscience, but because of the conscience of the other person who told you about the meat." The word translated **offered in sacrifice** must refer to the killing of animals for sacrifice.

I mean his conscience, not yours may also be expanded to "I am speaking about his conscience, not yours." ItCL restructures 28b and 29a as follows: "then for motive of conscience do not eat it because of the one who informed you; naturally I am speaking of his conscience, not yours."

Note that **do not eat it** occurs at the beginning of verse 28b in the Greek, as in TEV. It should be positioned wherever good style demands in the translator's language.

10.29b   RSV   TEV

For why should my liberty be deter-   "Well, then," someone asks, "why
mined by another man's scruples?   should my freedom to act be limited by
                                                                another person's conscience?

For suggests a logical connection with something that proceeds, probably Paul's main line of thought expressed in verse 27. However, ItCL, NEB, and TNT all agree with TEV that Paul is here quoting an objector. The weakness of this argument, though, is that Paul does not reply directly to the objection; nor does this interpretation make sense of the introductory **For** in the Greek. For this reason many translations, including RSV, GeCL, NAB, and JB, understand Paul to be speaking in his own name. This makes better sense, but translators must connect verse 29b with 27, not 29a. RSV has done this.

Héring gives a good translation of 29b, although he connects it with verse 29a: "What is the use of my freedom being judged by someone else's conscience?" One could also say "Why should someone else's conscience limit my freedom to do something?"

Liberty: see 9.1,19.

The end of this sentence is literally "by another conscience." But in many languages, as in English, it is unnatural to speak of the conscience as if it were independent of the person to whom it belongs. So it is better to say something like TEV's "by another person's conscience."

As elsewhere, a rhetorical question is often equivalent to a strong statement, in this case a negative one. One may say "For my liberty should not be determined by another person's conscience."

10.30   RSV   TEV

If I partake with thankfulness, why am I   If I thank God for my food, why should
denounced because of that for which I   anyone criticize me about food for
give thanks?   which I give thanks?"

In the comments on verse 16, it was explained that there is little difference between the Greek verbs meaning "bless" and "give thanks" (to God). In the present verse there is a play on the two senses of a similar Greek word for **give thanks.** (1) The Greek word used for **give thanks** is literally "to thank well," and this is contrasted with the "evil speaking" or the word translated **denounced.** This latter is the word from which the English "blaspheme" comes; it commonly means "to speak evil of" or "to slander" someone. (2) The word for **give thanks** is also related to the word for "grace," which in this context means "thanks" and which TEV translates "thank God." The whole phrase **partake with thankfulness** is literally "I partake in grace." However, this context is concerned with giving thanks for food. Paul may be implying that by saying grace over the food (that is, by giving thanks), the Christian makes all types of food pure to eat.

Translations generally make this verse a question, though it would be possible and perhaps more natural in some languages to translate it by a strong negative statement: "there is no reason why anyone should criticize me . . . ."

10.31   RSV   TEV

    So, whether you eat or drink, or whatever you do, do all to the glory of God.   **Well, whatever you do, whether you eat or drink, do it all for God's glory.**

The **So** (TEV's "Well") suggests that Paul begins a summary here which includes elements from the entire argument since the beginning of chapter 8.

Whatever you do should be understood as a summary of any activity that can be added to **whether you eat or drink.** Also, **whether you eat or drink** should not be understood as if **eat** and **drink** are alternatives. GeCL has "So I say: whether you eat or drink or do something else, do everything to the glory of God."

Glory of God too often is a set phrase used mainly in church circles. To give it its full meaning one may say "do everything in such a way that God will be honored."

10.32   RSV   TEV

Give no offense to Jews or to Greeks or to the church of God,   **Live in such a way as to cause no trouble either to Jews or Gentiles or to the church of God.**

Give no offense to follows the Greek quite literally, but TEV's expansion, "Live in such a way as to cause no trouble . . . to," makes the meaning much clearer in English. Continuous action over a period is implied. The root idea of the word translated **no offense** is the opposite of causing harm by causing someone to stumble over something. In the New Testament it is used metaphorically, for example, in Acts 24.16, speaking about having "a clear conscience," and Philippians 1.10, where the word has the meaning "undamaged." In the present verse it means "not causing (moral or spiritual) damage to anyone else."

Greeks: see comments on 1.22-24.

The church of God: see comments on 1.2. There and in this verse Paul probably means the local Christian community in Corinth.

10.33   RSV   TEV

just as I try to please all men in everything I do, not seeking my own advantage, but that of many, that they may be saved.   **Just do as I do; I try to please everyone in all that I do, not thinking of my own good, but of the good of all, so that they might be saved.**

This verse is linked grammatically with verse 32, but the thought is different. So TEV begins a new sentence. The best commentary on this verse can be found in 9.20-22. TEV's "Just do as I do" can be phrased as "You should follow my example."

Men should be translated as "people." It refers to both men and women.

Not seeking my own advantage: both the language and thought sound like those in verse 24a, where the same verb is translated "seek . . . own good." The Greek word in this verse is related to the word translated "helpful" in verse 23. These words include the idea of "gaining an advantage." One could then translate this clause as "not seeking to gain an advantage for myself."

Many is literally "the many"; see Isaiah 53.11; Mark 10.45; Romans 5.15-19; and especially the comments on 1 Corinthians 10.17. Commentators disagree on whether Paul means "the whole Christian community" or "the whole of mankind." The previous verses are mainly about the church, but Paul's thought is always prone to broaden rapidly. The following words, **that they may be saved,** suggest a wider reference to all of mankind.

11.1	RSV	TEV
	Be imitators of me, as I am of Christ.	Imitate me, then, just as I imitate Christ.

Be imitators of me overlaps in meaning with verse 33a, though the language is different. The rest of the verse carries the thought a step further, and to some extent prepares the reader for Paul's analogy in 11.2-12. It is important in translation to avoid expressions which may suggest something which is not genuine but "only an imitation." One can say, for example, "Follow my example" or "Use me as your model." For the idea of imitation in Paul's writings, see 1 Thessalonians 1.6; 2 Thessalonians 3.7,9.

Chapter 11

Covering the Head in Worship

2 I commend you because you remember me in everything and maintain the traditions even as I have delivered them to you. 3 But I want you to understand that the head of every man is Christ, the head of a woman is her husband, and the head of Christ is God. 4 Any man who prays or prophesies with his head covered dishonors his head, 5 but any woman who prays or prophesies with her head unveiled dishonors her head—it is the same as if her head were shaven. 6 For if a woman will not veil herself, then she should cut off her hair; but if it is disgraceful for a woman to be shorn or shaven, let her wear a veil. 7 For a man ought not to cover his head, since he is the image and glory of God; but woman is the glory of man. 8 (For man was not made from woman, but woman from man. 9 Neither was man created for woman, but woman for man.) 10 That is why a woman ought to have a veil *r* on her head, because of the angels. 11 (Nevertheless, in the Lord woman is not independent of man nor man of woman; 12 for as woman was made from man, so man is now born of woman. And all things are from God.) 13 Judge for yourselves; is it proper for a woman to pray to God with her head uncovered? 14 Does not nature itself teach you that for a man to wear long hair is degrading to him, 15 but if a woman has long hair, it is her pride? For her hair is given to her for a covering. 16 If any one is disposed to be contentious, we recognize no other practice, nor do the churches of God.

r Greek *authority* (the veil being a symbol of this)

2 I praise you because you always remember me and follow the teachings that I have handed on to you. 3 But I want you to understand that Christ is supreme over every man, the husband is supreme over his wife, and God is supreme over Christ. 4 So a man who prays or proclaims God's message in public worship with his head covered disgraces Christ. 5 And any woman who prays or proclaims God's message in public worship with nothing on her head disgraces her husband; there is no difference between her and a woman whose head has been shaved. 6 If the woman does not cover her head, she might as well cut her hair. And since it is a shameful thing for a woman to shave her head or cut her hair, she should cover her head. 7 A man has no need to cover his head, because he reflects the image and glory of God. But woman reflects the glory of man; 8 for man was not created from woman, but woman from man. 9 Nor was man created for woman's sake, but woman was created for man's sake. 10 On account of the angels, then, a woman should have a covering over her head to show that she is under her husband's authority. 11 In our life in the Lord, however, woman is not independent of man, nor is man independent of woman. 12 For as woman was made from man, in the same way man is born of woman; and it is God who brings everything into existence.

13 Judge for yourselves whether it is proper for a woman to pray to God in public worship with nothing on her head. 14 Why, nature itself teaches you that long hair on a man is a disgrace, 15 but on a woman it is a thing of beauty. Her long hair has been given

her to serve as a covering. 16 But if anyone wants to argue about it, all I have to say is that neither we nor the churches of God have any other custom in worship.

As we noted in the introduction to the last section, 11.1 "is much more closely connected with what precedes than with what follows" (Barrett). That is why we discussed it under the previous section. In an indirect and tactful manner Paul now prepares to discuss the behavior of women in worship. There is nothing to suggest that the Corinthians had asked him a question about this. It is more likely to have been something which Paul heard through friends (compare verse 18). In any case, in this section there are some points of contact with the last section and with earlier parts of the epistle. Related themes, especially that of women, are discussed in chapters 6—7. Also the comparisons in 10.33, and especially in 11.1, prepare the way for a series of comparisons between God, Christ, man, and woman, most clearly expressed in 11.3. Another minor point of contact is **glory,** found in 10.31 and 11.7.

The unity of the present section is marked by the references to **traditions** and **practice** in verses 2 and 16, though the Greek words are different. Verse 16 may be more specific. There is also a rather strongly implied contrast between **I commend you** in verse 2 and **I do not commend you** in verse 17 (compare verse 22).

This passage, first of all, is remarkably rich in connective words such as **but, nevertheless, for, as,** and so on. Secondly, there is a tendency for each stage of the argument to end with a mention of women, suggesting that they are at present Paul's main concern. However, as is common in Paul's writings, his thought broadens at various points which, as RSV's parentheses suggest, tend to interrupt the argument, even if they also enrich it. As RSV shows, and even more so TEV, it is not necessary or even possible to translate all the Greek connectives. However, the translator should begin by forming a clear idea in his own mind of the steps in Paul's argument as they appear in the text. We have prepared Table 3 to show where these connectives appear and how the idea of "woman" neatly divides the various sections. Words in parentheses (round brackets) in the table are not translated in RSV.

On one important matter this Handbook disagrees with TEV. The translator should note that the words "in public worship" in verses 4, 5, and 13 of TEV, and "in worship" in verse 16 of the same translation, are not expressed in the Greek text. Most commentators believe that Paul is speaking here about praying and prophesying in public worship, and this fact is made explicit in TEV, FrCL, GeCL, and Brc, and in verse 16 by AT. This example is not followed by other translations, including ItCL and NEB. If the present section really referred to public worship, there would be a contradiction with 14.34-35, where women are told to keep silent in church (see the comments). Some scholars have considered 14.34-35 to have been added by someone other than Paul, but there is no significant manuscript evidence to back up this claim. Others have said that the two passages belong to different epistles, in which case Paul would have changed his mind concerning the question of women in worship. Recent commentators still disagree about this. It should be remembered that in Paul's day, Christian worship differed from Jewish or pagan worship, for it was not conducted in buildings set aside for this purpose as in modern times. There is therefore no real connection between this passage and the later Christian tradition that women should wear a hat while inside a church building.

TABLE 4

THE STRUCTURE OF 1 CORINTHIANS 11.2-16

Verse

	2	(*de*)	Introduction				

A (3   <u>but</u>*   man/Christ, (*de*) woman/man, <u>and</u>* Christi/God

A (3 <u>but</u>* man/Christ, (*de*) woman/man, <u>and</u>* Christ/God

```
           ┌4        man
  B        │5                    but*    woman   (for)
           └6                    for     woman   but*    woman

           ┌7a  (men) for man
  C        │
           └7b                   but*    woman

(D)        ┌8   for     man      but⁺    woman
           │
           │9   (and for) man/woman,       but⁺      woman/man

  C  ──────┤10                   that is why  woman  because angels

           ┌11  nevertheless man/woman/Christ
  E        │
           └12  for as woman/man      so    man/woman    and*  God

           ┌13                   woman
  F        │14  (men) man
           └15                   but*    woman

           16   (de)  Conclusion
```

A (3   <u>but</u>*   man/Christ, (*de*) woman/man, <u>and</u>* Christ/God

B
- 4   man
- 5   <u>but</u>*   woman   (for)
- 6   <u>for</u>   woman   <u>but</u>*   woman

C
- 7a   (*men*) <u>for</u> man
- 7b   <u>but</u>*   woman

(D)
- 8   <u>for</u>   man   <u>but</u>⁺   woman
- 9   (<u>and for</u>) man/woman,   <u>but</u>⁺   woman/man

C
- 10   <u>that is why</u> woman <u>because</u> angels

E
- 11   <u>nevertheless</u> man/woman/Christ
- 12   <u>for as</u> woman/man   <u>so</u>   man/woman   <u>and</u>* God

F
- 13   woman
- 14   (*men*) man
- 15   <u>but</u>*   woman

16   (*de*)   Conclusion

* *de* = "and" or "but"

⁺ *alla* = "but," indicating a stronger contrast than *de*

The Greek *men* introduces the first part of a contrast.
It is not translated into English.

There is always the possibility that Paul does contradict himself. So we should avoid strained interpretations and translations of individual passages. TEV, by adding "in public worship," has avoided this danger. However, anyone reading chapter 11 as a whole is sure to be impressed by the heavy emphasis laid in verses 17-20 on the fact of "coming together." The same verb is used in verses 17, 18, and 20. TEV shows this more clearly than RSV, which uses the three English synonyms "come together," "assemble," and "meet together." Verse 18 also uses the phrase "as a church"; compare verse 22 and 14.34-35. In 11.22 church meetings are explicitly contrasted with ordinary meals in private houses (compare verses 33-34).

However, there appears to be a wider implied contrast between public worship in verses 17-34, and praying and prophesying, not necessarily in special meetings for worship, in verses 2-16. In these verses the only phrase which could be understood as referring to public worship is the "churches of God" in verse 16.

Other references in the New Testament to praying or even prophesying do not suggest that these activities were always carried out in the setting of worship by the whole Christian community. The addition of the phrase "in (public) worship" in references in 11.2-16 therefore appears to be unnecessary.

11.2	RSV	TEV
	I commend you because you remember me in everything and maintain the traditions even as I have delivered them to you.	I praise you because you always remember me and follow the teachings that I have handed on to you.

The Greek has the particle *de* (KJV "Now") to indicate that a new theme is being introduced. RSV and other modern translations omit it.

The Greek verb translated **commend** is not used by Paul outside of this chapter, except in a quotation from Psalm 117.1, in Romans 15.11, about praising the Lord. This verb of "praise" does not necessarily suggest worship. RSV, NEB, TNT, and Mft translate it **commend** in the present verse. Other translations expand or restructure it; for example, "You have done well" JB; "I must give you credit" Phps; "This is greatly to your credit" Brc; "I congratulate you" FrCL.

Remember here does not refer to "thinking about" or "fondly remembering," but rather refers to a remembering of Paul's way of life and teaching. It would be legitimate in many languages to expand this clause: "you always remember what I did and taught."

The word translated **maintain** sometimes means "possess," as in 7.30 and 2 Corinthians 6.10, but here it has the meaning of holding on or sticking closely to Paul's teaching (compare 15.2). It is possible, then, to translate this as "stick close to the things which I have taught you," or in some languages, "follow the things . . . ."

The words translated **traditions** (TEV's "teachings") and **delivered** (TEV's "handed on") are related to one another in Greek. The word **traditions** refers to a body of information or teaching which has been received from people of the past and **delivered** or "passed on" to others in the present. Paul is using this word in the present context to talk about Christian teaching which he received from others and has passed on to the Corinthians. It is difficult to know whether he is thinking here of basic Christian teachings, as in verse 23 and in 15.1,3, or of specific "customs" concerning the covering of women's heads. Another model for translating this verse is "I congratulate you because you always remember my actions and teaching, and you follow the Christian teachings which I received from others and have passed on to you."

<table>
<tr><td>11.3</td><td>RSV</td><td>TEV</td></tr>
</table>

RSV	TEV
But I want you to understand that the head of every man is Christ, the head of a woman is her husband, and the head of Christ is God.	But I want you to understand that Christ is supreme over every man, the husband is supreme over his wife, and God is supreme over Christ.

The structure of this verse consists largely of a comparison between three pairs of items: man and Christ, wife and husband, Christ and God. Between each of these pairs Paul uses the Greek connective *de*. RSV and TEV follow English usage in translating the first of these occurrences of *de* by a simple comma, and the second occurrence by a comma followed by **and.**

But suggests a contrast with verse 2. The contrast may be between (1) matters about which Paul can **commend** the Corinthians and (2) matters on which he must criticize them. However, he doesn't express this contrast until verse 17. It is more likely that the contrast of verse 3 is between the teaching already given by Paul and accepted by the Corinthians (verse 3), and new teachings which he is about to develop. If this is so, **I want you to understand** is probably different in meaning from the expression in 10.1 translated "I want you to know" (TEV's "remember"). The first expression **understand** refers to new teaching, whereas "know" refers to teaching which the Corinthians had already received from Paul (see the comments on 10.1, and compare 12.1).

The same Greek words are translated **man** or **husband,** and **woman** or "wife" (TEV; see the comments on 7.2). Each occurrence of these words must be considered to find out which is the more likely meaning in each case. In this verse Paul appears to be referring to the relationship between a man and a woman in marriage, not stating generally that man is **the head** of a woman. Elsewhere in this passage Paul appears to be speaking more generally of men and women, though verse 10 will raise special problems.

Some modern translations such as ItCL keep the word **head** because of a play on words in the Greek; it involves the literal meaning of "head" which occurs in verses 4-10. But in many languages it will be impossible to keep this play on words. Modern translations which do not use "head" in verse 3 tend to agree that Paul is thinking of the head as a symbol of authority; for example, Portuguese common langue translation (PoCL), "Christ has authority over all men as the man has authority over the woman and God over Christ." TEV's translation "supreme" also gives this meaning. (See Isa 7.8,9 for a similar problem.)

<table>
<tr><td>11.4</td><td>RSV</td><td>TEV</td></tr>
</table>

RSV	TEV
Any man who prays or prophesies with his head covered dishonors his head,	So a man who prays or proclaims God's message in public worship with his head covered disgraces Christ.

Prophesies (TEV "proclaims God's message"): this is the first of many references to "prophesying" in this letter (compare 12.10,28,29; 13.2,8,9; and the whole of chapter 14). Where Christian prophets are concerned, not Old Testament prophets, TEV generally translates "proclaim God's message" rather than "prophesy," which in English means only foretelling the future. The Greek word which Paul uses suggests not only that God gave the content of the message, but also that he provided the power to proclaim this message. However, Paul distinguishes clearly between Christian prophecy and speaking with tongues, and the Greek word here does not necessarily imply foretelling the future. GeCL has "proclaims the instructions of God," which distinguishes Christian prophecy from more general preaching of the Good News.

See the comments in the introduction to this section concerning TEV's addition of the words "in public worship."

With his head covered: in this and the following verses Mft uses the word "veil," suggesting a covering for the face. He does this because in verse 10 some Greek manuscripts have the word for "veil" rather than "authority." However, the evidence seems to favor "authority." In this verse Paul is probably referring to a garment hanging down from the head and covering the hair and the upper part of the body, rather than the face.

Dishonors his head: TEV is correct to translate this phrase as "disgraces Christ," for Christ is referred to as "the head of every man" in verse 3. Another possible rendering is "disgraces (dishonors) Christ who is the head." See discussion on **head** under verse 3. GeCL translates "dishonors Christ and himself," and adds a footnote giving the literal meaning, as in RSV. This may be the best solution.

11.5	RSV	TEV
	but any woman who prays or prophesies with her head unveiled dishonors her head—it is the same as if her head were shaven.	And any woman who prays or proclaims God's message in public worship with nothing on her head disgraces her husband; there is no difference between her and a woman whose head has been shaved.

Most of this verse so closely parallels verse 4 as to need no separate comment. The final part of the verse, introduced in Greek by "for," expands and emphasizes the words **dishonors her head.**

In verses 4 and 5 TEV makes it explicit that **his head** and **her head** are used metaphorically to suggest authority (see comments on verse 3), and to refer to Christ (verse 4) and the husband (verse 5). A number of CLTs follow this interpretation. ItCL, perhaps more satisfactorily, includes both in the text: "his head, which is Christ" in verse 4, and "her head, which is her husband," in verse 5. PoCL translates "offends the dignity of Christ" in verse 4, and "offends the dignity of her husband" in verse 5. The reference to Christ and husband is probably correct in verses 4 and 5a, though as 5b shows (**if her head were shaven**), the literal meaning of **head** is in Paul's thinking. In languages where the word for **head** can also refer metaphorically to "authority," one can maintain Paul's play on words.

Unveiled: in some cultures there will already be specific words for pieces of cloth or other material which women normally wear over their heads in religious gatherings. It would be good to use such words here.

The argument of verse 5b is not immediately clear, but there is no doubt about the meaning of the words. Paul probably means that by giving women a natural covering for their heads, God intends that women should give their heads a further covering when they pray or speak God's message. In Paul's time a woman's head would usually be shaven as a sign of shame or disgrace. There are, however, places in the modern world where women shave their heads as a custom. In such cultures it may be necessary for a translator to say "it is as if her head were shaved in order to disgrace her" or ". . . in order to make her feel ashamed." Translators may also need a footnote explaining the significance of shaving women's heads in Paul's time.

As if her head was shaven, of course, implies by someone else.

Another translation model for this verse is "Any woman who prays or proclaims God's message in public worship with nothing covering her head disgraces (brings shame to) her husband. There is no difference between her and a woman whose head has been shaved in order to disgrace her."

11.6   RSV   TEV

RSV	TEV
For if a woman will not veil herself, then she should cut off her hair; but if it is disgraceful for a woman to be shorn or shaven, let her wear a veil.	If the woman does not cover her head, she might as well cut her hair. And since it is a shameful thing for a woman to shave her head or cut her hair, she should cover her head.

Paul reinforces the argument of verse 5 by two contrasting conditions, introduced respectively in Greek by **For if** and **but if.** TEV translates these by two separate sentences. However, they are not very close in either meaning or language. In verse 6a **a woman** means "any woman." TEV's translation "her head" and "her hair" are implied throughout the verse, though, as we noted in verse 4, the garment which RSV calls **a veil** probably covered the shoulders as well as the hair.

She should cut off her hair: this seems to imply that the woman herself cuts her hair. In verse 5 the implication is that someone else did the cutting.

The word translated **disgraceful** is related to the verb translated **dishonors** in verses 4-5. It has a similar meaning. Paul is probably referring to both unmarried and married women. **Is disgraceful for a woman** can be rendered as "brings shame to a woman," or more idiomatically as "makes a woman sell (lose) her face."

To be shorn, literally "cut-her-hair" in Greek, probably referred to a regular trimming of her hair.

11.7   RSV   TEV

RSV	TEV
For a man ought not to cover his head, since he is the image and glory of God; but woman is the glory of man.	A man has no need to cover his head, because he reflects the image and glory of God. But woman reflects the glory of man;

This verse begins a new contrast in which first man and then woman is involved. The second half of the contrast is developed in verse 10.

For introduces a further argument to support the statement in 5a. But since the logical connection is not very close, most modern translations omit the word For.

Ought not to: here Paul uses negatively a Greek verb which literally means "to awe"; in verse 10 he uses it positively. It also has the extended meanings "to be under obligation" and "must, ought to." With a negative the meaning may be either (1) "is under no obligation," as probably in 2 Corinthians 12.14 (TEV), or (2) "ought not to," as in Acts 17.29. In the present verse most translations and commentaries agree with RSV in choosing (2), but others such as TEV, FrCL, ItCL, NEB, and Mft choose (1). The general trend of Paul's thought suggests that he is primarily concerned with women's obligation to wear a head covering, an obligation which does not apply to men. He is therefore not primarily concerned with any obligations which men may have. For this reason TEV's translation is to be preferred.

He is translates the Greek literally, but TEV is correct to choose the verb "reflects," which in English naturally extends the metaphor of image. He is the image means that a man "is made in the likeness of God." The language of this verse is similar to that in Genesis 1.26. However, Paul adds the word glory, which here refers to "the nature of God." Many translators will need to use nonmetaphorical language and translate the first part of this verse in a way similar to the following: "For a man does not need to put a covering over his head, because God has made him similar to himself and has given him a nature similar to his own."

In verse 7b RSV and TEV reproduce a difference in Greek between a man (literally "man") and woman (literally "the woman"), but there is probably no difference in meaning; Paul means "any man" and "any woman."

RSV   TEV

(For man was not made from woman,   for man was not created from woman,
but woman from man. 9 Neither was   but woman from man. 9 Nor was man
man created for woman, but woman for   created for woman's sake, but woman
man.)   was created for man's sake.

As the punctuation note in the UBS Greek text shows, experts disagree about how these verses are related to their context. The problem centers on the meaning of For at the beginning of verse 8. RSV treats this verse as an aside and follows Mft in putting the whole of these two verses in round brackets (parentheses); other translations do not. TEV, however, not only keeps For in the translation but links verse 8 to verse 7b, contrary to the UBS text. But verse 10 appears to follow more closely from verse 7b than do verses 8-9. It is even possible to see man's relation to God (verse 7a) as being, for Paul, in some way parallel to women's relation with the "angels" (see the comments on verse 10). Most translations, then, begin a new sentence at verse 8. Many omit the first For; and some, such as ItCL, make a distinct break: "in fact, man was not taken from woman." ItCL also brings out the full meaning of from woman and from man by using terms that more clearly refer to the story of how God made Eve from Adam's rib.

In languages which do not use the passive, a translator may restructure these verses as follows: "For God did not create man from woman, but created woman from man. Nor did God create man for woman, but rather created woman for man." For man (TEV "for man's sake") suggests that Paul is saying that woman is inferior to man. The meaning, though, seems to be "to meet his (man's) needs." One may not be too specific here.

11.10	RSV	TEV

That is why a woman ought to have a veil[r] on her head, because of the angels.

On account of the angels, then, a woman should have a covering over her head to show that she is under her husband's authority.

[r] Greek *authority* (the veil being a symbol of this)

This is one of the most difficult verses in the New Testament. The difficulties concern not only interpretation and background, but also text and translation.

Some ancient translations, but no Greek manuscript, replace the Greek word for "authority" by **veil**, understanding the veil as a symbol of authority (see RSV footnote). There is no doubt that Paul wrote "authority" (TEV). The difficulty is that there is no evidence outside this passage for using the veil as a symbol of authority. The context makes it clear that Paul intends some kind of connection between the head covering, authority, and angels, but what kind of connection is uncertain. Does he mean (1) that the veil is a sign that the woman is under authority, presumably the authority of her husband, as in TEV and some other CLTs, or (2) that the veil is a sign that the woman herself has some kind of authority, as Brc translates, "the veil which gives her her own authority," or even that the veil is "a symbol of her authority over her husband"? Against (2) we may argue that Paul has not talked about a woman's authority before; however, he goes on to speak of men and women as dependent on one another in verses 11-12.

The problem is complicated because we do not know to what Paul is referring when he writes **because of the angels**, though the meaning of the words themselves seems quite clear.

If Paul is referring in the present verse to the woman's own authority, **because of the angels** may imply "in order to protect herself from attacks of evil supernatural powers" or "so that she may have power over the evil spirits." Barrett does not agree with this interpretation, and comments that "it might have been thought that women would be safest when thus engaged," that is, when praying or prophesying. The most likely explanation is in two parts.[1] (1) A woman must wear a head covering in order that she may cease to fulfill her natural function of reflecting the glory of man, and instead be free to pray or prophesy to the glory of God alone. (2) The head covering is the sign of the authority which God now gives to a woman in order that she may speak to God in prayer and declare his word in prophecy. "That is, her veil represents the new authority given to the woman under the new dispensation to do things which formerly had not been permitted" (Barrett).[2]

---

[1] M.D. Hooker, 1964, " 'Authority on her Head': An examination of 1 Corinthians 11.10," New Testament Studies 10.410-416; summarized in Barrett, 254-255.

[2] A. Feuillet, 1973, "Le signe de puissance sur la tete de la femme. 1 Corinthians 11.10," Nouvelle Revue Théologique 95.945-954, suggests "freedom of choice or action."

If this argument is correct, the following expanded translation may be proposed: "That is why a woman should wear on her head the sign that she is authorized to pray and declare God's message, so that the angels may know that she has this authority." GeCL is even clearer: "For this reason the woman must wear a scarf on her head as a sign of her authority, and thus satisfy the order over which the angels watch."

That is why should refer back to verse 7b, and verses 8-9 should be placed in parentheses. Perhaps Paul thinks of the angels as watching to see that members of the Christian community (in this case women) behave properly.

11.11	RSV	TEV

(**Nevertheless, in the Lord woman is not independent of man nor man of woman;**

In our life in the Lord, however, woman is not independent of man, nor is man independent of woman.

RSV and TEV transfer the phrase **in the Lord** from the end of the Greek sentence to the beginning in English, since Paul's use of the word **Nevertheless** (TEV's "however") implies that there is a contrast between the category of creation (Gen 1-2), about which Paul has been speaking until now, and the new order established by Christ, to which Paul now turns. NEB makes this contrast clearer by translating **in the Lord** as "in Christ's fellowship." One could also translate this as "as we live our lives in fellowship with the Lord."

Nevertheless represents a strong and rather unusual Greek expression in Paul's writings. He uses it elsewhere to indicate that he is returning to the main point of his argument after a digression (see Eph 5.33 "however"; Phil 3.16 "Only"; 4.14 "Yet"). He does the same thing here. For most of this section Paul has been speaking about the distinct obligations of men and especially those of women. However, he had begun in verse 3 by placing this discussion in the setting of relations between men, women, Christ, and God. This wider perspective reappears in verses 11-12, following the reference to angels, and the more positive status recognized for women in verse 10. So in English some expression such as **Nevertheless** or "However that may be" may be appropriate. In terms of context, verses 11 and 12 may therefore be understood as the climax of the argument, though Paul returns to the lower level of man-woman relationships in verses 13-15.

This same interpretation is conveyed in various ways by modern translations; for example, NEB has "in Christ's fellowship woman is as essential to man as man to woman"; ItCL renders it as "However, before the Lord, woman does not exist without man or man without woman." If verse 11 stood alone it would be possible to translate "wife" and "husband," but the context, especially verse 12, speaks more generally of women and men, so this is probably the meaning of verse 11 also.

11.12	RSV	TEV

for as woman was made from man, so man is now born of woman. And all things are from God.)

For as woman was made from man, in the same way man is born of woman; and it is God who brings everything into existence.

Most translations, including both RSV and TEV, reproduce rather closely the structure of the Greek sentence, making it sound like a comparision between two similar events. In fact the two things which Paul compares, namely (1) the making of Eve out of Adam's rib (compare verse 8), and (2) the fact that it is woman that gives birth, are not so much similar as converse and complementary. GeCL brings this out clearly: "True, woman was made out of man, but man is born of woman." ItCL has "In fact, it is true that woman was taken from man, it is just as much true that every man is born of a woman." ItCL continues without a break: ". . . and that both come from God who made everything." The word "both" is not in the Greek but helps to make the progression in Paul's argument clear. Mft translates the final clause as ". . . while both, like all things, come from God."

The variations in Paul's use of prepositions, **from man** and **from God**, but **of woman**, is probably deliberate. The word translated **from** means "out of" (compare verse 8) and indicates origin, while the term translated **of** indicates the means by which man was made.

The parentheses (round brackets) in RSV around verses 11-12 do not seem as necessary as those around verses 8-9, since verse 13 does not follow immediately on the thought of verse 10. It is probably better to leave out the parentheses here, for they may suggest that these two verses contain material less important than the rest of the text. This is not the case here.

11.13	RSV	TEV

Judge for yourselves; is it proper for a woman to pray to God with her head uncovered?

Judge for yourselves whether it is proper for a woman to pray to God in public worship with nothing on her head.

Verses 13-15 bring Paul's argument on the practical level to a conclusion by appealing (1) to the reader's judgment (verse 13), (2) to nature itself (verse 14), and (3) to Christian custom (verses 15-16; also in Jewish custom).

In verse 13 Paul's appeal to the reader's judgment recalls 10.15, "judge for yourselves." This phrase may refer to judgment that is either "in your hearts" or "among yourselves." Since Paul is addressing a community of Christians, "among yourselves" is more probable.

The opening words of verse 13, **judge for yourselves,** show that the following question is not rhetorical, though Paul doubtless expected the answer "No." **Judge for yourselves** may also be expressed as "I want you to decide for yourselves."

Proper means "fitting," "right behavior."

Other translation models for this verse are: "I want you yourselves to decide whether it is right for a woman to pray to God in public worship with no covering over her head," or "I want you yourselves to decide: if a woman prays to God in public worship with no covering over her head, isn't she acting in a disgraceful manner?"

Does not nature itself teach you that | Why, nature itself teaches you that long
for a man to wear long hair is degrading | hair on a man is a disgrace, 15 but on a
to him, 15 but if a woman has long hair, | woman it is a thing of beauty.
it is her pride?

Verses 14-15a consist of a negative question in two parts; the first (verse 14) is about men, and the second (verse 15a) is about women. The question as a whole clearly expects the answer "Yes," so TEV translates it as a simple statement.

In Greek both halves of the question are conditional: "if a man/ woman . . . ." Paul is speaking quite generally, and other CLTs agree with TEV in not translating "if."

Paul's use of the word translated **nature** reflects both the culture in which he lived and his Christian convictions. Nowhere does Paul appear to contrast the natural and the supernatural, as modern theologians and philosophers often have done. Nor does **nature** for Paul consist only of plants, animals, and inanimate objects. Paul uses **nature** to refer either to plants, as in Romans 11.21,24, to human beings as divided by sex (Rom 1.26-27) or race (Rom 2.14; compare 2.27; Gal 2.15), or to divine beings (Gal 4.8). But he could also use **nature** to refer to man's sinful state (Eph 2.3). In each case the meaning of the word must be determined by its context. Here Paul is thinking of the order established by God in the world, and especially in human society. Therefore the word **nature** here could mean "the way God has ordered this world," or even ". . . created human society." And the clause **Does not nature itself teach you** may then be expanded to "Does not the way God has created human society show you . . . ?"

Long hair translates a verb meaning "to wear long hair," "to let one's hair grow long." In some languages the translation must be "to have much hair."

The word for **degrading** is not related to the verb translated "dishonors" in verses 4-5. There the meaning included the idea of shame. Here the thought is rather that of loss of honor or even worthlessness. RSV's translation is therefore more accurate.

For her hair is given to her for a | Her long hair has been given her to
covering. | serve as a covering.

This clause, like the end of verse 5, develops the side of Paul's argument which refers to women.

Is given: both the form of the verb and the context show that woman still possesses what she was once given. Paul is implying that her hair was a gift from God. So in languages which make little use of the passive, it may be better to make this clear: "For God gave her hair to her . . . ."

The word translated **to her** is omitted in some manuscripts, but it is usually more natural to add it in translation.

The word translated **covering** is a general word for a garment, possibly one used as an outer covering. Although it does not specify any particular piece of clothing, there seems to be an obvious relation between this verse and the discussion in verses 4 and 5 about a covering for the head.

RSV	TEV
If any one is disposed to be contentious, we recognize no other practice, nor do the churches of God.	**But if anyone wants to argue about it, all I have to say is that neither we nor the churches of God have any other custom in worship.**

In this verse Paul is putting an end to the discussion which he opened by his statements in verses 4-5. So in English the use of "But" (TEV) before **If** helps to conclude a section of Paul's argument. In certain other languages as well, it will be helpful to begin this verse with "But."

If anyone is disposed to be contentious may be translated as "But if anyone disagrees with me" or ". . . thinks that what I am saying is wrong."

It will be useful in many languages to add the words "about it," as TEV has done, to refer back to the question about "women's head coverings." One can also say "about this matter" or "about this problem."

It is necessary to add words such as "all I have to say is that" (TEV), to make the link with the second part of the verse clear. DuCL says "I answer that"; NEB has "let me tell you." Or one can say "I will say just this one thing."

It is not clear to whom the word **we** refers in this verse. The pronoun is limited by contrast with **the churches of God.** Some commentators think that Paul is speaking of himself alone; others, that he is including the Christian community in the place in which he is writing, or more narrowly, Sosthenes (see 1.1). If Paul is including a Christian community in the meaning of **we**, the end of the verse must be translated "the other churches of God." ItCL has followed this interpretation, "the other communities," but this is not in the Greek text. NEB gives a similar meaning without adding the word "other": ". . . or in any of the congregations of God's people." Phps has "we and the churches of God generally . . . ," meaning "most churches." This last is the most likely solution, since Paul speaks of himself, using the first person singular, in verse 17 of this chapter, and there is no suggestion anywhere else in the letter that Sosthenes played any significant part in its writing. In any case, "we" is exclusive, since Paul does not include the people in Corinth. A good sample translation is "neither I nor the churches of God generally . . . ."

The plural **churches** in this verse indicates local Christian communities rather than a wider group of churches as in **church of God** in 1.2; 10.32.

Concerning the addition of the words "in worship" in TEV and some other translations, see the introduction to 11.2-16.

RSV   **11.17-22**   TEV

The Lord's Supper

RSV	TEV
17 But in the following instructions I do not commend you, because when you come together it is not for the better but for the worse. 18 For, in the first place, when you assemble as a church, I hear that there are divisions among you; and I partly believe it,	17 In the following instructions, however, I do not praise you, because your meetings for worship actually do more harm than good. 18 In the first place, I have been told that there are opposing groups in your meetings; and this I believe is partly true. (19 No

<table>
<tr><td>

19 for there must be factions among you in order that those who are genuine among you may be recognized. 20 When you meet together, it is not the Lord's supper that you eat. 21 For in eating, each one goes ahead with his own meal, and one is hungry and another is drunk. 22 What! Do you not have houses to eat and drink in? Or do you despise the church of God and humiliate those who have nothing? What shall I say to you? Shall I commend you in this? No, I will not.

</td><td>

doubt there must be divisions among you so that the ones who are in the right may be clearly seen.) 20 When you meet together as a group, it is not the Lord's Supper that you eat. 21 For as you eat, each one goes ahead with his own meal, so that some are hungry while others get drunk. 22 Don't you have your own homes in which to eat and drink? Or would you rather despise the church of God and put to shame the people who are in need? What do you expect me to say to you about this? Shall I praise you? Of course I don't!

</td></tr>
</table>

RSV and many other translations take verses 17-34 as a single section dealing with the Lord's Supper.[3] This is generally correct, and verses 33-34, introduced by "So then," form the conclusion to the whole argument. However, it is convenient to distinguish three stages in the argument, corresponding to verses 17-22, 23-26, and 27-34. The UBS Greek text and ItCL make these separate sections, and other translations make them separate paragraphs. In verses 17-22 Paul presents the problem of abuses at the Lord's Supper.

In verses 23-26 Paul quotes the account of the Lord's Supper to show the true meaning of the Supper. In verses 27-34 he draws practical conclusions for the situation in Corinth. Verses 17-22, then, form a coherent whole in the general development of Paul's argument. These verses repeat phrases referring to the meeting of the Christian community; see the introduction to verses 2-6 and the detailed comments.

Translators may wish to give this section a title such as "Abuses at the Lord's Supper" or "The Corinthian Christians celebrate the Lord's Supper wrongly."

<u>11.17</u>　　　　　　RSV　　　　　　　　　　　　　　　TEV

But in the following instructions I do not commend you, because when you come together it is not for the better but for the worse.	In the following instructions, however, I do not praise you, because your meetings for worship actually do more harm than good.

The first part of this verse raises several related problems of (1) text, (2) grammar, and (3) meaning.

(1) The UBS Greek text, like most translations and commentaries, has literally "But this, instructing, I do not praise." Other manuscripts have different texts, the most important being "But this I instruct, not praising." The meaning is much the same.

(2) A more important problem is whether "this," in the word-for-word translation just given, refers to preceding or following instructions. This Greek pronoun normally refers to what precedes, but there are exceptions.[4] RSV, TEV,

---

[3] On the background, see G. Theissen, 1974, "Soziale Integration und sakramentales Handeln: Eine Analyse von I Kor. XI 17-34," <u>Novum Testamentum</u> 16.179-206.

and most CLTs understand "this" to refer to what follows. Other translations take "this" to refer to what precedes; for example, JB says "now that I am on the subject of instructions . . ."; NEB has "in giving you these injunctions . . ."; TOB has "having dealt with this . . . ." It is true that Paul uses a Greek conjunction which can imply a contrast with what precedes, but it can also indicate a transition from one thought to another. Some say that **the following instructions** is unlikely to be the correct translation, since Paul does not give any specific instruction until verse 33, or at least until verse 28. This argument is weak, since the phrase "in the first place" in verse 18 seems to refer forward to chapters 12 and 14, and because deviations are typical of Paul's writings.

(3) The word which RSV and TEV translate **because** may also mean "that," so that the whole sentence would mean "In giving you these injunctions I must mention a practice which I cannot commend: your meetings tend to do more harm than good" NEB.

It appears, then, that the more natural interpretation is to take "this" as referring forward, so it is good to add the words **following instructions.**

In some languages it may be necessary to make explicit that the **instructions** are from Paul, not from rules made by the Corinthians themselves. One can say "As I give these following instructions to you, however, I do not . . . ."

On TEV's "for worship," see introduction to 11.2-16.

The phrases **for the better** and **for the worse** seem to refer to the effect or result of the Corinthians' meetings.

Come together: Paul uses this verb in verses 18,20,33,34 and in 14.23,26 only.

11.18	RSV	TEV

<table>
<tr><td>For, in the first place, when you assemble as a church, I hear that there are divisions among you; and I partly believe it,</td><td>In the first place, I have been told that there are opposing groups in your meetings; and this I believe is partly true.</td></tr>
</table>

For indicates that Paul is about to sharpen the general criticism of verse 17. Barrett translates "Here is a particular example."

In the first place, in Greek as in English, suggests that Paul is beginning a list, as for example in 12.28. There is no clear indication that Paul ever continues the list, though he passes to other criticisms related to worship at Corinth in chapters 12 and 14.

When you assemble as a church comes at the beginning of the verse in Greek and is rather emphatic. The same phrase is repeated in verse 20, "when you meet together." The similarity in thought and language between verses 18a and 20a suggests that the phrase **as a church** (TEV's "in your meetings") and "together" (20a) are similar in meaning. Commentators discuss whether or not these phrases refer to an actual place. It seems unlikely, however, that Paul is referring to a special place where Christians met in Corinth for worship. He is, nevertheless, referring to physical meetings of the Corinthian Christians, not merely to a unity

---

[4] See 1 Timothy 1.9 for a similar construction; such phrases are frequent in the Johannine writings. See Moulton-Howard-Turner, Vol. 3, page 45; compare Arndt-Gingrich under *houtos* 1.a.

of spirit. In the New Testament, as in the Septuagint, the Greek word for **church** often refers to God's people gathered for worship. This is the likely meaning here. See also the comments on verse 20.

I hear that may also be translated as "People have told me."

The word **factions** (TEV "divisions") implies that the Corinthian Christians were dividing themselves into groups in their meetings and opposing or arguing with each other. The first part of the verse may be restructured in the following way: "The first thing I want to mention is that people have told me that when you meet together you split up into groups and oppose each other."

I partly believe it may be translated as "I am sure that there is some truth in what they say."

This verse can be restructured in the following way: "In the first place, people have told me that when you meet together you split up into opposing groups. I believe that there is some truth in this."

11.19	RSV	TEV
	for there must be factions among you in order that those who are genuine among you may be recognized.	(No doubt there must be divisions among you so that the ones who are in the right may be clearly seen.)

TEV, FrCL, and NEB put this verse in parentheses, to show the close links between verses 18 and 20. However, in the Greek, verse 19 is linked grammatically with verse 18 by the conjunction **for**. Paul may imply something like "such divisions are only to be expected," or even "such divisions are part of God's purpose." The verb translated **must** is often used in speaking of God's purpose, as in Mark 8.31.

Factions means the same as "divisions" in verse 18.

The ones who are genuine: the Greek probably implies that the crisis of division in the church will serve as a test or trial, after which it will be possible to tell who have remained faithful and who have not (compare 3.13; 9.27).

GeCL expresses this clause as ". . . so that one can see who has maintained himself in faith"; similarly ItCL, ". . . so that one can recognize who have overcome the test"; and FrCL, ". . . so that one can recognize those among you who are truly faithful."

In this verse Paul repeats twice the phrase **among you** which he has already used in verse 18. This emphasizes his concern in this passage for the corporate life of the Christian community.

11.20	RSV	TEV
	When you meet together, it is not the Lord's supper that you eat.	When you meet together as a group, it is not the Lord's Supper that you eat.

See the comments on verse 18, with which this verse is closely connected.

The Lord's translates an adjective meaning "belonging to the Lord." In Revelation 1.10 it is used of Sunday as the Lord's day.

The meaning of verse 20 must be partly understood in the light of the contrast with verse 21: "it is not *the Lord's* Supper that you are eating; it is your own selfish individual meals." Another possible translation is "even though you may think you are eating the Lord's Supper, it is not so."

For in eating, each one goes ahead with   For as you eat, each one goes ahead
his own meal, and one is hungry and   with his own meal, so that some are
another is drunk.   hungry while others get drunk.

The connection between this verse and verse 20 is brought out by the word
which RSV and TEV translate **For**. The Greek is literally "for each his own supper
takes—first in eating," but most translations put the phrase **in eating** (TEV's "as
you eat") at its natural place at the beginning of the sentence.

Each is emphatic in Greek, and "of you" is understood.

The word translated **meal** is the same as that translated **supper** in the
previous verse. At this time the Lord's Supper was a real meal.

Goes ahead with is literally "takes before or in advance." Verse 33 shows
what Paul means: the members of the church at Corinth sometimes eat together,
but do not wait for one another to arrive before beginning to eat. The first part
of this verse may well be translated as "each person hurries to eat his own meal."

Verse 21b consists of two brief contrasting clauses, **and one is hungry and
another is drunk**. The contrast is somewhat blurred by the fact that Paul here, as
in other places, is trying to convey two thoughts at once: (1) some do not have
enough to eat and others have too much, and (2) some do not have enough to drink
and others drink too much. However, Paul's text as he wrote it is perfectly clear.

What! Do you not have houses to eat   Don't you have your own homes in
and drink in? Or do you despise the   which to eat and drink? Or would you
church of God and humiliate those who   rather despise the church of God and
have nothing?   What shall I say to   put to shame the people who are in
you? Shall I commend you in this? No,   need? What do you expect me to say to
I will not.   you about this? Shall I praise you? Of
                                            course I don't!

This long verse may be divided into six parts, corresponding to the main
verbs (underlined) in Greek, literally:

(1) For do you not **have** houses to eat and drink (in)?
(2) or do you **despise** the church of God?
(3) and **humiliate** those who do not have (anything)?
(4) What am I to **say** to you?
(5) Shall I **praise** you?
(6) About this I do not **praise** you.

(1) to (5) form a new series of rhetorical questions with high emotional
impact. Paul is now challenging his readers to make a positive response.

(1) is a rhetorical question equivalent to the statement "surely you have
houses for eating and drinking in."

(2) and (3) are clearly separated from (1), are closely linked together, and
overlap in meaning. **Despise** has much the same meaning as **humiliate**, except that
humiliate suggests an active expression of a person's contempt. From another

point of view, (3) makes (2) more specific: Paul accuses some of his readers of despising the Christian fellowship by embarrassing those members who are in need.

Since there is no direct connection between (1) and (2), **Or** may be omitted in translation. "Rather" (TEV) is not in the text and does not improve the connection between (1) and (2). One should translate these as two independent questions.

(2) should be understood as **despise** in the sense of "treat as if it is unimportant." Paul means "does it mean nothing to you that you are members of God's people?"

(3) **Those who have nothing** is, of course, an exaggeration; the meaning is similar to the expression "the have-nots," people who have few material things.

Humiliate can be rendered as "bring shame upon" or "cause to receive shame."

"Am I to" in (4) is different in Greek from "shall I" in (5). The verb in (5) is future tense; in (4) the verb form suggests that Paul is considering what he will do. (4) is a real question, and (5) must, in this context, be understood as a real question too, since Paul answers it in (6). As the literal translation shows, Paul repeats the verb translated "praise" (TEV) or **commend**, probably recalling verses 2 and 17.

In this (TEV's "about this"), in the UBS Greek text, belongs to (6), as the literal translation shows. Some older translations agree with RSV in making **in this** part of (5). There is no manuscript evidence for making it part of (4). TEV, however, does so to make the meaning clear, since (4), (5), and (6) all refer to "this matter."

RSV   **11.23-26**   TEV

23 For I received from the Lord what I also delivered to you, that the Lord Jesus on the night when he was betrayed took bread, 24 and when he had given thanks, he broke it, and said, "This is my body which is for *s* you. Do this in remembrance of me." 25 In the same way also the cup, after supper, saying, "This cup is the new covenant in my blood. Do this, as often as you drink it, in remembrance of me." 26 For as often as you eat this bread and drink the cup, you proclaim the Lord's death until he comes.

s Other ancient authorities read *broken for*

23 For I received from the Lord the teaching that I passed on to you: that the Lord Jesus, on the night he was betrayed, took a piece of bread, 24 gave thanks to God, broke it, and said, "This is my body, which is for you. Do this in memory of me." 25 In the same way, after the supper he took the cup and said, "This cup is God's new covenant, sealed with my blood. Whenever you drink it, do so in memory of me."

26 This means that every time you eat this bread and drink from this cup you proclaim the Lord's death until he comes.

The place of this section within verses 17-34 is discussed in the introduction to verses 17-22. Most translations agree with the UBS Greek text in beginning the next section or paragraph at verse 27; TEV, GeCL, and Phps begin it at verse 26, and JB at verse 28. The argument in favor of TEV's division is that Paul's quotation of the tradition about the Lord's Supper goes only until the end of verse 25. However, the section in any case contains in verse 23a words which are not themselves part of the tradition, but an introduction, and verse 26 may be a kind of summary. In the Greek the **For** of verse 26 marks a less important transition than the "therefore" of verse 27. There is nothing in the Greek to suggest a major break at the end of verse 27.

Translators may well use "The Lord's Supper" (TEV) as the heading for this section. It is perhaps the best known passage in Paul's writings, since it is used in all Christian traditions which celebrate the Lord's Supper. Translators may therefore expect their work to be carefully scrutinized, and often criticized, by readers of a new translation. They may find people trying to pressure them to use traditional, word-for-word formulations. It is therefore even more necessary than usual that they should know, not only how to translate the passage, but also the reasons for their translation.

This section also offers a good example of the limitations of the translator's task. It is important to consult the parallel passages—Matthew 26.26-29; Mark 14.22-25; Luke 22.19-20—in order to avoid unnecessary variation in translating the same expressions. However, the translator's task is not, at this point, to translate the Gospels, but the Greek text as it stands in this chapter. The background information given in general commentaries is useful in helping the translator to understand the Greek text at places where its meaning and implications may not otherwise be clear.

11.23	RSV	TEV

For I received from the Lord what I also delivered to you, that the Lord Jesus on the night when he was betrayed took bread,

For I received from the Lord the teaching that I passed on to you: that the Lord Jesus, on the night he was betrayed, took a piece of bread,

For: the connection with the previous section is not very close, and the word is omitted in some modern translations. BJ and PoCL translate it "in fact." Héring thinks that the word "presupposes an unexpressed thought: 'if you had been faithful to the traditions which were passed on to you (11.1), you could not have behaved in this way. For—I repeat—this is the tradition . . . .'"

The first **I** in this verse is emphatic in Greek, underlining the contrast between the abuses at Corinth and the tradition which Paul received.

The verbs translated **I received** (compare 15.1,3) and **I also delivered** (see 11.2) were commonly used among Jewish and other teachers when speaking about traditional teaching. In the ancient world and in many places in the modern world, a personal relationship with a teacher counted at least as much in education as the reading of books.

The word translated **from** is not the preposition commonly used in speaking of direct personal communication found, for example, in Galatians 1.12; 1 Thessalonians 2.13; 4.1; 2 Thessalonians 3.6. Some scholars believe that Paul's choice of a less common preposition indicates that he is thinking of Jesus as beginning a tradition which Paul received indirectly, not directly, from Jesus. Others believe that he received this "teaching" directly from Jesus in some supernatural way. Others, though, take the view that the story of the founding of the Lord's Supper may have come to Paul through human channels, but that this tradition came to life for him through communion with the risen Lord. It is the context, particularly the close similarity between the accounts given here and in the synoptic Gospels (especially Luke), which suggests that Paul is relying on a tradition already being handed on within the church.

The Lord is Jesus, as usual in Paul's writings. This is made clear later in the verse. In many languages it would doubtless be smoother to have "the Lord Jesus" in the first part of the verse, and "Jesus" later. However, translators generally attempt to keep the wording of the text, showing the distinction between the tradition (verses 23b-25) and Paul's introduction to it (verse 23a). In languages which do not normally employ the passive, one may render this first clause as "For the Lord passed on to me that teaching which . . . ."

Most translators will find it helpful to add the words "the teaching," as TEV has done.

The verbs translated **delivered** and **betrayed** are the same in the Greek, but the two meanings are quite distinct and thus should be translated as "passed on" (TEV) or "handed down" for the first one, and **betrayed** or "handed over" for the second one.

Also links the two verbs **received** and **delivered.** As already noted, the second **I** is not expressed in the Greek. So it will be helpful in many languages to omit **also** as TEV has done. This will avoid the misunderstanding that Paul is implying that someone else as well "delivers" the tradition.

On the night wrongly suggests to the modern reader that the meal took place in the middle of the night. In fact, it was probably held soon after sunset.

As noted on 10.16, Greek has the same word for **bread** and "loaf." In the present verses, commentators who mention the matter tend to prefer "loaf" (Mft, Brc) rather than "some bread" (JB, AT) or the literal **bread** (RSV, NEB). There is nothing in the Greek to support TEV's suggestion that the loaf was already broken, so "a loaf" is preferable to "a piece of bread."

11.24	RSV	TEV

and when he had given thanks, he broke it, and said, **"This is my body which is for** ^{s} **you. Do this in remembrance of me."**

gave thanks to God, broke it, and said, **"This is my body, which is for you. Do this in memory of me."**

^{s} Other ancient authorities read *broken for*

In verses 23b-24 many translations agree with TEV in having a series of main verbs—"took," "gave thanks," "broke," and "said"—as in the Greek of Mark 6.41. However, RSV's more literal translation shows that giving thanks to God is a preliminary act closely related to breaking the loaf. The connection between the other actions of Jesus is less close. Perhaps one can begin a new sentence with verse 24: ". . . took a loaf of bread. Then when he had given thanks . . . ."

He had given thanks: "to God" (TEV) is implied as in 10.16 (see the comments). The same word is used in Luke 22.19. Mark 14.22 and Matthew 26.26 have "bless," but the meaning is much the same. JB makes the meaning even more explicit by translating "thanked God for it," that is, for the loaf.

Broke it: AT emphasizes this by adding "in pieces," and this may make the meaning clearer in some languages.

For you: some manuscripts add "broken" as in KJV, "given" as in Luke 22.19, and one manuscript even has a strong verb meaning "broken in pieces." The weight of manuscript evidence is on the side of the shorter text **for you.** However, one can fill out the meaning, as GeCL has done by rendering this phrase as "which is sacrificed for you."

The pronoun **This** occurs twice in verse 24 and twice more in verse 25. The second time in verse 25, TEV translates "so" to stress the importance of performing this ritual regularly. **Do this in remembrance of me** may also be rendered as "Eat this bread to make you remember me."

In remembrance of me: the Greek word has the meaning of a memorial or reminder. As the rest of the verse shows, Paul's thought is turned at least as much to the future as to the past. The Jews and the first Christians thought of sacred meals as events by which later generations were identified with historic events of the past, such as the exodus on the one hand, and the death and resurrection of Christ on the other. NEB has "as a memorial of me." Brc brings out the meaning using a verb: "to make you remember me."

A model translation for verse 24 can be "When he had thanked God, he broke the bread and said, 'This is my body which is for you. Eat this bread to make you remember me.' "

<u>11.25</u>

RSV	TEV
In the same way also the cup, after supper, saying, "This cup is the new covenant in my blood. Do this, as often as you drink it, in remembrance of me."	In the same way, after the supper he took the cup and said, "This cup is God's new covenant, sealed with my blood. Whenever you drink it, do so in memory of me."

In the same way: here, as in verse 24, attention is focused on the actions of Jesus rather than on the bread and wine themselves. Bruce comments: "as he had taken the bread and given thanks for it, so he took the cup and gave thanks for it."

The in front of **cup** shows that Paul is referring to a particular cup which was used during the Last Supper, not just any cup.

As in verse 20, **supper** should be translated in such a way as to make it clear that a real meal was in progress, both at the Last Supper itself, and in the Lord's Supper as it was celebrated at Corinth and elsewhere.

The idea of the **new covenant** can best be understood in the light of Jeremiah 31.31-34; the words **in my blood** recall Exodus 24.8. **New covenant** is found also in Luke 22.20. The basic meaning of **covenant** is that of an agreement, normally between two parties. In the Old Testament the term **covenant** was specially used of the inevitably one-sided agreement by which God claimed Israel as his special people and gave himself to Israel as their God. In many languages there is no parallel to this idea apart from language based on the Bible. TEV and some other CLTs try to bring out the meaning by adding "God's," but **covenant** is not used in modern secular English except in the sense of a financial arrangement. AT and Phps translate "agreement," which has a somewhat wider range of meaning in English than **covenant.** Brc translates "This cup stands for the new relationship with God made possible at the cost of my death." Whatever expression the translator chooses, he or she must carefully examine its meaning in common language to avoid misunderstanding or lack of understanding by the readers of the translation. See *A Translator's Handbook on the Letter to the Hebrews,* Appendix B, on "The Translation of Covenant."

In my blood (TEV's "sealed in . . ."): the Greek may mean "by means of" or "at the cost of my blood"; compare DuCL "ratified by," FrCL "guaranted by," ItCL "established with," TNT "made by my blood." The grammar of this sentence is understood in different ways. The two most likely meanings are (1) to take **my blood** with **This cup**, meaning "if the cup is a cup of the covenant, it is because of my blood"; and (2) to take the phrase "sealed with my blood" (TEV) with **new covenant.** TEV and most translations and commentaries favor the second.

In verse 25b the words translated **as often as you drink it** may mean "as often as you drink wine" (Barrett), suggesting that bread, but not wine, was a normal article of diet. However, the context suggests rather "as often as you drink wine in celebrating the Lord's Supper." In many languages, including English, it is not natural to speak of drinking a cup. In such cases it will be necessary for reasons of style to translate "each time you drink wine from it," that is, "from this cup," as in verse 26. There is nothing in the Greek to suggest how often the Lord's Supper was celebrated at Corinth.

The words **Do this** may be expanded to "You should do this."

In remembrance: see comments on verse 24.

The final sentence can be translated as "Whenever you drink wine from this cup, you should do it in memory of me."

11.26 RSV	TEV
For as often as you eat this bread and drink the cup, you proclaim the Lord's death until he comes.	This means that every time you eat this bread and drink from this cup you proclaim the Lord's death until he comes.

Although the language in this verse is similar to that of previous verses, Paul is now giving his own interpretation of the tradition rather than repeating the tradition itself.

The cup implies "the cup previously mentioned."

Here as elsewhere in the passage, bread may be translated as "loaf," giving a possible translation "each time you eat from this loaf and drink from this cup."

The word translated **you proclaim the Lord's death** may need some expansion or clarification in translation. The word for **proclaim** is often used of the work of Christian preachers such as the apostles in announcing the "good news" of what Jesus had done (compare 2.1; 9.14). In some languages it may be necessary to say "you are proclaiming the fact of the Lord's death," "you are telling the story of the Lord's death," or "you are telling people once again that Jesus has died."

Until he comes: the Greek expresses the certainty of a future event. In some languages, including English, a literal translation as in RSV and TEV can be misunderstood as implying that the Lord has not yet come to earth at all. For this reason several translations, including ItCL, AT, Phps, and Brc, have "returned," "comes back," or "comes again."

Even if **until he comes** is understood as "until he comes back," the connection of these words with the rest of the sentence is not very clear. It is possible that, as in other places, Paul is thinking more quickly than his secretary can write, and therefore leaving out certain stages in the argument. If this is so here, **until he comes** may be more connected with **as often** in the first clause, and with the same phrase in verse 25, than with **proclaim the Lord's death. Until he comes** would therefore be an afterthought, rather like "in eating" in verse 21, and "not distinguishing the body" in verse 29. This phrase can also mean "until the goal is reached that he comes." In such a case one may render this verse as "For until the Lord comes back, every time you eat this bread and drink wine from the cup, you proclaim his death."

 RSV   11.27-34   TEV

27 Whoever, therefore, eats the bread or drinks the cup of the Lord in an unworthy manner will be guilty of profaning the body and blood of the Lord. 28 Let a man examine himself, and so eat of the bread and drink of the cup. 29 For any one who eats and drinks without discerning the body eats and drinks judgment upon himself. 30 That is why many of you are weak and ill, and some have died.[t] 31 But if we judged ourselves truly, we should not be judged. 32 But when we are judged by the Lord, we are chastened[u] so that we may not be condemned along with the world.

33 So then, my brethren, when you come together to eat, wait for one another—34 if any one is hungry, let him eat at home—lest you come together to be condemned. About the other things I will give directions when I come.

[t] Greek *have fallen asleep* (as in 15.6,20)
[u] Or *when we are judged we are being chastened by the Lord*

27 It follows that if anyone eats the Lord's bread or drinks from his cup in a way that dishonors him, he is guilty of sin against the Lord's body and blood. 28 So then, everyone should examine himself first, and then eat the bread and drink from the cup. 29 For if he does not recognize the meaning of the Lord's body when he eats the bread and drinks from the cup, he brings judgment on himself as he eats and drinks. 30 That is why many of you are sick and weak, and several have died. 31 If we would examine ourselves first, we would not come under God's judgment. 32 But we are judged and punished by the Lord, so that we shall not be condemned together with the world.

33 So then, my brothers, when you gather together to eat the Lord's Supper, wait for one another. 34 And if anyone is hungry, he should eat at home, so that you will not come under God's judgment as you meet together. As for the other matters, I will settle them when I come.

This is the third and last part of the discussion which Paul began in verses 17-22 (see the introduction to that section). Having appealed in verses 23-26 to the facts and meaning of the Lord's Supper as instituted by Jesus, Paul now draws practical conclusions.

The main general difficulty in translating these verses is how to give full weight to several expressions which were generally used in law courts. These are mostly related to the word for "judge."

The simple Greek verb for "judge" is used in verse 32a. Grammatically related Greek words are those translated **discerning** (verse 29), **judged** (verse 31), **condemned** (verse 32), and **condemned** (verse 34). Terms which are related in meaning but not in form include **guilty** (verse 27), possibly **examine** (verse 28), and **give directions** (verse 34). How far translators should attempt to translate these words by related terms depends on the resources of the receptor language and the analysis of what each term means in its context.

We have already noted a similar group of legal terms in 6.1-6, where Paul's aim was to encourage the Corinthians to settle their disputes within the Christian community. In 5.3-5 Paul was much closer to acting as a judge, announcing his own verdict, though still with the cooperation of the Corinthians themselves.

Verse 34b suggests that Paul thinks of himself as "settling" things—in a sense judging the matter under discussion. However, his instructions in verses 28, 33, and 34a are balanced by further arguments by which Paul tries to help the Corinthians see the reason for his judgment. Then in verses 31-32 he places himself alongside his readers by the use of an inclusive **we.**

It seems likely that in this section, as in 5.3-5 and 6.1-6, Paul is not speaking about the last judgment. Rather he is talking about an immediate judgment by himself and the Corinthian church on the bad behavior described in verses 17-22.

An appropriate heading for this section can be "Eating the Lord's Supper in a wrong way."

11.27 RSV	TEV
Whoever, therefore, eats the bread or drinks the cup of the Lord in an unworthy manner will be guilty of profaning the body and blood of the Lord.	It follows that if anyone eats the Lord's bread or drinks from his cup in a way that dishonors him, he is guilty of sin against the Lord's body and blood.

Therefore, like "so then" in verse 33, is the same Greek word and indicates that Paul is drawing a conclusion from what precedes.

Here as in other passages, Paul uses different expressions to indicate that he is speaking generally and not about a particular individual. These expressions include **Whoever** (TEV's "anyone") in verse 27, "a man" (TEV's "everyone") in verse 28, and "any one" in verse 34.

Neither the Greek nor RSV makes it clear that the phrase **of the Lord** applies to both the bread and the cup. However, the context and the phrase **the bread** (not just "bread") show that Paul is still speaking of the loaf used in the Lord's Supper. TEV makes this clear by putting "the Lord's" before bread and writing "his cup" later in the verse. Translators would do well to restructure the verse in a similar way.

As in previous verses, the word for **bread** may be translated "loaf" or "loaf of bread"; see comments on verse 26.

Drink the cup is unnatural English, so TEV has "drink from his cup."

In an unworthy manner: the implied object here is Christ, so TEV has added "him": "In a way that dishonors him." The literal translation **unworthy** may be misunderstood as suggesting that there are other people who are "worthy" and who do in some way deserve the benefits of the Lord's Supper, but no such limitation or comparison is implied. The adverb "unworthily" is not used elsewhere in the New Testament, but in 6.2 the related adjective was translated "incompetent."[5] Mft translates "carelessly" in the present verse. Phps has "without proper reverence," and Brc, perhaps overtranslating, has "in a way that contradicts all the Lord meant it to be." TEV's "in a way that dishonors him" may be the best rendering.

---

[5] Where Paul uses the corresponding positive Greek adjective for "worthy," it is related to the activity of God (Phil 1.27; 1 Thes 2.12) or Christ (Gal 1.10), and to the calling (Eph 4.1) to belong to God's people (Rom 16.2); compare 2 Thessalonians 1.11, where Paul speaks of God's making the readers "worthy of the life he has called you to live" (TEV).

Guilty here refers to **profaning** or "sinning against" Christ's death on the cross rather than to being responsible for his death. So even though the Greek does not have a word corresponding to **profaning**, it should be added as RSV and TEV have done.

Commentators disagree about the meaning of **the body and blood of the Lord.** Some think that **body** refers to the church, but in that case it is difficult to see why Paul adds **blood.** It is best to read this verse in the light of verses 24-25 and to translate the key terms in the same way.

11.28	RSV	TEV

Let a man examine himself, and so eat of the bread and drink of the cup.	So then, everyone should examine himself first, and then eat the bread and drink from the cup.

This verse is closely connected with verse 27, about which see the comments.

The word translated **examine** is related to the adjective in verse 19 translated "genuine" and has a similar meaning: "check whether all is right." To "test oneself," as in NEB, Mft, and GeCL, is perhaps too narrow, as it suggests just one particular test. Some languages may have to say something like "look carefully into the heart," in order to avoid the idea of a physical examination.

And so: the **so** is emphatic, implying "and only when he has examined himself." This meaning is made explicit by GeCL, ". . . before he eats the bread"; ItCL says "Each one therefore should first examine himself, and then eat . . ."; and NEB, "a man must test himself before eating his share of the bread . . . . "

11.29	RSV	TEV

For any one who eats and drinks without discerning the body eats and drinks judgment upon himself.	For if he does not recognize the meaning of the Lord's body when he eats the bread and drinks from the cup, he brings judgment on himself as he eats and drinks.

For gives the reason for the statement in verse 28, and it links up and partly overlaps with the thought of verse 27.

Some manuscripts add "unworthily" after **drinks,** and "of the Lord" after **body,** as in verse 27. These additions are probably intended to make the text clear. Although it seems unlikely that "unworthily" is implicit in the text, it certainly is justified to add "of the Lord" after "body," as TEV has done.

The Greek of this verse is not very smooth. The phrase translated **without discerning the body** (of the Lord) is added loosely at the end of the verse. All translations we have consulted agree with TEV in translating these words as an "if" clause, and many languages will prefer to put this clause at the beginning of the verse, as in English.

TEV correctly expands RSV's literal translation to "the Lord's body," that is, the body of Jesus. GeCL translates "If he does not realize that he has to do with the Lord's body . . . ." Many scholars believe that Paul is thinking of the church as the body of Christ, but he leaves this implicit, and translators should probably do the same. Some translations such as NEB have capitalized "Body," but this is ineffective. When the verse is read aloud, the hearer will not catch the difference in meaning.

It seems better, on the whole, to understand verse 29 in the light of verse 27 as referring to someone who "does not realize the sacredness of Christ's body" as he eats the bread in the Lord's Supper (TNT translational notes).

This interpretation is partially reflected in TEV and more clearly by FrCL: "if anyone eats of the bread and drinks of the cup without recognizing their relationship with the body of the Lord." In a similar way GeCL renders it "If he has not made it clear to himself that he has to do with the Lord's body . . . ."

Judgment means a verdict—almost always, as here, of condemnation. One can render this clause as "God will condemn him as he eats and drinks" (see verse 34 in TEV).

<u>11.30</u>   RSV   TEV

That is why many of you are weak and ill, and some have died.[t]   **That is why many of you are sick and weak, and several have died.**

[t] Greek *have fallen asleep* (as in 15.6,20)

That is why: God's **judgment** (verse 29) can have physical consequences.

Many of you, literally "many among you," means "many members of your community." **Many** and **some** are different words in the Greek; some translations have "a number" for **some.** The difference in meaning between the two terms, though, is probably slight. The context, rather than the words themselves, suggests that more people at Corinth had been ill than had died.

The words translated "sick" (TEV) and **weak** are also quite similar in meaning. TEV appears to translate them in the opposite order than the Greek. **Weak** should be understood in a physical sense in this verse. "Sick" (TEV) is a less common Greek term used in Mark 6.5,13. Some languages such as ThCL can use one strong word to approximate the meaning of the two Greek words.

As RSV's footnote states, **have died** is literally "have fallen asleep." New Testament writers tend to use this expression in speaking of the death of Christians. It no doubt reflects the Christian belief that death is not the end. There is simply no basis for Phps' translation "many of you are spiritually asleep." The word used here is used in the same sense in 15.6,20; see especially 1 Thessalonians 4.13-16, where "those who are asleep" (verse 13) and "the dead in Christ" (verse 16) are the same people. In most present-day situations it is better to use the common word for "die," because euphemisms suggest old-fashioned church language rather than any difference of meaning.

<u>11.31</u>   RSV   TEV

But if we judged ourselves truly, we should not be judged.   **If we would examine ourselves first, we would not come under God's judgment.**

The passive **we should not be judged** probably refers to the judgment of Christ (as in verse 32) rather than the judgment of God (as in TEV). Paul means

"If we first examine ourselves, there will be nothing for Christ to condemn in our behavior as we share in his Supper."

11.32	RSV	TEV

But when we are judged by the Lord, we are chastened ^u so that we may not be condemned along with the world.	But we are judged and punished by the Lord, so that we shall not be condemned together with the world.

^u Or *when we are judged we are being chastened by the Lord*

But suggests a contrast with the immediately preceding clause. The Greek is literally "but being judged by the Lord we are disciplined . . . ." Most translations understand the participle "being judged" to refer to judgments which fall on both Paul and his readers, though the rest of the verse shows that they are not yet the final judgment of the world. If so, RSV's **when we are judged** is correct. However, the participle may also be understood as making a concession: "(even) if we are judged . . . ," as in ItCL and ThCL. The translation "if" would bring verse 32a closer in meaning to verse 31a: "But if we judged ourselves . . . ."

The word translated **chastened** may also mean "educated" or "disciplined." Paul's thought moves for a moment from the law courts to the family or the school. For the meaning, compare Hebrews 12.5-11. TNT has "we are being disciplined," implying the activity of Christ. NEB's "he is disciplining us" seems to give the meaning of this verb. "Correction" is also a possiblity. Both the acts of "judging" and "disciplining" are seen as being done by the Lord. So TEV's restructuring is probably better than RSV's rather literal translation.

So that we may not be condemned indicates the purpose of the discipline: "in order that Christians may not, in the end, fall under God's general condemnation of the world." The passive **be condemned** suggests the activity of God or Christ, probably God, if the last judgment is intended. Here, as elsewhere, **the world** means society, including nonhuman powers, organized in rebellion against God (compare 1.20-21; 2.12).

In languages which do not normally use the passive voice, the following is a possible model: "But the Lord judges and disciplines us so that in the end God will not have to condemn us along with the world."

11.33	RSV	TEV

So then, my brethren, when you come together to eat, wait for one another—	So then, my brothers, when you gather together to eat the Lord's Supper, wait for one another.

This verse and verse 34 partly repeat verses 21-22 and also form a conclusion to the entire argument begun in verse 17.

So then introduces the conclusion, like "therefore" (TEV's "it follows") in verse 27.

My brethren: again this phrase may be translated as "my fellow Christians" or "elders and youngers." It is referring to fellow believers, not true family members.

When you come together returns to the language and theme of verse 17. There is nothing in the Greek corresponding to the Lord's Supper. TEV assumes that when the whole Christian community gathered for a meal, this meal would include a celebration of the Lord's Supper. This is certainly correct and reminds the modern reader that the Lord's Supper at this time was associated with a real meal.

Wait for one another was made clear in verse 21.

11.34	RSV	TEV

if any one is hungry, let him eat at home—lest you come together to be condemned. About the other things I will give directions when I come.	And if anyone is hungry, he should eat at home, so that you will not come under God's judgment as you meet together. As for the other matters, I will settle them when I come.

The **if** in translations, including RSV, TEV, and others, may be misunderstood as meaning that, in contradiction to the rest of the passage, the Lord's Supper was not a real meal designed to satisfy hunger. What Paul really means is that if someone is so hungry that he cannot wait until everyone has arrived for the common meal (compare 33b), he should eat something at home first. GeCL makes this clear: "anyone who is hungry should eat at home first."

Lest you . . . be condemned recalls verse 17, especially in the Greek. In both places Paul is concerned not with the intention of the Corinthians but with the results of their behavior: "in order that when you meet together, you do not behave in such a way that as a result God will condemn you."

Condemned: see the comments on verse 29. God is probably the one condemning.

The final sentence of this chapter is quite general. We have no means of knowing whether the **other things** were also related to the Lord's Supper or not. The **other things** could mean and could even be translated "the other matters which you wrote about."

Will give directions: this Greek verb originally had the idea of setting in order; and many translations, including NEB's "arrange" and JB's "adjust," think this is the meaning here. However, the most common meaning of this verb in the New Testament is "to give orders" or "give instruction." Although this may sound harsh to modern readers, it is probably closer to Paul's meaning; compare 7.17, where Paul talks about **my rule.**

When I come does not suggest any particular time for Paul's visit or even that he is sure it will take place. In many languages **I come** needs to be translated by a future tense, since it refers to a future event. Some languages may require an explicit destination, "when I come to you."

Chapter 12

Gifts from the Holy Spirit

1 Now concerning spiritual gifts,[x] brethren, I do not want you to be uninformed. 2 You know that when you were heathen, you were led astray to dumb idols, however you may have been moved. 3 Therefore I want you to understand that no one speaking by the Spirit of God ever says "Jesus be cursed!" and no one can say "Jesus is Lord" except by the Holy Spirit.

4 Now there are varieties of gifts, but the same Spirit; 5 and there are varieties of service, but the same Lord; 6 and there are varieties of working, but it is the same God who inspires them all in every one. 7 To each is given the manifestation of the Spirit for the common good. 8 To one is given through the Spirit the utterance of wisdom, and to another the utterance of knowledge according to the same Spirit, 9 to another faith by the same Spirit, to another gifts of healing by the one Spirit, 10 to another the working of miracles, to another prophecy, to another the ability to distinguish between spirits, to another various kinds of tongues, to another the interpretation of tongues. 11 All these are inspired by one and the same Spirit, who apportions to each one individually as he wills.

[x] Or *spiritual persons*

1 Now, concerning what you wrote about the gifts from the Holy Spirit.

I want you to know the truth about them, my brothers. 2 You know that while you were still heathen, you were led astray in many ways to the worship of lifeless idols. 3 I want you to know that no one who is led by God's Spirit can say "A curse on Jesus!" and no one can confess "Jesus is Lord," unless he is guided by the Holy Spirit.

4 There are different kinds of spiritual gifts, but the same Spirit gives them. 5 There are different ways of serving, but the same Lord is served. 6 There are different abilities to perform service, but the same God gives ability to all for their particular service. 7 The Spirit's presence is shown in some way in each person for the good of all. 8 The Spirit gives one person a message full of wisdom, while to another person the same Spirit gives a message full of knowledge. 9 One and the same Spirit gives faith to one person, while to another person he gives the power to heal. 10 The Spirit gives one person the power to work miracles; to another, the gift of speaking God's message; and to yet another, the ability to tell the difference between gifts that come from the Spirit and those that do not. To one person he gives the ability to speak in strange tongues, and to another he gives the ability to explain what is said. 11 But it is one and the same Spirit who does all this; as he wishes, he gives a different gift to each person.

There are several indications that a new major section begins at this point. The word translated **concerning** is used to mark a new section in 7.1,25; 8.1 (compare 8.4); 16.1. As in 1.10 and elsewhere, **brethren** indicates a new theme.

The words translated **I do not want you to be uninformed,** literally "I do not want you not to know," were used in 10.1 at the beginning of a section and were translated positively as "I want you to know." "I want you to understand" in 11.3 is similar in meaning. In all three places, 10.1; 11.3; and 12.1, there is a contrast, either explicit or implicit, between something which the readers are presumed to know already and something more which Paul wants to tell them (**I want you to understand** in 12.3). That is why TEV adds the words "the truth" in 12.1. Paul is concerned, not just that his readers shall know of the existence of spiritual gifts—they know about these in any case—but that they should receive correct teaching about these gifts.

The subject of spiritual gifts will occupy Paul until the end of chapter 14. Chapter 13 forms a diversion from this main theme of gifts.

The inner structure of chapter 12 may be understood in different ways without greatly affecting the translation (see also the introduction to 12.12-31a). Most translations and commentaries agree with the UBS Greek text and TEV in making a more important break after verse 11 than after verse 3, though Barrett makes the division after verses 3 and 31. There are some similarities between the ways in which Paul's argument develops in this chapter and in chapter 11. 12.1-11, like 11.2-16, is concerned generally with prophecy. Chapter 12 also includes other gifts of the Spirit. In the second part of each chapter, Paul's attention turns to the complex unity of the church. The same pattern is repeated on a larger scale in chapters 13 and 14 respectively.

The structure of 12.1-11 is generally clear and, as the detailed comments will show, is of importance at several points for the translation. Verses 1-3 introduce the whole subject, and verse 3 lays the basic theological foundation. Verses 4-11 are almost poetic in character and therefore include a good deal of balance, rhythm, and repetition. Verses 4, 5, and 6 are closely parallel, the extra length of verse 6 giving this line greater emphasis. Verse 7 marks a change of grammatical structure and introduces a complementary theme: verses 4-6 emphasize the unity of God's action, but verses 7-10 emphasize its diversity. Verse 11 rounds off the list of spiritual gifts in verses 8-10, and also contains echoes of verses 4-6.

12.1   RSV   TEV

    Now concerning spiritual gifts,[x] brethren, I do not want you to be uninformed.

[x] Or *spiritual persons*

    Now, concerning what you wrote about the gifts from the Holy Spirit.
    I want you to know the truth about them, my brothers.

The Greek word for **Now** does not always need to be translated, but other indications of a change of theme show that **Now** should be translated, as RSV and TEV have done.

The word **concerning** may be expanded to "I want to talk to you about . . . ."

The word translated **spiritual gifts** or "gifts from the Holy Spirit" (TEV) may also mean "spiritual people" (see RSV footnote). Some commentators think "spiritual people" is the meaning here, though no translation which we consulted agrees with this interpretation. The immediate context does not help to settle the question since verses 4-6 are about spiritual gifts, verses 7-10 are about the various people to whom spiritual gifts are given, and verse 11 is about both.

However, where Paul speaks elsewhere in this letter about "spiritual people" (2.15; 3.1; 14.37), there is an explicit or implied contrast with other members of the Christian community who are not spiritual, but this does not seem to be Paul's point in this section. The translation **spiritual gifts,** meaning "the gifts from the Holy Spirit" (TEV), is therefore preferable.

Brethren, as in earlier passages, means "fellow believers" or "fellow Christians," not actual family members.

Here, as in 8.1, TEV adds "what you wrote about." Other translations do not follow TEV's example, and some scholars believe that Paul's information in chapter 12 was drawn, not only or mainly from the Corinthian's letter to him (7.1), but also from other reports such as those mentioned in 1.11 and 11.18. Some translations therefore refer more generally to previous information: "I want to clear up a wrong impression about spiritual gifts" JB; "I want to give you some further information in some spiritual matters" Phps. The basis for Phps' word "further" is the distinction Paul makes between what "you know" in verse 2 and what "I want you to understand" in verse 3. The double negative, **I do not want you to be uninformed,** is awkward in English, so TEV turns it into the positive statement, "I want you to know," as RSV did in 10.1. One possible translation, then, is "Now I want to talk with you further about gifts which come from the Holy Spirit. I want you to know the facts (or, the truth) about them, my brothers."

<table>
<tr><td>12.2</td><td>RSV</td><td>TEV</td></tr>
</table>

RSV	TEV
You know that when you were heathen, you were led astray to dumb idols, however you may have been moved.	You know that while you were still heathen, you were led astray in many ways to the worship of lifeless idols.

The statement **You know** is an equivalent of Paul's frequent question "Do you not know?" used, for example, in 3.16. Paul refers here to facts which his readers clearly know.

Nowhere else does Paul refer to Corinthian Christians as having been **heathen.** Since Paul uses the past tense, **when you were heathen,** he must be thinking about their beliefs and way of life which changed when they became Christians, rather than about their race. **Heathen** or "people who did not worship God" is probably a more adequate translation than "non-Jews" in this context.

The general meaning of the rest of the verse is clear, but the Greek is extremely difficult in detail. Both ancient scribes and modern editors have made or suggested various changes in trying to make the text clearer. The main options for the translator are represented by the NEB text, "you were swept off to those dumb heathen gods, however you happened to be led" (as in RSV and TEV), and the NEB footnote, "you would be seized by some power which drove you to those dumb heathen gods."

Led astray is literally "led away," but the extended meaning of "led into error" is the likely one here. Translators may wish to avoid the passive here and say "lifeless idols led you astray."

The word translated **dumb** (TEV's "lifeless") is literally "voiceless." The implied meaning expressed in various Old Testament passages is that pagan idols are lifeless and therefore cannot speak or answer. The literal translation "voiceless" should be avoided, since it appears to contradict verse 3a where people are said to speak under the influence of an evil spirit. "Lifeless" therefore gives the meaning better.

However (TEV's "in many ways") probably suggests repeated action. It also may be translated "in one way or another" (TNT).

12.3	RSV	TEV

RSV	TEV
Therefore I want you to understand that no one speaking by the Spirit of God ever says "Jesus be cursed!" and no one can say "Jesus is Lord" except by the Holy Spirit.	I want you to know that no one who is led by God's Spirit can say "A curse on Jesus!" and no one can confess "Jesus is Lord," unless he is guided by the Holy Spirit.

The relation between this verse and verse 2 is not altogether clear. RSV translates the connecting word **therefore,** which TEV omits. Perhaps it should be kept in translation. GeCL understands verse 2 to lay the basis for statements of verse 3. It translates the two verses as follows:

> When you were still unbelievers, you experienced something similar. You know how you came to be possessed by dead idols. Therefore, you must be careful to distinguish between good and bad spirits. When the Spirit of God takes possession of someone, this person cannot say, "Jesus be cursed!" Conversely, no one can say, "Jesus is the Lord!" if he is not filled by the Holy Spirit.

I want you to understand: Paul uses similar language, for example, in 15.1 and 2 Corinthians 8.1, and in each instance the words occur at the beginning of a section.

No one speaking by the Spirit of God ever says may be rendered as "No one who is led by God's Spirit can say" or "No one whom God's Spirit is leading . . . ."

A common Christian confession was **Jesus is Lord.** So **cursed** contrasts with this. Compare Romans 10.9. **No one . . . says "Jesus be cursed!"** in some languages may be better translated by indirect discourse: "no one . . . can curse Jesus."

The contrast between the two halves of this verse is clear. Emphasis falls on **speaking by the Spirit of God** and **except by the Holy Spirit.** Both phrases refer to the Holy Spirit guiding a person when that person speaks. The latter phrase may also be rendered as "unless the Holy Spirit is guiding that person."

References to the Holy Spirit, here and elsewhere in Paul's writings, should be clearly personal, corresponding to the use of the English pronoun "he" rather than "it." For example, "he" should be used in verse 11 to refer to the Holy Spirit.

RSV reflects the Greek by having **can** only once in the verse, whereas TEV has two instances. The first half is literally "no one says," and many languages will not need **can.** But in the second half **can** is expressed in the Greek and may have the strong meaning "no one has the power to say 'Jesus is Lord' . . . ."

12.4-6	RSV	TEV

RSV	TEV
Now there are varieties of gifts, but the same Spirit; 5 and there are	There are different kinds of spiritual gifts, but the same Spirit gives

varieties of service, but the same Lord; 6 and there are varieties of working, but it is the same God who inspires them all in every one.

them. 5 There are different ways of serving, but the same Lord is served. 6 There are different abilities to perform service, but the same God gives ability to all for their particular service.

For the structure of these verses, see the introduction to this chapter. In Greek all three verses are linked by **and.** TEV is right to omit these conjunctions and begin new sentences for two reasons: first, because verses 5a and 6a introduce no new information; and second, to make the sentence lighter.

The word translated **varieties** or "different ways" (TEV) is not used elsewhere in the New Testament. It is a compound of the word translated "factions" in 11.19, but without the negative meaning of that word.

The word for **gifts** (Greek *charismata*) is not related to the term used in verse 1. It emphasizes the "giving" nature of the gifts, while the term in verse 1 emphasizes the spiritual nature of the gift (see the comments on 1.7). Translators may add the word "spiritual" in these verses as TEV does.

In verse 3 Paul identifies the "Spirit of the Lord" or the "Holy Spirit" as the Spirit who works in Christians. In many languages it will be necessary to keep on using one of these terms in verses 4-13 so that readers are clear which Spirit is referred to. In many languages capitalization does not carry the effect it does in English, and also, when the text is read aloud, the effect of capitalization is lost on the listener.

But the same Lord can be expressed as "but people serve the same Lord" or "but it is the same Lord who is served."

The word translated **working** (TEV's "abilities to perform service") is used in the New Testament only here and in verse 10, where it is translated by TEV as "power to work." It seems likely that Paul uses these different expressions for variety, with little difference in meaning.

In the second part of verses 4, 5, and 6, Paul is not concerned with distinctions between the persons of the Trinity, **Spirit, Lord,** and **God,** but with emphasizing that they work together.

Translators would do well to use TEV as a model for translating these three verses. RSV's translation is too literal, thus resulting in poor English style.

12.7	RSV	TEV

To each is given the manifestation of the Spirit for the common good.

The Spirit's presence is shown in some way in each person for the good of all.

This verse is a general introduction to what follows, not simply the first of a new series of statements.

To each, as TEV shows, means "each person," "everyone."

Is given the manifestation of the Spirit refers to the activity of God in each believer's life. In some languages it will be better to use active verbs: "God reveals his Spirit's presence in some way to each person," or "God gives each person some proof of the Spirit's presence" or ". . . some proof that the Spirit is present."

Spirit: see the comment under verses 4-6. The meaning of the phrase **for the common good** is made clear in the following verses. TEV's translation, "for

the good of all," shows that the Spirit's purpose is not to help the individual necessarily, but the whole Christian community. This clause can be translated as "to be
used to help the whole church" or "to be used to help all the believers." So a
translation model for the whole verse is "God gives each person some proof of the
Spirit's presence to be used to help the whole church."

12.8	RSV	TEV
	To one is given through the Spirit the utterance of wisdom, and to another the utterance of knowledge according to the same Spirit,	The Spirit gives one person a message full of wisdom, while to another person the same Spirit gives a message full of knowledge.

The Greek sentence runs on without a break from verse 8 to the end of
verse 11. TEV and most modern translations divide this at various points. Translators should read these verses and decide where they would naturally make a
division in their languages. Both the language and thought of this verse are more
closely linked with verse 7 than are the following verses. Verses 9-11, on the
other hand, may be an extension of Paul's original point, or even an afterthought.

The grammar of verse 8 marks a contrast: "to one . . . ," "to another . . . ,"
yet the words which follow are similar in meaning. Bruce writes "Paul presumably
intends some distinction between *sophia* (**wisdom**) and *gnōsis* (**knowledge**), but the
distinction is not clear to us." Paul has used language similar to 8a in 2.7: "we
impart . . . a hidden wisdom." Verse 8b mirrors 1.5: "enriched in . . . all knowledge." The word for **wisdom** is often used in a negative sense, but clearly this is
not so here. Nor can we make a clear distinction between **wisdom** as something
practical, and **knowledge** as something more abstract or impractical. Both **wisdom**
and **knowledge** seem to have been words commonly used, and perhaps sometimes
misused, in discussion in Corinth.

In this verse Paul is less concerned to make precise distinctions between
the gifts than to show that all these gifts come from the same Spirit. His style in
verses 8-11 emphasizes the piling up of items rather than the differences between
them. He does, though, distinguish the people to whom the gifts are given from
the gifts themselves, with the puzzling exceptions of **wisdom** and **knowledge**.

"The same Spirit" is the expression used in verse 4; it will be repeated in a
more emphatic phrase "by one and the same Spirit" in verse 11. TEV brings out
the meaning of the Greek by translating "a word of wisdom/knowledge" by "a
message full of wisdom/knowledge." In some languages it may be preferable to
use an adjective such as in the English phrase "a wise message."

A possible translation model for this verse is "God's Spirit gives one person
the ability to speak a message which is full of wisdom, and the same Spirit gives
to another person the ability to speak a message which is full of knowledge."

12.9	RSV	TEV
	to another faith by the same Spirit, to another gifts of healing by the one Spirit,	One and the same Spirit gives faith to one person, while to another person he gives the power to heal.

To another faith may be rendered as "gives one person the ability to believe in Christ greatly."

Gifts of healing (TEV's "power to heal") probably means the power to heal various kinds of illnesses.

The same Spirit means the same as **the one Spirit,** and in most languages there is no reason to translate these phrases differently. The "identical Spirit" is accomplishing these things. In most languages it will be better to avoid using two different expressions referring to the Spirit, as it may wrongly suggest a difference in meaning.

See the comment on **Spirit** under verses 4-6.

12.10 RSV	TEV
to another the working of miracles, to another prophecy, to another the ability to distinguish between spirits, to another various kinds of tongues, to another the interpretation of tongues.	The Spirit gives one person the power to work miracles; to another, the gift of speaking God's message; and to yet another, the ability to tell the difference between gifts that come from the Spirit and those that do not. To one person he gives the ability to speak in strange tongues, and to another he gives the ability to explain what is said.

The working of miracles: it will be helpful to carry the idea of "gives . . . power" from verse 9 (see TEV) over to this verse. One can translate "The Spirit gives to another person the power to work miracles." **Working of miracles** is literally "abilities of powers." "Powers" is commonly used of miracles and is quite general in meaning. The central meaning is not that which is against the normal course of nature, but events which show in a special way the power of God in action (see the discussion of "nature" in 11.14).

The next two items in Paul's list, **prophecy** and the **ability to distinguish between spirits,** belong together for reasons which Paul develops in 14.26-28. However, in this verse the relationship between them is not stressed, and TEV perhaps overtranslates here. However, TEV's translation of **prophecy** as "speaking God's message" is truer to the meaning of the word as generally used in Paul's writings. **Ability to distinguish,** which is plural in Greek, is found in a similar sense in Hebrews 5.14 and is translated negatively in Romans 14.1 as "opinions." Paul is probably thinking of different occasions on which it may be necessary to distinguish between spiritual powers (compare verse 3). The related verb translated variously as "decide between," "discerning," and "weigh" is used in 6.5; 11.29,31; and 14.29. It seems possible that there was some discussion in Corinth of claims to possess spiritual judgment. TEV's translation "the ability to tell the difference between gifts that come from the Spirit and those that do not" makes the meaning clearer than RSV's rendering.

As in other verses in this section, it will be helpful in many languages to identify "the Spirit" (TEV) as "God's Spirit" or the "Holy Spirit."

Various kinds of tongues and **the interpretation of tongues,** like the two phrases we have just discussed, belong together for reasons which Paul will specify in 14.26-28. Translators need to clearly distinguish **prophecy** from **tongues.** **Prophecy** is preaching that is inspired by God, but in normal understandable human language. On the other hand, speaking in **tongues** in Paul's letters refers to a type of speech which could not be understood unless it was interpreted by someone having a special gift to do so. In some languages a literal translation of the word **tongues** will sound strange or may even have an incorrect meaning. In such cases the translator may use expressions such as "ecstatic speech," "strange sounds," or "unintelligible sounds." It is important for translators to avoid giving two wrong impressions: (a) that of normal speech including strange words, and (b) that of natural foreign languages.

The term translated **interpretation** may refer either to understanding, translation, or interpretation. The interpretation of otherwise unintelligible sounds fits the context best here, as in 13.1 and throughout chapter 14. The phrase **interpretation of tongues** therefore may be expanded to "explain what is meant by these strange sounds."

12.11	RSV	TEV

All these are inspired by one and the same Spirit, who apportions to each one individually as he wills.

But it is one and the same Spirit who does all this; as he wishes, he gives a different gift to each person.

This verse forms an emphatic conclusion to the section, particularly to verses 4-10.

All these refers to the various gifts mentioned in verses 8-10.

The verb translated **inspired,** more literally "empowers" or "works in," is related to the noun which is translated "working" in verses 6 and 10. So TEV's "does" is probably clearer here.

One and the same Spirit is a literal translation of the Greek, which happens to be idiomatic in English. In other languages it may be necessary to use a more emphatic equivalent of the phrase translated **the same Spirit** in verses 4 and 8, or to say, for example, "All these are inspired by God's Spirit alone" or "It is God's Spirit alone who does all this."

The verb translated **apportions** is related to the noun translated "varieties," which in verses 4-6 referred to God's activity in giving a variety of gifts. It might be well to follow TEV's example and make "gifts" explicit in this verse.

To each one individually recalls the language of verse 7, "to each is given," but is more emphatic, "to each individual."

RSV	12.12-31a	TEV

One Body with Many Parts

12 For just as the body is one and has many members, and all the members of the body, though many, are one body, so it is with Christ. 13 For by one Spirit we were all baptized into one body—Jews or Greeks, slaves or free—and all were made to drink of one Spirit.

12 Christ is like a single body, which has many parts; it is still one body, even though it is made up of different parts. 13 In the same way, all of us, whether Jews or Gentiles, whether slaves or free, have been baptized into one body by the same Spirit, and we have all been given the one Spirit to drink.

14 For the body does not consist of one member but of many. 15 If the foot should say, "Because I am not a hand, I do not belong to the body," that would not make it any less a part of the body. 16 And if the ear should say, "Because I am not an eye, I do not belong to the body," that would not make it any less a part of the body. 17 If the whole body were an eye, where would be the hearing? If the whole body were an ear, where would be the sense of smell? 18 But as it is, God arranged the organs in the body, each one of them, as he chose. 19 If all were a single organ, where would the body be? 20 As it is, there are many parts, yet one body. 21 The eye cannot say to the hand, "I have no need of you," nor again the head to the feet, "I have no need of you." 22 On the contrary, the parts of the body which seem to be weaker are indispensable, 23 and those parts of the body which we think less honorable we invest with the greater honor, and our unpresentable parts are treated with greater modesty, 24 which our more presentable parts do not require. But God has so composed the body, giving the greater honor to the inferior part, 25 that there may be no discord in the body, but that the members may have the same care for one another. 26 If one member suffers, all suffer together; if one member is honored, all rejoice together.

27 Now you are the body of Christ and individually members of it. 28 And God has appointed in the church first apostles, second prophets, third teachers, then workers of miracles, then healers, helpers, administrators, speakers in various kinds of tongues. 29 Are all apostles? Are all prophets? Are all teachers? Do all work miracles? 30 Do all possess gifts of healing? Do all speak with tongues? Do all interpret? 31 But earnestly desire the higher gifts.

14 For the body itself is not made up of only one part, but of many parts. 15 If the foot were to say, "Because I am not a hand, I don't belong to the body," that would not keep it from being a part of the body. 16 And if the ear were to say, "Because I am not an eye, I don't belong to the body," that would not keep it from being a part of the body. 17 If the whole body were just an eye, how could it hear? And if it were only an ear, how could it smell? 18 As it is, however, God put every different part in the body just as he wanted it to be. 19 There would not be a body if it were all only one part! 20 As it is, there are many parts but one body.

21 So then, the eye cannot say to the hand, "I don't need you!" Nor can the head say to the feet, "Well, I don't need you!" 22 On the contrary, we cannot do without the parts of the body that seem to be weaker; 23 and those parts that we think aren't worth very much are the ones which we treat with greater care; while the parts of the body which don't look very nice are treated with special modesty, 24 which the more beautiful parts do not need. God himself has put the body together in such a way as to give greater honor to those parts that need it. 25 And so there is no division in the body, but all its different parts have the same concern for one another. 26 If one part of the body suffers, all the other parts suffer with it; if one part is praised, all the other parts share its happiness.

27 All of you are Christ's body, and each one is a part of it. 28 In the church God has put all in place: in the first place apostles, in the second place prophets, and in the third place teachers; then those who perform miracles, followed by those who are given the power to heal or to help others or to direct them or to speak in strange tongues. 29 They are not all apostles or prophets or teachers. Not everyone has the power to work miracles 30 or to heal diseases or to speak in strange tongues or to explain what is said. 31 Set your hearts, then, on the more important gifts.

There are several points of contact between this and the preceding section. Verse 18b partly repeats the language and thought of verse 11b, though God, not the Holy Spirit, is the subject. The theme of "one and many" from verses 4-6 is developed in this section, with greater emphasis on diversity within the Christian "body." However, it is the subject, the "body," rather than the language which makes the present section a distinct unit. This theme is introduced in verse 12, given a preliminary application in verse 13, developed more fully in verses 14-26, and applied to the Corinthians' situation in verses 27-31a.

From the point of view of the general structure, however, the present section, together with 12.31b—13.13, may be considered as diverging from the subject of spiritual gifts which was introduced in 12.1, and which is taken up again in 14.1.

The end of the section is no more sharply marked than the beginning. The transitional sentence, verse 31b, will be discussed in the introduction to the following section. The theme of love, which dominates chapter 13, is anticipated by what is said in 12.25 about the different **members** of the body **having the same care for one another.**

Paul's illustrations from the natural world are not always the clearest parts of his writings. Jesus' parables from nature, for example, are generally more easily understood. The main difficulty in this section is that Paul's thought and language appear to vary between (1) comparing the church in its complex unity to a body and (2) identifying the two: **you are the body of Christ,** verse 27. He complicates his argument by using the idea of "Christ's body" in an extended and nonphysical sense. The development of Paul's thought thus leads him to break one of the basic rules of figurative language, namely, that metaphors and similes normally have a comparison which uses a particular common feature between two dissimilar objects. For example, the sentence "He is as wise as an owl" implies that he is only like an owl in this one respect, wise, and certainly should not be considered to be an actual owl.

Three lesser difficulties in understanding and translating this section also arise from the dynamic development of Paul's thought. (1) The theme of body and Spirit which Paul briefly mentions in verse 13 is carried over from the previous section, but is not developed any further in the present section. That is probably why TEV begins another paragraph at verse 14. (2) Verse 13 and verses 28-30 are quite different, though they do not contradict each other. Verse 13 is concerned with the diverse origins of different groups within the church, whereas verses 28-30 describe different functions within the Christian community. (3) Most of verses 22-24 is concerned with a deviation in Paul's thinking which we will mention in the detailed comments.

The TEV section heading, "One Body with Many Parts," may be rendered as "The body has many parts."

12.12	RSV	TEV
	For just as the body is one and has many members, and all the members of the body, though many, are one body, so it is with Christ.	Christ is like a single body, which has many parts; it is still one body, even though it is made up of different parts.

The language of verse 12 does not indicate any sharp break with what precedes it, but the conjunction **For** is rather weak in Greek, so it would be better omitted in translation, as TEV has done.

In this verse Paul's thought is quite condensed and he "takes two steps in one" (Barrett): (1) Christians in the church are like various parts of the body, and (2) the church is the body of Christ. For this reason GeCL goes to the other extreme from TEV by, so to speak, forcing Paul to take one step at a time: "One can compare the church of Christ with a body which has many members." Other English translations, including JB, TNT, and TOB, agree essentially with RSV's middle path: **so it is with Christ.** This solution is probably the better one.

The use of the words **body** and **members** in this section is fairly consistent. In most occurrences **body** has its literal meaning of a living physical body, including the head (verse 21). The context shows that the word translated **members** (TEV's "parts") is quite general, including not only arms and legs, but also other parts of the body. It is important for translators to choose terms which are live metaphors, that is, terms which are still capable of having a literal meaning. In that sense **members** is unsuitable in modern English, since it has almost lost its literal meaning of "limbs." TEV's translation "parts" is more suitable.

Many members: Paul's point here is not the large numbers of parts in the body, but their diversity. So "different parts" (TEV) is a better translation.

The position of **Christ** in the verse is different in RSV and TEV. In Greek its position at the end of the verse is emphatic, whereas it is more emphatic at the beginning of the sentence in English. CLTs and also NEB generally agree with this restructuring, which also makes the logic clearer.

12.13	RSV	TEV
	For by one Spirit we were all baptized into one body—Jews or Greeks, slaves or free—and all were made to drink of one Spirit.	In the same way, all of us, whether Jews or Gentiles, whether slaves or free, have been baptized into one body by the same Spirit, and we have all been given the one Spirit to drink.

See the comments in the introduction to this section, and compare Galatians 3.28.

For, which is repeated at the beginning of verse 14, indicates a development of the principle that is stated in verse 12, not a strictly logical deduction from it. From another point of view, however, verse 13 is a deviation from the main theme of this section. For this reason TEV first links verse 13 to verse 12 by adding the phrase "In the same way," and then links verse 14 back to verse 12 by adding "itself" after "the body."

As the dashes show, verse 13 consists of three parts. The first and the third of these contain the major statements, and the second contains illustrations of the various groups at Corinth. TEV links the first and third parts more closely together by moving the second part close to the beginning of the sentence. This is a simpler construction in English. The question arises whether we can consider that the two major statements, **we were all baptized into one body** and **all were made to drink of one Spirit,** as alternative ways of saying the same thing, or whether they complement each other. The verbs translated **baptized** and **made to drink** both refer to particular past events. The first of these events was clearly baptism, but in New Testament times the gift of the Spirit was also usually associated with baptism (see Mark 1.8 and perhaps John 7.37-39). A translator must avoid giving the impression that **baptized** and **made to drink** refer to the same event. **Made to drink** is metaphorical language. In some languages it will be impossible to use this metaphor. Translators may have to change the metaphor to a simile: "God has caused us all, as it were, to drink the Spirit." Some translators may need to say "God has given us all the same Spirit in our hearts," or "God has poured this one Spirit upon all of us" (compare Rom 5.5),[1] or "God has put the same Spirit in all our hearts."

For **baptized into,** see comments on 10.2.

We were all baptized can be expressed as "we have all received baptism."

Greeks: the context here, as in 1.22-24; 10.32, shows that "non-Jews" or "Gentiles" (TEV) is meant here.

Slaves or free may be rendered as "whether we are slaves or free people."

It will be helpful in many languages, especially those which do not normally use passive expressions, to restructure this verse; for example, "In the same way, all of us, whether we are slaves or free people, have received baptism into the one Spirit, and God has given us all the same Spirit in our hearts."

12.14	RSV	TEV
	For the body does not consist of one member but of many.	For the body itself is not made up of only one part, but of many parts.

Paul now begins his main development of the image of the body.

The body, in English as in Greek, is generic; that is, it does not refer to a particular body. This is a statement that is true of all human bodies. In other languages there are various ways of making this clear.

Consist is implied in the Greek.

12.15-16	RSV	TEV
	If the foot should say, "Because I am not a hand, I do not belong to the body," that would not make it any less a part of the body. 16 And if the ear should say, "Because I am not an eye, I do not belong to the body," that would not make it any less a part of the body.	If the foot were to say, "Because I am not a hand, I don't belong to the body," that would not keep it from being a part of the body. 16 And if the ear were to say, "Because I am not an eye, I don't belong to the body," that would not keep it from being a part of the body.

These two verses are very closely parallel in structure. As the punctuation note in the UBS Greek text shows, they have sometimes been taken as questions, like verses 17 and 19. However, verses 17-18 and 19-20 form separate units (the UBS text punctuates them as separate sentences), so most editions and translations take the present verses as statements.

---

[1] See the note on this verse in G.J. Cumming, 1981, "*Epotisthemen* (I Corinthians 12.13)," New Testament Studies 27.283-5.

The conditions introduced by **if** are unreal, as RSV's **should** and TEV's "were to" indicate. The two occurrences of **. . . should say** can be expressed as "suppose"; for example, "Suppose the foot should say."

The second half of each of these verses contains a double negative, literally "not for this reason is it not of the body." Most translations turn this into a positive statement which makes this phrase much clearer. TEV's "would not keep it from being a part" is easier in English than **make it any less a part.** Another way of translating this is "that does not mean it is no longer a part." In some cases it may be better to translate as a rhetorical question: "That would not keep it from being a part of the body, would it?"

12.17-20 RSV	TEV
If the whole body were an eye, where would be the hearing? If the whole body were an ear, where would be the sense of smell? 18 But as it is, God arranged the organs in the body, each one of them, as he chose. 19 If all were a single organ, where would the body be? 20 As it is, there are many parts, yet one body.	If the whole body were just an eye, how could it hear? And if it were only an ear, how could it smell? 18 As it is, however, God put every different part in the body just as he wanted it to be. 19 There would not be a body if it were all only one part! 20 As it is, there are many parts but one body.

Verses 17-18 and 19-20 are similar in structure, though not as close as 15-16 are in structure. Verse 17 is also more specific than verse 19. In each pair of verses, an unreal condition is followed by a statement of fact. The transition is clearly made by the words translated **as it is,** which may also be rendered as "the fact is that."

TEV's "however" after "As it is" in verse 18 is implied.

In verse 17 Paul mentions first two organs, the eye and the ear, and then two senses, hearing and smelling. In Greek the same term means both **ear** and **hearing.** In most languages it will be necessary to use two different words.

In verse 18 Paul emphasizes the words **each one of them** by placing them in a separate phrase. Each language has a different way to show emphasis. For example, in modern English one can add "different" after "every" ("each"), as TEV has done: "every different part."

The phrase **as he chose** can be translated as "just as he decided that it should be."

The form of verse 19 is similar to that of verse 17, though more general. This is a rhetorical question in Greek and translated as a question by RSV. However, TEV translates this rhetorical question as a strong negative statement. This is more forceful in English, but there is no change in meaning. In certain languages the "if" clause will appear at the beginning of the sentence: "If there is only one part, there won't be any body."

One body is literally "but the body (is) one." One may also say "but they form one body." There is no reference here to a number of different complete bodies.

TEV

RSV	TEV
The eye cannot say to the hand, "I have no need of you," nor again the head to the feet, "I have no need of you." 22 On the contrary, the parts of the body which seem to be weaker are indispensable, 23 and those parts of the body which we think less honorable we invest with the greater honor, and our unpresentable parts are treated with greater modesty, 24 which our more presentable parts do not require. But God has so composed the body, giving the greater honor to the inferior part,	So then, the eye cannot say to the hand, "I don't need you!" Nor can the head say to the feet, "Well, I don't need you!" 22 On the contrary, we cannot do without the parts of the body that seem to be weaker; 23 and those parts that we think aren't worth very much are the ones which we treat with greater care; while the parts of the body which don't look very nice are treated with special modesty, 24 which the more beautiful parts do not need. God himself has put the body together in such a way as to give greater honor to those parts that need it.

The course of Paul's argument in verses 21-24 is less clear than it has been so far in this section. He weaves together two main ideas: (1) the different parts of the body are interdependent and should therefore not despise one another; (2) those parts of the body which might be considered inferior receive special treatment. Idea (1) is mainly expressed in verse 21.

Idea (2) occupies verses 22, 23, and most of verse 24, excluding **God has so composed the body,** which prepares for the conclusion in verse 25a. This idea is both a development of idea (1) and also a preparation for the theme of mutual caring that is expressed in verse 25b and more fully in chapter 13.

In verse 21 the **head** is mentioned as one part of the body among others. A literal term, therefore, should be chosen here rather than some figurative expression meaning "chief" or "ruler."

It is not certain which are **the parts of the body which seem to be weaker.** In any case the translator needs to use a general term for **weaker** which will be the opposite of physically "stronger."

Seem may be translated "are thought of," similarly to verse 23 where the same Greek word is rendered **we think.**

In verse 23 **less honorable** implies "worth less than other parts." The Greek term means both "value" or "worth," and also "honor." It is perhaps "honor" which is in focus here. One can translate this phrase, then, as "those parts of the body which we consider to have little honor." However, in many languages a rendering similar to that of TEV will be adequate. In verse 23b the reference to **unpresentable parts** appears to be to the covering of sexual organs (see Gen 3.7,10,21). TEV's rendering, "don't look very nice," does not reproduce the meaning of the Greek, which is concerned, not with beauty, but with decency. Perhaps one could render this as "are not presentable" or "should not be shown in public." GeCL translates "the parts which are considered unpresentable we clothe with particular care, and we do the same with those parts which cause offense." ItCL combines both halves of the verse: "and the parts which we consider less noble and decent, we surround with greater care."

Verse 24b marks the beginning of a greater transition, back from the theme of diversity (verses 12-21) to that of unity (verses 4-11), and indeed further back to the theme of divisions within the church at Corinth, mentioned in similar language in 1.10 and 11.18. The successive waves of Paul's argument may be summed up as follows: (1) not disunity, but (2) unity; yet unity (3) not of uniformity, but (4) of mutual concern and love.

Inferior part (TEV's "parts that need it") may be expanded to "the parts that are lacking in honor" or "the parts which we feel do not have much value."

12.25 RSV	TEV
that there may be no discord in the body, but that the members may have the same care for one another.	And so there is no division in the body, but all its different parts have the same concern for one another.

That there may be is probably closer to the meaning of the Greek than TEV's "And so there is." One can also say "in order that there may be."

Some Greek manuscripts wrongly have "divisions" instead of "division" (TEV), under the influence of 1.10 and 11.18, where the plural of the same Greek word occurs. **Discord** is probably a better translation in this context. It may be expanded to "be no quarreling among the members . . . ."

The word translated **care** here has a positive meaning. The phrase **may have the same care for one another** may be rendered as "may exist for the good of all (parts)" or "may have love and concern for each other."

One possible translation model for this verse is "God did this so that the parts of the body may not quarrel with each other, but that they should have the same care (concern) for each other."

12.26 RSV	TEV
If one member suffers, all suffer together; if one member is honored, all rejoice together.	If one part of the body suffers, all the other parts suffer with it; if one part is praised, all the other parts share its happiness.

As Paul uses the figure of "the body," he sometimes thinks more about the figure "body," and sometimes thinks more about what it refers to, that is, the church. Here it is becoming increasingly clear that Paul is thinking more of the church at Corinth than of the parts of a physical body. It is scarcely true to say that all the parts of a physical body suffer if, for example, a finger is hurt, and in verse 26b it is difficult to think of parts of a physical body rejoicing together when one of them is honored. However, Paul's language is clear and should be translated as exactly as possible.

With both occurences of **all**, it may be well to expand it to "all the other parts" as TEV has done.

See verse 12 for a discussion of the use of the term **member** in modern English.

The word translated **one** before **member is honored** is omitted by some manuscripts, but translators, like some scribes, commonly add it in order to make the contrast between the two halves of the verse clearer. No change of meaning is involved. **One** before **member suffers** is certainly part of the text.

Is honored (TEV "praised") may be phrased as "receives honor" or "receives praise." Some languages can use a neutral phrase such as "if they honor . . ." or "if they praise . . ." instead of the passive construction **is honored.**

12.27	RSV	TEV

Now you are the body of Christ and individually members of it.

All of you are Christ's body, and each one is a part of it.

From this point on Paul explains the image of the body as referring to the church, the body of Christ. This verse takes up the thought of verse 12. For this reason and in order to make the contrast between verses 27a and 27b clearer, several translations agree with TEV in expanding **you** to "all of you." For example, JB has "Now you together are Christ's body."

Are the body of Christ may be expressed as "make up Christ's body." **The body of Christ** means not "the body which is Christ" but "the body which belongs to Christ."

A possible translation model of this verse is the following: "All of you are the body which belongs to Christ, and each one of you is a part of it."

12.28	RSV	TEV

And God has appointed in the church first apostles, second prophets, third teachers, then workers of miracles, then healers, helpers, administrators, speakers in various kinds of tongues.

In the church God has put all in place: in the first place apostles, in the second place prophets, and in the third place teachers; then those who perform miracles, followed by those who are given the power to heal or to help others or to direct them or to speak in strange tongues.

There is no reference to order in time in this verse, but rather to degrees of importance. To bring this idea out TEV has added the phrase "all in place" after "put." "All in place" may well be translated "all members in place" or "all parts in place."

The Greek sentence is confused because Paul moves without warning from nouns indicating groups of people in the church—**apostles, prophets, teachers**—to abstract nouns that indicate spiritual gifts such as **miracles** (see comments on verse 1).

First, second, third, and **then** probably suggests an order of importance.

Apostles: a number of other people were appointed as "apostles" after the original twelve. Paul was one of these.

Prophets can be translated as "those who proclaim God's message." Translator's should avoid using terms which suggest that this group of people are the same as the Old Testament prophets.

Teachers were probably people who gave instruction in the Christian faith (see Rom 12.7; 2 Tim 1.11; James 3.1 for further insight into this gift).

The latter part of this verse is literally "then powers," "gifts of support" (Barrett), "administration, kinds of tongues." These abstract nouns mean respectively "the power to perform miracles, the power to heal people, the ability to help, the ability to steer or direct, and various kinds of ecstatic speech." Most translations smooth the sentence by making all the nouns refer to people rather than directly to gifts; for example, "those who perform miracles," and so on.

Helpers: the context suggests that these were people who had the specific duty to aid the poor and needy.

Administrators refers to people who have the ability to steer or direct the affairs of the church.

Kinds of tongues: see the discussion under verse 10.

12.29-30 RSV	TEV
Are all apostles? Are all prophets? Are all teachers? Do all work miracles? 30 Do all possess gifts of healing? Do all speak with tongues? Do all interpret?	They are not all apostles or prophets or teachers. Not everyone has the power to work miracles 30 or to heal diseases or to speak in strange tongues or to explain what is said.

Paul returns for the last time to the subject of diversity of gifts in the church. There are differences between these verses and the list given in verse 28, but it is not the translator's task to smooth away these irregularities.

These are seven rhetorical questions that expect the answer "No." TEV translates them by negative statements. Many languages will need to use similar statements.

Are all may be expressed as "Is every person . . . ?" or "Not every person is."

Tongues: some languages may have to express this word as "strange sounds" or something similar. See also the discussion on verse 10.

In verse 30 the verb translated **interpret** is related to the word translated "interpretation" in verse 10 (see the comments on that verse). This appears to be interpretation of "strange sounds" or "ecstatic speech" rather than foreign languages. It will be helpful in many languages to expand **interpret** to "interpret what is said with these strange sounds" or "explain what is said . . . ."

12.31a RSV	TEV
But earnestly desire the higher gifts.	Set your hearts, then, on the more important gifts.

This sentence may be either (1) an order, "strive for spiritual gifts," or (2) a statement,[2] "you strive for." Most translations and commentaries choose (1), but (2) would make a good connection with verse 31b: "You Corinthians are struggling to obtain spiritual gifts, but I will show you a much better way," the way of love.

Earnestly desire: in languages which have a similar phrase to TEV's idiomatic expression, "Set your hearts," the translator may wish to expand this phrase by using the word "gain": "set your hearts, then, on gaining the more . . . ."

---

[2] See G. Iber, 1963, "Zum Verständnis von 1 Cor. 12.31," Zeitschrift für die Neutestamentliche Wissenschaft 54.43-52.

In this verse there is no need to put "spiritual" before **gifts,** since the previous verses have shown clearly what kind of gifts are in Paul's mind.

Higher gifts: some languages will prefer to express **higher** as "more important" (TEV). Verse 14.1 suggests that Paul is thinking here mainly of the gift of Christian prophecy or "proclaiming God's message." The highest gift of all, that of being an apostle, presumably could not be obtained by "setting one's heart" on it, but is given by a special appointment by God (see 1.1).

Chapter 13

31b And I will show you a still more excellent way.

13.1 If I speak in the tongues of men and of angels, but have not love, I am a noisy gong or a clanging cymbal. 2 And if I have prophetic powers, and understand all mysteries and all knowledge, and if I have all faith, so as to remove mountains, but have not love, I am nothing. 3 If I give away all I have, and if I deliver my body to be burned,^{v} but have not love, I gain nothing.

^{v} Other ancient authorities read *body that I may glory*

31b Best of all, however, is the following way.

Love

13.1 I may be able to speak the languages of men and even of angels, but if I have no love, my speech is no more than a noisy gong or a clanging bell. 2 I may have the gift of inspired preaching; I may have all knowledge and understand all secrets; I may have all the faith needed to move mountains —but if I have no love, I am nothing. 3 I may give away everything I have, and even give up my body to be burned^n —but if I have no love, this does me no good.

^{n} to be burned; *some manuscripts have in order to boast.*

The punctuation in the UBS Greek text shows that editions and translations differ in the paragraphing of 12.31 and 13.1. The UBS Greek text begins a new paragraph at 12.31b, but not at 13.1. This example is followed by ItCL, TNT, and AT. But most CLTs, like TEV, begin a new paragraph at 12.31b and a new section at 13.1. JB, on the other hand, begins a new section at 12.31a, and a new paragraph at 13.1. Most translations do not agree with JB's interpretation.

The connection between 12.31b and 13.1 is close. Most commentators think that chapter 13 was written by Paul as a separate hymn or poem about love, and inserted by him at this point in the letter. Verse 12.31b certainly reads like the introduction to a distinct section, a bridge leading to the hymn which begins in 13.1.

Most commentators and translators agree with the UBS Greek text in dividing the poem of chapter 13 into three sections: verses 1-3, 4-7, and 8-13. As Barrett puts it, "in verses 1-3 love is contrasted with other religious actions and attitudes . . . ; in verses 4-7 love is described mainly in negative terms . . . ; in verses 8-13 the theme of contrast returns, and it is brought out that when other things perish, love persists into the eternal world." There are points of contact between this chapter and the preceding section, but the links are not striking enough to prevent us from thinking of chapter 13 as a separate poem.

Both the style and to some extent the vocabulary of chapter 13 are rather different from what is found elsewhere in Paul's letters. However, both Jewish and secular Greek literature contain passages which are similar in form and, to a limited extent, in content.[1]

12.31b   RSV   TEV

    And I will show you a still more excellent way.   **Best of all, however, is the following way.**

    I will show can also be rendered "I will point out to you" or "I would like to introduce you to."

    The phrase **a still more excellent** is used only by Paul in the New Testament. It means something which is not only greater or better than something else, but *much* greater or better (compare Rom 7.13, "sinful beyond measure"; 2 Cor 1.8, "utterly"; 4.17, "beyond all comparison"; Gal 1.13, "violently"). NEB translates **more excellent way** as "the best way of all." One African language has "a way that far surpasses all others."

    "Following" is not explicit in the text but is added by TEV to make the connection with chapter 13 clear. It is implied in **I will show you.**

13.1   RSV   TEV

    If I speak in the tongues of men and of angels, but have not love, I am a noisy gong or a clanging cymbal.   **I may be able to speak the languages of men and even of angels, but if I have no love, my speech is no more than a noisy gong or a clanging bell.**

    Verses 1-3 all have a similar structure. Verse 1 begins with a condition, and verses 2 and 3 with two conditions each. In each case the conditional clauses are followed by the words **but have not love** and then by the main clause in the Greek. Problems in translation arise in deciding whether the conditions are likely to be fulfilled. For example, does Paul actually have **prophetic powers,** the ability to preach God's message (verse 2)? In 14.18 Paul certainly claims the gift of speaking with tongues, and in 14.6 he claims the gift of prophecy in the Christian sense (see comments on 12.10). However, it is quite uncertain whether he gave away everything he had (verse 3a), and he clearly had not given up his body to be burned (verse 3b). The whole section is so conditional in tone that Paul may be understood as taking his own situation, in very general terms, as an example (compare 4.6), rather than speaking directly of his personal experience. TEV's repeated "I may . . ." expresses this very well in English. NEB has a similar translation. Other ways of showing this possibly contrary to fact or hypothetical situation are: "If it should happen that I am able to speak . . . but I don't have love" or "Suppose that I should be able to speak . . . ." In some languages it may be necessary to use the word "one" instead of "I" and say "If it should happen that one . . . ."

    Men means human beings, both male and female. **Tongues of men** can be translated "human languages."

---

[1] See Conzelmann, page 220, note 18, and also Wisdom 7.22-30.

And of angels may be expressed as "even those of angels" or "even those which angels speak."

The Greek word translated **love** was not common in pre-Christian times. In the New Testament it is used primarily in speaking of God's or Christ's love for human beings. However, it is also used of the love of Christians, usually for one another, as in this chapter. In 12.25 the word "care" has a similar meaning. KJV's "charity" has in modern English the narrower meaning of generosity to the poor, and this meaning should be avoided in the translation of this chapter.

But have not love may also be rendered as "But if I do not love."

Gong: according to the context the Greek word means either a metal such as copper or bronze, or something made out of metal, such as coins, or it may refer to armor. The mention of a **cymbal** or "bell" (TEV) immediately after this word suggests that here a musical instrument such as a **gong** is intended. The **cymbal** in ancient times was a metal basin used like modern cymbals, in pairs, to produce a musical sound. TEV replaces **cymbal** by "bell" as being more widely understood. Other translators will have to decide what musical instruments in their cultures carry the same meaning, if there are no **gongs** or **cymbals**.

The term translated **noisy** (TEV's "clanging") is used in Mark 5.38 of the loud noise made by mourners. Some languages may use only one word to describe the sound of a **gong** and **cymbal**. One could say, for example, "a gong or cymbal which is sending out clanging noises."

13.2   RSV   TEV

And if I have prophetic powers, and | I may have the gift of inspired preach-
understand all mysteries and all knowl- | ing; I may have all knowledge and
edge, and if I have all faith, so as to | understand all secrets; I may have all
remove mountains, but have not love, I | the faith needed to move mountains—
am nothing. | but if I have no love, I am nothing.

Prophetic powers in most languages will need to be rendered as "have the ability to preach God's message," or ". . . to transmit messages received from God," or ". . . to speak messages which God has given to me." A word such as "preach" should probably be avoided as it gives the impression of modern day preaching from a pulpit.

The word translated **mysteries** (TEV's "secrets") is sometimes used by Paul to mean that part of Christian truth which can only be understood by mature believers (see comments on 2.1,7); but here it may refer more generally to hidden truths. **Knowledge** should be translated in a way that relates the term to earlier use in the letter; see "Detailed Comment" at 1.5.

All faith, so as to remove mountains: the thought is similar to Mark 11.23; compare Matthew 17.20; Luke 17.6; but the language is rather different. TEV's translation "needed to" is probably better than **so as to**. The appositional construction in TEV's "faith needed" can be expressed as "faith which is needed to" or ". . . strong enough to." The whole sentence may be rendered as "If I have strong enough faith in God so that I can move mountains."

To remove mountains may be rendered as "to cause mountains to move" or "to make mountains move." In some languages it may be necessary to say "move to another place."

The phrase **I am nothing** can be translated "I have no value at all."

　　　　　RSV　　　　　　　　　　　TEV

If I give away all I have, and if I deliver my body to be burned,^{v} but have not love, I gain nothing.

^{v} Other ancient authorities read *body that I may glory*

I may give away everything I have, and even give up my body to be burned^n— but if I have no love, this does me no good.

^{n} to be burned; *some manuscripts have* in order to boast.

The verb translated **give away** is related to the noun used in John 13.26,27, 30 to mean a small piece of bread. The meaning of the verb may vary according to the context between "feed" and "distribute," implying the distribution of food to the poor. In this verse the idea of selling possessions and distributing the proceeds seems to predominate. With this in mind, one may translate **all I have** as "all my possessions."

And if I deliver my body to be burned: as the RSV and TEV footnotes show, the text of this clause is uncertain and so is its meaning. All translations which we consulted, except AT, and most commentators prefer the text **to be burned.**[2] Any translation which indicates any variations in the Greek should give this variation in a footnote. In languages which do not favor passives, one may translate "even let them burn my body."

I gain nothing: DuCL has "it helps me nothing"; GeCL "all is useless." Another possible rendering is "it is of no use to me at all."

　　　　　RSV　　　　　**13.4-7**　　　　　TEV

4 Love is patient and kind; love is not jealous or boastful; 5 it is not arrogant or rude. Love does not insist on its own way; it is not irritable or resentful; 6 it does not rejoice at wrong, but rejoices in the right. 7 Love bears all things, believes all things, hopes all things, endures all things.

4 Love is patient and kind; it is not jealous or conceited or proud; 5 love is not ill-mannered or selfish or irritable; love does not keep a record of wrongs; 6 love is not happy with evil, but is happy with the truth. 7 Love never gives up; and its faith, hope, and patience never fail.

Here in this section and in verse 8a, love is spoken of as a person and is the subject of a series of verbs. In some languages this way of speaking may be unnatural or even impossible. In that case it will be necessary to decide whether the implied subject, that is, the person who loves, is Paul, Christians in general, God, or Christ. In the previous verses Paul seems to have been speaking of himself as an example rather than as an individual. Therefore in languages in which love cannot be spoken of as a person, it may be best to use some such general expression as "people who love are patient," leaving it to be understood that the people in question are Christians.

Another way to render these verses is to talk about the characteristics of true love; for example, "The characteristics of love are patience, kindness, lack of

---

[2] Metzger, pages 563-564, gives a good summary of the arguments on both sides.

jealousy, conceit, or pride . . . ." One may also say "Whoever loves in the Christian way has patience and kindness. Such a person is not jealous or boastful, arrogant or rude . . . ." Some languages may have a habitual verb form which would be proper here.

13.4	RSV	TEV

Love is patient and kind; love is not jealous or boastful;

Love is patient and kind; it is not jealous or conceited or proud;

The verb translated **is . . . kind** is not found elsewhere in the Greek Bible. However, it is clearly related to the adjective which is translated "good" in 15.33 and, when used as a noun in Romans 2.4, is translated as "kindness."

When used in a bad sense, as here, the verb translated **is . . . jealous** refers to envy of other people. See also James 4.2, where the verb is translated "covet."

Boastful translates two Greek verbs which TEV renders "conceited or proud." The first is a rare verb not used elsewhere in the Greek Bible. In secular Greek literature it has the meaning "boast." The second verb, "is . . . proud," is used in 4.6,18,19; 5.2; 8.1.

13.5	RSV	TEV

it is not arrogant or rude. Love does not insist on its own way; it is not irritable or resentful;

love is not ill-mannered or selfish or irritable; love does not keep a record of wrongs;

Is not arrogant or rude translates a single Greek verb which in 7.36 was translated "not behaving properly." The kind of action which is referred to here is not superficial matters of etiquette, but behavior in a wide sense, as RSV shows.

Does not insist on its own way is literally "does not seek its own." In many languages an equivalent of "unselfish" will give a clear meaning. The meaning, though not the words, of Philippians 2.4 is quite similar: "let each of you look not only to his own interests."

Irritable: a related noun is translated "a sharp contention" in Acts 15.39. Another possible translation, then, is "love is not . . . easily angered and argumentative."

Resentful is literally "keep a record of wrongs" (see TEV). In the New Testament context TEV's translation is a good model for other languages to use, unless a particular language has a single verb which equals this meaning. One may expand this a bit: "keep a record of wrongs done by other people."

13.6	RSV	TEV

it does not rejoice at wrong, but rejoices in the right.

love is not happy with evil, but is happy with the truth.

The two incidents of **rejoice** here come from two different but related Greek verbs. Paul obviously uses these synonyms for stylistic reasons, with no perceptible difference in meaning.

Wrong is too weak an English word here. TEV's "evil" renders the meaning of the Greek.

Right is more likely "truth," as in TEV. The Greek word implies speaking the truth, as in 5.8: "of sincerity and truth."

A possible translation model for this verse is the following: "People who have Christian love do not rejoice over evil, but they rejoice over the truth."

13.7	RSV	TEV

Love bears all things, believes all things, hopes all things, endures all things. | **Love never gives up; and its faith, hope, and patience never fail.**

It is difficult to say whether **all things**, which is repeated four times, refers in each case to the same things. It is necessary to examine these short clauses separately. In some languages it may be necessary to follow TEV's example, where **bears all things** is rendered by "never gives up," and the other instances of **all things** are reconstructed to "its . . . never fail" at the end of the verse.

Love bears all things: the Greek verb is related to the word for a roof. It may mean "supports or carries the universe," but more probably Paul means here that love bears or endures all kinds of ill-treatment. TEV expresses essentially the same meaning without the metaphor of "bearing." ItCL has "excuses everything."

RSV's repetition of **all things** tends in English to give a wrong meaning when combined with the verbs **believes, hopes,** and **endures**. For example, **believes all things** describes a naïve person rather than one who has strong faith. Barrett claims that **believes all things** means "never loses faith." One may also say "never stops believing."

Hopes all things: the word **hope** as Paul uses it has a main element of "confidence." So one can render this phrase as "is always confident." Some languages may need to state the goal of "confidence": ". . . confident in God."

Endures all things: endures has a similar meaning to **bears** in the first sentence. That is the reason why TEV structures the verse the way it does. The first **bear** is given a more general sense. Another possible translation model for this verse is "Love enables us to endure everything; it enables us in every circumstance to keep on believing, to keep our confidence in God, and to remain patient no matter what happens to us."

RSV	13.8-13	TEV

8 Love never ends; as for prophecies, they will pass away; as for tongues, they will cease; as for knowledge, it will pass away. 9 For our knowledge is imperfect and our prophecy is imperfect; 10 but when the perfect comes, the imperfect will pass away. 11 When I was a child, I spoke like a child, I thought like a child, I | 8 Love is eternal. There are inspired messages, but they are temporary; there are gifts of speaking in strange tongues, but they will cease; there is knowledge, but it will pass. 9 For our gifts of knowledge and of inspired messages are only partial; 10 but when what is perfect comes, then what is partial will disappear.

reasoned like a child; when I became a man, I gave up childish ways. 12 For now we see in a mirror dimly, but then face to face. Now I know in part; then I shall understand fully, even as I have been fully understood. 13 So faith, hope, love abide, these three; but the greatest of these is love.

11 When I was a child, my speech, feelings, and thinking were all those of a child; now that I am a man, I have no more use for childish ways. 12 What we see now is like a dim image in a mirror; then we shall see face-to-face. What I know now is only partial; then it will be complete—as complete as God's knowledge of me.

13 Meanwhile these three remain: faith, hope, and love; and the greatest of these is love.

TEV begins a new paragraph at verse 11 as well as at verse 8. This may be convenient for some readers, but there is no indication in verse 11 of a change of theme; and RSV, like the UBS Greek New Testament, treats these five verses as a single paragraph.

The main problem in translation is that of deciding how to translate personal pronouns. In this passage there are three main types of verbs. The first, in verses 8 and 13, are in the third person and refer to love and other spiritual gifts. These present no new problem, since translators will already have decided in verse 4 how to translate abstract nouns such as "love." In the introduction to verse 4 we suggested that in some languages one can say "the people who love . . . ." Secondly, there are first person plural "we" and "our" expressions in verses 9 and 12a; and thirdly, there are first person singular "I" and "me" expressions in verses 11 and 12b. These expressions present two problems: First, to whom does the "we" refer? And second, does the "I" refer to Paul alone, or to other people also? This raises a further question: are the "we" and the "I" really different, or are they just two ways of speaking of the same people?

A clue to the solution of these problems is found in verse 12, which is divided into two halves. The first words of each half can be translated literally: "We see . . . now . . . ; now I know." These expressions are so similar, both in language and meaning, as to suggest that there is no contrast and perhaps no difference between "we" and "I" in this passage. "We" includes Paul and the Christians in Corinth; "I" is not limited to Paul as an individual, but refers to Paul as an example of Christian experience (as probably in Rom 7.5-25). In some languages it may be natural to change from "I" to "we," but where it is not, expressions should be found which will maintain the continuity of thought and meaning.

13.8	RSV	TEV

Love never ends; as for prophecies, they will pass away; as for tongues, they will cease; as for knowledge, it will pass away.

Love is eternal. There are inspired messages, but they are temporary; there are gifts of speaking in strange tongues, but they will cease; there is knowledge, but it will pass.

Love never ends: the meaning is essentially the same as "love . . . endures all things" in verse 7. Here the statement serves to introduce a series of contrasts between love and other spiritual gifts.

The rest of the verse is divided into three parts. The verb translated **will pass away** here and in verse 10 is the same Greek word. TEV uses several synonyms for stylistic reasons: "are temporary," "it will pass," and in verse 10, "will disappear." **Will cease** translates an unrelated word with similar meaning. These two words seem to mean that the three gifts are temporary. In the following verse Paul states that they are "limited" or "incomplete," or even "imperfect" in relation to love, which is "perfect."

As in 12.28, **prophecies** are "messages which come from God" and refer to normal human speech. **Tongues,** on the other hand, as in 12.28,30, refer to "strange sounds" or "ecstatic speech" (TEV's "strange tongues"). TEV is correct to add the words "gifts of speaking" before "strange tongues."

In many languages it may be necessary to show the contrast between love which endures or never stops, and the three gifts which are limited and temporary. A possible translation model is: "Love never ends. However, the gifts of proclaiming God's message, speaking in strange sounds, and knowledge are only temporary or imperfect." Another possible translation model for this verse is the following: "Love lasts forever. There are messages from God, but they are temporary; there are gifts of speaking in strange sounds, but they will cease; there is knowledge, but it will pass away."

13.9-10   RSV   TEV

For our knowledge is imperfect and our prophecy is imperfect; 10 but when the perfect comes, the imperfect will pass away.

For our gifts of knowledge and of inspired messages are only partial; 10 but when what is perfect comes, then what is partial will disappear.

For marks the beginning of a new stage in Paul's thought. This will be expanded in verse 10, illustrated in verse 11 and verse 12a, and explained in more literal language in 12b, from "Now I know."

Imperfect is the phrase which in 12.27 was rendered "individually." The contrast is not between a whole community and its individual members, but between the wholeness or perfection of love, and the partial or imperfect nature of other gifts. Paul seems to be contrasting "imperfection" here with the "perfection" which will be established when he meets God face to face.

A possible translation model for this verse is: "For our gift of knowledge and the ability to proclaim God's message are incomplete; but when that which is complete and perfect comes, then that which is imperfect will no longer be needed."

13.11   RSV   TEV

When I was a child, I spoke like a child, I thought like a child, I reasoned like a child; when I became a man, I gave up childish ways.

When I was a child, my speech, feelings, and thinking were all those of a child; now that I am a man, I have no more use for childish ways.

The word **a child** is the same as "babes" used in 3.1, but in the present verse it has its literal meaning, as the rest of the verse shows. Translators should use a normal word for **child** here which contrasts with **man** or "adult male."

The Greek verbs translated **thought** and **reasoned** are quite close in meaning. The first refers to opinion, judgment, or attitude rather than emotion, and the second refers to logical processes.

The clause **when I became a man** can be more aptly expressed in many languages as "when I grew up" or "when I became an adult."

Childish ways is more literally "things to do with being a child." **I gave up childish ways** may be expressed as "I stopped behaving like a child" or "I left behind the affairs of small children."

13.12 RSV   TEV

For now we see in a mirror dimly, but then face to face. Now I know in part; then I shall understand fully, even as I have been fully understood.	What we see now is like a dim image in a mirror; then we shall see face-to-face. What I know now is only partial; then it will be complete—as complete as God's knowledge of me.

Reference to a mirror may suggest to readers a modern mirror made with glass and mercury. Ancient mirrors, however, were made of polished metal and therefore gave a generally less clear reflection, as the contrast shows.

See implies seeing God. The phrase **face to face** is not found elsewhere in the New Testament, but its meaning is plain. Numbers 12.8 similarly refers to God and Moses speaking "mouth to mouth." Languages will have differing ways of expressing **face to face,** such as "eyes to eyes."

The Greek verbs translated **know** and **understand fully** are related, the second being a stronger form than the first, as **fully** shows. **I have been fully understood** refers to the activity of God, and in many languages will be expressed as "even as God fully understands me" or "as complete as the way that God understands me." In some languages it will be more natural to provide an object for the verbs **know** and **understand.** In that case "I know God incompletely; then I shall understand him fully" is probably the best solution.

13.13 RSV   TEV

So faith, hope, love abide, these three; but the greatest of these is love.	Meanwhile these three remain: faith, hope, and love; and the greatest of these is love.

So (TEV's "Meanwhile") is literally "now." In some contexts it may refer to time. The word used in verse 13, however, often has a logical meaning; in 12.18, 20 it was translated "as it is." If this is the meaning here, there will be a contrast between complete knowledge which Paul hopes for, and the present in which faith, hope, and love remain. However, it is more likely that this verse is a summing up of what has gone before, and either **so** or "Meanwhile" would accurately fit the context.

These three may be expanded to "these three things" or "the following three things," moving this noun phrase before "faith, hope, and love," as in TEV.

The greatest is strictly "the greater," but in the New Testament the comparative form is often used with a superlative meaning, as in 12.31.

Chapter 14

More about Gifts from the Spirit

1 Make love your aim, and earnestly desire the spiritual gifts, especially that you may prophesy. 2 For one who speaks in a tongue speaks not to men but to God; for no one understands him, but he utters mysteries in the Spirit. 3 On the other hand, he who prophesies speaks to men for their upbuilding and encouragement and consolation. 4 He who speaks in a tongue edifies himself, but he who prophesies edifies the church. 5 Now I want you all to speak in tongues, but even more to prophesy. He who prophesies is greater than he who speaks in tongues, unless some one interprets, so that the church may be edified.

6 Now, brethren, if I come to you speaking in tongues, how shall I benefit you unless I bring you some revelation or knowledge or prophecy or teaching? 7 If even lifeless instruments, such as the flute or the harp, do not give distinct notes, how will any one know what is played? 8 And if the bugle gives an indistinct sound, who will get ready for battle? 9 So with yourselves; if you in a tongue utter speech that is not intelligible, how will any one know what is said? For you will be speaking into the air. 10 There are doubtless many different languages in the world, and none is without meaning; 11 but if I do not know the meaning of the language, I shall be a foreigner to the speaker and the speaker a foreigner to me. 12 So with yourselves; since you are eager for manifestations of the Spirit, strive to excel in building up the church.

13 Therefore, he who speaks in a tongue should pray for the power to interpret. 14 For if I pray in a tongue,

1 It is love, then, that you should strive for. Set your hearts on spiritual gifts, especially the gift of proclaiming God's message. 2 The one who speaks in strange tongues does not speak to others but to God, because no one understands him. He is speaking secret truths by the power of the Spirit. 3 But the one who proclaims God's message speaks to people and gives them help, encouragement, and comfort. 4 The one who speaks in strange tongues helps only himself, but the one who proclaims God's message helps the whole church.

5 I would like for all of you to speak in strange tongues; but I would rather that you had the gift of proclaiming God's message. For the person who proclaims God's message is of greater value than the one who speaks in strange tongues—unless there is someone present who can explain what he says, so that the whole church may be helped. 6 So when I come to you, my brothers, what use will I be to you if I speak in strange tongues? Not a bit, unless I bring you some revelation from God or some knowledge or some inspired message or some teaching.

7 Take such lifeless musical instruments as the flute or the harp—how will anyone know the tune that is being played unless the notes are sounded distinctly? 8 And if the man who plays the bugle does not sound a clear call, who will prepare for battle? 9 In the same way, how will anyone understand what you are talking about if your message given in strange tongues is not clear? Your words will vanish in the air! 10 There are many different languages in the world, yet none of them is without meaning.

my spirit prays but my mind is unfruitful. 15 What am I to do? I will pray with the spirit and I will pray with the mind also; I will sing with the spirit and I will sing with the mind also. 16 Otherwise, if you bless[w] with the spirit, how can any one in the position of an outsider[x] say the "Amen" to your thanksgiving when he does not know what you are saying? 17 For you may give thanks well enough, but the other man is not edified. 18 I thank God that I speak in tongues more than you all; 19 nevertheless, in church I would rather speak five words with my mind, in order to instruct others, than ten thousand words in a tongue.

20 Brethren, do not be children in your thinking; be babes in evil, but in thinking be mature. 21 In the law it is written, "By men of strange tongues and by the lips of foreigners will I speak to this people, and even then they will not listen to me, says the Lord." 22 Thus, tongues are a sign not for believers but for unbelievers, while prophecy is not for unbelievers but for believers. 23 If, therefore, the whole church assembles and all speak in tongues, and outsiders or unbelievers enter, will they not say that you are mad? 24 But if all prophesy, and an unbeliever or outsider enters, he is convicted by all, he is called to account by all, 25 the secrets of his heart are disclosed; and so, falling on his face, he will worship God and declare that God is really among you.

[w] That is, *give thanks to God*
[x] Or *him that is without gifts*

11 But if I do not know the language being spoken, the person who uses it will be a foreigner to me and I will be a foreigner to him. 12 Since you are eager to have the gifts of the Spirit, you must try above everything else to make greater use of those which help to build up the church.

13 The person who speaks in strange tongues, then, must pray for the gift to explain what he says. 14 For if I pray in this way, my spirit prays indeed, but my mind has no part in it. 15 What should I do, then? I will pray with my spirit, but I will pray also with my mind; I will sing with my spirit, but I will sing also with my mind. 16 When you give thanks to God in spirit only, how can an ordinary person taking part in the meeting say "Amen" to your prayer of thanksgiving? He has no way of knowing what you are saying. 17 Even if your prayer of thanks to God is quite good, the other person is not helped at all.

18 I thank God that I speak in strange tongues much more than any of you. 19 But in church worship I would rather speak five words that can be understood, in order to teach others, than speak thousands of words in strange tongues.

20 Do not be like children in your thinking, my brothers; be children so far as evil is concerned, but be grown up in your thinking. 21 In the Scriptures it is written,

"By means of men speaking
    strange languages
I will speak to my people, says
    the Lord.
I will speak through lips of
    foreigners,
    but even then my people will
        not listen to me."

22 So then, the gift of speaking in strange tongues is proof for unbelievers, not for believers, while the gift of proclaiming God's message is proof for believers, not for unbelievers.

23 If, then, the whole church meets together and everyone starts speaking in strange tongues—and if some ordinary people or unbelievers come in, won't they say that you are all crazy? 24 But if everyone is proclaiming God's message when some unbeliever or ordinary person comes in, he

will be convinced of his sin by what he
hears.   He will be judged by all he
hears, 25 his secret thoughts will be
brought into the open, and he will bow
down and worship God, confessing,
"Truly God is here among you!"

The TEV section heading "More about Gifts from the Spirit" can also be
rendered as "Other gifts which the Spirit gives."

There are two things which clearly show how this section fits into the
general structure of the letter. First, there is a close connection between 14.1
and 12.31a. Secondly, the real conclusion of the argument in this chapter is not
reached until the end of the chapter, where verse 39 overlaps in meaning with
verses 1-2. Links between chapters 13 and 14, on the other hand, are not clear,
and the connection at the beginning of 14.1, **Make love your aim**, seems artificial
(see the detailed comments).

It is more difficult to establish divisions within chapter 14 itself. All CLTs
which we have consulted, and also JB, NIV, and TOB agree with the UBS Greek
text in beginning a new section at verse 26. Some editions of NEB prefer to divide
the chapter before verses 20 and 36. The main problem in dividing the chapter
into paragraphs is whether verses 6 and 36 should be taken as the beginning or end
of paragraphs (see the comments on these verses). Some Greek manuscripts place
verses 34-35 at the end of the chapter. We discuss the special problems of these
verses below.

This chapter, and especially the present section, contains some repetition.
This repetition occurs mainly in different parts of the chapter rather than within
the same verse or sentence. No doubt this is because Paul is trying to persuade
his readers to make the right decision on a matter of great importance for them.
The translator should not remove this repetition. However, Paul uses a wide range
of words to describe spiritual gifts and happenings within the Christian community. Some of these, such as Christian prophecy and speaking with strange sounds,
are clearly distinguished and even contrasted by Paul. Others, such as "lesson"
and "revelation" (verse 26), are not clearly defined and will need to be given
special attention by translators.

In chapter 13 the key word was "love." In chapter 14 the central words are
terms which refer to the church and its corporate life.

14.1	RSV	TEV

**Make love your aim, and ear-
nestly desire the spiritual gifts, especially that you may prophesy.**

**It is love, then, that you should
strive for. Set your hearts on spiritual
gifts, especially the gift of proclaiming
God's message.**

This Greek sentence is simple but awkward. A literal translation would be
"Follow love, but be zealous for the spiritual gifts, but rather that you may prophesy." "Follow love" makes a real link with 12.31a, and "rather that you may
prophesy" introduces an important theme of chapter 14. The underlying thought is
"As I have just been saying, love is the supreme gift, but it is in a separate category, and we have no more to say about it. But now, returning to what I was
saying earlier, it is good to want to have spiritual gifts, but among these the most
important is 'the gift of prophecy.' "

Paul makes it clear in verse 39 that Christian prophecy, namely, proclaiming God's message, is much more important than speaking with tongues.

The phrase **Make love your aim** may be rendered as "So, you must strive above everything else to gain this ability to love."

Desire the spiritual gifts can also be expressed as "desire to gain spiritual gifts" or ". . . to gain abilities which the Spirit gives." Translators may use the term "ability" rather than **gifts,** if that is more natural in their language.

There is little difference in meaning between the verbs translated **Make . . . aim** and **earnestly desire** (compare 12.31; 14.39).

On the subject of Christian prophecy, see the comments on 11.4; 12.10.

Prophecy or "the gift of proclaiming God's message" (TEV) is certainly divinely inspired, but it is not ecstatic or unintelligible. There is also nothing in this chapter which would lead to our understanding of "prophecy" as foretelling the future.

14.2   RSV   TEV

RSV	TEV
For one who speaks in a tongue speaks not to men but to God; for no one understands him, but he utters mysteries in the Spirit.	The one who speaks in strange tongues does not speak to others but to God, because no one understands him. He is speaking secret truths by the power of the Spirit.

The phrase **speaks in a tongue** is the main theme which connects chapters 12, 13, and 14 (see the comments on 12.10). This theme is discussed in greater detail in the present chapter. Nothing in this letter would indicate that Paul used the term "tongues" to refer to actual human languages. In fact, in verses 10 and 11 he employs a different Greek word to speak about human languages. Both RSV and TEV show this difference clearly. Other modern translations such as DuCL and NIV have tended to translate "tongues" as "foreign languages." However, AT has "anyone who speaks ecstatically," and Brc says "when a man is speaking in ecstatic language." In the comments on 12.10 we suggested that if a literal translation of the word "tongues" has a strange meaning or is unintelligible, translators may use terms such as "ecstatic speech," "strange sounds," or "unintelligible sounds." The TNT glossary note on "tongues" (pages 577-578) is helpful but too long to reproduce here.

The phrase **one who** may be rendered as "the person who."

Men in this verse does not exclude women, so TEV translates "others."

Mysteries refers here to "secrets," things that are not generally known, as in 13.2: "understand all mysteries."

The final sentence of this verse can be translated as follows: "He is using the power of the Spirit to speak secret truths."

14.3   RSV   TEV

RSV	TEV
On the other hand, he who prophesies speaks to men for their upbuilding and encouragement and consolation.	But the one who proclaims God's message speaks to people and gives them help, encouragement, and comfort.

The meaning of this verse contrasts with the meaning of verse 2, as the words **On the other hand** show.

Men again includes women. GeCL has "others," and ItCL has "the community." They are probably anticipating "church" in verse 4.

There is some overlap in meaning between the terms translated **upbuilding, encouragement,** and **consolation.** The word for **upbuilding** is used in this chapter in the sense of "building up the church" as in verse 12. The word translated **encouragement** includes the idea of support and strengthening. The word for **consolation** is not used elsewhere in the New Testament. However, a related noun in Philippians 2.1 is translated "comforts" by TEV, and a related verb in 1 Thessalonians 5.14 is rendered "encourage" in RSV. If there is any significant distinction between these three terms, it is that **upbuilding** refers more to the strengthening of the church; **encouragement** means more generally help and support; and **consolation** means the fostering of good spirit among the Christian community.

14.4	RSV	TEV

He who speaks in a tongue **edifies himself,** but he who prophesies **edifies the church.**

The one who speaks in strange tongues helps only himself, but the one who proclaims God's message helps the whole church.

The two halves of this verse respectively sum up verses 2 and 3. Verse 4a, up to the word **himself,** is equivalent to verse 2. Verse 4b, from the phrase **but he who,** introduces the key word which is traditionally translated **church.** This key word has not been used since 12.28. In this passage it is clear that **church** refers to the local Christian community, an actual assembly of Christians (see especially verse 23). Barrett therefore translates "the assembled company." If the word which translators in a particular language have used for church refers mainly to a building, it may be better to translate the word in a way similar to Barrett: "the assembled group of believers," or ". . . group of Christians."

Tongue: see the comments on verse 2.

Prophesies here refers to "proclaiming God's word."

On **edifies,** see comments on 8.1.

14.5	RSV	TEV

Now I want you all to speak in tongues, but even more to prophesy. He who prophesies is greater than he who speaks in tongues, unless some one interprets, so that the church may be edified.

I would like for all of you to speak in strange tongues; but I would rather that you had the gift of proclaiming God's message. For the person who proclaims God's message is of greater value than the one who speaks in strange tongues—unless there is someone present who can explain what he says, so that the whole church may be helped.

Tongues: see the comments on verse 2.

Even more (TEV's "rather") is the usual meaning of the Greek word translated "especially" in verse 1. A contrast is implied here: although Paul would like all believers to **speak in tongues,** he feels that the gift of **prophecy** is a more important one and should be desired. The first sentence of this verse may be rendered as "I would like for all of you to speak with strange sounds; but more than that, I would like you to have the gift of proclaiming God's message."

To prophesy may be rendered as "to proclaim a message from God."

Greater is the word translated "more excellent" in 12.31. TEV is right to expand it to "of greater value," since Paul is not at present concerned with the importance of individuals in themselves, but with the value of their contributions to the Christian community. One can render this phrase as "has more importance" or "has greater usefulness."

The phrase **unless some one interprets** is awkward in Greek. It is not clear who is to do the interpreting or explaining. Barrett translates "the latter" instead of **some one,** meaning the one who is speaking in tongues. But since the speaker in tongues and his interpreter may, in fact, be different people (see 12.10,30), the translation in RSV and TEV of **some one** is quite adequate.

In many languages it will be helpful to add "what he says" (TEV) after **interprets:** "interprets what he says."

14.6	RSV	TEV
	Now, brethren, if I come to you speaking in tongues, how shall I benefit you unless I bring you some revelation or knowledge or prophecy or teaching?	So when I come to you, my brothers, what use will I be to you if I speak in strange tongues? Not a bit, unless I bring you some revelation from God or some knowledge or some inspired message or some teaching.

The Greek text suggests that Paul is introducing a new point, and this impression is strengthened by the use of the word **brethren.** Thus **Now** is preferable to TEV's "So." It also seems preferable to take verse 6 as part of the same paragraph as verse 11. For these reasons the UBS Greek text, RSV, GeCL, ItCL, and NIV begin a new paragraph with verse 6. **Now** seems to indicate a change in argument. Barrett translates "But now, brother, think . . . ."

How shall I benefit translates the same verb that was rendered as "I gain nothing" in 13.3.

Revelation here seems to refer to a particularly striking or unusual message from God, and in this context it is a message addressed through an inspired person such as Paul to the Christian community.

The clause **I bring you some revelation** may be rendered as "I bring you a message which God has revealed to me."

Knowledge: see 1.5; 12.8. In this context it should be noted that this is **knowledge** which is communicated to the believers, not secret knowledge which is kept to oneself.

Prophecy, again, means a "message from God."

Teaching: from this point on, Paul increasingly uses terms referring to learning and teaching. He does this to counteract the Corinthians' tendency to put too high a value on the more exotic gifts of the Spirit, especially speaking with tongues. The present-day reader needs to remember that Christian meetings in

New Testament times were concerned not only with worship but also with Christian instruction.

14.7   RSV   TEV

If even lifeless instruments, such as the   Take such **lifeless musical in-**
flute or the harp, do not give distinct   **struments as the flute or the harp—how**
notes, how will any one know what is   **will anyone know the tune that is being**
played?   **played unless the notes are**
                                             sounded distinctly?

The accent in the Greek word translated as **even** is uncertain, and so the meaning is also unclear. If the word is accentuated as in the UBS Greek text, it must mean "yet, still," and that is the basis of the translation **even.** However, the sequence of thought is not entirely clear, and for this reason many commentators prefer the form "in the same way": "In the same way, lifeless instruments such as . . . ."

As in verse 6, the rhetorical question expects the answer "No."

Lifeless: this word is not used elsewhere in the New Testament. Here the contrast is between inanimate objects and human beings.

The phrase **such as the flute or the harp** is literally "whether flute or harp." However, Paul is not contrasting two different types of musical instruments, but choosing two instruments at random. Thus RSV and TEV's rendering **such as** is correct.

What is played translates two Greek verbs, literally "what is being fluted or harped."

The final part of this verse can be restructured as follows: ". . . if people do not play them (the instruments) distinctly, how will the listener know what tune is being played?"

14.8   RSV   TEV

And if the bugle gives an indistinct   **And if the man who plays the bugle**
sound, who will get ready for battle?   **does not sound a clear call, who will**
                                             prepare for battle?

Bugle is the word also chosen by AT, Phps, NAB, and Brc. It fits in well with the military reference of this verse, but implies a modern setting, as bugles were not in use in New Testament times. For this reason all other translations consulted have "trumpet." This is the word chosen by TEV in all other places where this Greek word is used (for example, 15.51-52).

Indistinct here refers to something not clearly heard. One may say "If the bugle gives a sound which is not clearly heard . . ." or ". . . "does not play a distinct sound . . . ."

Get ready may have a general meaning, as in TEV's "prepare," or the more specific idea of a soldier getting his equipment together. Barrett even suggests the translation "who will arm himself for battle?"

One may render **for battle** as "to fight a battle."

14.9	RSV	TEV

So with yourselves; if you in a tongue utter speech that is not intelligible, how will any one know what is said? For you will be speaking into the air.

In the same way, how will anyone understand what you are talking about if your message given in strange tongues is not clear? Your words will vanish in the air!

Paul moves now from illustrations to literal statements. Here and in verse 12, **you** is emphatic. The order of words in the Greek is a little strange, and the meaning is not entirely clear, either in Greek or in RSV and TEV. The difficulty, as often in Paul's writings, arises because he is trying to say two things at once: (1) If you are speaking in a tongue, how will anyone be able to tell what you are saying? (2) How can anyone tell what you are saying if you do not give a clear message? The translator must avoid giving the impression that a message spoken in a "tongue" could of itself be distinct and intelligible. The implication, which Paul has expressed in verse 5, is that someone is needed to interpret whenever someone is speaking ecstatically.

RSV's literal translation of the last part of the verse may seem to give the impression that all speaking is really **speaking into the air.** TEV's expansion "your words will vanish in the air" gives the meaning more clearly. Many languages have similar idioms; for example, "speak the wind" (ThCL).

14.10	RSV	TEV

There are doubtless many different languages in the world, and none is without meaning;

There are many different languages in the world, yet none of them is without meaning.

Languages: here and in verse 11, the Greek word for "sound" is used in the sense of "language." By using this word Paul makes it clear that he is not talking about "tongues" in this verse. Some modern translations such as Phps and NEB translate this word as "sounds," but RSV, TEV, and many others render it as "languages." This latter translation is preferable.

The words translated **many different** convey the ideas (1) of a large number, and (2) that Paul is unwilling to say how many. Barrett translates "there are I don't know how many languages in the world."

The adjective translated **without meaning** means "incapable of speech," as in 2 Peter 2.16, which refers to Balaam's donkey. So the meaning may also be "incapable of meaning." One can render this double-negative clause positively as "yet all of them have meaning."

14.11	RSV	TEV

but if I do not know the meaning of the language, I shall be a foreigner to the speaker and the speaker a foreigner to me.

But if I do not know the language being spoken, the person who uses it will be a foreigner to me and I will be a foreigner to him.

Paul continues to draw an illustration from natural languages in order to show the danger of speaking ecstatically. In many languages this first sentence will need to be rendered as "If I do not understand the language which a person is speaking."

Foreigner: this is the Greek word from which the English "barbarian" is derived. However, here it refers to someone whose language cannot be understood rather than to a wild or fierce person.

For the last two clauses RSV follows the order of the Greek, while TEV reverses the order. At least in English, TEV's ordering is more logical: if someone is speaking in a language which I do not understand, the immediate effect is that I shall consider him a foreigner. The fact that he will also consider me a foreigner comes later. Even though they may understand each other when using normal speech, when they speak in strange tongues they are like foreigners to each other.

To me is literally "in me," meaning "in my sight" or "in my opinion."

14.12	RSV	TEV

So with yourselves; since you are eager for manifestations of the Spirit, strive to excel in building up the church.	Since you are eager to have the gifts of the Spirit, you must try above everything else to make greater use of those which help to build up the church.

The emphatic phrase **So with yourselves** introduces the point of Paul's argument. The following words are literally "if you are zealots of spirits." Paul is certainly not being ironic here. This word is related to the verb translated "make ... your aim" in verse 1. The literal "spirits" is here used to mean "spiritual gifts." So this sentence may be rendered as "you strive eagerly to get the gifts of the Spirit" or "you strive ... to get the abilities which the Spirit gives."

The rest of the verse is literally "towards the upbuilding of the church seek, in order that you may abound." TEV expands this slightly with the words "of those," which refer back to "the gifts of the Spirit." Translators should follow TEV's example here.

A model for translation of this verse is the following: "Since you yourselves strive eagerly to get the abilities which the Spirit gives, you must try above everything else to make the greater use of those abilities which help to build up the Christian community."

14.13	RSV	TEV

Therefore, he who speaks in a tongue should pray for the power to interpret.	The person who speaks in strange tongues, then, must pray for the gift to explain what he says.

Therefore indicates that this verse is linked with the previous sentence. From one point of view, it gives an example of what verse 12 states generally. However, it is an example of particular importance to Paul in this chapter. Within the general contrast between ecstatic sounds and intelligible language, the theme of prayer is central to verses 13-17. For this reason RSV, TEV, and other translations begin a new paragraph here.

Tongue may be rendered as "strange sounds," "unintelligible sounds," or "ecstatic speech."

TEV explains simply the meaning of **power to interpret.** One may say "the ability to explain what these strange sounds mean."

14.14	RSV	TEV

For if I pray in a tongue, my spirit prays but my mind is unfruitful.

For if I pray in this way, my spirit prays indeed, but my mind has no part in it.

For is omitted in some Greek manuscripts and is printed in square brackets in the UBS Greek text. Whether Paul wrote this word or not is unimportant. The connection with verse 13 is clear, and translators must decide for themselves whether a connecting word such as **For** is natural in their own language.

The question arises whether **I** here means strictly Paul alone, or whether Paul is using himself as an example. The same problem arises in chapter 13 (see the introduction) and in Romans 7. Most translations have "I," like RSV and TEV. GeCL, however, brings out the meaning that Paul is using himself as an example by translating "When someone . . . speaks" in verse 13, and using "he" in verse 14 (but not verse 15). This is possible, but it is important to keep the contrast between "I" in verse 15 and "you" in verse 16.

In a tongue may be rendered as "in strange sounds" or "in ecstatic speech" (see verse 13 and elsewhere in this chapter).

Mind here refers to a person's thinking apparatus or intellectual faculty, which is an integral part of human nature.

The **spirit,** on the other hand, is breathed into man by God (see Gen 2.7, which Paul quotes in 15.45). It is **my spirit,** but this does not mean here just one part or aspect of human nature; it is the human spirit acting under the inspiration of the Holy Spirit. GeCL brings this out by translating here "when [anyone] speaks in such languages, the Holy Spirit prays in him . . . ," and in verse 16, "but when you praise God in the language of the Spirit . . . ." This is possible, though NIV translates "your spirit" in verse 16.

Is unfruitful probably means "receives no benefit from."

14.15	RSV	TEV

What am I to do? I will pray with the spirit and I will pray with the mind also; I will sing with the spirit and I will sing with the mind also.

What should I do, then? I will pray with my spirit, but I will pray also with my mind; I will sing with my spirit, but I will sing also with my mind.

What am I to do may be rendered as "If that is the case, what should I do?" RSV, TEV, and most CLTs assume that Paul is asking a real question about his own future conduct. However, Mft's translation "Very well then" and Phps' "therefore" turn the question into a positive expression indicating a logical connection with verse 14. This interpretation seems preferable.

The rest of this verse consists of two closely parallel statements, each of which is divided into two halves. In languages where such repetition is not natural, it may be possible to shorten the whole text to say "I will pray and sing both with my spirit and also with my mind."

For the meaning of **spirit** and **mind,** see the comments on verse 14.

TEV introduces "my" in this verse, as it was used in the Greek in verse 14.

<u>14.16</u>   RSV   TEV

Otherwise, if you bless^w with the spirit,   When you give thanks to God in spirit
how can any one in the position of an   only, how can an ordinary person taking
outsider^x say the "Amen" to your   part in the meeting say "Amen" to your
thanksgiving when he does not know   prayer of thanksgiving? He has no way
what you are saying?   of knowing what you are saying.

^w That is, *give thanks to God*
^x Or *him that is without gifts*

This verse, like other details in the section, presupposes a church situation
in which worship is accompanied by teaching. Different verbs for "giving thanks"
are used here and in the following verse, but in both verses the ideas of praising
God and thanking him are closely linked.

With the spirit: see the comment on "spirit" in verse 14.

Translators may add the word "only" as TEV has done, since the content of
verses 14-15 implies this addition.

An outsider (TEV's "ordinary person") is rendered quite differently in different translations: DuCL "an ordinary churchgoer"; GeCL "someone who does not
understand this language" (that is, "the language of the spirit"); Phps "the ungifted
man." The basic problem seems to be that of deciding whether "ordinary people"
were members of the Christian community or not. On the one hand, Paul seems to
take it for granted that such people would be present in Christian meetings, so
outsiders as in RSV may be too negative a translation. On the other hand, those
"ordinary people" were clearly not mature members of the Christian community.
It is probably best to think of them as "members in training" or "uninstructed
Christians."

Most languages borrow the Hebrew term **Amen,** a word used at the end of
prayers to show that the hearers agreed with the content of the prayer. In languages where this is not the case, it may be possible to translate "how can an
uninstructed person be able to respond to your prayer of thanksgiving?" or ". . .
say 'I agree' to your prayer of thanksgiving?"

<u>14.17</u>   RSV   TEV

For you may give thanks well enough,   Even if your prayer of thanks to God is
but the other man is not edified.   quite good, the other person is not
                                                              helped at all.

In English **well enough** or "quite good" (TEV) is ambiguous. The meaning
here is "entirely good." NEB makes this clear: "your prayer of thanksgiving may
be all that could be desired."

Edified: see the comment on "upbuilding" in verse 3.

The final sentence may be rephrased as "you do not build up the other
person at all."

14.18	RSV	TEV

I thank God that I speak in tongues more than you all;

I thank God that I speak in strange tongues much more than any of you.

Tongues: see the comments on verse 2 and elsewhere in this chapter.

TEV's "much" is not in the text and is unnecessary in translation. The verse means that Paul has the gift of ecstatic speech in greater measure than his readers.

14.19	RSV	TEV

nevertheless, in church I would rather speak five words with my mind, in order to instruct others, than ten thousand words in a tongue.

But in church worship I would rather speak five words that can be understood, in order to teach others, than speak thousands of words in strange tongues.

In church means "in a meeting of Christians" (see the comments on verse 4).

With my mind, as in verse 15, probably means "with my understanding." TEV has tried to make this clearer by saying "that can be understood." This is probably a better translation, as nonecstatic speech is speech which can be understood.

14.20	RSV	TEV

Brethren, do not be children in your thinking; be babes in evil, but in thinking be mature.

Do not be like children in your thinking, my brothers; be children so far as evil is concerned, but be grown up in your thinking.

Brethren begins a new paragraph. It refers to "fellow Christians," not actual family members. The connection with what precedes this word is not entirely clear, but Paul appears to mean that the Corinthian Christians were "immature" in giving too much importance to speaking in tongues. This first sentence may be rephrased as "Fellow Christians, do not think like children" or ". . . like immature people."

The verb translated **be babes** is not related in form to **children** in the first part of the verse, but the meaning is the same. As elsewhere, Paul, a good writer, varies his language where possible. This sentence may be translated in some languages as "you must be innocent like babies in the ways of evil."

The word for **evil** refers to general activity which is wrong or sinful, rather than to evil persons or things. The sentence **be babes in evil** may be rendered in some languages as "You must be innocent like children in the ways of evil" or ". . . in not knowing evil doings."

Mature or "grown up" (TEV) was translated "spiritually mature" (TEV) in 2.6, and that is what **mature** means here. If verse 20b stood alone, it could be translated "become grown up . . . ," but this translation is not possible in verse 20a, so **be mature** is correct.

The whole verse may thus be translated: "My brothers, do not think in a spiritually immature way; you must be innocent like children, as far as evil is concerned, but think as people who are spiritually mature."

14.21

RSV	TEV
In the law it is written, "By men of strange tongues and by the lips of foreigners will I speak to this people, and even then they will not listen to me, says the Lord."	In the Scriptures it is written, "By means of men speaking strange languages I will speak to my people, says the Lord. I will speak through lips of foreigners, but even then my people will not listen to me."

Law here refers more generally to "scripture," since the quotation is almost certainly from Isaiah 28.11-12.[1] "Scriptures" (TEV) clearly refers to what Christians now call the Old Testament. Translators should avoid using the word Bible, as readers may think that the New Testament is included.

It is written: see comments on 1.19.

As in 1.19, Paul quotes a piece of Old Testament poetry in which the same thing is said twice in different words in successive lines. This is called "parallelism." RSV reproduces it, but TEV shows that it is not necessary to reproduce it in languages which do not have this kind of poetry. The quotation in this verse does not correspond exactly either to the Hebrew or to the Septuagint and may be based on another Greek translation. Here as elsewhere, translators should avoid adapting the New Testament quotation to fit in with the Old Testament text. The meaning of the quotation is different from the thought in earlier verses. The Old Testament text means that Israel will not listen obediently to God, even when God sends an invader against them who speaks a foreign language. Paul appears to make the text mean that speaking with tongues is not intended for the believing community, but for those outside it. Even this appears to conflict with what Paul has said earlier. Perhaps his meaning is that the ability to understand speaking with tongues is a sign by which believers may be distinguished from unbelievers.

The words **says the Lord** are not part of the text in Isaiah. However, it seems more natural to suppose that Paul added this common Old Testament refrain, intending it to be read as part of the quotation, rather than that he used it in his own name. If this is correct, **Lord** probably means "God," not "Christ."

The first part of this verse can be restructured as "I will use men who speak strange languages to speak to my people, says the Lord."

---

[1] The UBS Greek text notes a possible allusion to Deuteronomy 28.49, but this is more remote.

RSV	TEV
Thus, tongues are a sign not for believers but for unbelievers, while prophecy is not for unbelievers but for believers.	So then, the gift of speaking in strange tongues is proof for unbelievers, not for believers, while the gift of proclaiming God's message is proof for believers, not for unbelievers.

Thus introduces a conclusion from the scripture quotation in verse 21.

A sign is probably the better translation here. TEV's rendering "proof" seems to conflict with verse 24, where it is Christian prophecy, in contrast with speaking with tongues, which is said to "convict" the unbeliever who comes in from outside. Phps translates "a sign of God's power," suggesting that **tongues** are designed to impress unbelievers rather than to "convict" them.

Another possibility is that speaking with tongues is a sign by which unbelievers may be distinguished from believers, but the wording of the present verse, **not for believers, but for unbelievers,** does not make this clear. Paul seems to have been turned aside from his main argument by the word translated "strange tongues" (TEV's "strange languages") in the quotation in verse 21.

Prophecy means "the gift of proclaiming God's message" (TEV). It is inspired speaking in a human language, as in 12.10.

RSV	TEV
If, therefore, the whole church assembles and all speak in tongues, and outsiders or unbelievers enter, will they not say that you are mad?	If, then, the whole church meets together and everyone starts speaking in strange tongues—and if some ordinary people or unbelievers come in, won't they say that you are all crazy?

Therefore seems to mark a return to the main argument after Paul's deviation in the previous two or three verses.

The clause **the whole church assembles** emphasizes that Paul is speaking of a full assembly of the Christians at Corinth. This clause may also be expressed as "all the believers meet together."

All here refers to "everyone who can speak in tongues." It does not mean that every person in church has the ability to speak ecstatically.

Outsiders: some commentators and translators believe that **outsiders** in this verse are different from the **outsiders** (TEV's "ordinary people") in verse 16. NEB even translates this one Greek word three different ways in verses 16, 23, and 24, seemingly indicating three separate groups of people. However, this Greek word is so unusual and distinctive that it is unlikely that Paul would use it so differently in this short passage. We therefore suggest that **outsiders** refers to the same people in all three verses, namely, "uninstructed Christians." TEV's "ordinary person" is too general.

Unbelievers means "non-Christians"; Paul was probably thinking of the pagans who formed most of the non-Christian population of Corinth.

Mad: Barrett notes that this word "does not mean, You are suffering from mental disease, but You are possessed," that is, in the power of an evil spirit.

14.24 RSV	TEV
But if all prophesy, and an unbeliever or outsider enters, he is convicted by all, he is called to account by all,	But if everyone is proclaiming God's message when some unbeliever or ordinary person comes in, he will be convinced of his sin by what he hears. He will be judged by all he hears,

This verse begins as a contrast with verse 23, but is expanded for emphasis toward the end, and also in verse 25. These two verses complete the contrast between speaking with tongues and prophecy, which has been announced in verse 22.

The words **unbeliever or outsider** are used in the opposite order from verse 23 probably for reasons of style. For the meaning of these two words, see the comments on verse 23.

The word translated **convicted** commonly refers to moral influence on someone's conscience, rather than to persuasion by argument, as TEV shows by adding "of his sin." There is little difference in meaning between **convicted** and **called to account.** TEV uses the words "convinced" and "judged." TEV adds "he hears" to make clear what is implicit: the unbeliever or outsider will be listening to the proclaiming of God's message. What "he hears" will convict or judge him.

The clause **he is called to account by all** may also be rendered as "all the things which he hears will judge him."

14.25 RSV	TEV
the secrets of his heart are disclosed; and so, falling on his face, he will worship God and declare that God is really among you.	his secret thoughts will be brought into the open, and he will bow down and worship God, confessing, "Truly God is here among you!"

This verse, especially the first clause, is linked in grammar and meaning with verse 24.

The secrets of his heart is literally "the hidden things of his heart."

Disclosed appears to refer to "public confession," not just that the unbeliever comes to recognize his own sin. In languages which do not employ the passive, a translator will need to restructure **the secrets of his heart are disclosed;** for example, "He will confess his secret thoughts before the assembled Christians."

Falling on his face (TEV's "bow down") is a sign of unworthiness and humiliation. Translators should consider whether this is a normal attitude of prayer in the places where their translation will be used.

Declare is a more natural English translation here. "Confessing" as in TEV could be misunderstood to refer to "confession of sin."

Order in the Church

26 What then, brethren? When you come together, each one has a hymn, a lesson, a revelation, a tongue, or an interpretation. Let all things be done for edification. 27 If any speak in a tongue, let there be only two or at most three, and each in turn; and let one interpret. 28 But if there is no one to interpret, let each of them keep silence in church and speak to himself and to God. 29 Let two or three prophets speak, and let the others weigh what is said. 30 If a revelation is made to another sitting by, let the first be silent. 31 For you can all prophesy one by one, so that all may learn and all be encouraged; 32 and the spirits of prophets are subject to prophets. 33 For God is not a God of confusion but of peace.

As in all the churches of the saints, 34 the women should keep silence in the churches. For they are not permitted to speak, but should be subordinate, as even the law says. 35 If there is anything they desire to know, let them ask their husbands at home. For it is shameful for a woman to speak in church. 36 What! Did the word of God originate with you, or are you the only ones it has reached?

37 If any one thinks that he is a prophet, or spiritual, he should acknowledge that what I am writing to you is a command of the Lord. 38 If any one does not recognize this, he is not recognized. 39 So, my brethren, earnestly desire to prophesy, and do not forbid speaking in tongues; 40 but all things should be done decently and in order.

26 This is what I mean, my brothers. When you meet for worship, one person has a hymn, another a teaching, another a revelation from God, another a message in strange tongues, and still another the explanation of what is said. Everything must be of help to the church. 27 If someone is going to speak in strange tongues, two or three at the most should speak, one after the other, and someone else must explain what is being said. 28 But if no one is there who can explain, then the one who speaks in strange tongues must be quiet and speak only to himself and to God. 29 Two or three who are given God's message should speak, while the others are to judge what they say. 30 But if someone sitting in the meeting receives a message from God, the one who is speaking should stop. 31 All of you may proclaim God's message, one by one, so that everyone will learn and be encouraged. 32 The gift of proclaiming God's message should be under the speaker's control, 33 because God does not want us to be in disorder but in harmony and peace.

As in all the churches of God's people, 34 the women should keep quiet in the meetings. They are not allowed to speak; as the Jewish Law says, they must not be in charge. 35 If they want to find out about something, they should ask their husbands at home. It is a disgraceful thing for a woman to speak in a church meeting.

36 Or could it be that the word of God came from you? Or are you the only ones to whom it came? 37 If anyone supposes he is God's messenger or has a spiritual gift, he must realize that what I am writing to you is the Lord's command. 38 But if he does not pay attention to this, pay no attention to him.

39 So then, my brothers, set your heart on proclaiming God's message, but do not forbid the speaking in strange tongues. 40 Everything must be done in a proper and orderly way.

In this section Paul draws the consequences from his earlier discussion. Verses 39-40 form the conclusion of the whole chapter, or perhaps even of chapters 13-14. As in verse 20 and in many other places, **brethren** marks the beginning of a new paragraph or section.

<u>14.26</u>   RSV   TEV

What then, brethren? When you come together, each one has a hymn, a lesson, a revelation, a tongue, or an interpretation. Let all things be done for edification.

This is what I mean, my brothers. When you meet for worship, one person has a hymn, another a teaching, another a revelation from God, another a message in strange tongues, and still another the explanation of what is said. Everything must be of help to the church.

What then represents the same Greek phrase which is translated "what am I to do?" in verse 15. Most translations agree with RSV and TEV that the expression refers to action in verse 15, and to the course of the argument in verse 26. The reason for this is no doubt that verse 15b mentions something Paul will do, while in the present passage, verse 26b contains a brief description of the situation. Recommendations for action begin only at verse 27. However, AT ("then what is the right course, brothers?") and TOB think that Paul refers to action here. Such an interpretation is possible, since the general tone of the section is practical. Mft's translation "Very well then" leaves the matter open in both places.

Brethren refers to "fellow Christians," not to actual family members.

TEV adds the words "for worship" after **come together** ("meet"). Translators can also do this, as the rest of the verse and also verse 23 strongly suggest that Paul has a full church meeting in mind.

The **hymn** would probably be, not an Old Testament psalm, but a Christian hymn as in Ephesians 5.19. **Has a hymn** may be rendered as "sings a hymn."

A **lesson** (TEV's "teaching") is rather awkward in English. Another possible translation is "something to teach" or "teaches something." Paul does not mention Christian prophecy in this verse. This may indicate that the meanings of "prophecy" and "teaching" overlap. Prophecy in a Christian setting is inspired teaching.

A **revelation:** "from God" (TEV) is implied. For the meaning of **revelation,** see the comments on verse 6. There is no suggestion here of revelation at the end of time. In some languages it may be preferable to say "something to reveal from God" or "speaks a message which God has revealed."

A **tongue:** see the comments on verse 6. One may render this phrase as "speaks a message in strange sounds."

An interpretation is really "an explanation" (TEV). This clause may also be rendered as "can explain what is said in the strange sounds."

Let all things be done for edification can be rendered as "you should do everything in order to help and build up the believers."

TEV's linking words "one person . . . another . . . and still another" probably bring out the meaning more clearly than RSV's literal **each one.** However, throughout this passage (verses 23,24,26,31) Paul insists strongly that all the Corinthian Christians have, or at least can and should have, spiritual gifts. The translation should therefore avoid giving the impression that if a Christian had one spiritual gift, he could not have other gifts.

14.27 RSV	TEV
If any speak in a tongue, let there be only two or at most three, and each in turn; and let one interpret.	If someone is going to speak in strange tongues, two or three at the most should speak, one after the other, and someone else must explain what is being said.

After the introductory summary of verse 26, verses 27-28 are balanced by verses 29-30, and each pair of verses includes a contrast. Paul discusses speaking in tongues in verse 28, and not speaking in tongues in verse 29. In verse 29 he talks about prophesying, and in verse 30 his theme is not prophesying.

This verse is conditional. The content suggests that it describes a situation which had often arisen in Corinth. Paul is concerned with real circumstances, not with what might happen.

Speak (TEV's "going to speak"): the verb in Greek is present, not future, though naturally Paul's instructions could not be put into effect until his readers received them.

Two or at most three: the Greek implies that Paul means "on each occasion." Verse 31 shows that Paul is not suggesting a limitation in the number of Christian prophets in the community.

Each in turn is literally "one," implying here "one at a time."

Let one may be rendered "someone else must" (TEV) or "let another person."

Translators may add the words "what is being said" (TEV) after **interpret**.

14.28 RSV	TEV
But if there is no one to interpret, let each of them keep silence in church and speak to himself and to God.	But if no one is there who can explain, then the one who speaks in strange tongues must be quiet and speak only to himself and to God.

Them in **Let each of them keep silence** refers to the people speaking in tongues in verse 27. This is why TEV adds the words "the one who speaks in strange tongues must be quiet." Translators will do well to follow TEV's example.

Barrett points out that the word **to** in the phrases translated **to himself** and **to God** probably vary in meaning. The first phrase is better translated in many languages as "for himself," that is, silently and inwardly, and the second one "to God."

14.29 RSV	TEV
Let two or three prophets speak, and let the others weigh what is said.	Two or three who are given God's message should speak, while the others are to judge what they say.

Paul now discusses the second half of the contrast between speaking in tongues and Christian prophecy, which has been a main feature of this chapter.

Two or three: Paul does not repeat the phrase **at most** from verse 27, since he will now speak more positively of Christian prophecy than of speaking in tongues. Nor does he repeat **each in turn,** though this idea is probably implied. The danger of several people's talking at once would naturally be greater in the case of ecstatic speech than in inspired teaching using natural language.

The first sentence may be rendered as "Let two or three people to whom God has given a message speak."

The others may mean "other prophets" or "other members of the Christian community." The second, more general, meaning is preferable in translation.

Weigh (TEV's "judge") is the word used in 4.7 and in 11.29,31 referring to a similar situation (see the comments). Bruce suggests "discuss" as a possible translation. The Christians probably did discuss the messages from God. Their aim would be to apply the prophets' messages to the Corinthians' situation, rather than to judge the validity of what the prophets said or of the prophets' qualifications.

14.30   RSV   TEV

If a revelation is made to another   But if someone sitting in the meeting
sitting by, let the first be silent.   receives a message from God, the one
                                       who is speaking should stop.

The Greek text has the word "But" (see TEV) to introduce the second half of the contrast. Translators should probably include this word even though RSV omits it. The situation is probably not exactly the same as that in verse 28. That is why the same verb is translated "keep silence" in verse 28 and **be silent** in verse 30. In the present verse "stop (speaking)" as in TEV is a better translation.

The phrase **another sitting by** may be expressed as "another person who is sitting nearby."

The first can be expanded to "the first speaker." TEV's "the one who is speaking" is clearer English. This means one of those who are referred to in verse 29a.

This verse suggests that, as in Acts 2.14, people stood up in order to take a leading part in Christian meetings.

14.31   RSV   TEV

For you can all prophesy one by one, so   All of you may proclaim God's message,
that all may learn and all be encour-   one by one, so that everyone will learn
aged;   and be encouraged.

Can: it is not certain whether this Greek word should be translated **can,** "may" (TEV), or "have the power to." The context suggests that Paul is now thinking that a meeting must be carried on in an orderly fashion because there is a limited time (see verse 40). Most translations leave the question open by translating **can.**

All is repeated three times, showing emphasis. Translators should maintain this emphasis if possible. TEV adds "of you" after the first **all,** a necessary addition to make the meaning clear.

Learn: see 4.6 and 14.35.

14.31

Be encouraged: in this passage **be encouraged** has much the same meaning as "edification" in verse 26.

14.32   RSV   TEV

| **and the spirits of prophets are subject to prophets.** | **The gift of proclaiming God's message should be under the speaker's control,** |

RSV's translation is too literal; however, TEV brings out the meaning. **Spirits of prophets** probably means "the spiritual gift of prophecy" (see verse 12 and 12.10). TEV expresses the meaning by the singular "the speaker," meaning "any such speaker." Verses 14-15 help us to understand the present verse; in other words, Paul is saying that the prophet's reason and self-control should govern the way in which he uses his special gift.

It is possible to restructure this verse as follows: "The speaker who proclaims God's message must control his gift (ability)."

14.33   RSV   TEV

| **For God is not a God of confusion but of peace.**   **As in all the churches of the saints,** | **because God does not want us to be in disorder but in harmony and peace.**   **As in all the churches of God's people,** |

There is a difference in opinion as to whether the words **As in all the churches of the saints** belong with the first part of verse 33 or with verse 34 (see footnote C in the UBS Greek text). The problem is complicated by the fact that some manuscripts place verses 34-35 at the end of the chapter, following verse 40. If this is done, verse 33b must be taken with 33a. However, if verses 34-35 are kept in their traditional place, as the weight of manuscript evidence suggests, the question of the punctuation of verse 33 remains open. In favor of dividing verse 33 as in the UBS Greek text is the fact that verse 33a reads like the climax or conclusion of an argument and does not connect well with 33b.

In favor of linking verse 33b with 33a, it may be said (1) that the repetition of the phrases **in all the churches** (33b) and **in the churches** (34) is awkward; and (2) that Paul uses expressions very similar to 33b in 4.17 ("in every church") and 7.17 ("in all the churches"). In both cases these occur at the end of a sentence. It seems preferable, then, to link 33b with 33a. In this case, verse 33b will form the conclusion, not only of verses 32-33a, but also of the whole paragraph, and should be translated as a separate sentence. One may say, for example, "This is what happens in all the churches of God's people."

If, however, translators take verse 33b with verse 34, as TEV and many other translations have done, then translators may need to use different words for the two occurrences of **churches**. The first, in 33b, would refer to Christian communities everywhere, and the second to meetings of a particular community. TNT restructures: "the women must keep silent in the congregations, for they are not permitted to speak. This is the practice in all the congregations of God's people."[2]

Confusion: the same word is used in 2 Corinthians 12.20. It is possible that Paul means "God does not give spiritual gifts which are in conflict with one another." However, it is simpler to understand the text to mean "God is not a source of disorder in the Christian community." Therefore a translation similar to TEV's will fit the meaning more closely.

Peace: early Christian writers were very likely thinking of the Hebrew word for peace when they used the Greek word. The Hebrew had a wider meaning than that of the Greek or English. **Peace** for Christians, as in the Old Testament, was more than an absence of war or a peaceful feeling which an individual might have inside himself (see comments on 1.3; 7.15).

The first part of this verse can be restructured as "because God wants us to have harmony and peace among ourselves rather than confusion."

Churches clearly refers to local Christian communities.

Saints refers to God's people, meaning Christians everywhere. The meaning is similar to "God's holy people" in 1.2.

14.34 RSV	TEV
the women should keep silence in the churches. For they are not permitted to speak, but should be subordinate, as even the law says.	the women should keep quiet in the meetings. They are not allowed to speak; as the Jewish Law says, they must not be in charge.

As we noted in the introduction to 7.1-16, the same Greek word may mean "wife" and "woman." All translations consulted in languages which make a distinction between "wife" and "woman" take **women** to be the meaning here.

For the problem of reconciling this passage with 11.4, see the comments on that verse.

They are not permitted: "Christian custom" is probably the implied agent of this passive verb, not **the law** which Paul introduces in verse 34b as a fresh argument. In some languages it may be simpler to translate "we do not allow them to speak."

Verse 34b introduces a new argument based on the Old Testament, although Paul does not refer explicitly to any Old Testament text.[3]

Should be subordinate: TEV replaces RSV's positive expression by a negative one: "they must not be in charge." One may also say "they must not hold positions of leadership."

Law: "the Jewish" (TEV) is implied. One can also say "the law of Moses."

---

[2] The question of punctuation in verse 33, and the textual problem of the position of verses 34-35, should be distinguished from the question of whether Paul is the author of verses 34-35. Some commentators believe that Paul could not have written in this way, and that these verses crept into the text from a marginal note by a scribe, influenced perhaps by 1 Timothy 2.11-12. In many translations it may be good to state in a note that some manuscripts place verses 34-35 at the end of the chapter. However, there is no manuscript evidence for the omission of these verses, and where manuscript evidence is lacking, it is not advisable for translators, even in readers' helps, to enter into questions of authenticity. Quite apart from this, it may be said that the similarity of language between verses 34 and 35 and 1 Timothy 2.11-12 is not striking, and that there are several points of contact, indicated in the notes, between verses 34-35 and the wider context.

[3] Bruce suggests Genesis 1.26ff; 2.21ff (compare 1 Cor 11.3ff) rather than Genesis 3.16, suggested by earlier commentators.

There is no doubt in the Greek that "as the Jewish Law says" refers to "they must not be in charge" (TEV). The phrase "as the Jewish Law says" may be translated "as we find it written in the Jewish Law."

14.35   RSV   TEV

If there is anything they desire to know,   If they want to find out about some-
let them ask their husbands at home.   thing, they should ask their husbands at
For it is shameful for a woman to speak   home. It is a disgraceful thing for a
in church.   woman to speak in a church meeting.

In the first sentence it will be good in many languages to add the word "women"; for example, "If the women want to find out . . . ."

To know is the verb translated "learn" in verse 31, but the addition of "about something" in TEV suggests that here, learning involves asking questions; that is something which they should do at home.

The phrase **ask their husbands** can be expanded to "ask their husbands about it."

It is shameful probably means that the woman brings shame upon herself if she speaks in a church meeting. So a translation may say "For if a woman speaks in a church meeting she disgraces herself."

Speak: this is the ordinary verb for "speak" and should not be given any special meaning such as "chatter."

14.36   RSV   TEV

What! Did the word of God originate   Or could it be that the word of
with you, or are you the only ones it has   God came from you? Or are you the
reached?   only ones to whom it came?

As TEV makes clear, the two halves of this verse balance one another; the Christian message neither began nor ended in Corinth. The implication is that the Corinthians have no right to decide independently of other Christian communities how Christians should believe (see verse 33b).

The two rhetorical questions expect the answer "No." Paul is speaking ironically in contrast to his serious statements in 1.17; 11.23; and 15.3 about the source of his message.

What! is a rather idiomatic English expression. Most languages may leave this word out. In languages which do not use rhetorical questions, these two sentences can be rendered as positive statements: "The word of God did not originate with you. You are not the only ones . . . ."

The difficult English expression "Or could it be" in TEV can be rendered "Is it possible?"

The word of God generally has the meaning "a message from God," and only secondarily "a message about God." In the present context the expression refers to the Christian message. GeCL has "the Good News."

Originate is literally "went out." TEV adopts the point of view of the readers of the letter and uses the verb "came." Each translator must decide whether "go" or "come" is more natural in such a context.

14.37   RSV   TEV

If any one thinks that he is a   If anyone supposes he is God's messen-
prophet, or spiritual, he should ac-   ger or has a spiritual gift, he must
knowledge that what I am writing to   realize that what I am writing to you is
you is a command of the Lord.   the Lord's command.

Most of the textual differences noted in the UBS and other editions of the
Greek text affect the order of words rather than the meaning of the sentence as a
whole.

Thinks (TEV's "supposes") leaves open the question whether the person is
really "God's messenger" (TEV) or not.

Spiritual is literally "a spiritual (person)." The same term was used in the
plural in 14.1, but probably means "has a spiritual gift" as in TEV.

Acknowledge seems to refer to a mental acceptance or admission that Paul
is writing what the Lord has commanded. Other possible translations are "admit"
or "agree in his (or, one's) mind."

A few manuscripts omit **command,** giving the meaning "what I am writing
to you is from the Lord." Some manuscripts change **command** to "commands" in
order to agree with "the things I am writing to you." The most natural way of
understanding the phrase **command of the Lord** is as one particular order; but it
may also refer to the whole of the teaching in chapter 14 which Paul has given as
an apostle, and therefore with Christ's authority.[4]

14.38   RSV   TEV

If any one does not recognize this, he is   But if he does not pay attention to this,
not recognized.   pay no attention to him.

This may be expanded to "this command."

Both the text and the meaning of this verse are uncertain. The last word in
the Greek, translated **he is not recognized,** may be either "he is not known" (the
UBS Greek text), "let him not be known," or even as in one manuscript "you do not
know." The meaning of the verb may be either "not know" or "not pay attention,"
that is, "ignore." In both cases the implied agent of the verb may be either the
Corinthian Christians or God himself. GeCL has "God will not recognize him
either." NEB translates in a similar way. Most translations, however, interpret
this passage to mean that Paul is referring simply to recognition by the congregation.

14.39   RSV   TEV

So, my brethren, earnestly desire to   So then, my brothers, set your
prophesy, and do not forbid speaking in   heart on proclaiming God's message,
tongues;   but do not forbid the speaking in
                                            strange tongues.

---

[4] E. Sjöberg, 1957-58, "Herrens bud 1 Kor. 14.37," Svensk Exegetisk Årsbok
22-23.168-171.

So marks the beginning of the conclusion of the whole argument. This transition as usual is marked by **my brethren.**

My brethren, as throughout 1 Corinthians, refers to "fellow Christians."

Desire is the same verb as "make . . . aim" in verse 1. Many languages have idioms similar to TEV's "set your heart on," which will be effective in this context.

The phrase **forbid speaking** may be expressed as "forbid believers to speak."

<u>14.40</u>   RSV   TEV

| but all things should be done decently and in order. | Everything must be done in a proper and orderly way. |

Decently: Paul uses a word closely related to those translated by TEV as "right" in 7.35 and "beautiful" in 12.24. "Proper" (TEV) is probably better than RSV's **decently.**

One may translate this verse as follows: "You must do everything in a proper and orderly way."

Chapter 15

The Resurrection of Christ

1 Now I would remind you, brethren, in what terms I preached to you the gospel, which you received, in which you stand, 2 by which you are saved, if you hold it fast—unless you believed in vain.

3 For I delivered to you as of first importance what I also received, that Christ died for our sins in accordance with the scriptures, 4 that he was buried, that he was raised on the third day in accordance with the scriptures, 5 and that he appeared to Cephas, then to the twelve. 6 Then he appeared to more than five hundred brethren at one time, most of whom are still alive, though some have fallen asleep. 7 Then he appeared to James, then to all the apostles. 8 Last of all, as to one untimely born, he appeared also to me. 9 For I am the least of the apostles, unfit to be called an apostle, because I persecuted the church of God. 10 But by the grace of God I am what I am, and his grace toward me was not in vain. On the contrary, I worked harder than any of them, though it was not I, but the grace of God which is with me. 11 Whether then it was I or they, so we preach and so you believed.

1 And now I want to remind you, my brothers, of the Good News which I preached to you, which you received, and on which your faith stands firm. 2 That is the gospel, the message that I preached to you. You are saved by the gospel if you hold firmly to it—unless it was for nothing that you believed.

3 I passed on to you what I received, which is of the greatest importance: that Christ died for our sins, as written in the Scriptures; 4 that he was buried and that he was raised to life three days later, as written in the Scriptures; 5 that he appeared to Peter and then to all twelve apostles. 6 Then he appeared to more than five hundred of his followers at once, most of whom are still alive, although some have died. 7 Then he appeared to James, and afterward to all the apostles.

8 Last of all he appeared also to me—even though I am like someone whose birth was abnormal.[o] 9 For I am the least of all the apostles—I do not even deserve to be called an apostle, because I persecuted God's church. 10 But by God's grace I am what I am, and the grace that he gave me was not without effect. On the contrary, I have worked harder than any of the other apostles, although it was not really my own doing, but God's grace working with me. 11 So then, whether it came from me or from them, this is what we all preach, and this is what you believe.

[o] whose birth was abnormal; *or* who was born at the wrong time.

There is no apparent connection, either in theme or language, between this section and the one before. The divisions within chapter 15 are not very important; the chapter is bound together by the theme of resurrection. Indeed, it is only in the light of verses 12-58 that the point of verses 1-11 can be fully grasped.

Verse 12 shows clearly for the first time that Paul's purpose in reminding his readers of the basic Christian beliefs (verses 3-5) and of later appearances of the risen Christ (verses 6-7) is to counter false teaching at Corinth. However, once this has become clear, the structure of chapter 15 is seen to correspond broadly with that of other parts of this letter. Paul first states basic principles which his readers already know, and then he develops these in a more distinctive way (see comments on 12.1,3 and further references there). Paul's reference in verse 8 to having himself seen the risen Christ (compare 9.1) leads immediately to a description of Paul's own status and work (verses 9-10). The language here may reflect the fact that some people in Corinth were questioning his authority as an apostle (see again 9.1-2; also 2 Cor 10.13). Verse 11 rounds off the section in language which partly repeats and summarizes that of verses 1-2.

It is generally agreed that parts of this section, especially verses 3-4, probably also verse 5 and possibly even verses 6-7, are a very old summary of Christian beliefs.[1] The language is in places not typical of Paul; for example, nowhere else does he refer to **the twelve** (verse 5). This means that when translating this section, translators cannot follow Paul's usage in other places. Translators should consult general commentaries, especially on the points of contact and contrast between this section and gospel accounts of the resurrection.

15.1	RSV	TEV
	Now I would remind you, brethren, in what terms I preached to you the gospel, which you received, in which you stand,	**And now I want to remind you, my brothers, of the Good News which I preached to you, which you received, and on which your faith stands firm.**

Paul is now listing various ways in which readers are related to the gospel: (1) they had it preached to them, (2) they received it, (3) they stand firm in it, and (4) they are or will be saved by it (verse 2). Only in verse 3 does Paul state that he himself, like his readers, received the gospel from someone else.

Now is a legitimate addition in English to prepare the reader for the introduction of a completely new theme.

Brethren makes it clear that a new section is beginning. As in other places in this letter, **brethren** means "fellow Christians."

In what terms makes the English sentence hard to understand. TEV's "I want to remind you . . . of the Good News which I preached to you," reflects the meaning quite accurately.

Preached: translators should remember that the content of this first Christian preaching by Paul was the story of Christ's death and resurrection. Words which imply only moral exhortation should be avoided.

Gospel: see comments on 4.15.

Received is the same word, used in the same sense, as in 11.23. The word itself is quite common and general in meaning, but the context shows that Paul means something more active than merely hearing him preach. One may say "took to your hearts."

---

[1] See J. Kloppenborg, 1978, "An analysis of the pre-Pauline formula of 1 Corinthians 15.3b-5 in the light of some recent literature," Catholic Biblical Quarterly 40.351-367.

Stand: see comments on 10.12.

The clause **in which you stand** may be restructured: "as a foundation on which your faith can stand firm." TEV adds "faith" to make it clear that the "standing firm" is figurative. Compare also 7.37 and Romans 11.20.

15.2   RSV   TEV

by which you are saved, if you hold it fast—unless you believed in vain.	**That is the gospel, the message that I preached to you. You are saved by the gospel if you hold firmly to it—unless it was for nothing that you believed.**

Comparison with RSV shows how TEV has changed the order of the clauses. The structure of the sentence in Greek is difficult and may well require some restructuring in translation. Other CLTs, however, do not do this in the same way as TEV. For example, GeCL: "You will also be saved by it, if you hold it fast as I handed it over to you. Otherwise you would have come to faith in vain!"

The first clause, **by which you are also saved,** follows on naturally from verse 1. **Saved** in this context probably means "being saved," hence "you will be saved." It is quite common in New Testament Greek for the present tense to refer by anticipation to future events. NEB has "which is now bringing you salvation."

The main difficulties arise in the rest of the verse. NEB takes the following clause to be a direct question, "Do you still hold fast the Gospel as I preached it to you?" and then continues, "If not, your conversion was in vain." However, most translations and editions agree with the UBS Greek text in taking the second clause as an implied question, as for example in Brc "if you keep a tight grip of it, in the form in which I preached it to you."

15.3   RSV   TEV

For I delivered to you as of first importance what I also received, that Christ died for our sins in accordance with the scriptures,	**I passed on to you what I received, which is of the greatest importance: that Christ died for our sins, as written in the Scriptures;**

Of first importance is literally "in (the) first (plural)," an expression used only here in the New Testament. The phrase can mean "first in time" or "first in importance." It seems likely that Paul intended both meanings here: "first and foremost" (NEB); "of first importance" is another possibility.

What I also received: verse 3a may mean either "I delivered the gospel which I had first received" or "I, like you, received the gospel." However, **also** is clearly linked in the Greek with **received,** not with **I,** and the parallel with verses 1-2 suggests the former. In many languages it will be good to expand this clause to "the message which I also received."

A translator may restructure the first part of this verse as follows: "I received a message of the greatest importance and passed it on to you. It was that . . . ."

In the remainder of the verse the summary of the Christian faith now begins. TEV indicates this by a colon. The word "that" following the colon can be understood here as equivalent to opening quotation marks.

For in **for our sins** has a very general meaning as its English equivalent: "concerning," "with reference to," or "in order to deal with" (Barrett).

Here and in verse 4 it is uncertain whether **in accordance with the scriptures** refers to the simple fact that **Christ died** and "was raised" (verse 4), or whether the phrases **for our sins** and "on the third day" (verse 4) are also supposed by Paul to have been foretold in the Old Testament.[2] The order in the Greek, however, suggests that **in accordance with the scriptures**, both in verse 3 and in verse 4, refers to the entire preceding clause. Both RSV and TEV interpret the meaning in this way, making a smoother translation.

In accordance with the scriptures may be rephrased as "as written in the Scriptures" (TEV) or "fulfilling what is written in the scriptures."

15.4	RSV	TEV
	that he was buried, that he was raised on the third day in accordance with the scriptures,	that he was buried and that he was raised to life three days later, as written in the Scriptures;

In some languages **he was buried** needs to be rendered in the active voice as "they buried him."

He was raised: the tense of this verb indicates that the consequences of this event remain in force. The use of the passive indicates that God raised Christ from the dead. In many languages this phrase can be translated as "God raised him to life."

On the third day makes better sense than "three days later" (TEV) in areas where people do not count inclusively. Both the day of the death and the day of the resurrection are included in counting the three days.

15.5	RSV	TEV
	and that he appeared to Cephas, then to the twelve.	that he appeared to Peter and then to all twelve apostles.

He appeared is literally "he was seen," a verb form often used in Greek when speaking of supernatural appearances. In some languages it is possible to render this verb as "let himself be seen" or "he showed himself to."

Cephas: if translators have used "Peter" throughout 1 Corinthians (TEV), they should use that name here also (see comments on 1.12).

To the twelve: in some languages, or for some groups of readers, it may be necessary to make it appear that **the twelve** were the original apostles. However, since Paul mentions in verse 7 a group of apostles which was probably larger than twelve, it seems best in translation to omit TEV's "all" in the present verse.

---

2 This raises the further question, which does not immediately affect the translator, of whether these phrases formed part of the primitive creed, or were inserted by Paul as his own interpretation.

RSV   TEV

Then he appeared to more than five   Then he appeared to more than five
hundred brethren at one time, most of   hundred of his followers at once, most
whom are still alive, though some have   of whom are still alive, although some
fallen asleep.   have died.

    Appeared: see comment on verse 5.

    Brethren: usually in 1 Corinthians this word means "fellow Christians," but in this verse "his followers" (TEV) would be more correct.

    Are . . . alive is literally "remain," but in most languages "are alive" will be more meaningful.

    Though: this Greek word is usually translated "but." However, there is no emphasis on the last clause, as there would be if "but" were used in English. Paul's point is that there are many people still alive who can confirm that Jesus rose from death. Therefore **though** is the more natural word here.

    The phrase **have fallen asleep** will be misunderstood in most languages. The meaning is "have died," as in TEV.

15.7   RSV   TEV

Then he appeared to James, then to all   Then he appeared to James, and after-
the apostles.   ward to all the apostles.

    James: here Paul almost certainly means the brother of Jesus (see Matt 13.55; Gal 1.19). In certain languages where the translation of **James** presents particular problems, the translator should consult "Guiding Principles for Inter-confessional Cooperation in Translating the Bible," published in 1968 by the United Bible Societies and the Vatican's Secretariat for Promoting Christian Unity, page 4.

    All the apostles: all is expressed here in the Greek, though not in verse 5. The order of the Greek words may also suggest that **all** is emphasized, perhaps indicating a group larger than **the twelve.** The following verses strongly suggest that although Paul became an apostle later, he was not included in the group mentioned here.

15.8   RSV   TEV

Last of all, as to one untimely born, he   Last of all he appeared also to
appeared also to me.   me—even though I am like someone
                                        whose birth was abnormal.[o]

                                        [o] whose birth was abnormal; or who was
                                        born at the wrong time.

    Last of all: Last means "last in time."

    As to one untimely born: this phrase and the rest of the verse present serious problems for the translator, as TEV's text and footnote suggest. The difficulties do not lie on the surface. The phrase may be literally translated "like" or "as if to the miscarriage." The word for "miscarriage" is not found elsewhere in the New Testament, but its meaning is clear from other literature.

The use of the article in the phrase "the miscarriage" may be understood in various ways: (1) as generic, meaning "any"; (2) as referring to an insult made against Paul by people in Corinth; or (3) as referring to some previous or widely known use of the expression, as one might refer, for example, to "the fiery furnace," with Daniel 3 in mind. This would explain why Paul, immediately after placing himself **last of all** in the list of apostles and others who saw the risen Christ, should apply to himself the image of a baby born not too late, but **untimely born** or "too soon." Paul's figurative language is often unclear, but a translator should make every reasonable effort to resolve so direct a contradiction.

If this explanation is correct, the basis of comparison is not that of the time at which Paul became an apostle, but the "abnormal" (TEV footnote) or even "monstrous" fact of a persecutor becoming an apostle. This interpretation fits in with verse 9.

The translation **as to one untimely born** is not very meaningful in English. A possible translation is "I am like someone who was born at the wrong time." In many languages the word for "miscarriage" will be preferable here.

To me is heavily emphatic and should be emphasized by translators if possible.

15.9	RSV	TEV

For I am the least of the apostles, unfit to be called an apostle, because I persecuted the church of God.

For I am the least of all the apostles—I do not even deserve to be called an apostle, because I persecuted God's church.

Least of the apostles: "all" (TEV) is implied and may be added to make the meaning clear.

Unfit: literally "who am not worthy." The word translated "worthy" conveys the idea of adequacy, and in this context refers to competence for a particular work or office. The clause can also be translated "I am really disqualified from being an apostle."

To be called: in some languages this may be translated as "for people to call me an apostle."

Persecuted: the Greek root means "run after," implying "in order to harm someone."

15.10	RSV	TEV

But by the grace of God I am what I am, and his grace toward me was not in vain. On the contrary, I worked harder than any of them, though it was not I, but the grace of God which is with me.

But by God's grace I am what I am, and the grace that he gave me was not without effect. On the contrary, I have worked harder than any of the other apostles, although it was not really my own doing, but God's grace working with me.

Grace means "God's gift" (see comments on 1.3).

I am what I am is Paul's tactful way of saying "I have become an apostle." One may say "But what I am today, I am by God's grace" or "But God's grace has made me what I am today, that is, an apostle."

His grace toward me is rather literal. TEV's "the grace that he gave me" brings out more clearly the meaning of **grace** as God's gift—here, specifically, the gift of being an apostle.

Was not in vain: literally "did not become in vain." It means "was not wasted," "was not worthless," or the positive statement "was effective." The whole clause can be rendered as "God's gifts to me were not wasted" or ". . . were effective."

Most translations smooth away an awkward double contrast or change of direction in Greek; literally ". . . his grace toward me did not prove to be without effect, *but* I worked more than they all, (but) not I *but* the grace of God which was with me." On the level of style, the awkwardness arises from the repetition of the word *but* (the "but" in parentheses translates a different and weaker word). On the level of meaning the problem is that, as in other places, Paul is trying to express two contrasts at the same time: (1) "God's grace did not prove to be without effect; on the contrary, I worked harder than everyone else," and (2) "God's grace, not I, did the work." In the immediate context (the middle of verse 10) contrast (2) is an afterthought, but in the wider context (verses 9-10) God's grace is the main theme. In translation the simplest solution is probably to translate the two *buts* differently, as RSV and TEV do with **on the contrary** and **though.** Within (2), languages vary as to whether it is more effective to put the negative or the positive half of the contrast first. The Greek emphasizes the clause **the grace of God which is with me** by putting it at the end of the sentence.

Any of them means "the other apostles" (TEV). This should be made clear in translation.

15.11	RSV	TEV

Whether then it was I or they, so we preach and so you believed.

So then, whether it came from me or from them, this is what we all preach, and this is what you believe.

Paul sums up the section before turning to the problem of disbelief in the resurrection of the dead.

They refers to the other apostles.

Whether then it was I or they may be expanded to "whether it was what I preached or what the other apostles preached."

So may be expanded to "this is the message that."

We: the context makes it clear that Paul is speaking of himself and other apostles or evangelists who had worked at Corinth. The Corinthians are excluded.

You believed, as in verse 2, refers to the Corinthian Christians' first decision to believe. This phrase may also be rendered as "this is the message that you believed."

A model for translation of this verse is as follows: "So then, whether it was what I preached or what the other apostles preached, this is the message we continue to preach and which you believed."

Our Resurrection

12 Now if Christ is preached as raised from the dead, how can some of you say that there is no resurrection of the dead? 13 But if there is no resurrection of the dead, then Christ has not been raised; 14 if Christ has not been raised, then our preaching is in vain and your faith is in vain. 15 We are even found to be misrepresenting God, because we testified of God that he raised Christ, whom he did not raise if it is true that the dead are not raised. 16 For if the dead are not raised, then Christ has not been raised. 17 If Christ has not been raised, your faith is futile and you are still in your sins. 18 Then those also who have fallen asleep in Christ have perished. 19 If for this life only we have hoped in Christ, we are of all men most to be pitied.

20 But in fact Christ has been raised from the dead, the first fruits of those who have fallen asleep. 21 For as by a man came death, by a man has come also the resurrection of the dead. 22 For as in Adam all die, so also in Christ shall all be made alive. 23 But each in his own order: Christ the first fruits, then at his coming those who belong to Christ. 24 Then comes the end, when he delivers the kingdom to God the Father after destroying every rule and every authority and power. 25 For he must reign until he has put all his enemies under his feet. 26 The last enemy to be destroyed is death. 27 "For God^z has put all things in subjection under his feet." But when it says, "All things are put in subjection under him," it is plain that he is excepted who put all things under him. 28 When all things are subjected to him, then the Son himself will also be subjected to him who put all things under him, that God may be everything to every one.

29 Otherwise, what do people mean by being baptized on behalf of the dead? If the dead are not raised at all, why are people baptized on their behalf? 30 Why am I in peril every hour? 31 I protest, brethren, by my pride in you which I have in Christ Jesus our Lord, I die every day!

12 Now, since our message is that Christ has been raised from death, how can some of you say that the dead will not be raised to life? 13 If that is true, it means that Christ was not raised; 14 and if Christ has not been raised from death, then we have nothing to preach and you have nothing to believe. 15 More than that, we are shown to be lying about God, because we said that he raised Christ from death—but if it is true that the dead are not raised to life, then he did not raise Christ. 16 For if the dead are not raised, neither has Christ been raised. 17 And if Christ has not been raised, then your faith is a delusion and you are still lost in your sins. 18 It would also mean that the believers in Christ who have died are lost. 19 If our hope in Christ is good for this life only and no more,^{p} then we deserve more pity than anyone else in all the world.

20 But the truth is that Christ has been raised from death, as the guarantee that those who sleep in death will also be raised. 21 For just as death came by means of a man, in the same way the rising from death comes by means of a man. 22 For just as all people die because of their union with Adam, in the same way all will be raised to life because of their union with Christ. 23 But each one will be raised in his proper order: Christ, first of all; then, at the time of his coming, those who belong to him. 24 Then the end will come; Christ will overcome all spiritual rulers, authorities, and powers, and will hand over the Kingdom to God the Father. 25 For Christ must rule until God defeats all enemies and puts them under his feet. 26 The last enemy to be defeated will be death. 27 For the scripture says, "God put all things under his feet." It is clear, of course, that the words "all things" do not include God himself, who puts all things under Christ. 28 But when all things have been placed under Christ's rule, then he himself, the Son, will place himself under God, who placed all things under him; and God will rule completely over all.

32 What do I gain if, humanly speaking, I fought with beasts at Ephesus? If the dead are not raised, "Let us eat and drink, for tomorrow we die." 33 Do not be deceived: "Bad company ruins good morals." 34 Come to your right mind, and sin no more. For some have no knowledge of God. I say this to your shame.

z Greek he

29 Now, what about those people who are baptized for the dead? What do they hope to accomplish? If it is true, as some claim, that the dead are not raised to life, why are those people being baptized for the dead? 30 And as for us—why would we run the risk of danger every hour? 31 My brothers, I face death everyday! The pride I have in you, in our life in union with Christ Jesus our Lord, makes me declare this. 32 If I have, as it were, fought "wild beasts" here in Ephesus simply from human motives, what have I gained? But if the dead are not raised to life, then, as the saying goes, "Let us eat and drink, for tomorrow we die."

33 Do not be fooled. "Bad companions ruin good character." 34 Come back to your right senses and stop your sinful ways. I declare to your shame that some of you do not know God.

p If our hope in Christ is good for this life only and no more; or If all we have in this life is our hope in Christ.

Most translations agree with the UBS Greek text in treating this passage as a single section. Phps inserts section headings at verses 20 and 29 which correspond to the UBS paragraphs. Verse 29 introduces briefly a more specific aspect of the question of the resurrection, but Paul does not develop this theme. The words **if the dead are not raised** in verse 32 mark a return to the main theme. Verses 33-34 mark an apparently impatient aside by Paul, similar in some respects to 11.16 and 14.34-35. The present section therefore does not seem to have a clear conclusion. The division is made because verse 35 marks a new beginning within the general theme. The conclusion of the whole argument will not be reached until verse 58.

The TEV section heading "Our Resurrection" may be translated as "Christians will rise from death."

As we noted in the introduction to this chapter, verses 1-11 can only be understood in the light of the following verses, especially verse 12. The firmest link between this section and the previous one is formed by Paul's emphatically repeated statement that "Christ has been raised." Paul's point in verses 12-19 is that, since his readers already believe that Christ has been raised from the dead, they should also believe that Christians will rise with him. Paul develops this argument in verses 12-19 in largely negative terms, showing what would be the consequence if Christians did not rise from the dead. Verses 20-28 develop in a more positive way the consequences of belief in the resurrection of Christ.

In verses 29-32 Paul returns in a more disjointed fashion to note some additional negative consequences if this belief in resurrection were not well-founded.

15.12	RSV	TEV

Now if Christ is preached as raised from the dead, how can some of you say that there is no resurrection of the dead?

Now, since our message is that Christ has been raised from death, how can some of you say that the dead will not be raised to life?

Verses 12, 13, and 14 begin in the same way in Greek: "if," followed by a Greek word which has a range of meanings including "and" and "but." In verse 12 this word marks the introduction to a new thought, so it should be translated "Now," as in RSV and TEV. But in verses 13-14 the word introduces further links in Paul's chain of argument and thus is translated differently. See the comments on verses 13 and 14.

Paul begins this verse with the common and basic Christian belief that Christ was raised and is still alive (see comments on verse 4). The verb **is preached**, then, implies a preaching that is done by any Christian evangelist.

Now if Christ is preached as raised from the dead may be rendered as "Now since people preach that God has raised Christ from the Dead."

How can some of you say: some is slightly emphasized; Mft has "certain individuals among you."[3]

There is no resurrection of the dead is a literal translation of the Greek. Most languages will need to use a verb for **resurrection** to show that it is an event or action. TEV's "the dead will not be raised to life" is a good translation. However, in languages which do not have a passive, one may say "the dead will not receive life again."[4]

This verse makes it clear that Paul is discussing the resurrection in reply to false teaching in Corinth. Outside this chapter Paul uses the word for resurrection only in speaking of Christ, except in Philippians 3.11, and 2 Timothy 2.18. Normally he uses a different verb translated "raised." In the passive this verb usually indicates the activity of God.

15.13	RSV	TEV

But if there is no resurrection of the dead, then Christ has not been raised;

If that is true, it means that Christ was not raised;

The clause **But if there is no resurrection of the dead** largely repeats the content of verse 12b. The form, however, is different. In verse 12 the "if" clause means "if, as is the case, Christ is preached as raised from the dead." In verses 13, 14, 16, 17, and 19 Paul is speaking about what would happen if things were different, and all the "if" clauses in these verses mean "if . . . , which is not the case . . . ." Throughout this passage Paul uses repetition to emphasize the different elements of his argument. TEV translates this sentence as "If that is true" to avoid the repetition. This is good style in English, but each group of translators must decide whether in their language repetition of this kind adds emphasis or merely makes the sentence heavier.

---

[3] See R.A. Horsley, 1978, " 'How can some of you say that there is no resurrection of the dead?' Spiritual elitism in Corinth," Novum Testamentum 20.203-231.

[4] J. Jeremias, Abba, pages 303-304, quoted by Conzelmann.

No resurrection of the dead: see the comment on verse 12.

Then may be translated as "it means" (TEV). This interpretation is implied by the fact that verse 13b follows logically from verse 13a: "If no one is raised from the dead, then Christ was not raised either."

Christ has not been raised may be expressed in the active voice: "then God has not raised Christ from death either."

<u>15.14</u>   RSV   TEV

if Christ has not been raised, then our preaching is in vain and your faith is in vain.	and if Christ has not been raised from death, then we have nothing to preach and you have nothing to believe.

This verse and verse 15 state a negative consequence of something which has already been proved in verse 13. However, as verses 18-19 make clear, these are matters of life and death to Paul and his readers. Therefore they should not be underemphasized in translation. Because verses 14-15 depend logically on verses 12-13, TEV's translation of the opening words "and if" is stronger and clearer than RSV's **if.**

If Christ has not been raised: see comment on translating this phrase in verse 12.

Our preaching may be a little more specific than "is preached" in verse 12. It probably includes all the evangelists who worked in Corinth, but excludes the readers (compare verse 11).

Just as 13a repeated 12b, so 14a repeats 13b. Before taking a new step, Paul, so to speak, brings his second foot up to the step on which he is standing.

Our preaching is in vain is literally "our preaching is empty"; similarly **your faith is in vain** is literally "your faith is empty." It is possible to understand "empty" as the opposite of verse 10, where the "grace of God" is "effectual" or "produces results." GeCL has "then neither our preaching nor your faith would have any meaning"; ItCL says "our preaching is without foundation and your faith is without value"; NEB translates "our gospel is null and void"; NIV and JB use the word "useless." Both **preaching** and **faith** here refer to the content of what is preached and believed, rather than to the actual act of preaching and believing.

Some manuscripts have an additional "and" which somewhat changes the structure of the sentence. The UBS Greek text prints it in square brackets. If the additional "and" is taken as part of the text, the meaning will be "Both our preaching and your faith are empty" ("both . . . and . . ." linking two whole clauses, as in 1.22). If the "and" is omitted, the meaning will be "our preaching is empty, and your faith also."

Some manuscripts have "our faith" instead of **your faith;** the Greek words for "our" and "your" were often confused. **Your faith** makes a better balance with **our preaching;** compare verses 11 and 17.

A model for the translation of this verse can be "And if Christ has not been raised from death, then the message we preach and your belief in Christ have no meaning at all."

15.15	RSV	TEV

We are even found to be misrepresenting God, because we testified of God that he raised Christ, whom he did not raise if it is true that the dead are not raised.	More than that, we are shown to be lying about God, because we said that he raised Christ from death—but if it is true that the dead are not raised to life, then he did not raise Christ.

Even, literally "and" or "also," marks the beginning of a further consequence of the argument in verses 12-13. TEV expresses this Greek word by "More than that."

We are . . . found to be: this Greek verb is often used in speaking of the results of examination in a law court or some similar situation. One may also render this phrase as "it will be evident that we" or "it will also show that we." The following words **misrepresenting God** confirm that Paul is thinking for the moment in legal terms.

Misrepresenting is literally "false witnesses." This is an unusual noun which is related to the Greek verb for "bearing false witness," used in the Ten Commandments in the Septuagint of Exodus 20.16 and Deuteronomy 5.20 (verse 17 in Hebrew); compare Mark 10.19 and parallels in Matthew 26.60. Paul is not thinking about lying in general; he is comparing Christian preaching with giving witness in a court of law.

Most translations agree generally with TEV's translation, "lying about God." Phps expands to "we are lying in our witness for God." However, the Greek preposition translated "about" in TEV often means "against," especially in legal contexts. So in the present verse Arndt-Gingrich translates "give testimony in contradiction to God." The meaning of the whole clause would therefore be "What we have said in our preaching is proved to be the opposite of what God was doing." The rest of the verse would explain in what respect this was so.

We testified is literally "we witnessed," continuing the metaphor of the law court.

The clause **if it is true** is a dependent clause in grammar. However, it represents a step back in the argument and may be better expressed as a separate sentence; for example, "However, if it is true that the dead are not raised to life, then God did not raise Christ," or in languages which do not favor the passive, one could say ". . . that the dead do not receive life, then God did not raise Christ."

The dead are not raised: see the comment on verse 12.

15.16	RSV	TEV

For if the dead are not raised, then Christ has not been raised.	For if the dead are not raised, neither has Christ been raised.

Paul stresses his point by a further repetition of the content of verse 13, this time expressed in the same order. As usual, the passive verb **are . . . raised** implies that God is at work, as verse 15 has stated.

RSV   TEV

If Christ has not been raised, your faith   And if Christ has not been raised, then
is futile and you are still in your sins.   your faith is a delusion and you are still
                                                  lost in your sins.

If Christ has not been raised may be expressed also as "If God has not
raised Christ."

Is futile is similar in meaning to "empty" in verse 14. This phrase may be
rendered as "your faith in Christ is useless" or "your faith in Christ will gain you
nothing."

Verses 17b-18 show that the purpose of preaching about the resurrection
and believing in it is that people should be saved from their sins and from being
destroyed at the last judgment.

Still in your sins: "lost" (TEV) is implied. In the context of this verse the
phrase suggests a condition of domination by sin. Other possible renderings are
"you are still under the power of sin," or "sin still rules your lives," or even "your
sins have not been forgiven."

RSV   TEV

Then those also who have fallen asleep   It would also mean that the believers in
in Christ have perished.   Christ who have died are lost.

Then (TEV's "it would also mean") draws a further consequence, not directly
from verse 17 but from the basic statement of verse 16.

Those also who have fallen asleep in Christ: the metaphor of "sleep" will be
unclear in many languages. TEV's translation "the believers in Christ who have
died" is much clearer.

Perished here is the opposite of "salvation." If Christ has not risen from
the dead, then the Christian who has died has not been saved, but is lost—presumably separated from God. Other translation models for this verse are "If Christ
has not been raised it would also mean that the believers in Christ who have died
have already perished" or ". . . are receiving punishment."

RSV   TEV

If for this life only we have hoped in   If our hope in Christ is good for this life
Christ, we are of all men most to be   only and no more, [p] then we deserve
pitied.   more pity than anyone else in all the
                                                world.

                                                [p] If our hope in Christ is good for this
                                                life only and no more; *or* If all we have
                                                in this life is our hope in Christ.

The first part of this verse presents a serious problem. It is difficult to be
certain how the word **only** relates to the rest of the clause. The interpretation
which underlies RSV's text and TEV's footnote would be unique in Paul's writings,

for nowhere else does he use expressions like "only hope." The main difficulty is that this clause appears to suggest that hope continues in a future life, which would contradict Romans 8.24 and possibly 1 Corinthians 13.13.

If for this life only we have hoped in Christ: "hoping" here seems to mean "placing our confidence in Christ" or "trusting in Christ with confidence that he will save us." TEV's "and no more" is added to stress the emphatic nature of the Greek word. Only this life is involved, not the next one. Another translation model for this first sentence is "If we can trust Christ to save us only in this life and not in the next one . . . ."

However, in the present verse Paul seems to be emphasizing **this life** at the beginning of the clause, and **only** at the end. Paul is not thinking explicitly, at the moment, about a future life. Other CLTs agree with TEV's interpretation and sometimes express it more concisely: FrCL "If our hope in Christ is valid only for this life."

We are . . . most to be pitied translates an adjective meaning "more to be pitied." Another possible translation is "people should pity us more than . . . ."

Of all men is literally "than all people." This last clause can then be translated "We deserve the most pity of anyone in the world."

15.20	RSV	TEV

> But in fact Christ has been raised from the dead, the first fruits of those who have fallen asleep.

> But the truth is that Christ has been raised from death, as the guarantee that those who sleep in death will also be raised.

Paul now expresses positively what follows from belief in the resurrection of Christ. **But in fact** marks this transition emphatically; the same words were translated "as it is" in 12.18,20. This phrase may also be rendered as "But the truth is that" (TEV).

Christ has been raised from the dead: here and in other places in this chapter, the agent in the event of "raising" is God. In many languages an active statement is preferable; for example, "God has raised Christ from death," or "God has caused Christ to come alive" or ". . . Christ to live again."

The first fruits: Paul uses here the image of the first sample from a crop. This fruit or grain was offered to God, especially on the day following the Passover sabbath. The first installment of the crop was understood as a symbol of God's promise and the people's hope that the rest of the harvest would follow. Thus TEV's "guarantee" is a good English rendering.

Those who have fallen asleep: "in death" (TEV) is implied; see verse 18 and the comments on 7.39. The tense of the verb indicates the state of being dead, not the event of their dying.

It is possible to restructure this verse as follows: "But the truth is that God did raise Christ from death, as the guarantee that he will also raise those who have died."

15.21-22	RSV	TEV

For as by a man came death, by a man has come also the resurrection of the

For just as death came by means of a man, in the same way the rising from dead. 22 For as in Adam all die, so also in Christ shall all be made alive.

death comes by means of a man. 22 For just as all people die because of their union with Adam, in the same way all will be raised to life because of their union with Christ.

These two verses have a similar structure and complement one another in meaning. Paul begins by appealing to something which Jewish Christians, like other Jews, would have readily admitted, namely, that sin came into the world through Adam. The language of the first clause is condensed; the meaning is "since, as we agree, death entered the world by or through a man . . . ." The same Hebrew word means **Adam** and "human being," but Paul does not use the proper name **Adam** until verse 22. So his indirect reference to **Adam** in verse 21 should be kept in translation, if possible. There is a danger that readers may understand **a man** in the two halves of the verse to refer to the same man. In that case translators should render the second one as "by means of another man."

A possible model for translating verse 21 is as follows: "For just as people die because of what a man did, in the same way people rise from death because of what another man did."

In verse 22 Paul states the comparision more emphatically: **as** and **so also** are expressed here but implied in verse 21. TEV rightly expands the phrases which RSV translated **in Adam** and **in Christ.** The latter expression is frequent in Paul's writings; see comments on 1.30. AT translates "because of their relation to Adam" and ". . . to Christ." This is slightly weaker than TEV's "union" but may be a more correct rendering.

There is nothing in the Greek corresponding to **has come, came,** or "comes" (TEV). In most languages it will be necessary to supply a verb in the first part of the sentence referring to a distant past event, and in the second part a verb referring to a recent past event. Another way to translate these verbs or events, **came death** and **come . . . the resurrection,** are "people had to die" and "people will be raised from death." A possible translation model for verse 21 is "For just as people had to die because of what one man did, so people can be raised from death by what a man has done." The following verse explains who these two men were.

Scholars disagree about whether the second half of this verse implies that everyone, whether Christian or not, would be brought to life again in the resurrection, and if so, whether this means that all will be saved. Translators are not concerned with the last question, but it is possible to translate verse 22b as "so also all who are in Christ will be brought to life." However, this requires verse 22a to be translated "all who are in Adam die," and it is clear that for Paul, Adam gathered up into his person the whole human race. Adam thus symbolized the whole human race, so that the whole human race is thought of as identical with Adam. Thus, when Adam sinned, all humans sinned, and when Adam died, all died. It is therefore best to follow TEV in translating simply "all will be raised to life." Paul is probably at this point not asking questions concerning the fate of those who do not believe. In any case, verse 22b should be understood in the light of verse 21b, which implies that there is no resurrection of the dead apart from Christ.

But each in his own order: Christ the
first fruits, then at his coming those
who belong to Christ.

But each one will be raised in his proper
order: Christ, first of all; then, at the
time of his coming, those who belong to
him.

Some commentators begin a new paragraph here on the grounds that verses
23-28, like 50-57, are concerned with the end of time. These two passages are
also linked by the use of military terms such as **order** in verse 23 (see the comments) and "trumpet" in verse 52 (compare 14.8).

But leads the reader to expect a contrast, probably between "all" in verse
22 and **each** here. Paul may also have in mind a third group of people (verse 51),
who will not be raised from death because they are still alive when Christ returns.

Each in his own order: in many languages it will be helpful to add the words
"will be raised" as in TEV. One may also say "But God will raise each one in his
proper order."

The word translated **order** generally has a military meaning, referring
either to a troop of soldiers or to a rank. But that meaning would not apply to
Christ here. The passage seems to refer to succession in time or a progression of
events. To show this meaning one can say in the following sentence "God raised
Christ first . . . ."

First fruits: the same Greek word was translated "guarantee" in verse 20
(see the comments). "First of all" (TEV), though, is a more natural rendering here.

The word translated **coming** may also be translated as "appearance." The
meaning here, as in 1 Thessalonians 2.19, is that of the arrival of some important
person such as a ruler or judge. It may also be used more widely, as in 16.17, of
the arrival, or simply of the presence, of an ordinary person. One may say, then,
"when he appears" or "when he returns."

Those who belong to Christ: the language is similar to, though not quite the
same as, "Chloe's people" in 1.11; the meaning is similar to "God's holy people"
(TEV) in 1.2.

Then comes the end, when he delivers
the kingdom to God the Father after
destroying every rule and every authority and power.

Then the end will come; Christ will
overcome all spiritual rulers, authorities, and powers, and will hand over the
Kingdom to God the Father.

Then comes the end: this is the plain meaning of the text, and the one
preferred by recent commentators. **The end** refers to "the end of the age" or "the
end of the world." One may render this clause as "after that the end of the world
comes" or "after that this age will come to an end."

In the rest of the verse, RSV follows the Greek order quite literally, whereas TEV rearranges the events to correspond more closely to their ordering in
time. Many languages will find it helpful to follow TEV's ordering.

It is impossible to establish clearcut distinctions between **rule, authority,**
and **power.** These words overlap considerably in meaning with the word translated
kingdom, though **kingdom** refers in this verse to a power different from the other

terms. Paul is referring to angels or spirits (obviously "evil") which were thought of as controlling the area between heaven and earth (see comment on 8.5).

TEV's "spiritual" in "spiritual rulers" is not in the Greek text but is almost certainly implied here. Translators in some languages will have to translate this phrase as "ruling spirits."

Destroying does not mean that the spiritual powers will be absolutely destroyed, but that they will be made completely ineffective. TEV uses the word "overcome."

15.25   RSV   TEV

For he must reign until he has put all his enemies under his feet.

For Christ must rule until God defeats all enemies and puts them under his feet.

Most of this verse is a free quotation of Psalm 110.1: "Sit at my right hand, till I make your enemies your footstool."

Translators in most languages should add the names "Christ" and "God" to this verse in order to make clear in each case who the word **he** refers to: "For Christ must rule until God defeats all enemies and puts them under his feet" (TEV). In the psalm God is speaking to a king of Israel. In the New Testament this verse is always understood to mean that God is speaking to the Messiah, that is, to Christ.

Must in this context suggests that Christ's rule is part of God's will or plan. The same word is used in the same sense in verse 53.

Reign is related in Greek to the word "kingdom" used in verse 24. Barrett translates "reign in his kingdom" to make this meaning clear. One may also say "rule as king." The tense of the verb implies "Christ must go on ruling until . . . ."

Until he has put all his enemies under his feet: There are ancient pictures of kings with their feet on the necks of defeated enemies. Translators should keep this metaphor if in their language it is clear that the meaning is "defeat his enemies." However, in languages which do not speak in this way, TEV's "God defeats all enemies and puts them under his feet" is a clear translation.

The context, especially verse 26, suggests that the enemies are not only Christ's but also ours. For this reason TEV has "all enemies" instead of **all his enemies.** Greek manuscripts differ on this, but TEV follows the more reliable manuscripts.

His feet means Christ's feet, not God's, as Psalm 110.1 shows.

15.26   RSV   TEV

The last enemy to be destroyed is death.

The last enemy to be defeated will be death.

The main theme of this entire chapter is the resurrection. So in this verse Paul is applying the text he has just used to this main theme.

This sentence is literally "Last enemy [that] is-destroyed, death." "Paul uses the present tense (though the defeat of death lies in the future) because he looks at the process as a whole" (Barrett).

Destroyed here is a strong verb. GeCL has "annihilated," that is, "made nonexistent." The word means that all the power of death is to be removed. The word for **destroyed** is sometimes used in the New Testament in speaking about the destruction of Satan as the one who has power over death (Heb 2.14). Paul may be thinking of death itself as one of the "spiritual rulers, authorities, and powers" mentioned in verse 24. In the light of all this, TEV's translation "defeated" seems a little weak.

15.27	RSV	TEV

"For God^z has put all things in subjection under his feet." But when it says, "All things are put in subjection under him," it is plain that he is excepted who put all things under him.

For the scripture says, "God put *all* things under his feet." It is clear, of course, that the words "all things" do not include God himself, who puts all things under Christ.

^z Greek *he*

For links verse 27, not directly to verse 26, but to the earlier argument, especially verse 24. It may therefore be better to omit **For** in translation, especially since it is not part of the quotation.

TEV's "the scripture says" is implied and may be added to make the meaning of the text clear. The words which follow come from Psalm 8.6. Paul's readers would have known that these words were an Old Testament quotation. See comments on 1.19.

As in verse 25, **God** is implied but should be added by translators to show clearly who is doing the action **put . . . under his feet.** In Psalm 8.6 God is speaking to "the son of man," meaning "man" in the sense of "humanity." The fact that Jesus often spoke of himself as "the Son of man" may have made New Testament writers understand that in this psalm, as in Psalm 110.1, God is speaking to Christ (see also Heb 2.6-9).

The word translated **put** is stronger than "put" ("set," "placed") in verse 25, but the same as **put** at the end of this verse. The word explicitly expresses the idea of being subordinate or subject to another power. Paul understands the second quotation in the light of the first.

TEV prints "all" in italics for emphasis, contrary to the usual TEV style. There is, of course, nothing corresponding to italics in the Greek manuscripts. However, translators may use italics here to help the reader see in advance that this is the key word of the quotation, and to suggest that it be given vocal emphasis or stress when read aloud.

His feet: Paul is applying the word **his** in the quotation to Christ. However, a translator may not expand **his feet** to "Christ's feet." The reference in Psalm 8.6 is to "the son of man."

But when it says . . . it is plain: many languages cannot talk about written texts saying or speaking. Also, in some languages it will be appropriate to place the phrase **it is plain** in front of "but where it says." TEV's translation, "It is clear, of course, that the words . . . ," will be a good model for many languages.

RSV translates verse 27b quite literally, whereas TEV abbreviates the text for stylistic purposes by avoiding some of the repetition. In many languages TEV's abbreviated version will be adequate.

In repeating the verb **put in subjection under,** Paul changes the tense to make it refer to a continuous process covering both past and present. He is conscious that the process is not yet complete. However, Paul's comment here has another purpose, namely, to show that God is not included in the **all things** which will be subjected to Christ. The clause **who puts all things under him** may be rendered as "who causes Christ to rule over all things."

He is excepted is quite difficult English. TEV's "do not include God himself" gives the meaning clearly.

15.28	RSV	TEV

When all things are subjected to him, then the Son himself will also be subjected to him who put all things under him, that God may be everything to every one.	But when all things have been placed under Christ's rule, then he himself, the Son, will place himself under God, who placed all things under him; and God will rule completely over all.

Are subjected represents another change of tense and mood. The context clearly requires the meaning "when all things have been placed" (TEV) or "when God has placed all things."

Subjected to him means "under his rule." The preceding verses suggest a picture of God placing everything under Christ, and this would make good sense of the rest of the verse, especially the emphatic **the Son himself.** This is the most likely explanation and the one preferred by translators generally.

The situation is slightly complicated by the fact that some manuscripts insert an additional "and" or "also" before **the Son himself.** (The UBS Greek text prints this "and" in square brackets.) The addition of this "and" could require the meaning "but when God has subjected everything to himself, then the Son himself will also be subjected to God who subjected all things to him." Such a meaning would raise the same difficulty as noted in verse 25, since "to him" can scarcely mean "to himself." It is simpler, then, to follow the interpretation which underlies both RSV and TEV. The following is a possible translation of this first phrase: "But when God has placed all things under Christ's rule, then Christ himself, the Son . . . ."

Will also be subjected to him can be translated in languages which do not use passives as "will place himself under God" (TEV).

That God may be everything to every one: it is difficult to be certain of the exact meaning of this clause. Paul uses the same or similar language in 12.6 and in Ephesians 1.23, always at the climax of a paragraph. It is possible, therefore, that the traditional translation "all in all" may come closer to Paul's meaning than any attempt to define more narrowly the meaning of the two "alls." The first "all" cannot refer to people; the second "all" may refer either to people or to things. GeCL has "then God alone is the Lord who works everything and in everyone"; ItCL "and then God will reign effectively in all"; Phps "Thus, in the end, shall God be wholly and absolutely God." Mft and AT make it clear that they think the second "all" refers to people: "so that God may be everything to everyone." RSV follows this interpretation.

15.29 RSV	TEV
Otherwise, what do people mean by being baptized on behalf of the dead? If the dead are not raised at all, why are people baptized on their behalf?	Now, what about those people who are baptized for the dead? What do they hope to accomplish? If it is true, as some claim, that the dead are not raised to life, why are those people being baptized for the dead?

Some of the difficulties which commentaries discuss arise because we do not know enough about the situation to which Paul refers. In the present verse these difficulties are impossible to separate from problems of translation.

Otherwise (TEV's "Now"): Paul is digressing here from the main subject of the resurrection of Christ and of the believers. Other possible renderings of this sentence are "Just for a moment let us think about those people who are baptized on behalf of dead people" or ". . . those people who receive baptism on behalf of people who have died."

Nowhere else does the New Testament mention baptism on behalf of the dead. Some ancient Greek commentators have claimed that "baptism on behalf of the dead" refers, not to baptism on behalf of others who have died, but means baptism in order to ensure one's own resurrection. This interpretation is unlikely, for one reason, because **people** in the final sentence of the verse seems to refer to a particular group in the church. All translations which we consulted agree with the interpretation which underlies RSV and TEV.

What do people mean? is literally "what will they do?" The use of the future tense is unexpected and difficult. RSV's **What do people mean** and TEV's "What do they hope to accomplish?" represent two main interpretations. TEV seems to make better sense of the future tense. TNT's translation, "what good will those people do who are baptised for the dead?" agrees with TEV.

As the UBS Greek text's punctuation note shows, the clause **If the dead are not raised at all** may be connected either with the earlier part of the sentence or the last part. In verses 12-19, conditional clauses beginning with **If** have been placed at the beginning of the sentences. So it is probably more natural here to begin a new sentence with **If** and connect this clause with what follows.

TEV's "as some claim" is added as a reminder of what was said in verse 12; other CLTs do not follow TEV's example.

RSV's **the dead are not raised at all** shows the emphatic quality of the Greek; this is missing in TEV. Some languages can render this clause as "If God does not raise the dead to life at all . . . ."

The last clause, beginning with **why are people . . .** , is also emphatic. It can be phrased "What possible reason can those people have for being baptized for the dead?"

15.30 RSV	TEV
Why am I in peril every hour?	And as for us—why would we run the risk of danger every hour?

There is a sudden change of theme at this point, from the experience of the Corinthians to Paul's own experience. TEV shows this by the words "And as for us." NEB marks this sudden change of theme by beginning a new paragraph. However, verse 30 logically, though not grammatically, depends on the condition "If the dead are not raised," expressed in verse 29. It may be good to begin this verse "If there is no resurrection, why then would we . . . ?"

Some commentators and translators take "we" (TEV) to refer to Paul alone. However, in verse 32 he uses singular words in speaking of his personal experience. He could have done this in the present verse if other evangelists were not included. TEV's "we" is probably a better translation.

15.31	RSV	TEV

I protest, brethren, by my pride in you which I have in Christ Jesus our Lord, I die every day!

My brothers, I face death everyday! The pride I have in you, in our life in union with Christ Jesus our Lord, makes me declare this.

In the Greek the first phrase of this verse is "each day I die." This reflects the final clause of verse 31: "we are in danger every hour." It is likely, then, that these verbs have approximately the same meaning. I die, of course, is not to be taken literally, nor is Paul referring to the natural process of aging. The context, especially verse 32, shows that Paul has in mind the risk of a violent death. TEV's "I face death" is therefore a more natural translation.

I protest (TEV "declare") translates a Greek word used to introduce a solemn and emphatic statement.

By my pride in you: Paul is swearing here, not by God, but by his own pride, which is something distinctively human. Neither the text nor the language is entirely clear. TEV has the support of most commentators in taking the words to refer, not to the Corinthians' boasting about Paul, but to Paul's pride in the church he helped to found. Paul emphasizes that this is not human pride but pride in union with Christ Jesus our Lord. Translators would do well, then, to translate this phrase in a similar way to that in TEV: "The pride I have in you . . . makes me declare this."

It is unusual for Paul to use the word brethren in the middle of a sentence. In other parts of 1 Corinthians the word has always introduced a new theme. Here it is omitted in certain Greek manuscripts. The UBS Greek text has "brothers" in square brackets. Brethren, of course, refers to fellow Christians.

15.32	RSV	TEV

What do I gain if, humanly speaking, I fought with beasts at Ephesus? If the dead are not raised, "Let us eat and drink, for tomorrow we die."

If I have, as it were, fought "wild beasts" here in Ephesus simply from human motives, what have I gained? But if the dead are not raised to life, then, as the saying goes, "Let us eat and drink, for tomorrow we die."

The first part of this verse raises various problems.

(1) Fought with beasts is a single verb in Greek, not used elsewhere in the Bible. Most scholars agree that the beasts are human beings acting like wild

beasts, and that the "fighting" is figurative too. That is why TEV puts "wild beasts" in quotation marks and adds "as it were." Related words are used to describe human beings as "evil beasts" in a quotation in Titus 1.12, and in speaking of "fighting" (TEV's "quarrels") in 2 Corinthians 7.5. However, the strong language used in previous verses ("in peril," verse 30; "I die," verse 31) suggests that in the present verse the "fighting" must have involved some physical risk. Roman citizens such as Paul were not punished by being set to fight with wild beasts. However, before we exclude a literal meaning for **fought with beasts,** let us examine the following questions.

(2) A majority of commentators believe that the conditional clause beginning **If . . .** refers to some conflict in which Paul was actually engaged. It is, however, grammatically possible to understand this clause as an unfulfilled condition: "if I were to fight with wild beasts." In this case the objection that Paul could not legally undergo such a punishment would lose much of its force. If this argument is correct, "wild beasts" is more likely to be figurative.

(3) **Humanly speaking** may be connected either with **I fought** or with **beasts.** Both RSV and TEV choose the first option, which implies "I fought for my life like someone who expects no life after death"; compare TNT "as a mere mortal." The second option would probably mean "I fought with people who can only be described, in human language, as 'wild beasts.' " This would be Paul's way of softening his otherwise hard language. It is difficult to choose between these two options, since in the Greek "I-fought-with-wild-beasts" is a single word. However, the first is probably better.

What do I gain: this rhetorical question implies "if I have no resurrection to hope for, there would be no point in my living such a hard and dangerous life."

The words "as it were" (TEV) are implied and have the same function as the quotation marks around "wild beasts" in TEV.

At Ephesus: TEV's addition of "here" is probably not justified. We simply are not sure whether Paul was writing from Ephesus or not.

Let us eat and drink, for tomorrow we die is an exact quotation from Isaiah 22.13.

TEV's "as the saying goes" is implicit. The words are added to make it clear that the following words are a quotation. Isaiah 22.13 is part of scripture, but the quoted words are spoken by people whom the prophet condemns. Therefore, to introduce them by "as the scripture says," as TEV did in 10.26, might misleadingly suggest that Paul approves the attitude expressed in the quotation. The phrase "as the saying goes" may also be rendered as "as people often say" or "according to the popular saying."

15.33	RSV	TEV

Do not be deceived: "Bad company ruins good morals."

Do not be fooled. "Bad companions ruin good character."

Do not be deceived: in this verse the bad influence of other people is suggested. Perhaps one may translate "Do not let people deceive you."

The word translated **company** sometimes means "conversation" but has also the wider meaning of **company.** TEV makes this word more concrete with the translation "Bad companions."

Some languages will have proverbs which have a meaning equivalent to the saying in this verse. For example, ThCL has a proverb in the form of a poetic couplet which says literally "Associate bad people—mischievously lead to badness."

15.34   RSV   TEV

Come to your right mind, and sin no more. For some have no knowledge of God. I say this to your shame.	Come back to your right senses and stop your sinful ways. I declare to your shame that some of you do not know God.

Come to your right mind suggests a return to a more balanced way of life; literally "Come to your senses rightly." The adverb translated **right** commonly means "righteously" but has apparently no theological meaning here. Barrett uses a slightly different metaphor here: "wake up properly." Possibly one may translate "Get control of yourself."

Come (TEV's "Come back") is an order to perform a single action. **Sin no more**, on the other hand, suggests action over a period of time: "continue to avoid sins." The context suggests that the period of not sinning includes present and future rather than past and present time. So "stop your sinful ways" (TEV) is probably more appropriate than **sin no more.**

Some, as TEV shows, is better rendered as "some of you."

Knowledge in the Bible frequently refers to an intimate personal relationship with someone. **No knowledge** in this context presumably refers to a sinful condition which prevents a right relationship with God. Another way to render the clause is "For some among you do not have a right relationship with God" or ". . . have not been put right with God."

I say this to your shame is virtually a separate sentence in Greek and is emphasized because of its position at the end of the verse. This clause may be rendered "You ought to be ashamed because of this" or "This lack of knowledge should make you lose face." Some languages, as in English, may need to put this clause at the beginning of the verse and stress it in a way similar to TEV; for example, "Some of you should feel very ashamed that you do not know God."

              RSV   **15.35-58**   TEV

The Resurrection Body

35 But some one will ask, "How are the dead raised? With what kind of body do they come?" 36 You foolish man! What you sow does not come to life unless it dies. 37 And what you sow is not the body which is to be, but a bare kernel, perhaps of wheat or of some other grain. 38 But God gives it a body as he has chosen, and to each kind of seed its own body. 39 For not all flesh is alike, but there is one kind for men, another for animals, another for birds, and another for fish. 40 There are celestial bodies and there are

35 Someone will ask, "How can the dead be raised to life? What kind of body will they have?" 36 You fool! When you plant a seed in the ground, it does not sprout to life unless it dies. 37 And what you plant is a bare seed, perhaps a grain of wheat or some other grain, not the full-bodied plant that will later grow up. 38 God provides that seed with the body he wishes; he gives each seed its own proper body.

39 And the flesh of living beings is not all the same kind of flesh; human beings have one kind of flesh, animals

terrestrial bodies; but the glory of the celestial is one, and the glory of the terrestrial is another. 41 There is one glory of the sun, and another glory of the moon, and another glory of the stars; for star differs from star in glory.

42 So it is with the resurrection of the dead. What is sown is perishable, what is raised is imperishable. 43 It is sown in dishonor, it is raised in glory. It is sown in weakness, it is raised in power. 44 It is sown a physical body, it is raised a spiritual body. If there is a physical body, there is also a spiritual body. 45 Thus it is written, "The first man Adam became a living being"; the last Adam became a life-giving spirit. 46 But it is not the spiritual which is first but the physical, and then the spiritual. 47 The first man was from the earth, a man of dust; the second man is from heaven. 48 As was the man of dust, so are those who are of the dust; and as is the man of heaven, so are those who are of heaven. 49 Just as we have borne the image of the man of dust, we shall^a also bear the image of the man of heaven. 50 I tell you this, brethren: flesh and blood cannot inherit the kingdom of God, nor does the perishable inherit the imperishable.

51 Lo! I tell you a mystery. We shall not all sleep, but we shall all be changed, 52 in a moment, in the twinkling of an eye, at the last trumpet. For the trumpet will sound, and the dead will be raised imperishable, and we shall be changed. 53 For this perishable nature must put on the imperishable, and this mortal nature must put on immortality. 54 When the perishable puts on the imperishable, and the mortal puts on immortality, then shall come to pass the saying that is written:
"Death is swallowed up in
    victory."
55 "O death, where is thy victory?
O death, where is thy sting?"
56 The sting of death is sin, and the power of sin is the law. 57 But thanks be to God, who gives us the victory through our Lord Jesus Christ.

58 Therefore, my beloved brethren, be steadfast, immovable, always abounding in the work of the Lord, knowing that in the Lord your labor is not in vain.

another, birds another, and fish another.

40 And there are heavenly bodies and earthly bodies; the beauty that belongs to heavenly bodies is different from the beauty that belongs to earthly bodies. 41 The sun has its own beauty, the moon another beauty, and the stars a different beauty; and even among stars there are different kinds of beauty.

42 This is how it will be when the dead are raised to life. When the body is buried, it is mortal; when raised it will be immortal. 43 When buried, it is ugly and weak; when raised, it will be beautiful and strong. 44 When buried, it is a physical body; when raised, it will be a spiritual body. There is, of course, a physical body, so there has to be a spiritual body. 45 For the scripture says, "The first man, Adam, was created a living being"; but the last Adam is the life-giving Spirit. 46 It is not the spiritual that comes first, but the physical, and then the spiritual. 47 The first Adam, made of earth, came from the earth; the second Adam came from heaven. 48 Those who belong to the earth are like the one who was made of earth; those who are of heaven are like the one who came from heaven. 49 Just as we wear the likeness of the man made of earth, so we will wear^q the likeness of the Man from heaven.

50 What I mean, brothers, is that what is made of flesh and blood cannot share in God's Kingdom, and what is mortal cannot possess immortality.

51-52 Listen to this secret truth: we shall not all die, but when the last trumpet sounds, we shall all be changed in an instant, as quickly as the blinking of an eye. For when the trumpet sounds, the dead will be raised, never to die again, and we shall all be changed. 53 For what is mortal must be changed into what is immortal; what will die must be changed into what cannot die. 54 So when this takes place, and the mortal has been changed into the immortal, then the scripture will come true: "Death is destroyed; victory is complete!"
55 "Where, Death, is your victory?
Where, Death, is your power to
    hurt?"

a Other ancient authorities read *let us*

56 Death gets its power to hurt from sin, and sin gets its power from the Law. 57 But thanks be to God who gives us the victory through our Lord Jesus Christ!

58 So then, my dear brothers, stand firm and steady. Keep busy always in your work for the Lord, since you know that nothing you do in the Lord's service is ever useless.

q we will wear; *some manuscripts have* let us wear.

TEV's section heading "The Resurrection Body" can be rendered "The body which has been resurrected," or "What will the new body be like?" or "The nature of the new body after death."

In the last section Paul was addressing people who denied the possibility of resurrection altogether. In this section he moves on to deal with the arguments of those who admitted the possibility of resurrection, but raised questions about how it would happen. They were particularly concerned with the type of body which people would have after resurrection. This question is posed in verse 35. As in 14.7-11, Paul answers with a series of illustrations. These are followed in verses 42-49 by an application using literal language, and backed up by arguments from scripture. Verses 50-57 return to the theme of the end of time, introduced in verses 22-28. Paul also includes evidence from scripture. The final verse draws a general conclusion.

15.35	RSV	TEV

But some one will ask, "How are the dead raised? With what kind of body do they come?"

Someone will ask, "How can the dead be raised to life? What kind of body will they have?"

The strong **But** with which the verse opens appears to have a double function. (1) It marks the transition between the resurrection itself and how it would happen. (2) It may also imply a narrower contrast between "some of you" in verse 34, who are absolutely condemned, and others at Corinth who have genuine difficulties. Function (1) is fulfilled by the section heading and the paragraphing of a modern translation. Function (2) is adequately expressed by the repetition of "some" in verse 34 and this verse, referring to two separate groups of people. TEV uses "Someone" for the second occurrence of "some." Paul, however, almost certainly has no particular individual in mind. He is simply answering a typical objection. One may also translate **some** in the present verse as "other people."[5]

---

[5] As the punctuation note in the UBS Greek text shows, it is uncertain whether the rest of the verse consists of one or two questions. By placing the two questions side by side, without any connecting "and," RSV and TEV imply, probably rightly, that the two questions are similar in meaning, the second making the first more specific.

RSV's translation **How are the dead raised?** seems more accurate than TEV's "How can the dead be raised to life?" Paul is asking a hypothetical question about the means used in raising the dead, not casting doubt on whether it is possible for the dead to be raised. Other possible renderings are "Someone will ask, 'How are dead people raised to life?' " or ". . . 'How will God raise dead people to life?' " or ". . . 'In what way will God . . . ?' "

Body: see comments on 5.3. In this verse Paul is speaking of a literal body. Paul does not intend a contrast between **body** in verses 35-38; 40-44, and "flesh" in verse 39. In some languages it may be necessary to translate both terms in the same way. On the other hand, in other languages translations will need separate terms for the body of a human being, an animal, a plant, and "celestial bodies" such as the sun. A footnote may then be added stating that only one term is used in Greek.

Do they come: the future is implied. It is uncertain whether Paul means "come out of these tombs" or "go up to heaven." Therefore TEV's neutral translation "What kind of body will they have?" is appropriate.

15.36   RSV   TEV

You foolish man! What you sow does   You fool! When you plant a seed in the
not come to life unless it dies.   ground, it does not sprout to life unless
                                           it dies.

You foolish man! is unusually blunt for Paul, but the same language is used in Luke 11.40; 12.20; similar language in Ephesians 5.17; and an equally strong expression in Matthew 15.14. It should be remembered that Paul is addressing, not a real individual, but a typical objector. Some translations use softer expressions: GeCL "how can you ask such a question?"; NEB has "how foolish!"; JB "They are stupid questions."

Man means "person."

The second **you** is singular and emphatic, meaning not "someone" but "you who are asking the question."

Sow in Greek simply refers to scattering seed on the surface, as in Mark 4.3 and the following verses. However, "plant a seed" (TEV) will in many languages be a better picture, especially in the light of **a bare kernel** (TEV's "bare seed") in verse 37.

Does not come to life unless it dies may be expanded as "unless it first dies, it will not come to life again as a plant." **Dies** is what the text says, and therefore what must be translated. Paul does not write as a modern botanist; he means that the seed must cease to exist as a seed before it can become a plant.

15.37   RSV   TEV

And what you sow is not the body which   And what you plant is a bare seed,
is to be, but a bare kernel, perhaps of   perhaps a grain of wheat or some other
wheat or of some other grain.   grain, not the full-bodied plant that will
                                          later grow up.

And correctly leads the reader to expect that the theme of sowing will be continued, and also that something new will be said about it. In fact, it is in this verse that Paul begins to turn to the central theme of contrast between the earthly body and the risen body.

Body: see comment on verse 35.

Not the body which is to be (TEV "not the full-bodied plant") can be rendered as "not the full-grown plant."

Bare means literally "naked." However, in some languages it may be unnatural to speak of a "bare seed" (TEV) or a "naked seed," in which case an expression meaning "just a seed" may be chosen.

Some other grain: grain is implied. NEB has "some other kind," NIV "something else," but RSV and TEV are clearer.

15.38   RSV   TEV

But God gives it a body as he has   God provides that seed with the body he
chosen, and to each kind of seed its own   wishes; he gives each seed its own
body.   proper body.

In this verse Paul makes a statement which can be applied equally to illustrations from the natural world and to that which they are chosen to illustrate, namely the resurrection.

The clause **God gives it . . .** may be expanded to "God gives that seed a body which he has chosen for it."

He has chosen is literally "he wished." The meaning is that God first decided which kind of organism was appropriate to each type of seed and then gave it to the seed in question. However, the two events "choosing" and "giving" are not sharply distinguished. So rather than raising questions about when God did the choosing or deciding, it is better to use a present tense for both verbs, as in TEV. The language, and to some extent the thought, recalls 12.18.

The two halves of the verse are connected in Greek by **and,** but TEV rightly omits this word, since the second statement contains little new information.

"He gives" in TEV is implied, and so is the word "proper." This latter word emphasizes the word **own.** The final clause can be also rendered as "he gives to each seed the body which is most suited to it."

15.39   RSV   TEV

For not all flesh is alike, but there is   And the flesh of living beings is
one kind for men, another for animals,   not all the same kind of flesh; human
another for birds, and another for fish.   beings have one kind of flesh, animals
                                            another, birds another, and fish an-
                                            other.

As we mentioned in the comments on verse 35, there is no great difference in meaning in this passage between **flesh** and "body." Languages differ according to whether or not they use the same term to describe the "flesh" of humans, animals, and plants. In languages where distinctions are made, translators should always use what is natural in the receptor language rather than word-for-word correspondence with the Greek terms.

15.39

Not all flesh is alike: TEV's expanded translation "the flesh of living beings is not all the same kind of flesh" is much clearer in English. The words "of living beings" prepares the reader for the range of examples given later in the verse. In fact, all the examples are given from the animal kingdom.

15.40-41	RSV	TEV

There are celestial bodies and there are terrestrial bodies; but the glory of the celestial is one, and the glory of the terrestrial is another. 41 There is one glory of the sun, and another glory of the moon, and another glory of the stars; for star differs from star in glory.

And there are heavenly bodies and earthly bodies; the beauty that belongs to heavenly bodies is different from the beauty that belongs to earthly bodies. 41 The sun has its own beauty, the moon another beauty, and the stars a different beauty; and even among stars there are different kinds of beauty.

The TEV paragraphing shows that these two verses belong closely together.

Terrestrial bodies (TEV's "earthly bodies") probably includes all the examples which were given earlier in this section. They contrast with the **celestial** or "heavenly" bodies about to be mentioned. "Heavenly" here simply means "in the sky." One may translate this first sentence as "There are bodies in the sky and there are bodies on this earth."

Glory (TEV's "beauty"): TEV avoids the traditional translation **glory** here for various reasons. (1) **Glory** is not much used in present-day English apart from church language and poetic language. (2) **Glory** in English is generally used as an abstract noun that can have different degrees of stress but not different varieties, so that phrases such as "one glory," "a different glory" are unnatural. (3) If **glory** is used at all in modern English, it refers almost exclusively to God, and this usage does not fit the present passage. The word "beauty," then, is a more natural word in English. Other languages may need one or more words for **glory,** depending on whether a "heavenly" or "earthly" body is being described.

RSV's literal **for** is difficult to understand, since the last part of the verse makes a different point rather than drawing a conclusion from what has been already said. TEV's "even" is better here.

15.42	RSV	TEV

So it is with the resurrection of the dead. What is sown is perishable, what is raised is imperishable.

This is how it will be when the dead are raised to life. When the body is buried, it is mortal; when raised it will be immortal.

At this point Paul begins to give the nonfigurative meaning of his illustrations. Translators should begin a new paragraph here. In the first sentence there is no verb in the Greek, but TEV's "will be" is clearly implied.

So it is compares what follows with what precedes—the reality (resurrection) with the image (heavenly bodies).

The resurrection of the dead: in most languages it will be helpful to render **resurrection** as a verbal expression to show that it is an event: "when God raises the dead to life." See comments on verse 12.

What is sown: TEV has removed the metaphorical language to bring out the meaning of the passage: "When the body is buried." Another solution is Brc's translation: "what is buried in the earth, like a seed . . . ." Such a translation keeps the figure of speech but expands it.

The words **perishable** and **imperishable** mean respectively "in a state of being subject to death and decay," and the opposite. These words have to be understood in this particular context. Paul's argument makes it clear that the resurrection body is **imperishable** or "immortal" (TEV) because God has raised it to a new kind of life which it did not have before.

15.43	RSV	TEV

It is sown in dishonor, it is raised in glory. It is sown in weakness, it is raised in power.

When buried, it is ugly and weak; when raised, it will be beautiful and strong.

The two halves of this verse are similar in structure to 42b. RSV keeps the structure of the Greek. TEV has combined these two sentences, making them more specific applications of verse 42b. This interpretation, however, is not certain. It is perhaps more likely that Paul makes three overlapping statements which are of equivalent importance and similar meaning. If translators think that such rhetorical repetition is natural and effective in their language, the three statements in verses 42b and 43 must be translated separately. Otherwise, not only the two halves of verse 43, but all three statements can be combined. Many translations keep the two halves of verse 43 separate.

The phrases **It is sown** and **it is raised** may be expressed as "When the body is buried" and "when the body is raised."

Dishonor in the context of burial refers to "ugliness" (see TEV), the opposite of **glory**, which refers to "beauty" (see comments on verse 40).

Glory: see the comments on verse 40. TEV's "it will be beautiful" or FrCL's "it will be glorious" make the meaning clear.

In weakness . . . in power may be translated "as something weak . . . as something strong."

In some languages translators will be able to render this verse in a way similar to RSV's translation, but with some expansion: "When the body is buried it is ugly, but when it is raised it will be beautiful. When it is buried it is weak, but when it is raised it will be powerful." Many languages, however, will need to render this verse in a way similar to TEV: "When the body is buried, it is ugly and weak; when God raises it, it will be beautiful and strong."

15.44-49

Throughout verses 44-49 Paul establishes a series of contrasts between (1) **the physical, from earth,** and (2) **the spiritual,** which is **of heaven.** The argument includes in verse 45 a quotation of Genesis 2.7; the words **of the dust** (verses 48,49) also allude to this verse. Paul gives it an emphasis different from that of the Old Testament passage. There God takes dust of the earth and, by breathing into it, makes the first man a living being. Paul is not concerned with the

[317]

distinction between the dust and the divine breath, but between Adam as a whole and Christ. This means that, although a translator may use different terms, the basic contrast is between the two concepts Adam and Christ—not three concepts. Similarly, the physical is the same as that which is from earth.

15.44	RSV	TEV

It is sown a physical body, it is raised a spiritual body. If there is a physical body, there is also a spiritual body.	When buried, it is a physical body; when raised, it will be a spiritual body. There is, of course, a physical body, so there has to be a spiritual body.

In this verse Paul begins to define the new body.

It is sown and **it is raised:** see the comments on verse 43.

Physical . . . spiritual: see comments on "spiritual . . . natural" in 2.13.

Spiritual body is a literal translation of the Greek. It does not mean a ghostly entity; on the contrary, Paul means that the source of life in the new body is the Holy Spirit. FrCL translates "a body animated by the Spirit"; or one may say "a body to which the Holy Spirit gives life."

The last sentence of this verse can be understood as an aside or as a footnote to verse 44a. Verse 45 follows on smoothly from verse 44a. This can be shown in translation by the use of parentheses around the last sentence in verse 44.

If there is a physical body: this is not really a conditional clause but rather a statement of fact. Therefore TEV's translation "There is, of course, a spiritual body" is a clearer rendering. One may also express this clause as "Just as there is a physical body, so also there is a spiritual body" or "Since there is a physical body, there is also . . . ."

15.45	RSV	TEV

Thus it is written, "The first man Adam became a living being"; the last Adam became a life-giving spirit.	For the scripture says, "The first man, Adam, was created a living being"; but the last Adam is the life-giving Spirit.

The word **Thus** shows that Paul is now comparing his previous statements with the scriptural evidence for them.

It is written may be expressed as "it is written in the Scriptures." See comments on 1.19.

The words **first** and **Adam** are not in the Old Testament text; Paul is inserting a little explanation in order to make a closer parallel to the last part of the sentence. The clause **the first man Adam became a living being** may also be translated as "God created the first man, Adam, as a living being."

Became represents a rather general word in Greek. TEV's "created" is possibly too technical. In any case, Paul is not stating that Christ was created by God the Father, and so "created" should not be used in the last clause.

The last Adam is identified with Christ, as in verses 21-22.

A life-giving spirit does not mean one spirit among others, or even in the case of TEV's "life-giving Spirit," the Holy Spirit. The difficulties of translation may be solved or avoided by an unusually literal translation: "the first human being, Adam, was made [into] a living being; but the last Adam a life-giving spirit."[6]

15.46

RSV	TEV
But it is not the spiritual which is first but the physical, and then the spiritual.	It is not the spiritual that comes first, but the physical, and then the spiritual.

Not . . . first in this context is in the sense of importance. Jewish interpreters of the Old Testament had a saying: "A new act of God supersedes the old." Paul may have meant something similar. A translation model can be "The physical is of less importance than the spiritual. For the physical comes first and then the spiritual replaces it" or ". . . and then comes the spiritual, which is more important." It is also possible to say "For the physical being comes first, and then comes the spiritual being."

15.47

RSV	TEV
The first man was from the earth, a man of dust; the second man is from heaven.	The first Adam, made of earth, came from the earth; the second Adam came from heaven.

This verse must be understood in reference to verse 45 and to the Old Testament text quoted there. In the immediate context Paul says that "God formed man of dust from the ground." TEV's "earth" is a more natural English translation.

Man: as verse 45 and verses 21-22 showed, Paul can use **man** in place of "Adam" (TEV). Doubtless he was thinking of the Hebrew word which is the same for both **man** and "Adam." However, a literal translation such as that of RSV creates problems for the reader, since **the second man** more naturally refers to Cain than to Christ (see Gen 4.1). TEV's "the second Adam," meaning "the second type of man" or "the founder of a new human race," brings out the sense. **Second** in this context means the same as "last" in verse 45.

In both halves of the verse, TEV's "came" is implied. Paul is thinking of the origins of Adam and Christ, not of movement from a particular place.

After **the second man** many Greek manuscripts add "the Lord." However, modern translations are based on the shorter text, which is that of the UBS Greek New Testament.

15.48

RSV	TEV
As was the man of dust, so are those who are of the dust; and as is the man of heaven, so are those who are of heaven.	Those who belong to the earth are like the one who was made of earth; those who are of heaven are like the one who came from heaven.

---

6 On this predicate nominative use of the Greek *eis*, see Arndt-Gingrich under *eis*, 8.a.β.

15.48

RSV follows the order of the Greek very literally, whereas TEV begins with the grammatical subject and rearranges the text accordingly. This verse makes a contrast between Adam's descendants, with their natural bodies made of dust, and believers in Christ, who are given new, heavenly, or spiritual bodies.

The man of dust is too literal in English. TEV's "the one who was made of earth" is better. There is no suggestion that women are excluded.

Those who are of the dust may also be rendered as "Those who belong to the earth" (TEV).

Both "made" and "came" in TEV are implied.

15.49   RSV   TEV

Just as we have borne the image of the man of dust, we shall[a] also bear the image of the man of heaven.

Just as we wear the likeness of the man made of earth, so we will wear[q] the likeness of the Man from heaven.

[a] Other ancient authorities read *let us*

[q] we will wear; *some manuscripts have* let us wear.

In the Greek text this verse is linked by "and" to verse 48. Paul immediately applies his last statement to Christians, doubtless including himself and his readers. At the same time, he makes it clear that "those who are of the dust" and "those who are of heaven" are not two completely separate categories of people, fixed for all time.

In the second half of the verse, "let us" is in many Greek manuscripts (see RSV and TEV footnotes), but the context calls for a statement rather than for an appeal. The appeal is left until verse 58. The Greek verbs translated **we have borne** and "let us also bear" (RSV footnote) were pronounced in the same way, so mistakes in dictation are to be expected. The UBS Greek text has "we shall bear."

TEV's translation "wear" is supported by the words "put on" in verse 53. Paul is clearly thinking of a "likeness" (TEV) or **image** which is an integral part of the person "bearing" or "wearing" it. JB changes and thereby strengthens the metaphor: "we, who have been modelled on the earthly man, will be modelled on the heavenly man." GeCL removes the figurative language altogether: "Now we are like the man who was made of earth. Later we will be like the one who has come from heaven"; similarly ItCL.

15.50   RSV   TEV

I tell you this, brethren: flesh and blood cannot inherit the kingdom of God, nor does the perishable inherit the imperishable.

What I mean, brothers, is that what is made of flesh and blood cannot share in God's Kingdom, and what is mortal cannot possess immortality.

Paul now begins to develop the thought of the double nature of man before and after the resurrection. **I tell you this, brethren** (TEV "What I mean") introduces a teaching about the end of time (see also 7.29). Scholars disagree about the relationship between the two parts into which the rest of the verse is divided. Older commentators generally believed that the two statements, **flesh and**

blood cannot inherit the kingdom of God, and **nor does the perishable inherit the imperishable,** meant essentially the same. Recent commentators, however, tend to believe that **flesh and blood** refers to the living, and **the perishable** refers to the dead, so that the two statements are not the same but complementary. Verses 51-52 certainly distinguish between those who will be alive at the time of judgment, and those who will have died. However, such a distinction is less clear in verse 53, where the language is similar to that of the present verse. It is difficult to be certain which commentators are right, since the only other places in Paul's letters where **flesh and blood** is used are Galatians 1.16, meaning "human beings," and Ephesians 6.12, where it means human beings as contrasted with the supernatural powers of evil. TEV's "and" before "what is mortal" suggests that the two statements are *not* equivalent.

Brethren refers to "fellow Christians." In 1 Corinthians this word usually introduces a new paragraph or theme.

Inherit means "take possession of."

Kingdom of God: see comments on 4.20.

Perishable: see comments on verse 42; Barrett has "corpses in decomposition," following the second interpretation mentioned above.

The noun which is translated **imperishable** (TEV "immortality") is used in the New Testament only in this chapter and in 1 Timothy 6.16. New Testament writers avoided the idea that human beings possessed eternal life in themselves, apart from God's gift.

15.51-52   RSV   TEV

    Lo! I tell you a mystery. We shall not all sleep, but we shall all be changed, 52 in a moment, in the twinkling of an eye, at the last trumpet. For the trumpet will sound, and the dead will be raised imperishable, and we shall be changed.

    Listen to this secret truth: we shall not all die, but when the last trumpet sounds, we shall all be changed in an instant, as quickly as the blinking of an eye. For when the trumpet sounds, the dead will be raised, never to die again, and we shall all be changed.

It is important for translators to compare TEV's restructured translation with RSV's more literal version, and to consider what rearrangement may bring out the meaning most clearly in their own language.

Lo! is the Greek interjection traditionally translated "behold." Both words are no longer used in everyday English. TEV's "Listen" is good modern English. This word is used to call attention to the following words.

Mystery here means a special teaching revealed to Paul so that he may pass it on. JB, perhaps more precisely than TEV, translates "I will tell you something that has been secret"; see comments on 2.7 and 13.2. "Will" in JB means "about to," as implied in the Greek.

We shall not all sleep, but we shall all be changed: manuscripts vary, probably because later scribes found the text difficult to understand or accept. The UBS Greek text gives an "A" rating to the text which is translated by RSV and TEV. This means that this text is virtually certain. For the variants, see Metzger and general commentaries.

The words translated **We shall not all sleep** would normally mean "none of us will sleep (that is, die) before the last judgment." It is likely that Paul, when he wrote this letter, expected to be alive when Christ returned to earth. Nowhere else does he state that no further deaths would take place before Christ's return. For this reason, all translations consulted, and most commentaries, understand the words to mean "we shall not all die" (TEV), meaning that, although some of us may die, not all of us will die. However, the translation "none of us will die" is perhaps worth giving as an alternative in a footnote.[7] In any case, throughout the verse "we" and "us" include both Paul and his readers.

We shall all be changed: see last paragraph of comments on these verses.

In a moment: literally "atom," meaning here a unit of time, not of matter, so small that it cannot be divided again.

Twinkling: more precisely, "in the time it takes to cast a glance at something."

At the last trumpet: Paul does not say who is to sound the trumpet. If it is necessary in translation to give the verb a subject, one may translate "when people hear the sound of the last trumpet" or "when they blow the last trumpet."

Trumpet is the normal translation of the Greek word; "bugle" was chosen in 14.8 because that verse referred to a military instrument (see comments).

The phrase **the dead will be raised** may be rendered as "God will raise the dead to life."

Imperishable is the opposite of the condition described as "mortal" (TEV) in verse 42 (see the comments). The Greek therefore implies, not only that the dead *will* never die again (TEV), but that they *can* never die again.

We shall be changed: this clause almost certainly refers to different people from the dead whom God will raise, never to die again. The people here are the ones mentioned in verse 51 who will still be alive when Christ returns. The **we** in Greek is emphatic, suggesting a change of subject. It is therefore significant that **all** is expressed in the Greek of verse 51, but not in verse 52. It may even be that **we shall be changed** is a clarification or correction by Paul of **we shall all be changed** in verse 51, to show that "we all" refers only to Christians who are still alive in the last days. TEV's "all" is not in the Greek text of verse 52. GeCL makes this contrast clear: "when the trumpet sounds, the dead will be awakened to everlasting life. But we, who are still alive, (will) receive a new body." Other CLTs are less explicit but do not follow TEV in repeating "all" from verse 51. The distinction between the renderings of verses 51 and 52 should be kept in translation.

15.53   RSV   TEV

RSV	TEV
For this perishable nature must put on the imperishable, and this mortal nature must put on immortality.	For what is mortal must be changed into what is immortal; what will die must be changed into what cannot die.

For appears to draw a conclusion from what precedes, but in fact this verse is largely a restatement of what has already been said.

---

[7] The opposite view is presented by Hurd, pages 230-231 (especially page 230, note 1), who paraphrases: "We are, as you know, going to live to see the Parousia [return of Christ]. When that Day comes none of us will have to pass through death to attain resurrection bodies. Instead, all of us will be transformed instantaneously at the last trumpet."

And: the two halves of the verse also largely repeat one another. For this reason TEV omits the **and** which is present in the Greek before **this mortal** (see comments on verse 50). The phrases **this perishable nature** and **this mortal nature** may be expressed in many langauges as "For this nature of ours which will decay must be changed into a nature which will live for ever."

Put on: the metaphor of "putting on" or "wearing" clothes is continued from verse 49. TEV removes this figurative language. NEB and Brc have "clothed," which is clearer. Phps somewhat intensifies the metaphor by translating "wrapped in."

This perishable nature means "what is subject to decay," perhaps implying "what is decaying" (see verses 42, 50, and 54, where the same or related terms are used).

15.54a	RSV	TEV
	When the perishable puts on the imperishable, and the mortal puts on immortality, then shall come to pass the saying that is written:	So when this takes place, and the mortal has been changed into the immortal, then the scripture will come true:

The first part of this verse overlaps with verse 53. That is why TEV has started with the phrase "So when this place," and then combined the first two clauses into one: "and the mortal has been changed into the immortal." However, the overlap in meaning between verses 54 and 53 is even greater than what TEV suggests. The clause **When the perishable puts on the imperishable** largely repeats verse 53a, and the clause **the mortal puts on immortality** largely repeats verse 53b, in each case with a change of tense. So logically the two clauses **the perishable puts on . . . the mortal puts on immortality** could be omitted. The content of these clauses is included in TEV's "when this takes place." Another way of treating this repetition would be to repeat the word **when** before the words **the mortal;** for example, "when the mortal." The repetition of "when" would indicate the overlap of thought and language. Some CLTs, including earlier editions of TEV, agree with RSV in repeating all the material from verse 53. GeCL, however, has simply "when this happens."

Several scribes omitted the words corresponding to **put on the imperishable, and the mortal,** and there are other Greek manuscripts where the whole of verse 54 is omitted. Translations and commentaries generally prefer the longer text, as it seems typical of Paul's use of repetition, such as that found in verses 42-44.

The saying that is written: in many languages there is clash between "say" and "write." TEV rightly removes this, and TEV also makes it plain that Paul refers to "scripture," not to some popular "saying" or proverb.

15.54b-55	RSV	TEV
	"Death is swallowed up in victory."	"Death is destroyed; victory is complete!
55	"O death, where is thy victory? O death, where is thy sting?"	55 "Where, Death, is your victory? Where, Death, is your power to hurt?"

Paul quotes an otherwise unknown Greek version of Isaiah 25.8, followed by Hosea 13.14. The key words in both are **death** and **victory**.

Swallowed up is figurative language which TEV replaces by the literal language "is destroyed." Brc expands the metaphor to make it clearer: "Death is swallowed up, and victory is complete!" In languages where poetry is popular, it may be possible to translate these two lines as poetry. GeCL and ItCL set out both quotations as poetry, but also divide the first quotation into two lines.

Death is spelled with a capital in TEV because **death** is addressed as if it were a person. Translators should consider whether this is natural in their own language, or whether it is better to speak of death in the third person in verse 55 as well as in verse 54. The questions in verse 55 are rhetorical. In some languages these will need to be replaced by statements; for example, "Your victory, Death, has gone."

Sting: the word for sting can also mean "goad," as in Acts 26.14, and in Revelation 9.10 it refers to a scorpion's sting, pain, and harm, though death is not suggested. It is impossible to be sure what Paul's meaning is, since he does not use this word in his writings outside of this passage. It seems evident, then, that the two possible translations are the figurative **sting** and the nonfigurative "power to hurt" (TEV).

15.56   RSV   TEV

RSV	TEV
The sting of death is sin, and the power of sin is the law.	**Death gets its power to hurt from sin, and sin gets its power from the Law.**

Paul comments in this verse on the second half of the quotation in verse 55, and in verse 57 on the first half of that quotation.

Like verse 27b, this verse is an aside. In modern books it would have been put in a footnote or in parentheses.

This verse begins in the Greek with a word meaning "and" or "but." RSV and TEV agree in omitting this word here, where it is a very weak transitional.

Sting: see the comments on verse 55.

Power implies "power to hurt," or perhaps even better, "power to kill," as in FrCL.

The law: this **law** is considered as coming from God, so TEV capitalizes "the Law." Some translations which do not use capitalization may need to say "the law written by Moses."

15.57   RSV   TEV

RSV	TEV
But thanks be to God, who gives us the victory through our Lord Jesus Christ.	**But thanks be to God who gives us the victory through our Lord Jesus Christ!**

This verse is a comment on verse 55a; but more than that it is also a brief thanksgiving which brings the argument of the whole chapter to its climax.

But here marks a return to the triumph song of verses 54b-55.

Thanks be to God may be expressed as "we should thank God" or "we thank God."

Victory is the key word of the quotations in verses 54-55 and should be translated in the same way here if possible. The clause **who gives us the victory**

through our Lord Jesus Christ can be restructured as follows: "who lets us have the victory through what our Lord Jesus Christ has done."

15.58   RSV   TEV

Therefore, my beloved brethren, be steadfast, immovable, always abounding in the work of the Lord, knowing that in the Lord your labor is not in vain.

So then, my dear brothers, stand firm and steady. Keep busy always in your work for the Lord, since you know that nothing you do in the Lord's service is ever useless.

Therefore introduces the practical result of the chapter; see comments on 1.7, where the same Greek word is translated so that.

My beloved brethren is a particularly affectionate phrase used by Paul only here and in Philippians 4.1. The phrase also has the function of calling special attention to the words which follow. Brethren, as usual, means "fellow Christians."

The words abounding, your labor, and in vain recall verse 10. See the comments.

The clause in the Lord your labor is not in vain means "your work is not useless when you do it as Christians," or even "the Lord (Christ) will make sure that your work does not prove useless." The words in the Lord are strongly emphasized in the Greek by being at the end of the sentence.

Chapter 16

The Offering for Fellow Believers

RSV	TEV
1 Now concerning the contribution for the saints: as I directed the churches of Galatia, so you also are to do. 2 On the first day of every week, each of you is to put something aside and store it up, as he may prosper, so that contributions need not be made when I come. 3 And when I arrive, I will send those whom you accredit by letter to carry your gift to Jerusalem. 4 If it seems advisable that I should go also, they will accompany me.	1 Now, concerning what you wrote about the money to be raised to help God's people in Judea. You must do what I told the churches in Galatia to do. 2 Every Sunday each of you must put aside some money, in proportion to what he has earned, and save it up, so that there will be no need to collect money when I come. 3 After I come, I shall give letters of introduction to the men you have approved, and send them to take your gift to Jerusalem. 4 If it seems worthwhile for me to go, then they can go along with me.

Chapter 16 is loosely constructed, as is usual at the end of Paul's letters. Therefore there are short sections and paragraphs both in the UBS Greek text and in TEV. It is pointless to look for any common theme of harmonious development connecting the whole chapter. All that can be said about the structure of chapter 16 as a whole is that it generally continues the practical tone of 15.58, and that some of the language, especially in verses 1-12, refers to matters of organization. In verses 13-24, on the other hand, the language generally reflects the situation of the Corinthian church at worship.

Verses 1-4 are concerned with the collection of money which Paul agreed to make on behalf of the poor and persecuted Christians in Jerusalem (see Gal 2.10). This is the oldest New Testament writing which refers to this collection. It will be discussed in greater detail in 2 Corinthians 8—9. However, the sudden introduction of this subject, and the use of the definite article **the contribution** in verse 1, imply that the readers had already heard about the collection. Paul is concerned here, not to present the subject to his readers or even to command them to take up the collection, but to give instructions about its organization.

The TEV section heading "The Offering for Fellow Believers" may be rendered as "Corinthian Christians give money to help fellow Christians."

RSV	TEV
Now concerning the contribution for the saints: as I directed the churches of Galatia, so you also are to do.	**Now, concerning what you wrote about the money to be raised to help God's people in Judea. You must do what I told the churches in Galatia to do.**

Concerning can be expressed as "I want to speak about."

TEV's "what you wrote about" is not in the Greek text, though some commentators believe that it is implied here, in 12.1, and even in 16.12, where the Greek is similar. However, it is not certain that this phrase is implied, and other translations do not include it (see comments on 12.1).

Contribution translates a Greek word not found elsewhere in the Bible, except in some manuscripts of 2 Maccabees 12.43. In secular Greek writings it refers to the collection of taxes or of funds for pagan temples. Here the context shows that it is a voluntary collection. In many languages it will be helpful to expand **the contribution** to "the money that you need to raise."

The saints, as in 1.2 and elsewhere, means the Christian community, hence TEV's "God's people." TEV has added "in Judea" to supply information which the first readers certainly had, but most modern readers do not have (compare 2 Cor 8.4). Some CLTs have "in Jerusalem" instead. By adding "in Judea" or "in Jerusalem" here, translators will make it clear that **the saints** in this verse is not the same group mentioned in verse 15.

Directed: the same verb was "my rule" in 7.17 (see the comments). In the present verse the main idea is that of giving instructions, but perhaps refers to organizing too.

You is emphasized in the text, contrasting with **the churches of Galatia.**

16.2	RSV	TEV

On the first day of every week, each of you is to put something aside and store it up, as he may prosper, so that contributions need not be made when I come.

Every Sunday each of you must put aside some money, in proportion to what he has earned, and save it up, so that there will be no need to collect money when I come.

The first day of the week means "Sunday" (TEV).

Aside certainly implies that for the time being, each member's contribution is to be saved up in his own home. FrCL has "at home," and Brc "each of you must personally lay aside and save up." The last part of the verse must therefore imply that the collection should be started before Paul's visit.

In this context, **something** obviously means "some money" (TEV), as the rest of the verse makes clear.

There is some disagreement about the meaning of the words translated **as he may prosper.** Héring translates "whatever he can succeed in saving." The Greek originally meant "to have a successful journey," and was then more widely applied to success in business. Some translations express this phrase in a slightly different way: "as much as he can spare." *Maxfield would say no to this translation*

When I come: compare 11.34.

16.3	RSV	TEV

And when I arrive, I will send those whom you accredit by letter to carry your gift to Jerusalem.

After I come, I shall give letters of introduction to the men you have approved, and send them to take your gift to Jerusalem.

When I arrive: the meaning is the same as "come" in verse 2. Perhaps, as often in Paul's writings, a different verb is used simply for stylistic variety.

Letter: TEV's "letters of introduction" is better.

The words **I will send those whom you accredit by letter** can be understood in two ways, depending on whether the **letter** is understood to be written by Paul himself, or by representatives of the church at Corinth. Translators should contrast RSV with TEV and also NEB. One may argue that "letters of introduction" would be better received in Jerusalem if they were signed by someone like Paul who was well known there. However, two details make it perhaps more likely that the letters would be written by the Corinthian leaders, as RSV suggests. (1) The Greek makes it clear that the Corinthians themselves would choose people to take the fund to Jerusalem. (2) There would be little point in Paul's writing letters if, as verse 4 suggests, there was a possibility of his going to Jerusalem himself.

Accredit: it is impossible to tell from the Greek whether the Corinthians had already approved people or had still to do so. TEV "have approved" suggests the first, but the context rather suggests the second.

Gift means simply the money which expresses the Corinthian Christians' generosity.

16.4	RSV	TEV

If it seems advisable that I should go also, they will accompany me.

If it seems worthwhile for me to go, then they can go along with me.

If it seems advisable: most commentators and translators understand the text to mean "worthwhile" (TEV); "If it seems worthwhile," or "If it is proper" or ". . . a good thing."

They will accompany me: the text says nothing about who would be the most important member of the party. The literal translation, which in this case also gives the meaning, is "If it seems proper for me to travel too, they will travel with me."

RSV	16.5-12	TEV

Paul's Plans

5 I will visit you after passing through Macedonia, for I intend to pass through Macedonia, 6 and perhaps I will stay with you or even spend the winter, so that you may speed me on my journey, wherever I go. 7 For I do not want to see you now just in passing; I hope to spend some time with you, if the Lord permits. 8 But I will stay in Ephesus until Pentecost, 9 for a wide door for effective work has opened to me, and there are many adversaries.

10 When Timothy comes, see that you put him at ease among you, for he is doing the work of the Lord, as I

5 I shall come to you after I have gone through Macedonia—for I have to go through Macedonia. 6 I shall probably spend some time with you, perhaps the whole winter, and then you can help me to continue my trip, wherever it is I shall go next. 7 I want to see you more than just briefly in passing; I hope to spend quite a long time with you, if the Lord allows.

8 I will stay here in Ephesus until the day of Pentecost. 9 There is a real opportunity here for great and worthwhile work, even though there are many opponents.

am. 11 So let no one despise him. Speed him on his way in peace, that he may return to me; for I am expecting him with the brethren.

12 As for our brother Apollos, I strongly urged him to visit you with the other brethren, but it was not at all his will *b* to come now. He will come when he has opportunity.

b Or *God's will for him*

10 If Timothy comes your way, be sure to make him feel welcome among you, because he is working for the Lord, just as I am. 11 No one should look down on him, but you must help him continue his trip in peace, so that he will come back to me; for I am expecting him back with the brothers.

12 Now, about brother Apollos. I have often encouraged him to visit you with the other brothers, but he is not completely convinced*r* that he should go at this time. When he gets the chance, however, he will go.

r he is not completely convinced; *or* it is not at all God's will.

See the introduction to 16.1-4.

| 16.5 | RSV | TEV |

I will visit you after passing through Macedonia, for I intend to pass through Macedonia,

I shall come to you after I have gone through Macedonia—for I have to go through Macedonia.

Passing through is literally "I go through," meaning "I intend to go through."
Macedonia: in many languages one will need to make it clear that Macedonia is a province, that is, a subdivision of a country or territory. In this case Macedonia was a Roman province which corresponded to the northern part of Greece today.

| 16.6 | RSV | TEV |

and perhaps I will stay with you or even spend the winter, so that you may speed me on my journey, wherever I go.

I shall probably spend some time with you, perhaps the whole winter, and then you can help me to continue my trip, wherever it is I shall go next.

And: many languages will prefer to begin a new sentence here, as TEV has done.
The winter: TEV's "whole" is implied. In ancient times it was dangerous to cross the Mediterranean in winter (see Acts 27.9-12).
Speed me on my journey: TEV's "help me to continue my trip" is clearer English. It implies that the Corinthians will give material support to Paul for the next stage of his journey.
Wherever I go: TEV adds "next," which means "after my visit to Corinth."

16.7	RSV	TEV

For I do not want to see you now just in passing; I hope to spend some time with you, if the Lord permits. | **I want to see you more than just briefly in passing; I hope to spend quite a long time with you, if the Lord allows.**

Now should be understood as "immediately" or "soon." Paul is saying "I do not want to visit you in the near future and only have a short time with you. Rather . . . ." So the two halves of this verse include a double contrast: (1) not now but later, and (2) not in passing but for a long visit. TEV does not express the first contrast; RSV does.

The two halves of the sentence are connected in Greek by "for," though neither RSV nor TEV has this word. The meaning is that there is no point in Paul's paying a brief visit to Corinth soon, because he plans a longer stay with them later.

16.8	RSV	TEV

But I will stay in Ephesus until Pentecost, | **I will stay here in Ephesus until the day of Pentecost.**

Stay in Ephesus: the word "here" (TEV) is implied in the word **stay.**

Pentecost was the Jewish festival described in Leviticus 23.15-21, Numbers 28.26,31, and called in Numbers 28.26 the "feast of weeks" (TEV's "Harvest Festival"). There is no evidence that in Paul's time Christians had any distinctive celebration at this time. AT translates "the Harvest Festival" in this verse, but other translations have "Pentecost," sometimes with an explanatory note.

"The day of" (TEV) is implied here, though expressed in Acts 2.1; Pentecost was a one-day celebration. In some languages it may be advisable to translate "the festival of Pentecost" or more simply "the Harvest Festival," for readers who may not otherwise recognize that Pentecost was a festival.

16.9	RSV	TEV

for a wide door for effective work has opened to me, and there are many adversaries. | **There is a real opportunity here for great and worthwhile work, even though there are many opponents.**

For a wide door for effective work has opened to me: TEV's "there is a real opportunity for great and worthwhile work" makes the meaning of Paul's metaphor clear. The image of the open door is used, for example, in 2 Corinthians 2.12. There TEV has "way," while in this verse it has "opportunity." In each case Paul is speaking about an opportunity for preaching the Christian message.

For effective work may also be rendered as "for me to do an effective work."

And (TEV's "even though") translates a Greek word commonly used to introduce a contrast. TEV's translation is an appropriate one.

Adversaries refers, not to people who merely fail to accept the Christian message, but to those who actively oppose it also, as in Galatians 5.17; Philippians

1.28. **There are many adversaries** can be rendered as "though many people oppose me."

16.10   RSV   TEV

When Timothy comes, see that   If Timothy comes your way, be
you put him at ease among you, for he   sure to make him feel welcome among
is doing the work of the Lord, as I am.   you, because he is working for the Lord,
                                          just as I am.

When: the Greek clearly conveys uncertainty about whether Timothy will visit Corinth. TEV's "If Timothy comes" expresses this correctly. There is no basis for RSV's **When.**

Comes: TEV's "your way" is implied. One can also say "If Timothy arrives in Corinth." Paul speaks in very similar language in 2.3 of his own arrival in Corinth. Several translations therefore have "arrives."

Put him at ease among you: this rendering seems to weaken the meaning (so also TEV). JB has "show him that he has nothing to be afraid of in you," and TNT "see that he has nothing to fear while he is with you." These latter translations are closer to the force of the Greek.

The phrase **as I am** may be expanded to "as I work for the Lord."

16.11   RSV   TEV

So let no one despise him. Speed him   No one should look down on him, but
on his way in peace, that he may return   you must help him continue his trip in
to me; for I am expecting him with the   peace, so that he will come back to me;
brethren.   for I am expecting him back with the
                                          brothers.

Let no one despise him may be rendered as "Don't let any person among you look down on him." They may have been inclined to do so because Timothy was young (see 1 Tim 4.12). **Despise** is more literally "treat as nothing."

Speed him on his way: see verse 6. **Speed** here does not mean "fast"; it rather refers to "help" (TEV): "you must help him to continue his trip." TEV's "you must" translates a Greek imperative "send him on," literally "send him forward in peace" (see 7.15).

Expecting him can be rendered as "expecting him to return."

Brethren probably refers to male fellow workers in this verse.

16.12   RSV   TEV

As for our brother Apollos, I   Now, about brother Apollos. I
strongly urged him to visit you with the   have often encouraged him to visit you
other brethren, but it was not at all his   with the other brothers, but he is not
will[b] to come now. He will come when   completely convinced[r] that he should
he has opportunity.   go at this time. When he gets the
                                          chance, however, he will go.

^{b} Or *God's will for him*

^{r} he is not completely convinced; *or* it is not at all God's will.

Brother: as found in **brother Apollos,** see comments on verse 11. On **Apollos** himself, see comments on 1.12.

Strongly and "often" are equally possible meanings of the Greek, and the context gives no help in choosing between them.

Brethren as usual means "fellow Christians."

Most translations agree with RSV and TEV in linking **to visit you** with **the other brethren,** but the translation "I have more than once encouraged him, together with the other (brothers), to go to you" (DuCL) is also possible, implying that Paul also encouraged others to go.

The following words **it was not at all his will** do not make it clear in Greek whether Paul means God's will or Apollos's, as the footnotes in RSV and TEV show. Paul's language may be deliberately indirect in referring to a strong expression of Apollos's will, with which Paul himself may not have agreed. RSV and TEV's solution seems best.

When he has opportunity: "when he gets the chance" (TEV) is a common language English rendering of this phrase.

	RSV	**16.13-24**	TEV

Final Words

13 Be watchful, stand firm in your faith, be courageous, be strong. 14 Let all that you do be done in love.

15 Now, brethren, you know that the household of Stephanas were the first converts in Achaia, and they have devoted themselves to the service of the saints; 16 I urge you to be subject to such men and to every fellow worker and laborer. 17 I rejoice at the coming of Stephanas and Fortunatus and Achaicus, because they have made up for your absence; 18 for they refreshed my spirit as well as yours. Give recognition to such men.

19 The churches of Asia send greetings. Aquila and Prisca, together with the church in their house, send you hearty greetings in the Lord. 20 All the brethren send greetings. Greet one another with a holy kiss.

21 I, Paul, write this greeting with my own hand. 22 If any one has no love for the Lord, let him be accursed. Our Lord, come!^{c} 23 The grace of the Lord Jesus be with you. 24 My love be with you all in Christ Jesus. Amen.

13 Be alert, stand firm in the faith, be brave, be strong. 14 Do all your work in love.

15 You know about Stephanas and his family; they are the first Christian converts in Achaia and have given themselves to the service of God's people. I beg you, my brothers, 16 to follow the leadership of such people as these, and of anyone else who works and serves with them.

17 I am happy about the coming of Stephanas, Fortunatus, and Achaicus; they have made up for your absence 18 and have cheered me up, just as they cheered you up. Such men as these deserve notice.

19 The churches in the province of Asia send you their greetings; Aquila and Priscilla and the church that meets in their house send warm Christian greetings. 20 All the brothers here send greetings.

Greet one another with a brotherly kiss.

21 With my own hand I write this: *Greetings from Paul.*

^{c}Greek *Maranatha*

22 Whoever does not love the
Lord—a curse on him!
Marana tha—Our Lord, come!
23 The grace of the Lord Jesus
be with you.
24 My love be with you all in
Christ Jesus.

See the introduction to 16.1-4.

16.13	RSV	TEV

Be watchful, stand firm in your faith, be courageous, be strong.   **Be alert, stand firm in the faith, be brave, be strong.**

Be watchful "in the sense of looking out for eschatological events, expected to happen shortly" (Barrett).

Stand firm in your faith: the Greek could mean either (1) "stand firm in your acceptance of Christian teaching" (compare 11.2 "maintain the traditions") or (2) "stand firm in your trust in God and Christ." RSV chooses (2) as AT does. Most translations, including TEV, choose (1), the meaning of which is implied in the literal words "in the faith."

Be courageous: this verb is not used elsewhere in the New Testament but is common in the Greek Old Testament, almost always with other verbs meaning "be strong." See, for example, Deuteronomy 31.6,7,23.

Strong refers to strength of faith rather than muscular strength. The two words **courageous** and **strong** reinforce the words **stand firm** earlier in the verse.

16.14	RSV	TEV

Let all that you do be done in love.   **Do all your work in love.**

All you do is quite general in Greek. TEV's "work" is too narrow.
In love can be rendered "lovingly."

16.15	RSV	TEV

Now, brethren, you know that the household of Stephanas were the first converts in Achaia, and they have devoted themselves to the service of the saints;   **You know about Stephanas and his family; they are the first Christian converts in Achaia and have given themselves to the service of God's people. I beg you, my brothers,**

KJV places most of this verse and 16a in parentheses so that the main sentence reads "I beseech you, brethren . . . that ye submit yourselves . . . ." This interpretation is the basis of TEV and other CLTs, which begin verse 15 with the words which KJV places in parentheses. They then place the words "I beg you, my brothers" at the end of this verse. The alternative is to take the opening words of verse 15 as an unfinished sentence, as "I have a request to make of you, my brothers" (NEB), and to understand verse 16 as a direct imperative, "be subject to such men." The difference in meaning between these two alternatives is slight.

You know that the household of Stephanas: TEV makes it clear that Stephanas is included in the **household:** "Stephanas and his family." On **Stephanas,** see 1.16. The word translated **household** or "family" could mean either a house, as in 11.22, or the people who lived in it. This would generally be a family, but sometimes someone's servants also lived in the house and were considered part of the **household** (see Phil 4.22).

The first converts: the Greek is literally "the first fruits." The addition of the word "Christian" (TEV) is helpful in translating this phrase.

Achaia was a province of the Roman empire (see also comment on verse 5).

Devoted themselves: the Greek is literally "appointed themselves," that is, they saw a need and took upon themselves the responsibility of meeting it.

Saints means "God's people" (TEV).

The clause **devoted themselves to . . . of the saints** may be rendered as "used all of their energies to work on behalf of God's people."

| 16.16 | RSV | TEV |

I urge you to be subject to such men and to every fellow worker and laborer.

to follow the leadership of such people as these, and of anyone else who works and serves with them.

This verse begins in Greek with a strangely emphatic "you also be subject to such people." This suggests that Stephanas and his family had served God's people in places other than Corinth, or at least that they had served other Christians than those to whom this letter was addressed. We do not know for sure. Most translations ignore the emphasis, but JB makes sense of it by translating "I want you in turn to put yourselves in the service of people like this."

I urge you: in Greek this clause stands at the beginning of verse 15.

Be subject to means "follow the leadership of" (TEV), or "be submissive to," or "obey."

Such men: "such people" (TEV) is a better translation. It is very likely that Stephanas' family included women.

The participles translated **worker** and **laborer** refer to "those who work." The second participle implies hard work. The first participle includes a prefix meaning "with," but there is nothing to indicate whether it means "work with them," that is, with Stephanas and his family, or "work with me," that is, Paul. All translations consulted agree with RSV and TEV to leave the matter vague, applying to fellow workers in general.

This verse may also be rendered as ". . . to obey leaders such as these people, and any other person who works with them."

| 16.17 | RSV | TEV |

I rejoice at the coming of Stephanas and Fortunatus and Achaicus, because they have made up for your absence;

I am happy about the coming of Stephanas, Fortunatus, and Achaicus; they have made up for your absence

I rejoice at the coming . . . : this first sentence may be rephrased as "I am very happy that Stephanas, Fortunatus, and Achaicus have come here."

They have made up for your absence: or ". . . represented you in your absence." This clause is introduced in the Greek, as in RSV, by **because,** giving the reason why Paul is happy. RSV and TEV give the most likely meaning, but Paul may be referring to something more specific. If that is so, Barrett's translation "they . . . have supplied what you could not do for me" is also possible.

16.18   RSV   TEV

for they refreshed my spirit as well as yours. Give recognition to such men.   **and have cheered me up, just as they cheered you up. Such men as these deserve notice.**

The meaning of **refreshed** is probably in this context "setting someone's mind at rest." If so, **they refreshed my spirit as well as yours** would mean that the Corinthian Christians' minds were set at rest when Stephanas and his companions brought them good news about Paul.

The verb translated **give recognition** is not commonly used in the sense of recognizing someone's authority, though in the light of verse 16 this may be the meaning here. Probably no more than "pay attention to what they say" is meant here. This final sentence may thus be rephrased as "You must pay close attention to what these people say."

Such men is the same phrase as in verse 16, where it referred probably to males. However, in the present verse there is no reason why the word can not have a more general meaning; for example, "such people."

16.19   RSV   TEV

     The churches of Asia send greetings. Aquila and Prisca, together with the church in their house, send you hearty greetings in the Lord.   **The churches in the province of Asia send you their greetings; Aquila and Priscilla and the church that meets in their house send warm Christian greetings.**

Asia: it will be well to add the word "province" (TEV) in translation to make it clear that Paul does not mean the entire continent which is now called Asia.

Prisca is in the Greek text, as in Romans 16.3 and 2 Timothy 4.19. But it is in Acts 18.2,18,26 where the diminutive form "Priscilla" is used. It is confusing for modern readers if a translation refers to the same person by two forms of the same name. So translators should choose whichever form is more familiar or more simple in their own language.

Church in their house: as TEV makes clear, the church in the New Testament is people, the Christian community, not the place where they meet.

Hearty or "warm" (TEV) is the word translated "strong" in verse 12.

In the Lord: TEV's "Christian" gives the essential meaning, and FrCL makes it more explicit by translating ". . . in the Lord who unites us."

16.20	RSV	TEV

All the brethren send greetings. Greet one another with a holy kiss.

All the brothers here send greetings. Greet one another with a brotherly kiss.

Brethren as usual means "fellow Christians" and seems to refer to a larger group than that mentioned in verse 19.

TEV adds "here" after "brothers." Most translations will need this word to make it clear that Paul is talking about people in the place from which he is writing.

Holy kiss means the kind of greeting appropriate for members of God's people (verse 15). Kissing, of course, has various connotations in different cultures and at different times. If its use will have the wrong meaning here, a term for greeting with a more general meaning is preferable; for example, "Give a warm Christian greeting to each other" or "Greet each other in a warm Christian fashion."

16.21	RSV	TEV

I, Paul, write this greeting with my own hand.

With my own hand I write this: *Greetings from Paul.*

As in Galatians 6.11, Paul guarantees that this letter is genuine by taking over the pen from his secretary for the last few lines. The phrase "Greetings from Paul" in italics in TEV suggests that only these words are in Paul's own hand. But it is perhaps more likely that the whole of verses 21-24 were personally written by Paul. RSV's paragraphing suggests this.

16.22	RSV	TEV

If any one has no love for the Lord, let him be accursed. Our Lord, come! [c]

Whoever does not love the Lord —a curse on him! *Marana tha*—Our Lord, come!

[c] Greek *Maranatha*

The word translated **love** was common in secular Greek and occurs also in Titus 3.15, but is never used by Paul of God or Christ. In John 21.15,17 it is used alongside the usual Christian word for "love," with no apparent difference of meaning. Perhaps Paul used it because in verse 20 he had just used the related word for **kiss.**

The Lord, as usual, refers to Jesus.

Let him be accursed: see 12.3. What is probably implied is exclusion from the Christian fellowship, implying destruction by God when Christ returns.

Our Lord, come! is "Marana tha" in the Greek. It was evidently an ancient prayer used by Aramaic-speaking Christians. Like such words as "Amen," "Hosanna," and "Hallelujah," it was carried over into communities which spoke other languages. Most scholars understand this word to mean **Our Lord, come!**

16.23   RSV   TEV

The grace of the Lord Jesus be with   **The grace of the Lord Jesus be**
you.   **with you.**

The letter ends as it began (compare 1.3) and similarly to other letters (compare Rom 16.20).

16.24   RSV   TEV

My love be with you all in Christ   **My love be with you all in Christ**
Jesus. Amen.   **Jesus.**

In the Greek **in Christ Jesus** may be connected with **my love,** with **you all,** or with the whole sentence. The final option is the more likely; for example, "my love goes out to you all. Through Jesus Christ we are bound together with one another" (GeCL).

Bibliography

BIBLE TEXTS AND VERSIONS CITED

Texts

The Greek New Testament. 3rd edition (corrected), 1983. K. Aland, M. Black, C.M. Martini, B.M. Metzger, and A. Wikgren, eds. Stuttgart: United Bible Societies. (Cited as UBS Greek New Testament.)

Novum Testamentum Graece. 26th edition, 1979; corrected, 1981. Erwin Nestle and Kurt Aland, eds. Stuttgart: Deutsche Bibelgesellschaft. (Cited as Nestle-Aland.)

Versions

Die Bibel in heutigem Deutsch: Die Gute Nachricht des Alten und Neuen Testaments. 1982. First edition of New Testament, 1971. Stuttgart: Deutsche Bibelgesellschaft. (Cited as GeCL.)

The Bible: A New Translation. 1925. James Moffatt. New York: Harper and Brothers; London: Hodder and Stoughton. (Cited as Mft.)

La Bible de Jérusalem. 1973. First edition of New Testament, 1971. Paris: Les Éditons du Cerf. (Cited as BJ.)

La Bible en français courant. 1982. First edition of New Testament, 1971. Paris: Alliance Biblique Universelle. (Cited as FrCL.)

The Complete Bible: An American Translation. 1923. J.M. Powis Smith and Edgar Goodspeed. Chicago: University of Chicago Press. (Cited as AT.)

Dios Habla Hoy: La Biblia con Deuterocanónicos. Versión Popular. 1979. First edition of New Testament, 1966. New York: Sociedades Bíblicas Unidas. (Cited as SpCL.)

Good News Bible: The Bible in Today's English Version. 1976, 1979. New York: American Bible Society. (Cited as TEV.)

Groot Nieuws Bijbel: vertaling in omgangstaal. 1983. Boxtel: Katholieke Bijbelstichting; Haarlem: Nederlands Bijbelgenootschap. (Cited as DuCL.)

The Holy Bible (Authorized or King James Version). 1611. (Cited as KJV.)

The Holy Bible: New International Version. 1978. Grand Rapids, Michigan: Zondervan Bible Publishers; London: Hodder and Stoughton. (Cited as NIV.)

The Holy Bible: Revised Standard Version. 1952, 1971, 1973. New York: Division of Christian Education of the National Council of the Churches of Christ in the United States of America. (Cited as RSV.)

The Jerusalem Bible. 1966. London: Darton, Longman & Todd. (Cited as JB.)

The New American Bible. 1970. Camden, New Jersey: Thomas Nelson, Inc. (Cited as NAB.)

The New English Bible. First edition of the New Testament, 1961; Second edition, 1970. London: Oxford University Press and Cambridge University Press. (Cited as NEB.)

The New Testament: A new translation by William Barclay. Volume 2: The Letters and the Revelation. 1969. London and New York: Collins. (Cited as Brc.)

The New Testament in Modern English. 1972. J.B. Phillips. New York: Macmillan. (Cited as Phps.)

O Novo Testamento: a Boa Nova para toda gente. 1978. Lisbon: Sociedade Bíblica. (Cited as PoCL.)

Parola Del Signore: Il Nuovo Testamento: Traduzione interconfessionale dal testo greco in lingua corrente. 1976. Leumann: Elle Di Ci; Rome: Alleanza Biblica Universale. (Cited as ItCL.)

Traduction Oecuménique de la Bible: Nouveau Testament. 1974. Paris: Sociétés Bibliques/Les Éditions du Cerf. (Cited as TOB.)

The Translator's New Testament. 1973. London: British & Foreign Bible Society. (Cited as TNT.)

(The Word for the New Age: The New Testament Thai Common Language Version.) 1977. Bangkok: Church of Christ in Thailand. (Cited as ThCL).

GENERAL BIBLIOGRAPHY

Grammars

Blass, F., and A. Debrunner. 1961. A Greek Grammar of the New Testament and Other Early Christian Literature. Translated and revised by Robert W. Funk. Chicago and London: University of Chicago Press.

A Grammar of New Testament Greek. Vol. 1: J.H. Moulton. 1908. Prolegomena. Vol. 2: J.H. Moulton and W.F. Howard. 1919. Accidence and Word Formation. Vol. 3: N. Turner. 1963. Syntax. Vol. 4: N. Turner. 1976. Style. Edinburgh: T. & T. Clark.

Lexicons

Arndt, William F., and F. Wilbur Gingrich. 1979. A Greek-English Lexicon of the New Testament and Other Early Christian Literature. 2nd edition, revised by F.W. Gingrich and F.W. Danker. Chicago and London: University of Chicago Press.

Commentaries

Barrett, C.K. 1971. 2nd edition. A Commentary on the First Epistle to the Corinthians. London: Adam & Charles Black; New York: Harper & Row.

Bratcher, R.G. 1982. A Translator's Guide to Paul's First Letter to the Corinthians. New York: United Bible Societies.

Bruce, F.F. 1971. 1 and 2 Corinthians. London: Oliphants; Grand Rapids, Michigan: Eerdmans.

Conzelmann, Hans. 1975. First Corinthians. Philadelphia: Fortress Press.

Héring, Jean. 1949. La première épître de saint Paul aux Corinthiens. Neuchatel and Paris: Delachaux & Niestlé. English translation, 1955. The First Epistle of Paul to the Corinthians. London: Epworth Press.

Hurd, John C. 1965. The Origins of I Corinthians. New York: Seabury Press.

Martin, Ralph P. 1984. The Spirit and the Congregation: Studies in 1 Corinthians 12-15. Grand Rapids, Michigan: Eerdmans.

Orr, William D., and James Arthur Walther. 1975. 1 Corinthians. Garden City, New York: Doubleday.

Robertson, Archibald T., and Alfred Plummer. 1911. A Critical and Exegetical Commentary on the First Epistle of Paul to the Corinthians. Edinburgh: T & T Clark.

Zuntz, Günther. 1953. The Text of the Epistles. London: Oxford University Press.

Other Works

Beekman, John, and John Callow. 1974. Translating the Word of God. Grand Rapids, Michigan: Zondervan.

Concise Oxford Dictionary. 6th edition, 1975. London and New York: Oxford University Press. (Cited as COD.)

Ellingworth, Paul, and Eugene A. Nida. 1983. A Translator's Handbook on the Letter to the Hebrews. New York: United Bible Societies.

Metzger, B.M. 1975. A Textual Commentary on the Greek New Testament. London and New York: United Bible Societies.

Nida, E.A. 1975. Componential Analysis of Meaning. The Hague and Paris: Mouton.

————, and Charles R. Taber. 2nd edition, 1974. The Theory and Practice of Translation. Leiden: E.J. Brill for the United Bible Societies.

Glossary

This Glossary contains terms which are technical from an exegetical or a linguistic viewpoint. Other terms not defined here may be referred to in a Bible dictionary.

abstract noun is one which refers to a quality or characteristic, such as "beauty" or "darkness."

active. See voice.

adjective is a word which limits, describes, or qualifies a noun. In English, "red," "tall," "beautiful," and "important" are adjectives.

adverb is a word which limits, describes, or qualifies a verb, an adjective, or another adverb. In English, "quickly," "soon," "primarily," and "very" are adverbs.

agent is one who accomplishes an action, whether the grammatical construction is active or passive. In the expressions "John struck Bill" (active) and "Bill was struck by John" (passive), the agent in either case is "John."

ambiguous describes a word or phrase which in a specific context may have two or more different meanings. For example, "Bill did not leave because John came" could mean either (1) "the coming of John prevented Bill from leaving" or (2) "the coming of John was not the cause of Bill's leaving." It is often the case that what is ambiguous in written form is not ambiguous when actually spoken, since features of intonation and slight pauses usually make clear which of two or more meanings is intended. Furthermore, even in written discourse, the entire context normally serves to indicate which meaning is intended by the writer.

aorist refers to a set of forms in Greek verbs which denote an action completed without the implication of continuance or duration. Usually, but not always, the action is considered as completed in past time.

apposition (appositional) is the placing of two expressions together so that they both refer to the same object, event, or concept; for example, "my friend, Mr. Smith."

article is a grammatical class of words, often obligatory, which indicate whether the following word is definite or indefinite. In English the definite article is "the," and the indefinite article is "a" (or "an").

central meaning is that meaning of a word which is generally understood when the word is given without a context. This is also called the "unmarked meaning." For example, the central meaning of tree is a large perennial plant. However, tree may have a wide variety of other meanings, depending on the context. (See referential meaning.)

chiasmus is a reversal of words or phrases in the second part of an otherwise parallel construction. For example: "(1) I / (2) was shapen / (3) in iniquity // (3) in sin / (2) did my mother conceive / (1) me."

clause is a grammatical construction, normally consisting of a subject and a predicate. The main clause is that clause in a sentence which can stand alone as a complete sentence, but which has one or more dependent or subordinate clauses related to it. A subordinate clause is dependent on the main clause, but it does not form a complete sentence. See also phrase.

comparative refers to the form of an adjective or adverb that indicates that the object or event described possesses a certain quality to a greater degree than does another object or event. "Richer" and "smaller" are adjectives in the comparative degree, while "sooner" and "more quickly" are adverbs in the comparative degree. See also superlative.

components are the parts or elements which go together to form the whole of an object. For example, the components of bread are flour, salt, shortening, yeast, and water. The components of the meaning (semantic components) of a term are the elements of meaning which it contains. For example, some of the components of "boy" are "human," "male," and "immature."

compound refers to forms of words or phrases consisting of two or more parts.

conditional refers to a clause or phrase which expresses or implies a condition, in English usually introduced by "if."

conjunctions are words which serve as connectors between words, phrases, clauses, and sentences. "And," "but," "if," and "because" are typical conjunctions in English.

connective is a word or phrase which connects other words, phrases, clauses, etc. See conjunctions.

construction. See structure.

context is that which precedes and/or follows any part of a discourse. For example, the context of a word or phrase in Scripture would be the other words and phrases associated with it in the sentence, paragraph, section, and even the entire book in which it occurs. The context of a term often affects its meaning, so that a word does not mean exactly the same thing in one context that it does in another context.

culture (cultural) is the sum total of the beliefs, patterns of behavior, and sets of interpersonal relations of any group of people. A culture is passed on from one generation to another, but undergoes development or gradual change.

definite article. See article.

direct object is the goal of an event or action specified by a verb. In "John hit the ball," the direct object of "hit" is "ball."

dummy subject is an element introduced into a sentence to satisfy formal grammatical requirements, even though the word may be empty of any meaning, and as a means of putting so-called "new information" in the predicate position. For example, in "it is raining" or "there is a book on the table," "it" and "there" do not refer to anything but simply occupy the subject position in the sentence, as demanded by English grammar.

emphasis (emphatic) is the special importance given to an element in a discourse, sometimes indicated by the choice of words or by position in the sentence. For example, in "Never will I eat pork again," "Never" is given emphasis by placing it at the beginning of the sentence.

euphemism is a mild or indirect term used in the place of another term which is felt to be impolite, distasteful, or vulgar; for example, "to pass away" is a euphemism for "to die."

event is a semantic category of meanings referring to actions, processes, etc., in which objects can participate. In English, most events are grammatically classified as verbs ("run," "grow," "think," etc.), but many nouns may also refer to events, as for example, "baptism," "song," "game," and "prayer."

exclusive first person plural excludes the person(s) addressed. That is, a speaker may use "we" to refer to himself and his companions, while specifically excluding the person(s) to whom he is speaking. See inclusive.

explicit refers to information which is expressed in the words of a discourse. This is in contrast to implicit information. See implicit.

feminine. See gender.

figure, figure of speech, or figurative expression involves the use of words in other than their literal or ordinary sense, in order to bring out some aspect of meaning by means of comparison or association. For example, "raindrops dancing on the street," or "his speech was like thunder." Metaphors and similes are figures of speech.

first person. See person.

full stop, or period, is a marker indicating the end of a sentence.

future tense. See tense.

future perfect is the tense which indicates that the event expressed by the verb will be completed before a specific time or before another specific event will occur. For example, in "John will have returned before tomorrow," "will have returned" is in the future perfect tense. See also tense.

gender, with respect to the Greek language, refers to any of three grammatical subclasses of Greek nouns and pronouns (called masculine, feminine, and neuter), which determine agreement with and selection of other words or grammatical forms. In most languages the classification of nouns is not related to the identity of male or female sex.

generic has reference to a general class or kind of objects, events, or abstracts; it is the opposite of specific. For example, the term "animal" is generic in relation to "dog," which is a specific kind of animal. However, "dog" is generic in relation to the more specific term "poodle."

genitive case is a grammatical set of forms occurring in many languages, used primarily to indicate that a noun is the modifier of another noun, as in "people of God," "pound of flour," "child's toy," or "Garden of Eden." The genitive often indicates possession, but it may also indicate measure, origin, apposition, characteristic, separation, or source.

goal is the object which receives or undergoes the action of a verb. Grammatically, the goal may be the subject of a passive construction ("John was hit," in which "John" is the goal of "hit"), or of certain intransitives ("the door shut"), or it may be the direct object of a transitive verb (as "John" in "the ball hit John").

grammar refers to the arrangement and interrelations of words in phrases, clauses, and sentences.

hendiadys is a figure in which a single complex idea is expressed by two words or structures, usually connected by a conjunction. For example, "weary and worn" may mean "very tired."

idiom (idiomatic) is a combination of terms whose meanings cannot be understood by adding up the meanings of the parts. "To hang one's head" and "to have a green thumb" are English idioms. Idioms almost always lose their meaning or convey a wrong meaning when translated literally from one language to another.

immediate context is that context which immediately precedes or follows a discourse or segment of discourse, with no intervening context. For example, John 3.17 is a passage in the immediate context of John 3.16.

imperative refers to forms of a verb which indicate commands or requests. In "Go and do likewise," the verbs "Go" and "do" are imperatives. In many languages, imperatives are confined to the grammatical second person; but some languages have corresponding forms for the first and third persons. These are usually expressed in English by the use of "may" or "let"; for example, "May we not have to beg!" or "Let them work harder!"

implicit (implied) refers to information that is not formally represented in a discourse, since it is assumed that it is already known to the receptor, or evident from the meaning of the words in question. For example, the phrase "the other son" carries with it the implicit information that there is a son in addition to the one mentioned. This is in contrast to explicit information, which is expressly stated in a discourse. See explicit.

inclusive first person plural includes both the speaker and the one(s) to whom that person is speaking. See exclusive.

indefinite article. See article.

indicative refers to forms of a verb in which an act or condition is stated as an actual fact rather than as a potentiality, a hope, or an unrealized condition. The verb "won" in "The king won the battle" is in the indicative form.

indirect discourse is the reporting of words of one person embedded grammatically in an altered form in the discourse of another person. For example, the direct discourse expression "I will go" may be transformed into indirect discourse in the expression "He said that he would go."

instrument (instrumental) is the object used in accomplishing an action. In the sentence "John opened the door with a key," the "key" is the instrument. See also agent.

irony (ironic) is a sarcastic or humorous manner of discourse in which what is said is intended to express its opposite; for example, "That was a smart thing to do!" when intended to convey the meaning "That was a stupid thing to do!"

kernel is a sentence pattern which is basic to the structure of a language. Kernels may also be called "basic sentence patterns," out of which more elaborate sentence structures may be formed.

literal means the ordinary or primary meaning of a term or expression, in contrast with a figurative meaning. A literal translation is one which represents the exact words and word order of the source language; such a translation is frequently unnatural or awkward in the receptor language.

main clause. See clause.

manuscript evidence is also called textual evidence. See text, textual.

manuscripts are books, documents, or letters written by hand. Thousands of manuscript copies of various Old and New Testament books still exist, but none of the original manuscripts. See text.

masculine. See gender.

metaphor is likening one object, event, or state to another by speaking of it as if it were the other; for example, "flowers dancing in the breeze." Metaphors are so commonly used and so well established in all languages that speakers and writers often use them without being conscious of the fact that they are using figurative language. See simile.

neuter. See gender.

nonfigurative. See figure, figure of speech, figurative expression.

noun is a word that names a person, place, thing, or idea, and often serves to specify a subject or topic of discussion.

object of a verb. See direct object.

paragraph is a distinct segment of discourse dealing with a particular idea, and usually marked with an indentation on a new line.

parallel, parallelism, generally refers to some similarity in the content and/or form of two parts of a construction; for example, "Hear this, all peoples! Give ear, all inhabitants of the world." The structures that correspond to each other in the two statements are said to be parallel. Parallels, or parallel passages, refers to two or more portions of biblical text that resemble each other, often by using a series of words that are identical. For example, the Lord's Prayer as recorded in Matthew 6.9-13 has as its parallel Luke 11.2-4.

paraphrase, as some linguists use the term, is a restatement of a meaning but in a different form. Paraphrases are of two principal types: (1) grammatical (for example, "John hit the man" and "the man was hit by John") and (2) lexical (for example, "the man refuses to work" and "he declines all employment").

participle is a verbal adjective, that is, a word which retains some of the characteristics of a verb while functioning as an adjective. In "singing children" and "painted house," "singing" and "painted" are participles.

particle is a small word whose grammatical form does not change. In English the most common particles are prepositions and conjunctions.

passive. See voice.

past tense. See tense.

person, as a grammatical term, refers to the speaker, the person spoken to, or the person or thing spoken about. First person is the person(s) speaking (such as "I," "me," "my," "mine," "we," "us," "our," or "ours"). Second person is the person(s) or thing(s) spoken to (such as "thou," "thee," "thy," "thine," "ye," "you," "your," or "yours"). Third person is the person(s) or thing(s) spoken about (such as "he," "she," "it," "his," "her," "them," or "their"). The examples here given are all pronouns, but in many languages the verb forms have affixes which indicate first, second, or third person and also indicate whether they are singular or plural.

personal pronoun is one which indicates first, second, or third person. See person and pronoun.

personify (personification) is to refer to an inanimate object or an abstract idea in terms that give it a personal or a human nature; as in "Wisdom is calling out," referring to wisdom as if it were a person.

phrase is a grammatical construction of two or more words, but less than a complete clause or a sentence. A phrase is usually given a name according to its function in a sentence, such as "noun phrase," "verb phrase," or "prepositional phrase." See also clause.

plural refers to the form of a word which indicates more than one. See singular.

preposition is a word (usually a particle) whose function is to indicate the relation of a noun or pronoun to another noun, pronoun, verb, or adjective. Some English prepositions are "for," "from," "in," "to," and "with."

pronouns are words which are used in place of nouns, such as "he," "him," "his," "she," "we," "them," "who," "which," "this," or "these."

present tense. See tense.

referential meaning is that aspect of the meaning of a term which most closely relates to the portion of the nonlinguistic world which the term symbolizes. For example, the referential meaning of the central meaning of father consists of such components as human, male, immediately preceding generation, and direct line of descent. This referential meaning is in contrast with certain connotative or emotive meanings of father, which suggest care, love, protection, and discipline. (See central meaning.)

reflexive has to do with verbs where the agent and goal are the same person. Sometimes the goal is explicit (as in "He dresses himself"); at other times it is implicit (as in "He dresses").

relative pronoun is a pronoun which refers to a noun in another clause, and which serves to mark the subordination of its own clause to that noun; for example, in "This is the man who came to dinner," "who" is the relative pronoun referring to "the man" in the previous clause. The subordinated clause is also called a relative clause.

restructure. See structure.

<u>rhetorical question</u> is an expression which is put in the form of a question but which is not intended to ask for information. Rhetorical questions are usually employed for the sake of emphasis.

<u>second person</u>. See <u>person</u>.

<u>sentence</u> is a grammatical construction composed of one or more clauses and capable of standing alone.

<u>Septuagint</u> is a translation of the Hebrew Old Testament into Greek, made some two hundred years before Christ. It is often abbreviated as LXX.

<u>simile</u> (pronounced SIM-i-lee) is a <u>figure of speech</u> which describes one event or object by comparing it to another, using "like," "as," or some other word to mark or signal the comparison. For example, "She runs like a deer," "He is as straight as an arrow." Similes are less subtle than metaphors in that metaphors do not mark the comparison with words such as "like" or "as." See <u>metaphor</u>.

<u>singular</u> refers to the form of a word which indicates one thing or person, in contrast to <u>plural</u>, which indicates more than one. See <u>plural</u>.

<u>specific</u> is the opposite of <u>generic</u>. See <u>generic</u>.

<u>structure</u> is the systematic arrangement of the elements of language, including the ways in which words combine into phrases, phrases into clauses, clauses into sentences, and sentences into larger forms of discourse. Because this process may be compared to the building of a house or bridge, such words as <u>structure</u> and <u>construction</u> are used in reference to it. To separate and rearrange the various components of a sentence or other unit of discourse in the translation process is to <u>restructure</u> it.

<u>style</u> is a particular or a characteristic manner in discourse. Each language has certain distinctive <u>stylistic</u> features which cannot be reproduced literally in another language. Within any language, certain groups of speakers may have their characteristic discourse styles, and among individual speakers and writers, each has his own style.

<u>subjunctive</u> refers to certain forms of verbs that are used to express an act or state as being contingent, possible, or probable (sometimes also as wish or desire), rather than as actual fact. For example, in "If John were here, he would help us," the verbs are traditionally called subjunctive. See <u>indicative</u>.

<u>subordinate clause</u>. See <u>clause</u>.

<u>superlative</u> refers to the form of an adjective or adverb that indicates that the object or event described possesses a certain quality to a greater degree than does any other object or event implicitly or explicitly specified by the content. "Most happy" and "finest" are adjectives in the superlative degree, while "least" and "most quickly" are adverbs in the superlative degree. See also <u>comparative</u>.

<u>synonyms</u> are words which are different in form but similar in meaning, such as "boy" and "lad." Expressions which have essentially the same meaning are said to be <u>synonymous</u>. No two words are completely synonymous.

tense is usually a form of a verb which indicates time relative to a discourse or some event in a discourse. The most common forms of tense are past, present, and future.

text, textual, refers to the various Greek and Hebrew manuscripts of the Scriptures. Textual evidence is the cumulative evidence for a particular form of the text. See also manuscripts.

theme is the subject of a discourse.

third person. See person.

transition in discourse involves passing from one thought-section or group of related thought-sections to another. Transitional words, phrases, or longer passages mark the connections between two such sets of related sections and help the hearer to understand the connection.

translation is the reproduction in a receptor language of the closest natural equivalent of a message in the source language, first, in terms of meaning, and second, in terms of style.

verbs are a grammatical class of words which express existence, action, or occurrence, such as "be," "become," "run," or "think."

verbal has two meanings. (1) It may refer to expressions consisting of words, sometimes in distinction to forms of communication which do not employ words ("sign language," for example). (2) It may refer to word forms which are derived from verbs. For example, "coming" and "engaged" may be called verbals, and participles are called verbal adjectives. See verbs.

versions are translations. The ancient, or early, versions are translations of the Bible, or of portions of the Bible, made in early times; for example, the Greek Septuagint, the ancient Syriac, or the Ethiopic versions.

voice in grammar is the relation of the action expressed by a verb to the participants in the action. In English and many other languages, the active voice indicates that the subject performs the action ("John hit the man"), while the passive voice indicates that the subject is being acted upon ("The man was hit").

Index

This index includes concepts, key words, and terms for which the Handbook contains a discussion useful for translators.

A Handbook on Paul's first Letter to the Corinthians rev. ed. LC 93-21894
UBS Handbook Ser., $15.00
398p.

United Bible Society
0-8267-0161-2, 105361

Printed in the United States of America